Positive Psychology on the College Campus

Positive Psychology on the College Campus

EDITED BY JOHN C. WADE, LAWRENCE I. MARKS,
and
RODERICK D. HETZEL

OXFORD
UNIVERSITY PRESS

OXFORD

UNIVERSITY PRESS

Oxford University Press is a department of the University of
Oxford. It furthers the University's objective of excellence in research,
scholarship, and education by publishing worldwide.

Oxford   New York

Auckland   Cape Town   Dar es Salaam   Hong Kong   Karachi
Kuala Lumpur   Madrid   Melbourne   Mexico City   Nairobi
New Delhi   Shanghai   Taipei   Toronto

With offices in

Argentina   Austria   Brazil   Chile   Czech Republic   France   Greece
Guatemala   Hungary   Italy   Japan   Poland   Portugal   Singapore
South Korea   Switzerland   Thailand   Turkey   Ukraine   Vietnam

Oxford is a registered trademark of Oxford University Press
in the UK and certain other countries.

Published in the United States of America by
Oxford University Press
198 Madison Avenue, New York, NY 10016

Library of Congress Cataloging-in-Publication Data
Positive psychology on the college campus / edited by John C. Wade, Lawrence I. Marks and Roderick D. Hetzel.
pages cm. — (Series in positive psychology)
Summary: "The field of positive psychology has blossomed over the past several years. A positive psychology course has
become the most popular elective at Harvard, and leaders in many fields regularly draw upon concepts and strategies from
the field's growing body of research. Because positive psychology provides a framework for enhancing individual, group, and
institutional well-being, it is particularly relevant for college campuses, which are ripe for such strength-based interventions.
Positive Psychology on the College Campus provides innovative strategies that can be employed with students to enhance
both their personal development and educational experiences. The book also provides an overview of the state of college
students' mental health and relevant developmental issues. Individual chapters, all written by experts in their fields, describe
practical strategies for readers to use with students. Additionally, the authors explain how positive psychology can be applied
in general to the college experience. With its wide-ranging topics and distinguished contributors, Positive Psychology on the
College Campus is a must-have resource for all those who work with college students, including faculty, academic advisors,
administrators, residence-life staff, counselors, and student-activities staff" Provided by publisher.
Summary: "Positive Psychology on the College Campus provides innovative strategies that can be employed with
students to enhance their personal development and educational experience. A wide range of areas is covered, making it
a must-have book for all those who work with college students"—Provided by publisher.
Includes bibliographical references.
ISBN 978–0–19–989272–3 (hardback)
1. Counseling in higher education.   2. College students—Mental health.   3. Positive psychology.   I. Wade,
John C., editor of compilation.
LB2343.P62 2015
378.1′97—dc23
2015019054

1 3 5 7 9 8 6 4 2
Printed in the United States of America
on acid-free paper

To my parents, who instilled a love of learning, and to my wife, Susan, and daughters, Angelica and Andrea, for their unending love, support, and patience through the process of working on the book.
—John

To my daughter, Eden Dawn Marks, who fills my life with so many positive emotions, to my wife, Yaela, for her love and ongoing support, and to my family and friends who have been there with me through all of life's big and small events.
—Larry

To my professor, mentor, and friend Donna Davenport, PhD, who taught me how to integrate head and heart as a psychologist; to my clients and students, who have shared with me their light as well as their darkness; and to my wife, Susan Matlock-Hetzel, whose unwavering love and support has sustained me on the journey.
—Rod

CONTENTS

Preface   ix
About the Editors   xiii
List of Contributors   xv

1. Positive Psychology and Higher Education: The Contribution of
   Positive Psychology to Student Success and
   Institutional Effectiveness   1
   LAURIE A. SCHREINER

2. Millennials in Higher Education: As Students Change, Much about
   Them Remains the Same   27
   FRANK SHUSHOK JR. AND VERA KIDD

3. Positive Psychology 101   57
   JEANA L. MAGYAR-MOE

4. Cultural Competence in Positive Psychology: History, Research,
   and Practice   81
   JENNIFER TERAMOTO PEDROTTI

5. Enhancing Intellectual Development and Academic Success in
   College: Insights and Strategies from Positive Psychology   99
   MICHELLE C. LOUIS

6. Positive Psychology in the Classroom   133
   JEANA L. MAGYAR-MOE

7. Positive Career Counseling   167
   JOHN C. WADE

8. Positive Supervision and Training   191
JANICE E. JONES AND JOHN C. WADE

9. Personal Growth and Development   219
CHRISTINE ROBITSCHEK AND MEGAN A. THOEN

10. Social Development and Relationship Enhancement   239
SARAH L. HASTINGS AND TRACY J. COHN

11. The Role of Positive Psychology in Fostering Spiritual Development and a Sense of Calling in College   261
BRUCE W. SMITH, BELINDA VICUNA, AND GLORY EMMANUEL

12. The Intersection of Positive Psychology and Leadership Development   279
SHARRA DURHAM HYNES

13. Positive Psychology in College Sport and Exercise   299
LISA M. MILLER

14. Life Coaching for Students   319
LAWRENCE I. MARKS

15. Creating a Positive Campus Culture   343
TIM HODGES AND JESSICA KENNEDY

Index   359

PREFACE

The idea for this book actually was first developed quite a few years ago, after the editors had all participated in a workshop at the American Psychological Association annual convention on applications of positive psychology in university counseling centers. Each of us was employed as a psychologist in a counseling center at that time, and the presenters in this workshop talked about different aspects of counseling center work. As we continued to dialog in the days after our program, we talked with enthusiasm about how positive psychology has applications beyond the counseling center and to almost all areas of student affairs work. Although an idea for an edited book came up right away, it took some time for the project to get off the ground. In the intervening time, other scholarly work on positive psychology applications on campus began to emerge paralleling our work and highlighting the growing interest in this approach.

The past several years also have been a uniquely challenging time for higher education, reflecting even larger economic and social issues in society, including strained budgets (for students and institutions), stressed students (and staff), expectations for measuring and promoting effectiveness, and meeting the needs of changing student demographics. We imagine most readers are well aware of the many factors that contribute to these issues that confront both university personnel and students. Of course, at any stage in the history of higher education there have been and will be challenges present, and many of the staff, faculty, and administration who work in higher education are often open to embracing the inevitable challenges and ready to work hard to find solutions. Those who view and manage problems as opportunities for growth will likely find positive psychology and its applications to be a welcomed approach.

Positive psychology offers a refreshing, valuable, and scientifically based perspective and strategies for meeting the contemporary needs and struggles within higher education. Positive psychology is often misunderstood by the public as being simply an updated form of positive thinking—basically choosing to focus on the positive and ignoring the negative. A much more accurate and certainly more empowering understanding of positive psychology is that it is the study and science of the factors associated with creating success. To be clear, positive psychology does not propose ignoring problems or weaknesses, but it does advocate for examining the often neglected other side of a situation—what is working well. Furthermore, through using powerful positive psychology-related strategies and constructs that will be discussed in this book, one may be in a better position to face real individual and institutional level challenges.

Indeed, the field of positive psychology has been burgeoning over the past 15 years, with applications being welcomed as energizing and effective in domains such as business, sports, health care, as well as education. Positive psychology provides a framework for focusing on and enhancing individual, group, and institutional well-being, and college campuses are ripe for such strength-based interventions. The purpose of this book is to provide those who work with college students a valuable resource that examines applications of positive psychology on campus, including innovative strategies that can be used with students to enhance their personal development and educational experience. A wide range of areas are covered, making the book of interest to academic advisors, administrators, counselors, faculty, residence life staff, student activities staff, and all others who work with college students.

The book begins with an exploration of the current nature of the university and an examination of the characteristics and talents of today's diverse college students, with a focus on the contribution of positive psychology to student success and institutional effectiveness. In Chapter 1, Laurie Schreiner discusses the role of positive psychology in higher education and how it contributes to student thriving. Frank Shushok and Vera Kidd further the discussion in Chapter 2 by describing the culture of the Millennial generation, emphasizing the strengths and assets that they bring to campus. We continue with an introduction to positive psychology and its foundational principles, provided in Chapter 3 by Jeana Magyar-Moe, and in Chapter 4, Jennifer Teramoto Pedrotti explains how positive psychology constructs and strengths based work are culturally embedded.

The subsequent chapters each focus on a particular area of student development and/or area of intervention on university campuses. The chapter authors were invited to write on their areas of expertise and to include a review of theory, research, or other relevant literature in the content area, specific suggestions for application and practice, a case study to illustrate key points, and a discussion of multicultural and diversity considerations as they pertain to the chapter's topic, all in a scientifically based but also engaging and readable style.

In Chapter 5, Michelle Louis discusses how student learning and achievement can be enhanced with positive psychology constructs. In Chapter 6, Jeana Magyar-Moe offers information regarding positive psychology applications for teaching. John Wade describes an approach to providing positive career counseling in Chapter 7. In Chapter 8, Janice Jones and John Wade explain the factors in their model of strengths based supervision of students. In Chapter 9, Christine Robitschek and Megan Thoen review the research on the benefits of having an intentional personal growth perspective and how this can be increased with students. Social development and relationship enhancement in college students is explored in Chapter 10 by Sarah Hastings and Tracy Cohn. In Chapter 11, Bruce Smith, Belinda Vicuna, and Glory Emmanuel explore the role of positive psychology in relation to spiritual development. The integration of existing leadership theories and select positive psychology principles is reviewed by Sharra Durham Hynes in Chapter 12. Lisa Miller writes in Chapter 13 about the benefits of enhancing physical development and athletic performance through positive psychology interventions. In Chapter 14, Lawrence Marks describes the connections between positive psychology, life coaching, and student development and success. Finally, in Chapter 15, Tim Hodges and Jessica Kennedy discuss creating a positive campus culture through reporting research on strengths, hope, engagement, and well-being.

As can be seen by this brief overview, no matter where your office is located on the campus map, positive psychology can be applied to your work. We hope that you will find the book useful and will find ways in your daily professional life to put into practice the ideas presented.

We would like to express our sincere gratitude to all of the university students, administrators, faculty, and staff with whom we have had the privilege of working over our careers and who have made working on campus such a stimulating and growth-filled environment. Thank you to all the chapter authors who took on the task of writing and editing in order to share their knowledge and ideas. Finally, thank you to Molly Balikov, Abby Gross, Suzanne Walker, and their team at Oxford University Press for the kind help and guidance along the way.

ABOUT THE EDITORS

John C. Wade is Associate Professor of Psychology and Director of the Clinical Psychology Program at Emporia State University, and earned his Ph.D. in counseling psychology from Pennsylvania State University. He frequently conducts workshops on positive psychology, training, and supervision, as well as current psychotherapy approaches. He is the co-author of *Strength-Based Clinical Supervision: A Positive Psychology Approach to Clinical Training.*

Lawrence I. Marks is a licensed psychologist at the University of Central Florida Counseling and Psychological Services, and earned his Ph.D. in counseling psychology from the University of Tennessee, Knoxville. He has extensive experience providing individual and group counseling and coaching, and has conducted over 200 presentations focusing on college student mental health and wellness including positive psychology applications.

Roderick D. Hetzel is a licensed psychologist in independent practice at Waco Psychological Associates. He also holds an appointment as Adjunct Professor of Practical Theology at George W. Truett Theological Seminary at Baylor University. He earned his Ph.D. in counseling psychology from Texas A&M University, and his areas of professional interest include mind-body health, positive psychology, and college student mental health.

LIST OF CONTRIBUTORS

Tracy J. Cohn
Department of Psychology
Radford University
Radford, Virginia

Glory Emmanuel
Department of Psychology
University of New Mexico
Albuquerque, New Mexico

Sarah L. Hastings
Department of Psychology
Radford University
Radford, Virginia

Tim Hodges
Gallup
Omaha, Nebraska

Sharra Durham Hynes
Experiential Learning
University of Central Oklahoma
Edmond, Oklahoma

Janice E. Jones
College of Education and
    Leadership
Cardinal Stritch University
Milwaukee, Wisconsin

Jessica Kennedy
Gallup
Omaha, Nebraksa

Vera Kidd
Division of Student Affairs
Virginia Tech University
Blacksburg, Virginia

Michelle C. Louis
College of Arts & Sciences
Bethel University
St. Paul, Minnesota

Jeana L. Magyar-Moe
Department of Psychology
University of Wisconsin-Stevens
    Point
Stevens Point, Wisconsin

Lawrence I. Marks
Counseling and Psychological Services
University of Central Florida
Orlando, Florida

Lisa M. Miller
School of Health Sciences
American Military University
Manassas, Virginia

Christine Robitschek
Department of Psychological
  Sciences
Texas Tech University
Lubbock, Texas

Laurie A. Schreiner
Department of Higher
  Education
Azusa Pacific University
Azusa, California

Frank Shushok, Jr.
Division of Student Affairs
Virginia Tech University
Blacksburg, Virginia

Bruce W. Smith
Department of Psychology
University of New Mexico
Albuquerque, New Mexico

Jennifer Teramoto Pedrotti
Department of Psychology and Child
  Development
California Polytechnic State
  University
San Luis Obispo, California

Megan A. Thoen
Institute for Forensic Science
Texas Tech University
Lubbock, Texas

Belinda Vicuna
Department of Psychology
University of New Mexico
Albuquerque, New Mexico

John C. Wade
Department of Psychology
Emporia State University
Emporia, Kansas

Positive Psychology on the College Campus

Positive Psychology and Higher Education

The Contribution of Positive Psychology to Student Success and Institutional Effectiveness

LAURIE A. SCHREINER

In the face of significant economic challenges in higher education, colleges and universities are increasingly interested in interventions that can enhance student success and institutional effectiveness. Yet the statistics are discouraging: 43% of students who enter college do not complete a bachelor's degree within 6 years, and this number has changed little in the last three decades despite significant investments of resources and programming (Hennessy, 2010). Among developed nations, the United States is now ranked 19th of the 23 Organization for Economic Cooperation and Development countries in college completion rates, raising concerns about the nation's future economic and social health (Organization for Economic Cooperation and Development, 2013). Of more concern is the difference in achievement and graduation rates across ethnic groups: Asian and White first-time, full-time college students experience the highest success rates (67% and 60%, respectively), whereas Hispanic, African American, and Native American students continue to lag significantly behind with 6-year graduation rates of 50.6%, 40.1%, and 40.3%, respectively (National Center for Education Statistics, 2012). Arum and Roksa (2011) conclude from their extensive longitudinal study of college outcomes that higher education reproduces rather than reduces social inequality, with the initial achievement gap across ethnicity widening over the college years. Such disparity across ethnic groups is a reminder that much remains to be done to ensure that access to higher education is translated into success.

The gap in degree attainment across ethnic groups is one of the major challenges of the changing future facing higher education. In 2001, Carnevale and

Fry projected that students of color would comprise over 80% of the growth in new students entering higher education by 2015. As that date nears, the striking lack of progress in closing the achievement gap presents higher education with not only a significant challenge, but also an opportunity to explore new pathways to student success that will enable a greater percentage of students to reach their educational goals.

This chapter serves as an introduction to the landscape of higher education, with its emphasis on student success and institutional effectiveness. The chapter also focuses on ways in which positive psychology can inform and influence the policies and practices on college campuses so that a greater percentage of students from all backgrounds are able to succeed. The chapter begins with an overview of the core outcomes and goals of higher education; it then targets two of those major outcomes, student success and institutional effectiveness, as rich opportunities for the principles of positive psychology to make a significant difference in the way higher education approaches its work. Specific implications for faculty, staff, student life professionals, and administrators are incorporated throughout the chapter.

The Purposes and Priorities of Higher Education

At its inception, higher education in the United States served a small but elite segment of society, had a religious mission, and was "deliberately organized to pursue two important objectives: training the intellect and building character" (Bok, 2006, p. 13). Colleges and universities embraced both mental discipline and moral education as legitimate institutional functions and goals, with as much emphasis on character development as on intellectual development (Reuben, 1996). With the end of World War II and the availability of the GI bill to finance a college education for returning veterans, there was a dramatic increase in the number and types of students enrolling in higher education. Colleges and universities increased in size, curricula increased in scope and variety, and faculty became more specialized. Institutions began to focus more narrowly on the preparation of graduates to fill professional and managerial positions and on the production of scientific knowledge, rather than on moral education or character development (Arum & Roksa, 2011; Gardner, 2005).

As the Vietnam War ended, an even greater diversity of entering students was evident as access to higher education widened. Student Life professionals were more common and co-curricular programming became widespread, along with an institutional mindset toward student-centeredness. In the 1980s, this student-centeredness moved further toward a consumer mentality, with higher education becoming more market driven and viewed as a commodity (Arum & Roksa, 2011). Gardner (2005) described this institutional stance as *cross-eyed,* where one eye is on the bottom line and the other is on the demands and desires of the student; he warned that "to the extent that colleges become indistinguishable from other commercial entities, they lose their reason for existence" (p. 98).

Today's colleges and universities have continued this trajectory toward market-driven education, with an even greater emphasis on national reputation and rankings and attracting prospective students through an increasing array of amenities and services (Arum & Roksa, 2011). At the same time, revenue shortfalls and budget crises at the federal, state, and local levels have increased the concern for financial stability, with the result that the primary function of a college president is fundraising, and senior leaders of the institution are more often business people than academics (Zemsky, 2009). The economic difficulties faced by most institutions also have resulted in a two-tiered system of full-time and part-time faculty, with tenure-track faculty pressured and rewarded more for their research than their teaching (Arum & Roksa, 2011). The unintended consequence of this market-driven logic of education, as Arum and Roksa (2011) noted, is that it "encourages students to focus on its instrumental value—that is, as a credential—and to ignore its academic meaning and moral character" (p. 16). As a result, a college education is now perceived as a right, what Wadsworth (2005) called "the ticket of admission to a good job and a middle-class lifestyle" (p. 25). In recent surveys, 91% of the U.S. public sampled thinks that every high school graduate who wants a four-year college degree should be able to earn one (Wadsworth, 2005).

This environment is creating what some believe is a "perfect storm" in higher education (Wadsworth, 2005). A "third tidal wave" (Kerr, 2001) of diverse students is entering college at the same time that higher education is experiencing serious revenue shortfalls, a less committed and less teaching-oriented faculty, and a greater societal emphasis on a college education as a career- and income-enhancing commodity all should be able to afford. Add to this mix an increasing number of students who bring to college diagnosable mental health issues (American College Health Association, 2010) that often outstrip the ability and resources of counseling centers to provide direct treatment, and the storm on the horizon is more than a thunder cloud. Yet this perfect storm also could be perceived as an unprecedented opportunity to provide an entire college-bound generation with what Schneider (2005) called "the full benefits of an empowering and horizon-expanding education" (p. 63) that can prepare students for the intellectual and social demands of a global knowledge economy and a changing world. The timing could not be better for positive psychology to be in a position to influence higher education!

As higher education has increasingly moved away from its moral roots and its emphasis on character development toward credentialism and job skills, the practical benefits of a college education have become more tangible, but we have lost a sense of the deeper and more far-reaching benefits that are intangible: the power to enrich one's life, to open new horizons and develop new perspectives, to engender open-minded compassion, to develop habits of mind and spirit that can sustain one in difficult times, and to develop moral and ethical principles for participating as a contributing citizen of the world—in short, the "power to change lives" (Kidd, 2005, p. 196). The central features of a meaningful life and broad preparation for civic engagement and productive work were historically the focus of higher education. A return to those goals, but in the context of a diverse and rapidly changing world, could provide the impetus for U.S. higher education to regain its position as a world leader; more importantly, it could lead to richer lives and greater well-being among the students who graduate.

The Intersection of Higher Education and Positive Psychology

Positive psychology is the scientific study of positive emotion, positive character, and positive institutions (Seligman, Steen, Park, & Peterson, 2005). The "fulfilled individual and the thriving community" (Seligman & Csikszentmihalyi, 2000, p. 5) are the targets of attention in this emerging science. These objectives are mirrored in higher education as student success and institutional effectiveness, yet they tend to be narrower targets in colleges and universities that have focused almost exclusively on grades and graduation rates. For higher education to realize its full potential to empower and equip the next generation of diverse students for meaningful, productive lives, these definitions are in need of expansion. As Schreiner, Hulme, Hetzel, and Lopez (2009) noted, "the challenge is for positive psychology to inform the field of higher education by applying their principles to the work of faculty, staff, and administrators on college campuses" (p. 569).

The goal of positive psychology is to enable a greater percentage of the world's population to *flourish* (Seligman, 2011). Flourishing people have high levels of emotional, psychological, and social well-being; they are productively engaged with other people, in their work, and in society, experiencing fulfillment and a sense of purpose in their engagement. They are resilient, rising to meet the challenges of life and realistically optimistic about the future. They also look beyond themselves and help others find meaning, purpose, and satisfaction in life. Vitally engaged and functioning well in work and in relationships, they are enthusiastic about life and exhibit an acceptance of self and others that encourages growth (Keyes, 2003). Using this definition, current estimates are that only one fifth of the U.S. adult population is flourishing (Keyes, 2009). Through the empirical study of optimal functioning, strengths, well-being, effective coping, health, creativity, altruism, hope, and the characteristics of positive institutions and situations, positive psychologists desire to increase levels of flourishing and influence public policy so that a greater percentage of the world is able to experience a life well lived.

The goal of flourishing exists within a broader theory of well-being (Seligman, 2011) that is useful in understanding how positive psychology can best influence the work of college faculty, staff, and administrators. Although the construct of subjective well-being has a long and distinguished history spanning Aristotle, the Utilitarian philosophers, Freud, and modern-day researchers such as Diener (1984, 2000) and colleagues (Diener, Oishi, & Lucas, 2009), former American Psychological Association president and one of the founders of positive psychology, Martin Seligman (2011), suggested a theory of well-being that goes beyond subjective self-report. He maintained that there are five elements of well-being that enable humans to flourish: positive emotion, engagement, meaning, accomplishment, and positive relationships. Extending this theory to higher education could enable a greater proportion of students to not only survive the college experience, but actually thrive within it. This particular intersection of positive psychology and higher education will be the focus of the remainder of this chapter.

Student Success: Thriving in College
Definitions of Student Success

In the current environment, equating student success with increased graduation rates is a straightforward way to address the concerns of legislators and the general public; however, this traditional definition offers little insight into the complexities of student success. With its focus on the percentage of students who remain enrolled at a specific institution from year to year, along with grade point average as an indicator of their progress to graduation (Venezia, Callan, Finney, Kirst, & Usdan, 2005), this definition conceptualizes the problem simply as reversing the dropout rate and increasing completion rates. Too often, it also leads to the position that admissions selectivity is the best pathway to improved graduation rates, because students with better academic preparation, higher test scores, higher parental education, and higher family income are more likely to graduate from college (Adelman, 2006). However, admitting solely those students whose background characteristics predispose them to graduate would not only fail to help the United States reach its ambitious goals for more college-educated adults, but it would also contradict all the efforts to expand college access to a wider range of students. As Kinzie (2012) noted,

> The laser focus on completion may also overshadow other important college processes and outcomes, including the quality of students' experiences in undergraduate education, student behaviors and level of

engagement in educationally purposeful activities, learning outcome attainment, preparation for the world of work and lifelong learning, personal growth and development, and many other desirable outcomes of college. The singular focus on graduation rates also provides limited insight into the full scope of what may be contributing to lagging completion rates and, more importantly, what action should be taken to improve student success. Finally, the emphasis on simple survival to earn a degree can eclipse important quality educational experiences that engage students at high levels and help them make the most of their college experience. (p. xx)

Expanded definitions of student success are beginning to emerge, incorporating not only persistence, but also satisfaction, learning, and personal development (Kuh, Kinzie, Shuh, & Whitt, 2005; Kuh, Kinzie, Buckley et al., 2006). However, there remains an emphasis on the behaviors of students. For example, the National Survey of Student Engagement focuses on student engagement in "educationally purposeful activities" (Kuh, 2001b, p. 1), measuring how often students use the library, rewrite a paper, and use tutoring services and the like. It also assesses the extent to which institutions support participation in those activities (Carini, Kuh, & Klein, 2006; Kuh, 2001a, 2001b, 2003). Such an approach ignores psychological engagement in favor of behavioral engagement, missing a potential opportunity to craft a more holistic view of student success. However, one particular approach to student success that considers psychosocial factors and is beginning to garner attention in higher education is the strengths development perspective.

Talent and Strengths Development

When student success is defined solely in terms of grades and graduation, not only does the institutional emphasis shift to admissions standards, but it also shifts to the deficits students bring to the college environment that must be remediated in order for students to succeed. The deficit remediation model is the dominant paradigm in U.S. higher education, and it is founded on the belief that there are certain abilities and skills a student must possess in order to succeed in college and that those who do not possess these skills at entrance must spend most of their first college year acquiring them (Schreiner, 2013a). As a result, in the U.S., billions of dollars are spent on remedial education at higher education institutions, with up to 40% of all college students taking developmental courses (Attewell, Lavin, Domina, & Levey, 2006). However, decades of evidence indicate that this approach to student success is not particularly effective: After controlling for academic preparation, high school skills, and family background, Attewell and colleagues (2006) found that enrolling in remedial coursework actually *reduced* the likelihood that a student would graduate. Likewise, other researchers using matched samples have found that students who take remedial classes are less likely to complete a year of college or graduate compared to similar students who do not receive developmental education (Bettinger & Long, 2008; Calcagno & Long, 2008).

The deficit remediation approach to student success has overlooked a key ingredient in learning and achievement: motivation. Spending most of one's time remediating weakness rarely energizes a student. Thus, a shift in perspective is needed, one that taps into student motivation. A strengths development approach to student success builds on what energizes students, what they do best, and capitalizes on the talents that students bring with them into the college environment to help them gain the knowledge and skills necessary to develop their talents into strengths (Louis & Schreiner, 2012; Shushok & Hulme, 2006). This approach is congruent with and has been informed by the positive psychology movement.

The strengths development perspective has an interdisciplinary history within social work (Saleebey, 1992), organizational development (Buckingham & Clifton, 2001; Clifton & Harter, 2003), positive psychology (Aspinwall & Staudinger, 2003), and higher education (Astin, 1985; Kuh et al., 2005; Lopez & Louis, 2009). In higher education, this perspective originated in Astin's (1985) theory of talent development that emphasized the institution's role in promoting student learning and success. Those who subscribe to this view of student success believe that every student can learn under the right conditions; as a result, the institution must organize its resources and create conditions for teaching and learning to optimize success (Kuh et al., 2005).

Implicit within the talent development approach is a philosophy that capitalizing on one's areas of greatest talent is likely to lead to greater success than investing comparable time and effort to remediate areas of weakness (Clifton & Harter, 2003). Lopez and Louis (2009) expanded this notion into strengths development, emphasizing the importance of identifying students' talents at entry and then teaching them how to develop the talents into strengths by investing effort to acquire the necessary knowledge and skills that will lead to excellence. They noted that this approach represents a return to basic educational principles that were evident in the early theories of Binet (Binet & Simon, 1916), Terman (Terman & Oden, 1947), Dewey (1938), and Chickering (1969), who studied "the best of the best" or what helped students succeed and develop.

This view of student success as developing student talent into strengths has particular relevance for an increasingly diverse student population. A strengths development approach emphasizes the need to embrace the wide variety of talents students possess (Chickering, 2006); as a result, it sends a far different message to students at entrance to college. Rather than focusing on students' deficits at entrance, a strengths development approach focuses on the talents they possess and what they are able to contribute to the academic community, talents that can form the foundation for addressing the challenges they will likely face as a college student. Instead of communicating that there is one pathway to success, a strengths development approach conveys that success lies in leveraging one's unique gifts and talents, becoming the best version of oneself (Louis & Schreiner, 2012). Furthermore, as students have the opportunity to act on their strengths and do what they do best, the likelihood increases that they will flourish (Frederickson, 2009). Developing students' strengths holds the potential for energizing students to become engaged in the learning experience, to invest the effort necessary to succeed, and to connect with others in positive ways.

Thriving as an Integrative Definition of Student Success

The current approaches to student success have tended to focus on either the behaviors that lead to learning outcomes (National Survey of Student Engagement, 2006), the institutional supports for engagement in those behaviors (Kuh et al., 2005), or the programs and services that are available to students (Kramer, 2007). Such research has significantly advanced higher education's understanding of student success; however, a component largely missing is the individual motivation and psychological processes that lead students to engage and fully benefit from the opportunities presented in the college environment (Bean, 2005). Such processes are malleable (Robbins et al., 2004), meaning that strategically developed interventions could enable a greater percentage of students entering college to not simply survive but thrive in the collegiate environment.

Representing an intersection of the principles of positive psychology and the goals of higher education, the construct of *thriving* was derived from the research on flourishing (Keyes, 2003; Keyes & Haidt, 2003; Seligman, 2011) and the psychosocial factors most predictive of college student retention (Bean & Eaton, 2000; Berger & Milem, 1999). Thriving is defined as being "fully engaged intellectually, socially, and emotionally in the college experience" (Schreiner, 2010a, p. 4). This integrative view of student success as thriving in college incorporates not only academic performance and graduation, but it also includes vital engagement and deriving optimal benefits from the college experience. Thriving students are engaged in the learning process, invest effort to reach important educational goals, manage their time and commitments effectively, connect in healthy ways to other people, are optimistic about their future and positive about their present choices, are appreciative of differences in others, and are committed to enriching their community (Schreiner, 2010a). Empirical evidence suggests that each of these qualities is amenable to intervention and connected to academic success and persistence to graduation (Schreiner, Pothoven, Nelson, & McIntosh, 2009).

Confirmatory factor analysis with large national samples of college students indicates that the construct of thriving is a higher-order factor comprising five latent variables: Engaged Learning, Academic Determination, Positive

Perspective, Social Connectedness, and Diverse Citizenship (Schreiner, 2012). Each of the factors represents an element of *academic, intrapersonal,* or *interpersonal* thriving that has been empirically demonstrated to be amenable to change within students, rather than a fixed personality trait over which there is little control (Schreiner, McIntosh, Nelson, & Pothoven, 2009). In a national study of 14,067 students from 53 public and private 4-year institutions, these aspects of thriving were found to account for an additional 11–23% of the variation in important outcomes such as college grades and intent to graduate, over and above what was explained by institutional differences and individual student demographic characteristics (Schreiner, Nelson, Edens, & McIntosh, 2011). From this national research, the 25-item Thriving Quotient was developed as an instrument to measure the extent to which college students are gaining optimal benefits from their college experience. Research has demonstrated strong internal consistency (α = .89), excellent fit of the model to national samples of college students ($\chi^2_{(114)}$ = 1093.83, $p < .001$, comparative fit index = .954; root mean square error of approximation = .054 with 90% confidence intervals from .052 to .058), and evidence of predictive validity connecting scores on the instrument to intent to graduate, institutional fit, satisfaction, learning gains, perception of the value of tuition, and grade point average (Schreiner, Kalinkewicz, McIntosh, & Cuevas, 2014; Schreiner, Nelson, Edens, & McIntosh, 2011; Schreiner, Pothoven, Nelson, & McIntosh, 2009).

Academic Thriving

Students who are thriving academically are engaged in the learning process, and they are investing the necessary effort to set goals, manage their time, and regulate their own learning process. The Engaged Learning factor is described as "a positive energy invested in one's own learning, evidenced by meaningful processing, attention to what is happening in the moment, and involvement in learning activities" (Schreiner & Louis, 2011, p. 6). Congruent with Seligman's (2011) *engagement* component in his well-being theory, this aspect of thriving also incorporates Langer's (1997) concept of *mindfulness,* with its focus on attentiveness in the present moment. The Academic Determination factor is similar to Seligman's *accomplishment* component of well-being, but it also includes elements from Snyder's (1995) hope theory, with its emphasis on goal setting, pathways, and agency. Academic Determination combines hope theory with self-regulated learning principles (Pintrich, 2004), Ryff and Keyes' (1995) concept of *environmental mastery,* theories of effort regulation (Pintrich et al., 1993; Robbins et al., 2004), and the ability to apply one's strengths to academic tasks (Lopez & Louis, 2009).

Research with large samples of 4-year college students across the United States, Canada, and Australia demonstrates that engaged learning and academic determination can be enhanced by rewarding interactions with faculty, as well as by family support for the student attending college, being sure of one's major, and experiencing a sense of community on campus. However, this same research indicates that the specific pathways to engaged learning and academic determination vary by ethnicity. For example, Asian students tend to engage in learning to a greater degree when they interact with faculty within their major or conduct research with faculty, whereas African American students engage to a greater degree when their interactions with faculty are within the context of ethnic organizations, as advisors, or when they discuss career and graduate school plans with faculty. In contrast, Latino students experience the least benefit of faculty involvement, but they are more likely to engage when their interactions with faculty are social in nature (McIntosh, 2012; Schreiner, Kammer, & Primrose, 2011). Because interventions are planned to enhance student thriving, attention to cultural nuances such as these will be an important dimension of programming.

Intrapersonal Thriving

The Positive Perspective factor of thriving represents the way students view life. Comprising two constructs from positive psychology, *optimism* (Carver, Scheier, Miller, & Fulford, 2009) and *subjective well-being* (Diener, 2000), this factor is congruent with Seligman's (2011) *positive emotion* component of well-being. Students who are thriving intrapersonally view the world and their future with confidence, expecting good things to happen and reframing negative events into learning experiences, with the result that they tend to be more satisfied with their lives and enjoy the college experience more. Students with a positive perspective are able to take a long-term view of events that happen to them and are able to see those events from multiple viewpoints. As a result, they are able to experience more positive emotions on a regular basis, which leads to higher levels of satisfaction with the college experience (Schreiner, Pothoven et al., 2009).

When a student's family is supportive of the college chosen and encourages him or her to graduate, it fuels intrapersonal thriving. In the same manner, students who report that their religious or spiritual beliefs provide strength during difficult times and offer a guiding framework for decision making are also highly likely to report a positive perspective on life. However, the role that spirituality contributes to a positive perspective differs by ethnicity, with African American and Asian students seeming to rely on spirituality as a pathway to intrapersonal thriving to a greater degree than Caucasian or Latino students (McIntosh, 2012; Schreiner, Kammer, & Primrose, 2011). Thus, potential new pathways to enhance student success, particularly in underrepresented populations on campus, become available by recognizing and validating students' spiritual beliefs and experiences. Within the campus context, there is evidence that participating in community service and experiencing a sense of community on campus are also predictive of a positive perspective; however, on predominantly White campuses, these experiences are often very different for historically underrepresented groups than for majority students (Collins, 2012).

Interpersonal Thriving

As Seligman (2011) noted when he advanced *positive relationships* as an important component of his well-being theory, "very little that is positive is solitary" (p. 20). Thus, thriving in college incorporates healthy relationships and interactions with others. Two aspects of interpersonal thriving are reflected in the factors of the Thriving Quotient: Social Connectedness and Diverse Citizenship (Schreiner, 2012). Although both of these factors describe interpersonal connections, the former captures students' beliefs about the sufficiency of their personal relationships, whereas the latter emphasizes the attitudes and values that drive their interactions with others.

Based on Ryff and Keyes' (1995) construct of *positive relations*, Social Connectedness is the presence of healthy relationships in students' lives. This factor comprises having good friends, being in relationship with others who listen to them, and feeling connected to others so that one is not lonely. The ability to form and maintain healthy relationships is an important element in college students' growth emphasized in higher education theories of student development (Chickering & Reisser, 1993).

Diverse Citizenship is a combination of openness and valuing of differences in others, along with a desire to make a contribution to one's community and the confidence to do so. It is derived from higher education research on *openness to diversity* (Miville et al., 1999) and *citizenship* (Tyree, 1998). Thriving students give time to help others and respond to others with openness and curiosity, believing that those who are different from themselves have something important to contribute to the relationship. They want to make a difference in their community and the larger society (Schreiner, 2012; Schreiner, McIntosh et al., 2009), a goal that is consistent with the civic engagement objectives that have historically characterized higher education.

These interpersonal dimensions of thriving are enhanced most by campus experiences, but they are also framed by the connections students maintain with others outside of the campus environment, such as their family, friends, and work colleagues. Interpersonal thriving is most affected by a sense of community on campus—the feeling students have that they belong, are connected in important and meaningful ways to others, and matter to the institution. For underrepresented students, this sense of community matters even more to their success and well-being: it is the major predictor of their thriving, not only interpersonally but also intrapersonally and academically (McIntosh, 2012; Schreiner, Kammer, & Primrose, 2011). The students least likely to be thriving on a university campus are those who are most disconnected from others and most out of their comfort zone: international students, ethnic and religious minority students, and low-income students. Any application of positive psychology principles to the university setting must be interpreted through these cultural lenses.

The holistic view of student success that is represented in the construct of thriving has the potential to refocus higher education toward not only intellectual engagement but also positive relationships, meaningful contribution to society, and healthy psychosocial coping mechanisms. Such a refocusing provides many opportunities to apply the principles of positive psychology to the work of higher education, with specific implications for the college classroom, as well as for academic advising, counseling centers, and a wide variety of student life programming. In each section below, specific applications of positive psychology principles in the university context will be discussed.

Thriving in the Classroom: Applying Principles of Positive Psychology

Engaging and motivating students in the learning process is the major challenge facing educators, particularly within diverse classrooms where students bring a variety of needs and levels of preparation for college work (Perry, Hall, & Ruthig, 2005; Pintrich & Zusho, 2002). Applying positive psychology principles derived from self-determination theory (Ryan & Deci, 2000) could provide educators with tools for a more positive impact on students' motivation, leading to higher levels of engagement that enable students to succeed and persist to graduation. Ryan and Deci (2000) referred to *authentic motivation* as motivation that is self-initiated and self-regulated, in contrast to extrinsic motivation. They noted that this type of motivation results in higher levels of "interest, excitement, and confidence, which in turn is manifest both as enhanced performance, persistence, and creativity" (Ryan & Deci, 2000, p. 69). Environments that support students' needs for autonomy, competence, and relatedness can lead to authentic motivation, which fuels student engagement in the learning process and contributes to their development and optimal functioning.

Engaged learning is the ultimate goal, whereby students meaningfully process what they are learning, attending to what is happening in the moment, and actively participating in the learning experience (Schreiner & Louis, 2011). Faculty development programs that equip instructors with strategies for meeting students' needs for autonomy, competence, and relatedness (Ryan & Deci, 2000) as a way of fostering engaged learning are an example of how the principles of positive psychology can be applied to teaching and learning. As faculty learn to provide clear expectations, optimal challenges, and timely informative feedback, students' competence levels increase. Teaching faculty how to design their assign-ments and course activities to optimize students' choices in the context of con-tent mastery can meet students' needs for autonomy and thereby increase levels of authentic motivation. Providing tools and strategies to help faculty structure collaborative, active learning in their classrooms builds positive emotions that expand students' engaged learning (Fredrickson, 2009) and also meet students' needs for relatedness (Schreiner & Louis, 2011).

Explicitly teaching positive psychology in the classroom, whether as a stand-alone course in the psychology curriculum or woven into existing courses, also affords the opportunity for students to benefit from the research and empha-sis on fulfilled individuals and thriving communities. Fineburg (2004) notes that infusion into existing courses is "the more efficient and holistic way of teaching positive psychology" (p. 203), because students will gain a more complete and nuanced perspective on the field of psychology as a whole. However, courses on positive psychology are becoming more common (Froh & Parks, 2012), often structured around the three pillars of positive psychology: positive emotions, positive individual traits, and positive institutions:

> Understanding positive emotions entails the study of contentment with the past, happiness in the present, and hope for the future. Understanding positive individual traits consists of the study of the strengths and virtues, such as the capacity for love and work, courage, compassion, resilience, creativity, curiosity, integrity, self-knowledge, moderation, self-control, and wisdom. Understanding positive institutions entails the study of the strengths that foster better communities, such as justice, responsibility, civility, parenting, nurturance, work ethic, leadership, teamwork, pur-pose, and tolerance. (Positive Psychology Center, http://www.ppc.sas.upenn.edu/)

By intentionally teaching college students the principles of positive psychol-ogy, whether woven into first-year seminar courses or introductory psychology classes, or taught as a singular focus of a course, educators have the potential to equip students with the tools they need to thrive in the college years.

Positive Psychology and the Advising Relationship

The advising relationship is the ideal vehicle for applying positive psychology prin-ciples to enable more students to thrive in college, because it is a preexisting struc-ture within every institution whereby each student has the opportunity for an ongoing individual interaction with a representative of the institution (Schreiner, 2013a). These institutional representatives, whether faculty or professional advisors, know the institution well and also are cognizant of students' strengths and needs. When advising is structured toward hope building, strengths development, and equipping students with an optimistic explanatory style, the best of positive psychology is aimed strategically at helping students grow and thrive (Schreiner, Hulme, Hetzel, & Lopez, 2009).

Students with high levels of hope are able to conceptualize their goals and then create specific strategies they are motivated to use consistently to reach those goals (Lopez et al., 2004). In a 6-year study of college students that statistically controlled for their entrance exam scores, previous academic performance, self-esteem, and intelligence, those students who entered college with higher levels of hope earned higher grades and were more likely to graduate (Snyder et al., 2002). Hope building within the advising relationship involves assisting students in setting meaningful, realistic goals and brainstorming multiple pathways to reach their goals. Because advisors help students reframe potential obstacles to success as challenges that can be overcome with effort, they are able to provide students with the encouragement and support necessary to sustain the motivation for reaching their goals (Schreiner, Hulme, Hetzel, & Lopez, 2009).

A strengths development approach to the advising relationship represents a paradigm shift for higher education from failure prevention and a survival mentality to success promotion and a thriving perspective (Schreiner, 2013b). Rather than focusing exclusively on problems the student is encountering, this approach emphasizes possibilities. Instead of assessing where the student is deficient and in need of remediation, strengths development advising assesses the personal assets or talents that the student brings into the college environment and considers how they can be multiplied by gaining the necessary knowledge and skills to develop them into strengths. As students learn how to develop their strengths and apply them to meet challenges and reach important goals, they experience a level of self-efficacy that can sustain them through difficult times. They also develop a wider repertoire of success strategies and proactive coping skills because they learn to use their strengths as pathways to their goals and as the foundation for addressing the inevitable challenges of college life (Schreiner, 2013a). Advisors who use a strengths development approach apply the best of empirically established positive psychology principles represented in appreciative inquiry (Bloom, Hutson, & He, 2008; Cooperrider & Whitney, 1999), life coaching (Linley & Harrington, 2006), and signature strengths interventions (Seligman, Steen, Park, & Peterson, 2005).

Finally, positive psychology can be integrated into the advising relationship as advisors help students develop an optimistic explanatory style. This positive perspective on life is foundational to thriving in college, because it engenders persistence during difficult times (Schreiner, 2010a). Teaching students to attribute their successes and failures to controllable causes builds resilience and hope, enabling them to approach future events with greater confidence that success is possible. For example, an advisor can turn a discussion of low grades into an opportunity to teach the student to reframe the situation and strategize for success the next time. Students equipped with this optimistic explanatory style are more likely to engage in the learning process, leading to higher levels of academic performance (Pintrich & Zusho, 2002).

Positive Psychology and the Counseling Center

Increasing numbers of students enter college with low levels of psychological well-being, experiencing "difficulties in relationships and developmental issues, as well as the more severe problems such as anxiety, depression, suicidal ideation, sexual assault, and personality disorders" (Benton et al., 2003, p. 69). These increased clinical demands in the context of limited resources pose significant challenges to university counseling centers. Positive psychology offers a unique framework for expanding the traditional role of the counseling center and has significant potential for addressing the growing mental health needs of college students (Schreiner, Hulme, Hetzel, & Lopez, 2009).

In addition to incorporating well-being therapy (Ruini & Fava, 2004), quality of life therapy (Frisch, 2006), and positive psychotherapy (Seligman, Rashid, & Parks, 2006) into the traditional therapeutic strategies offered by the counseling center, positive psychology principles can be applied to preventive outreach services, so that more students are taught proactive coping strategies that enable them to thrive. Web-based positive psychology interventions (Seligman, Steen, Park, & Peterson, 2005) and resilience workshops (Hetzel et al., 2005) are examples of applying positive psychology in a proactive manner to the vast numbers of students who are languishing in college but may never seek counseling. Infusing strengths development into new student orientation and first-year student seminars (Louis & Schreiner, 2012; Schreiner, Hulme, Hetzel, & Lopez, 2009) applies a primary prevention perspective to student success by equipping students with coping skills before they are in crisis.

Positive Psychology and Student Life Programming

The co-curricular realm of college life also affords an opportunity for positive psychology to influence higher education and promote thriving. Two key areas where the principles of positive psychology can be applied include service learning and student leadership development.

Service learning is often a partnership between academic affairs and student life, because faculty design the curriculum and assignments and Student Life professionals manage the community service logistics (Einfeld & Collins, 2008). The best service-learning programs provide prolonged engagement in the community, offer students an opportunity to reflect and discuss their experiences with one another, and tie the service experience to academic content (Astin, Vogelsgang, Ikeda, & Yee, 2000). When done well, service learning results in "an increased sense of personal efficacy, an increased awareness of the world, an increased awareness of one's personal values, and increased engagement in the classroom experience" (Astin, Vogelsgang, Ikeda, & Yee, 2000, p. 4). Positive psychology could be applied to a service-learning context by incorporating principles of empathy and altruism, so that students not only engage in short-term efforts to improve the welfare of others, but they gain a long-term perspective that enables them to respond more sensitively to the needs around them. Encouraging perspective taking and developing empathy-induced altruism has been used effectively in other settings to improve racial attitudes and attitudes toward stigmatized outgroups, as well as to promote greater cooperation in competitive situations and to improve long-term relationships (Batson, Ahmad, & Lishner, 2009). Applying these principles in service learning thus has the potential to increase the Diverse Citizenship and Social Connectedness components of thriving (Schreiner, 2010b).

Student leadership development programming is a ubiquitous feature of the co-curricular environment on college campuses. This area holds considerable potential for the application of positive psychology principles, because the research on authentic leadership and psychological capital is particularly relevant to developing leadership skills in college students (Schreiner, Hulme, Hetzel, & Lopez, 2009). As student leaders learn to develop their own psychological capital by increasing their hope, efficacy, resilience, and optimism (Luthans, Youssef, & Avolio, 2007), they become more authentic leaders. Authentic leaders, according to Luthans and Avolio (2003), use individual strengths, engender positive emotions, stimulate hope, and reinforce consistent morals and values, with the result that the organizations they serve engage in a continuous process of self-development that results in sustained performance. For student leaders, these principles translate to empowering the student members of their organization and fostering their development so that the organization is more likely to meet its goals.

Institutional Effectiveness: The Thriving Community

Along with student success, one of the primary goals within higher education is institutional effectiveness. Institutional effectiveness has been conceptualized in myriad ways over the years, beginning with a focus on academic inputs such as library resources, faculty/student ratios, average admissions test scores, and faculty credentials. In the past two decades, the focus has shifted from inputs to outcomes, such that indicators of institutional effectiveness now include graduation rates, student satisfaction levels, and job placement rates (Ruben, 2004). However, as Pascarella and Terenzini (2005) have noted, considerably more attention has been devoted to measuring the reputation and resources of institutions than to determining the actual impact they have on student learning.

An encouraging trend is seen in the efforts to quantify student engagement in educationally purposeful activities and measure the institution's supports for such behaviors through the National Survey of Student Engagement (Kuh, 2001b). In addition, accrediting bodies are increasingly demanding assessment of student learning outcomes as measures of institutional effectiveness (Maki, 2010). From an accreditation perspective, the most comprehensive definition of institutional effectiveness is the extent to which the institution delivers on its promises or the congruence between the stated institutional mission and outcomes of its curricula, programs, and services. The net result is that many colleges and universities are collecting a wider variety of evidence about their effectiveness. However, there is considerable opportunity for positive psychology to influence how higher education responds to this evidence.

Effective institutions are proactive and responsive to the data they collect. This stance necessitates an organizational climate in which feedback is valued, collaboration and trust characterize daily work, and there is a commitment to keeping the promises implicit in the mission of the institution (Park & Peterson, 2003). Positive organizational scholarship and community psychology both have garnered significant empirical support for two constructs that could be particularly helpful for colleges and universities as they address organizational climate. *Positive organizational behavior* and a *psychological sense of community*, which combine to form the ideal of "the thriving community" that was foundational to Seligman and Csikszentmihalyi's (2000) original conceptualization of positive psychology, have the potential to dramatically change the way higher education approaches institutional effectiveness.

Positive Organizational Behavior

Positive organizational behavior is defined as "the study and application of positively oriented human resource strengths and psychological capacities that can be measured, developed, and effectively managed for performance improvement in today's workplace" (Luthans, 2002, p. 59). What distinguishes positive organizational behavior from other aspects of positive psychology is its emphasis on state-like qualities that can be developed, rather than on traits that are relatively fixed, and its intended outcome of institutional performance impact, rather than optimal individual functioning (Luthans & Youssef, 2009). As colleges and universities strive to improve their effectiveness, several principles based in positive organizational behavior may be helpful.

Psychological capital (Luthans, Youssef, & Avolio, 2007) is an individual-level construct composed of hope, efficacy, resilience, and optimism that Luthans and Youssef (2009) posit has synergistic effects on performance and satisfaction. The creation of a positive organizational climate does not occur by hiring only people who possess high levels of psychological capital, however. Organizational climate is fluid and dynamic; it requires the development of its human resources. Authentic leaders are those who attend to their own levels of psychological capital while also developing the psychological capital of others; as a result, an organizational climate of inclusion, caring, support, and trust develops. Organizational cultures characterized by information sharing, cooperation, ownership, and interdependence exhibit the highest levels of performance and satisfaction (Luthans & Youssef, 2009), offering much after which higher education can pattern itself. Park and Peterson (2003) assert that organizations also have virtues; the best organizations are those that have an articulated moral vision or goal that is embraced by members and constituents alike. These organizations have explicit and equitable reward structures, treat people as individuals, "allow them to do what they do best" (Park & Peterson, 2003, p. 41), and follow through on the promises they make. These characteristics, when applied to colleges and universities, offer a strategy for impacting institutional effectiveness.

A Psychological Sense of Community

Some of these same themes from the field of positive organizational scholarship have existed within the discipline of community psychology since the early 1970s. For instance, Sarason's (1974) conceptualization of a psychological sense of community emphasized interdependence and ownership as key elements. Although researchers have studied the concept of sense of belonging, particularly among students of color (Hurtado & Carter, 1997), the focus has been at the individual student level. By expanding this focus to include a psychological sense of community, there are multiple pathways for affecting institutional effectiveness and the broader organizational climate.

A psychological sense of community is defined as "a feeling that members have of belonging and being important to each other, and a shared faith that their needs will be met by their commitment to be together" (McMillan & Chavis, 1986, p. 9). Students, faculty, and staff who report a strong sense of community on campus feel they are part of a stable and dependable network of people who care about them, are committed to their growth and well-being, and are able to meet their needs (Lounsbury & DeNeui, 1995). Recent adaptations of this definition have focused on four aspects of a sense of community that provide a roadmap for enhancing campus climate. These four aspects include membership, ownership, relationship, and partnership (Schreiner, 2010b).

Membership refers to a sense of belonging, feeling that one is part of something larger than oneself, and feeling valued by others in the community (McMillan & Chavis, 1986). The use of rituals, traditions, honor codes, and symbols of the university conveys membership. Celebrating the accomplishments of students and faculty can be a powerful way of tangibly demonstrating the value the university places on members of its community (Schreiner, 2010b). *Ownership* refers to voice and contribution; members of the community perceive that their input matters and that they have something to offer the community (McMillan & Chavis, 1986). Including students, faculty, and staff in institutional decision making and soliciting their regular feedback thus bolsters their sense of community. The *relationship* aspect of a sense of community refers to the development of emotional connections and positive interactions with other community members (McMillan & Chavis, 1986). Frequent opportunities to celebrate and to experience shared positive emotions enhance this element of a sense of community. Finally, *partnership* refers to interdependence, working together toward common goals, and experiencing the synergy that occurs when accomplishment is shared (McMillan & Chavis, 1986). Student-faculty research, interdisciplinary teaching and scholarship, and cross-departmental projects are examples of the types of partnerships that build a psychological sense of community (Schreiner, 2010b).

By focusing on the development of each aspect of a sense of community, colleges and universities can increase their institutional effectiveness. Because previous studies have demonstrated that a strong sense of community is the best single predictor of individual student thriving (Schreiner, Kalinkewicz et al., 2014; Schreiner, Nelson, Edens, & McIntosh, 2011), fostering a sense of community on campus can lead to higher levels of student success, as well. Other research has discovered that satisfaction with the campus climate is one of the best predictors of student retention (Schreiner & Nelson, 2013–2014); in addition, Braxton, Hirschy, and McClendon (2004) note that a positive campus climate that communicates institutional integrity and a commitment to student welfare is predictive of student persistence to graduation. Thus, the benefits of developing aspects of the campus climate that are conducive to a sense of community span the entire student experience and involve the contributions of faculty, staff, and administrators alike.

Conclusion

As higher education encounters the pressures and demands of a rapidly changing global society that is based on a knowledge economy and promises educational access to a wide variety of diverse learners, the principles of positive psychology are particularly relevant for higher education to fulfill its original mission of developing the intellect and character of the next generation. Whether those principles are applied in the classroom, the advising relationship, the counseling center, the co-curricular programs and services, or through the development of a positive campus climate and sense of community, the emphasis on strengths and virtues that enable students and universities to thrive provides a strong foundation for meeting the needs of a changing world.

References

Adelman, C. (2006). *The toolbox revisited: Paths to degree completion from high school through college.* Washington, DC: U.S. Department of Education.

American College Health Association. (2010). *National College Health Assessment: Fall 2010 reference group executive summary.* Retrieved from http://www.achancha.org/docs/ ACHA-NCHA- II_ReferenceGroup_ ExecutiveSummary_Fall2010.pdf

Arum, R., & Roksa, J. (2011). *Academically adrift: Limited learning on college campuses.* Chicago, IL: University of Chicago Press.

Aspinwall, L. G., & Staudinger, U. M. (Eds.). (2003). *A psychology of human strengths: Fundamental questions and future directions for a positive psychology.* Washington, DC: American Psychological Association.

Astin, A. W. (1985). *Achieving educational excellence.* San Francisco, CA: Jossey-Bass.

Astin, A. W., Vogelsegang, L. J., Ikeda, E. K., & Yee, J. A. (2000). *How service learning affects students.* Los Angeles, CA: Higher Education Research Institute, University of California, Los Angeles.

Attewell, P. A., Lavin, D. E., Domina, T., & Levey, T. (2006). New evidence on college remediation. *Journal of Higher Education, 77*(5), 886–924.

Batson, C. D., Ahmad, N., & Lishner, D. A. (2009). Empathy and altruism. In S. J. Lopez & C. R. Snyder (Eds.), *Oxford Handbook of Positive Psychology,* 2nd edition (pp. 417–426). Oxford, England: Oxford University Press.

Bean, J. P. (2005, November). *A conceptual model of college student engagement.* Paper presented at the annual meeting of the Association for the Study of Higher Education, Philadelphia, PA.

Bean, J. P., & Eaton, S. B. (2000). A psychological model of college student retention. In J. M. Braxton (Ed.), *Reworking the student departure puzzle* (pp. 48–61). Nashville: Vanderbilt University Press.

Benton, S. A., Robertson, J. M., Tseng, W. C., Newton, F. B., & Benton, S. L. (2003). Changes in counseling center client problems across 13 years. *Professional Psychology Research and Practice, 34*(1), 66–72.

Berger, J. B., & Milem, J. F. (1999). The role of student involvement and perceptions of integration in a causal model of student persistence. *Research in Higher Education, 40,* 641–664.

Bettinger, E., & Long, B. T. (2008). *Addressing the needs of under-prepared students in higher education: Does college remediation work?* (NBER Working Paper 11325). Cambridge, MA: National Bureau of Economic Research. Retrieved from the National Bureau of Economic Research website: http://www.nber.org/papers/w11325

Binet, A., & Simon, T. (1916). *The development of intelligence in children* (E. S. Kit, Trans.). Baltimore, MD: Williams and Wilkins.

Bloom, J., Hutson, B., & He, Y. (2008). *The appreciative advising revolution.* Champaign, IL: Stipes Publishing.

Bok, D. (2006). *Our underachieving colleges: A candid look at how much students learn and why they should be learning more*. Princeton, NJ: Princeton University Press.

Braxton, J. M., Hirschy, A. S., & McClendon, S. A. (2004). *Toward understanding and reducing college student departure*. ASHE-ERIC Higher Education Research Report Series (No. 30). San Francisco: Jossey-Bass.

Buckingham, M., & Clifton, D. O. (2001). *Now, discover your strengths*. New York, NY: The Free Press.

Calcagno, J. C., & Long, B. T. (2008). *The impact of postsecondary remediation using a regression discontinuity approach: Addressing endogenous sorting and noncompliance* (NBER Working Paper 14194). Cambridge, MA: National Bureau of Economic Research. Retrieved from the National Bureau of Economic Research website: http://www.nber.org/papers/w14194

Carini, R. M., Kuh, G. D., & Klein, S. P. (2006). Student engagement and student learning: Testing the linkage. *Research in Higher Education, 47*(1), 1–32.

Carnevale, A. P., & Fry, R. A. (2001). *Economics, demography, and the future of higher education policy*. Washington, DC: National Governors Association.

Carver, C. S., Scheier, M. F., Miller, C. J., & Fulford, D. (2009). Optimism. In S. J. Lopez & C. R. Snyder (Eds.), *Oxford Handbook of Positive Psychology, 2nd edition* (pp. 303–312). Oxford, England: Oxford University Press.

Chickering, A. (1969). *Education and identity*. San Francisco: Jossey-Bass.

Chickering, A. W. (2006). Creating conditions so every student can learn. *About Campus, 11*(2), 9–15.

Chickering, A. W., & Reisser. L. (1993). *Education and identity*. San Francisco: Jossey-Bass.

Clifton, D. O., & Harter, J. K. (2003). Investing in strengths. In K. S. Cameron, J. E. Dutton, & R. E. Quinn (Eds.), *Positive organizational scholarship* (pp. 111–121). San Francisco, CA: Berrett-Koehler.

Collins, K. P. (2012). Thriving in students of color on predominantly White campuses: A divergent path? In L. A. Schreiner, M. C. Louis, and D. D. Nelson (Eds.), *Thriving in transitions: A research-based approach to student success* (pp. 65–85). Columbia, SC: The University of South Carolina, National Resource Center for the First-Year Experience and Students in Transition.

Cooperrider, D. L., & Whitney, D. (1999). *Appreciative inquiry*. San Francisco, CA: Berret-Koehler.

Dewey, J. (1938). *Experience in education*. New York, NY: Collier.

Diener, E. (1984). Subjective well-being. *Psychological Bulletin, 93*, 542–575.

Diener, E. (2000). Subjective well-being: The science of happiness and a proposal for a national index. *American Psychologist, 55*, 34–43.

Diener, E., Oishi, S., & Lucas, R. E. (2009). Subjective well-being: The science of happiness and life satisfaction. In S. J. Lopez & C. R. Snyder (Eds.), *Oxford handbook of positive psychology, 2nd edition* (pp. 187–194). Oxford, England: Oxford University Press.

Einfeld, A., & Collins, D. (2008). The relationships between service learning, social justice, multicultural competence, and civic engagement. *Journal of College Student Development, 49*(2), 95–109.

Fineburg, A. C. (2004). Introducing positive psychology to the introductory psychology student. In P. A. Linley & S. Joseph (Eds.), *Positive psychology in practice* (pp. 197–209). Hoboken, NJ: John Wiley and Sons.

Fredrickson, B. L. (2001). The role of positive emotions in positive psychology: The broaden-and-build theory of positive emotions. *American Psychologist, 56*(3), 218–226.

Fredrickson, B. L. (2009). *Positivity*. New York: Crown Publishers.

Frisch, M. B. (2006). *Quality of life therapy: Applying a life satisfaction approach to positive psychology and cognitive therapy*. Hoboken, NJ: John Wiley and Sons.

Froh, J. J., & Parks, A. C. (2012). *Activities for teaching positive psychology: A guide for instructors*. Washington, DC: American Psychological Association.

Gardner, H. (2005). Beyond markets and individuals: A focus on educational goals. In R. H. Hersh & J. Merrow (Eds.), *Declining by degrees: Higher education at risk* (pp. 97–112). New York, NY: Palgrave Macmillan.

Hennessy, E. (2010). *New data indicate educational attainment continues to flat-line.* Retrieved from American Council on Education website: http://www.acenet.edu/AM/ Template. cfm?Section=Search&template=/CM/HTMLDisplay.cfm&ContentID=38695

Hetzel, R. D., Matlock-Hetzel, S., & Marsh, J. G. (2005). Positive psychology and university counseling centers: The Baylor experience. *Section on Counseling and University Counseling Centers Newsletter, 1*(2), 8–9.

Hurtado, S., & Carter, D. F. (1997). Effects of college transition and perceptions of the campus racial climate on Latino college students' sense of belonging. *Sociology of Education, 70,* 324–345.

Kerr, C. (2001). *The uses of the university.* Cambridge, MA: Harvard University Press.

Keyes, C. L. M. (2003). Complete mental health: An agenda for the 21st century. In C. L. M. Keyes & J. Haidt (Eds.), *Flourishing: Positive psychology and the life well-lived* (pp. 293–309). Washington, D.C.: American Psychological Association.

Keyes, C. L. M. (2009). Toward a science of mental health. In S. J. Lopez & C. R. Snyder (Eds.), *Oxford handbook of positive psychology (2nd ed.)* (pp. 89–96). New York: Oxford University Press.

Keyes, C. L. M, & Haidt, J. (Eds.). (2003). *Flourishing: Positive psychology and the life well-lived.* Washington, D.C.: American Psychological Association.

Kidd, J. J. (2005). It is only a port of call: Reflections on the state of higher education. In R. H. Hersh & J. Merrow (Eds.), *Declining by degrees: Higher education at risk* (pp. 195–208). New York, NY: Palgrave Macmillan.

Kinzie, J. (2012). A new view of student success. In L. A. Schreiner, M. C. Louis, & D. Nelson (Eds.), *Thriving in transitions: A research-based approach to college student success* (pp. xi–xxx). Columbia, SC: University of South Carolina, National Resource Center for the First-Year Experience and Students in Transition.

Kramer, G. (2007). *Fostering student success in the campus community.* San Francisco, CA: Jossey-Bass.

Kuh, G. D. (2001a). Assessing what really matters to student learning: Inside the National Survey of Student Engagement. *Change, 33*(3), 10–17, 66.

Kuh, G. D. (2001b). The National Survey of Student Engagement: Conceptual framework and overview of psychometric properties. Bloomington, IN: Indiana University, Center for Postsecondary Research.

Kuh, G. D. (2003). What we're learning about student engagement from NSSE. *Change, 35*(2), 24–32.

Kuh, G. D., Kinzie, J., Buckley, J. A., Bridges, B. K., & Hayek, J. C. (2006). *What matters in student success: A review of the literature.* Washington, DC: National Postsecondary Education Cooperative.

Kuh, G. D., Kinzie, J., Schuh, J. H., & Whitt, E. J., and associates. (2005). *Student success in college: Creating conditions that matter.* San Francisco, CA: Jossey-Bass.

Langer, E. J. (1997). *The power of mindful learning.* Reading, MA: Addison Wesley.

Linley, P. A., & Harrington, S. (2006). Strengths coaching: A potential-guided approach to coaching psychology. *International Coaching Psychology Review, 1,* 37–46.

Lopez, S. J., & Louis, M. C. (2009). The principles of strengths-based education. *Journal of College and Character, 10*(4), 1–8.

Lopez, S. J., Snyder, C. R., Magyar-Moe, J. L., Edwards, L. M., Pedrotti, J. T., Janowski, K., Turner, J. L., & Pressgrove, C. (2004). Strategies for accentuating hope. In P. A. Linley & S. Joseph (Eds.), *Positive psychology in practice* (pp. 388–404). Hoboken, NJ: John Wiley and Sons.

Louis, M. C., & Schreiner, L. A. (2012). Helping students thrive: A strengths development model. In L. A. Schreiner, M. C. Louis, & D. D. Nelson (Eds.), *Thriving in transitions: A research-based approach to college student success* (pp. 19–40). Columbia, SC: University of South Carolina, National Resource Center for the First-Year Experience and Students in Transition.

Lounsbury, J., & DeNeui, D. (1995). Psychological sense of community on campus. *College Student Journal, 29*(2), 270–277.

Luthans, F. (2002). Positive organizational behavior: Developing and managing psychological strengths. *Academy of Management Executive, 16*(1), 57–72.

Luthans, F, & Avolio, B. J. (2003). Authentic leadership: A positive developmental approach. In: K. S. Cameron, J. E. Dutton, & R. E. Quinn (Eds.), *Positive organizational scholarship,* (pp. 241–261). San Francisco, CA: Barrett-Koehler.

Luthans, F., & Youssef, C. M. (2009). Positive workplaces. In C. R. Snyder, & S. Lopez (Eds.), *Handbook of positive psychology,* 2nd edition (pp. 579–588). Oxford, UK: Oxford University Press.

Luthans, F., Youssef, C. M., & Avolio, B. J. (2007). *Psychological capital: Developing the human competitive edge.* Oxford, England: Oxford University Press.

Maki, P. (2010). *Assessing for learning: Building a sustainable commitment across the institution.* Sterling, VA: Stylus Publishing.

McIntosh, E. J. (2012). *Thriving in college: The role of spirituality and psychological sense of community in students of color.* (Order No. 3521901, Azusa Pacific University). ProQuest Dissertations and Theses, 229. (1035327809).

McMillan, D. W., & Chavis, D. M. (1986). Sense of community: A definition and theory. *Journal of Community Psychology, 14*(1), 6–23.

Miville, M. L., Gelso, C. J., Pannu, R., Liu, W., Touradji, P., Holloway, P., et al. (1999). Appreciating similarities and valuing differences: The Miville-Guzman University-Diversity Scale. *Journal of Counseling Psychology, 46*(3), 291–307.

National Center for Education Statistics. (2012). *Higher education: Gaps in access and persistence study.* Washington, DC: National Center for Education Statistics, Institute of Education Sciences, U.S. Department of Education.

National Survey of Student Engagement. (2006). *Engaged learning: Fostering success for all students.* Annual report of the National Survey of Student Engagement. Retrieved from: http://nsse.iub.edu/NSSE_2006_Annual_Report/docs/NSSE_2006_Annual_Report.pdf

Organization for Economic Cooperation and Development. (2013). *Education at a glance 2013.* OECD Indicators, OECD Publishing. Retrieved from: http://dx.doi.org/10.1787/eag-2013-en

Park, N., & Peterson, C. M. (2003). Virtues and organizations. In K. S. Cameron, J. E. Dutton, & R. E. Quinn (Eds.), *Positive organizational scholarship: Foundations of a new discipline* (pp. 33–47). San Francisco, CA: Berrett-Koehler.

Pascarella, E. T., & Terenzini, P. T. (2005). *How college affects students: A third decade of research* (Vol. 2). San Francisco, CA: Jossey-Bass.

Perry, R. P., Hall, N. C., & Ruthig, J. C. (2005). Perceived (academic) control and scholastic attainment in higher education. In J. C. Smart (Ed.), *Higher education: Handbook of theory and research* (Vol. 20, pp. 363–436). Norwell, MA: Springer.

Pintrich, P. R. (2004). A conceptual framework for assessing motivation and self-regulated learning in college students. *Educational Psychology Review, 16*(4), 385–407.

Pintrich, P. R., Smith, D. A. F., Garcia, T., & McKeachie, W. J (1993). Reliability and predictive validity of the Motivated Strategies for Learning Questionnaire (MSLQ). *Educational and Psychological Measurement, 53,* 801–813.

Pintrich, P. R., & Zusho, A. (2002). Student motivation and self-regulated learning in the college classroom. In J. C. Smart & W. G. Tierney (Eds.), *Higher education: Handbook of theory and research* (Vol. 16, pp. 55–128). The Netherlands: Springer.

Positive Psychology Center. (2011). Retrieved from the University of Pennsylvania Positive Psychology Center website: http://www.ppc.sas.upenn.edu/

Reuben, J. A. (1996). *The making of the modern university: Intellectual transformation and the marginalization of morality*. Chicago, IL: University of Chicago Press.

Robbins, S. B., Lauver, K., Le, H., Langley, R., Davis, D., & Carlstrom, A. (2004). Do psychosocial and study skill factors predict college outcomes? A meta-analysis. *Psychological Bulletin, 130*(2), 261–288.

Ruben, B. D. (2004). *Pursuing excellence in higher education: Eight fundamental challenges*. San Francisco, CA: Jossey-Bass.

Ruini, C., & Fava, G. A. (2004). Clinical applications of well-being therapy. In P. A. Linley & S. Joseph (Eds.), *Positive psychology in practice* (pp. 371–387). Hoboken, NJ: John Wiley and Sons.

Ryan, R. M., & Deci, E. L. (2000). Self-determination theory and the facilitation of intrinsic motivation, social development, and well-being. *American Psychologist, 55*(1), 68–78.

Ryff, C. D., & Keyes, C. L. M. (1995). The structure of psychological well-being revisited. *Journal of Personality and Social Psychology, 69*, 719–727.

Saleebey, D., (Ed.). (1992). *The strengths perspective in social work practice*. New York, NY: Longman.

Sarason, S. B. (1974). *The psychological sense of community: Prospects for a community psychology*. San Francisco, CA: Jossey-Bass.

Schneider, C. G. (2005). Liberal education: Slip-sliding away? In R. H. Hersh & J. Merrow (Eds.), *Declining by degrees: Higher education at risk* (pp. 61–76). New York, NY: Palgrave Macmillan.

Schreiner, L. A. (2010a). The "Thriving Quotient": A new vision for student success. *About Campus, 15*(2), 2–10.

Schreiner, L. A. (2010b). Thriving in community. *About Campus, 15*(4), 2–11.

Schreiner, L. A. (2012). From surviving to thriving during transitions. In L. A. Schreiner, M. C. Louis, & D. D. Nelson (Eds.), *Thriving in transitions: A research-based approach to college student success* (pp. 1–18). Columbia, SC: University of South Carolina, National Resource Center for The First-Year Experience and Students in Transition.

Schreiner, L. A. (2013a). Strengths-based advising. In J. K. Drake, P. Jordan, and M. A. Miller Eds.), *Academic advising approaches: Strategies that teach students to make the most of college* (pp. 105–120). San Francisco, CA: Jossey-Bass.

Schreiner, L. A. (2013b). Thriving in college. In P. C. Mather and E. Hulme (Eds.), *Positive psychology and appreciative inquiry in higher education* (pp. 41–52). New Directions in Student Services, no. 143.

Schreiner, L., Hulme, E., Hetzel, R., & Lopez, S. (2009). Positive psychology on campus. In S. J. Lopez & C. R. Snyder (Eds.), *Oxford handbook of positive psychology* (2nd ed.) (pp. 569–578). New York, NY: Oxford University Press.

Schreiner, L. A., Kalinkewicz, L., McIntosh, E. J., & Cuevas, A. P. (2014). *Advancing a psychosocial model of college student success: The role of thriving*. Manuscript submitted for publication.

Schreiner, L. A., Kammer, R., & Primrose, B. (2011, November). *Predictors of thriving in students of color: Differential pathways to college success*. Paper presented at the annual meeting of the Association for the Study of Higher Education, Charlotte, NC.

Schreiner, L., & Louis, M. C. (2011). The Engaged Learning Index: Implications for faculty development. *Journal of Excellence in College Teaching, 22*(1), 5–28.

Schreiner, L. A., McIntosh, E. J., Nelson, D., & Pothoven, S. (2009). *The Thriving Quotient: Advancing the assessment of student success*. Paper presented at the annual meeting of the Association for the Study of Higher Education. Vancouver, British Columbia.

Schreiner, L. A., Nelson, D., Edens, D., & McIntosh, E. J. (2011). *The Thriving Quotient: A new vision for student success*. Paper presented at the annual conference of the National Association of Student Personnel Administrators, Philadelphia, PA.

Schreiner, L. A., & Nelson, D. (2013–2014). The contribution of student satisfaction to persistence. *Journal of College Student Retention, 15*(1), 77–123.

Schreiner, L. A., Pothoven, S., Nelson, D., & McIntosh, E. J. (2009). *College student thriving: Predictors of success and retention.* Paper presented at the annual meeting of the Association for the Study of Higher Education. Vancouver, British Columbia.

Seligman, M. E. P. (2011). *Flourish: A visionary new understanding of happiness and well-being.* New York, NY: Free Press.

Seligman, M. E. P., & Csikszentmihalyi, M. (2000). Positive psychology: An introduction. *American Psychologist, 55*(1), 51–82.

Seligman, M. E. P., Rashid, T., & Parks, A. C. (2006). Positive psychotherapy. *American Psychologist, 61*(8), 774–788.

Seligman, M. E. P., Steen, T. A., Park, N., & Peterson, C. (2005). Positive psychology progress: Empirical validation of interventions. *American Psychologist, 60*(5), 410–421.

Shushok, F., & Hulme, E. (2006). What's right with you: Helping students find and use their personal strengths. *About Campus, 11*(4), 2–8.

Snyder, C. R. (1995). Conceptualizing, measuring, and nurturing hope. *Journal of Counseling & Development, 73*(3), 355–360.

Snyder, C. R., Shorey, H. S., Cheavens, J., Pulvers, K. M., Adams, V. H., III, & Wiklund, C. (2002). Hope and academic success in college. *Journal of Educational Psychology, 94*(4), 820–826.

Terman, L. M., & Oden, M. H. (1947). *The gifted child grows up: Twenty-five years' follow-up of a superior group.* Stanford, CA: Stanford University Press.

Tyree, T. M. (1998). Designing an instrument to measure the socially responsible leadership using the social change model of leadership development. *Dissertation Abstracts International, 59* (06), 1945. (UMI No. 9836493).

Venezia, A., Callan, P. M., Finney, J. E., Kirst, M. W., & Usdan, M. D. (2005, September). *The governance divide: A report on a four-state study on improving college readiness and success.* San Jose, CA: The Institute for Educational Leadership, the National Center for Public Policy and Higher Education, and the Stanford Institute for Higher Education Research.

Wadsworth, D. (2005). Ready or not? Where the public stands on higher education reform. In R. H. Hersh & J. Merrow (Eds.), *Declining by degrees: Higher education at risk* (pp. 23–38). New York, NY: Palgrave Macmillan.

Zemsky, R. (2009). *Making reform work: The case for transforming American higher education.* New Brunswick, NJ: Rutgers University Press.

2

Millennials in Higher Education

As Students Change, Much about Them Remains the Same

FRANK SHUSHOK JR. AND VERA KIDD

Perhaps a chapter about how to best work with students from a "new" genera-tion would start with a summary of their characteristics in an attempt to define or aggregate their commonly held beliefs, behaviors, and expectations. Those of us working on college campuses have become accustomed to the broad brush strokes that get painted about each successive generation of students—the cur-rent "Millennial" generation is no exception. Sometimes it seems that those brush strokes, rendered by those in the older generations, emphasize and generalize per-ceived negative images of our young adults—images communicated about and directly to students. This chapter challenges these practices, incorporating the philosophy of positive psychology and giving Millennials credit and support for their strengths and potential for good.

Writing in *Time Magazine*, Stein and Sanburn (2013) capture the dichot-omy of these broad brush strokes in an article entitled, "The New Greatest Generation: Why Millennials Will Save Us All." While describing Millennials' strong tendencies toward narcissism, their sense of entitlement, high expecta-tions, strong brand identification, and dependence on technology as the "Me Me Me Generation," the authors explain that burgeoning technology in the new digi-tal world, material abundance, and "peer-enting" style of parental relationships have shaped this generation, not as rebels, but as self-determining extensions of their parents' generation. They state ". . . millennials' self-involvement is more a continuation of a trend than a revolutionary break from previous generations. They're not a new species; they've just mutated to adapt to their environment" (Stein and Sanburn, 2013, p. 31). Stein and Sanburn (2013) point to the positive traits of millennials, describing them as accepting of differences in people, cau-tious in life decisions, earnest, nice, positive, and optimistic—young people who are good at navigating and negotiating with traditional institutions, when they choose to join them, and who are "pragmatic idealists" (p. 34).

This chapter will indeed provide information about the Millennial generation, generally defined as being born after 1981, but it will not purport a narrow list of characteristics unattached to the context of their environment. Philosophically, we have begun to wonder about the usefulness of the current practice of analyzing generations of students and doling out prescriptive tips about how to best work with them, individually and as a group. It is no doubt true that students change and become shaped by historical circumstances, their upbringing and parental practices, and prevailing educational philosophies. Clearly, we must understand demographic and cultural shifts in society and their impact on young people, but some cautionary reminders about the potential pitfalls of the oversimplification of these analyses, and resulting interventions, seems worthwhile.

This chapter will instead portray the *culture* of the Millennials through the societal, technological, and global forces at work that both shaped young adults and are shaped by them. The authors urge readers to think widely about the world shared by the younger and older generations and our varied ways of adapting to the opportunities and stresses that encompass us. As discussed below in "A World of Change" and "A World of Technology," a time-stamped overview of generational attributes is no longer helpful to the college educator when the speed at which our cultures change far outpaces any previous time in history.

Furthermore, as we discuss in "A World of Diversity," how can we define the characteristics of "typical" young adults amidst the burgeoning diversity of today's colleges? Surely, studies of homogeneous "generations" have become less conclusive as access to higher education grows and cadres of students from different socioeconomic, racial, ethnic, and religious backgrounds from across the globe learn on our college and university campuses and online.

Essentially, the current "generation" of students is difficult to generalize without devaluing the diversity and complexity of their cohort. Levine and Dean (2012) explain:

> ***The portrait is a composite***, [italics added] a picture of a generation, not of the individuals who make up that generation. The portrait is multifaceted, a report on a generation's attitudes, values and experiences replete with the contradictions and inconsistencies that are part of the lives of all human beings. The portrait is complex, looking backward and forward across a span of more than two centuries with multiple historic anchor points and a number of different comparison groups. (pg. *x*)

If a generation is a composite, it also presents a moving target, more akin to a film. Levine and Dean (2012) continue:

> The problem is that the names describe only a facet of a generation, not the whole. In this sense, they conceal more than they reveal. College

student attitudes, values, and experiences are continually shifting and changing. For the most part, these changes are matters of degree rather than kind. Generational names focus on the most visible of the changes. With time, however, the stereotype becomes more real than the generation itself. (p. 6)

Stein and Sanburn (2013) also warn about treating this group as homogeneous, stating that the rate of change is already segmenting the millennial generation into "microgenerations," emerging every few years so that even siblings can perceive real differences between them. The authors predict that members of the next group after millennials are likely to be even more empowered than their predecessors. This "micro-fracturing" of the age group, especially in light of the expanding diversity of the population, will continue to challenge our attempts to create generational titles.

Most likely, however, the best reason to relax our temptation to describe generations of students with overgeneralizations is that such characterizations are most frequently undergirded with negative overtones. As an unscientific test of this theory, we sent an e-mail to a dozen colleagues across the campus and asked them to describe this generation of students, as well as to compare and contrast students of today with students from the educator's generation. Although a reasonable number of more charitable descriptions were returned, the weight of responses hinted that something had gone awry. Listen carefully to how educators describe the "current generation." The hard working, relationally astute, family-focused, values-centered students of their generation had been replaced by a "technology-obsessed," "money-focused," and "egocentric" generation of today. Organizational theorists give this tendency a name—retrospective sense-making (Weick, 1979). In short, there may be an inclination to remember our college-age years as the good old days, largely because we who lived them conveniently forgot what we care not to remember.

Several years ago, Birnbaum and Shushok (2001) studied claims of "crises" in the higher education literature from 1970 to 1994. In summary, they found a consistent pattern across the decades of declaring problems of today more vivid and intense than the half-forgotten terrors of yesterday, even though at the time the crises of the past were considered just as intense. It may well be the same with new generations of college students—the issues and challenges are much more the same than we remember.

We have a colleague who is fond of the bayou country saying *plus les choses changent, plus ca reste la meme*: "In times like these, it is good to remember there have always been times like these." Regardless of the generation, students of yesterday and today have been and will continue to be in pursuit of answering some really important questions: who am I and what do I value? What is the meaning and purpose of life? What are my gifts and talents? Why am I in college and will I be successful? What kind of relationships should I pursue? How can I matter in the world? Whether in the 15th century or the 22nd, human beings pursue mostly the same questions. The difference, of course, is the surrounding and ever-changing context in which they ask these questions. Understanding the continuity in general needs and dispositions of humanity helps center our approach to help students learn, minimize cynicism, and remain relentless in our care for humanity.

What's Right with Your Generation?

In 2006, Frank Shushok joined colleague Eileen Hume in calling for higher education leaders to reframe their thinking, interactions, and pedagogy in a way that emphasizes the positive about individual students and their generation. They challenged readers to pay attention to how often they discussed what was wrong with a student, a colleague, or a situation. There is no doubt, too, that each generation comes with unique strengths that need to be considered and exploited by college educators. Perhaps the question should not be "what's wrong with a generation?" but "what's right with a generation that will help us make a better world?" (Shushok & Hulme, 2006).

Western culture often tends toward the pathological; we are trained to look for disease, speculate on its cause and potential consequences, and, most importantly, remedy it. We must remember that generational differences are not blights, nor should we treat younger generations as needing remediation to conform to the characteristics of their elders. Focusing on their positive traits—nurturing the unique strengths, talents, and skills of the youth in society—is a more holistic and forward-thinking approach. When students learn what is right about themselves and their generation, they begin to identify their strengths and initiate a process of learning that includes how their unique attributes can be used through vocational paths and civic opportunities. The result is frequently a new energy and passion for learning—through both curricular and cocurricular activities (Shushok & Hulme, 2006).

Therefore, what is good for the individual student could hold true for cohorts or generational groupings of students. In short, given the "strengths" of the current generation, how can we optimize these strengths in ways that improve the functioning of society? If we ask these questions in an ongoing manner, we position ourselves to be constant learners about our students. In our discussion of characteristics below, we offer examples of the "strengths" inherent in how we describe students.

Shushok and Hulme (2006) also recommend framing a discussion about how the tendency toward seeking pathology may affect student learning, especially as it relates to how students discover meaning, purpose, and their potential influence on the world. They counsel colleges and universities to take advantage of new research offered through the positive psychology movement by engaging in at least the following three activities: (1) study and understand successful students on campus; (2) establish a campus ethos that facilitates students' discovery and understanding of their strengths; and (3) assist students in finding groups, organizations, or communities that they can serve with their strengths.

Traditional academic or behavioral remediation approaches will continue to serve colleges and universities well in working with individual students. However, although we have engaged in remediation for the few, we have neglected to ask ourselves in any serious and organized manner what is it, within an individual student or a generation of students, that creates success? We suggest that educators spend an amount of time equivalent to that spent on remediation in the pursuit of learning about the traits, habits, and thought processes of *highly successful students*. Through rigorous empirical examination, we can determine which of these traits can be replicated in all students through proven interventions (Shushok & Hulme, 2006).

Although the newer characteristics attributed to Millennials, such as use of technology, are unquestionably descriptive, the development of definable generational *culture* is most helpful. Howe and Strauss (2000) cite three basic principles of rising generations that apply in societies such as the United States, where there is sufficient freedom for young people in numbers to redirect society. The new generation: (1) approaches and solves a problem that the prior youth generation has been unable to solve; (2) seeks to make corrections for what it perceives are behavioral excesses in their parents' generation; and (3) fills the social role being vacated by the elder generation. Although older generations may perceive these challenges as negative rebellion, Howe and Strauss (2000) explain otherwise:

> In a durable society, the rebellion of every new youth generation serves an invaluable function: curbing the excesses and complimenting the strengths of older generations—who may not be getting the kids they expect, but who usually get the kids they need. No generation can fairly be described as better, or worse, than any other. They simply have different locations in history, and thus different needs, desires, fears, obsessions, blind spots, opportunities for greatness, and tendencies toward tragedy. Each generation does what it must, within the context of the history and generational constellation into which it is born. (p. 70)

In the 1960s and 1970s for example, there was a focus on the environment as members of the idealistic, consciousness-awakened "Boomer" generation protested the effects on the planet of industrial air and water pollution and society's apathy about these issues. During this time, organizations such as the Environmental Protection Agency and legislation such as the Clean Air Act of 1970 were created and implemented. Civic-minded Millennials, who have reaped some of the benefits of these efforts, have also inherited many persistent environmental problems, including escalating rates of climate change. Given their own generational outlook, Millennials have taken up the banner of individual, national, and global sustainability—an approach they see as a rational initiative to impact the ills of the planet from a citizen's grass-roots perspective.

The Boomers (born between the mid-1940s and mid-1960s) and the X'ers (born between the mid-1960s and 1980) may have made the world aware of global environmental challenges, but the Millennials are emphasizing the role of the individual and concerned groups of citizens in addressing local and regional problems. Due to the internet and social media, they also have affiliations with a network of interconnected national and world organizations. They are essentially incorporating technological innovations and redirecting focus on issues that their parents and grandparents have been unable to solve, in ways they perceive to be more efficient and potentially successful.

Education in the Boomers' time involved identifying ecological problems and their scientific and societal causes, creating national awareness, accommodating social unrest, and training future lawyers and congressional members to tackle macrosolutions around issues. However, in the current climate, educational institutions teach courses on the techniques and potency of social media, sustainability, and recovery strategies for damaged ecosystems; campus organizations support the viability of microgrants to help curb destruction of natural resources, encourage international student trips to impact education in rain forest areas, and sponsor campus-wide recycling and energy conservation programs. Millennials have chosen to tackle these issues in a way that fits their own style. Educational institutions with offerings and missions that support their belief systems are the most likely to thrive and help effect needed change.

If we attribute future success to the Millennials or any subsequent youth generation, how can we as the older adults in society help shape that generation in a way that optimizes their talents, both for the betterment of the individual young adults and for society? Simply put, we must study success in order to promote success. George Vaillant's (2002) book, *Aging Well*, reports on his analysis of human development with an eye toward understanding those who reach their later years of life feeling fulfilled. Likewise, Keen, Keen, Parks, and Daloz's (1996) book, *Common Fire*, examines the lives of 100 people who sustained long-term commitment to the common good in the face of overwhelming odds. Colleges and universities can follow the lead of such authors and move away from a disposition toward studying the least successful to focusing on students who are fulfilled, accomplished, and, most importantly, learning. Two notable examples of this type of work are provided by George Kuh and his colleagues in *Involving Colleges* (1991) and in *Student Success in College* (2010).

To facilitate student understanding of their strengths, educators should first be aware of their own personal strengths and how they have used them to create success. Role models who understand their strengths can help dispel myths that anyone can be competent at anything, or that the greatest room for growth is in one's areas of weakness. As Palmer (1999) advises, "Before you tell your life what you intend to do with it, listen for what it intends to do with you" (p. 3). Students who watch faculty, staff, and alumni model this philosophy may be inspired to explore what their life intends to do with them. Colleges and universities should also be intentional about providing mechanisms through which students can identify their strengths.

Characteristics of Current College Students

With the philosophical ground work laid for our discussion about the appropriate use of generational research on college students, and our concerns and caveats about group characteristics being automatically applied to individuals in that group, we are ready to explore the characteristics that are widely attributed to today's college students. In discussing these descriptors of Millennials, it should be noted that what is offered herein mostly reflects Western and European society and industrialized, open nations such as Japan. Clearly, in some parts of the world, due to governmental or religious intervention in personal freedoms or communications, or the lack of resources—particularly in the area of technology—these attributes will manifest in varying degrees.

There are several excellent books that delve deeply into the details of defined characteristics of young adults. There are too many attributes to discuss in one chapter among all these well-researched and well-written resources, including an early comprehensive view in "Millennials Rising—The Next Great Generation" (Howe and Strauss, 2000) and most recently "Generation on a Tightrope—A Portrait of Today's College Student" (Levine and Dean, 2012). In between there are hundreds of books and articles that provide both characteristics and context for further research. However, it takes but a cursory review of this multitude of articles and books, each defining the current generation of college students, to realize that the focus on the major characteristics attributed to them, and the degree of positivity or alarm predicted, relies largely upon the author. As further evidence of the difficulty in defining this generation, witness some of the names by which they have been labeled: Millennials, Echo Boom, Generation Y, Gen Y, Net Generation, Generation Tech, Generation Next, The Therapy Generation, Generation 9/11, and Generation Why? Howe and Strauss (2000) determined that members of this generation prefer the name "Millennials." This label is as independent as its namesakes, because it stands on its own and is not attributed to a previous generation (Gen Y), to an attribute (Net Generation), nor some type of defining event (Generation 9/11).

Demographically, we know that current college students are the children either of older "Baby Boomer" parents, generally defined above as having been born between the mid-1940s and mid-1960's, or younger "Generation X" parents who are generally defined as having been born from 1965 through 1980. For the purposes of this discussion, Millennials can be understood to be born beginning after 1981, which means the oldest began entering college near the change of the Millennium, beginning in 1998 (Taylor & Keeter, pg. 4).

In summary, even though each generation deliberately takes on its own language, music, and style, thereby creating its own unique definition of relevance, young people cannot help but be, to some greater or lesser degree, the evolutionary product of the prior generation(s) with whom they share their family, community, and world. They have continuously been adapting to the world they were handed, and they have, even as children and teenagers, already influenced that world dramatically. Thus, the following conversation about the general characteristics of the Millennials who have reached college age should be viewed in the context of their place in the evolution of society, science, and technology.

A World of Change

Although it can be said that every generation in over 225 years of American history has dealt with societal change that was considered to be rapid at the time, the pace and saturation of change has accelerated wildly during Millennials' formative years. Their parents may be "Baby Boomers" or "Generation X's," depending on their age. Baby Boomers lived through and experienced their own explosion of change, with the beginnings of the space program, mainframe computers, hippies, station wagons, birth control, network news programs, the Civil Rights Movement, Vietnam, Watergate, the Cold War, the Cuban Missile Crisis, Motown, Woodstock, and 8-track tapes. Parents who are younger Generation X'ers have seen the continued evolution of the social and world changes that burgeoned in the Boomers' formative years, and they lived through the upsurge in the number of two-career couples, "latchkey kids" and daycare, the increase in divorce and single-parent households, the delay of parenthood, the increase in sales of foreign automobiles and manufacturing, outsourcing of domestic production, MTV, cassette audio and video tapes, spiraling supply and cost issues associated with fossil fuels and the degradation of the environment, the introduction of super stores and online shopping, and the AIDS pandemic. Millennials born in 1980 have seen the fall of the Berlin Wall, dissolution of the Union of Soviet Socialist Republics (USSR), the introduction of personal computing capabilities and truly portable cell phones, CDs and DVDs, construction of the International Space Station and Hubble Telescope, escalating global climate change, and the rise of terrorism—most notable in the United

States were the Oklahoma City bombing in 1995 and the events of September 11, 2001.

The unprecedented speed of change in our social, international, religious, and technological worlds means that Millennials have "lived" with these and many other changes subsequent to their parent's youth, either personally or through family and cultural stories. Although older adults clearly can see change in terms of "how it was before" and "how it is now," Millennials do not have the historical context to understand how dramatic these changes actually are in the fabric of history; it has simply been their *modus operandi*. Their world transformed rapidly throughout their childhood and adolescence; change is "no big deal."

Thus, some of the more negative comments about Millennials, such as impatience or a tendency to become bored easily, make sense in light of the rate of societal transformation in their lifetimes. This point is succinctly made by Arthur Levine and Diane R. Dean (2012) in the preface to their book "Generation on a Tightrope," describing "a generation of college students who were born, grew up and will live their lives in a nation undergoing a transformation from an analog, national, industrial society to a global, digital, information economy" (p. *x*).

Should not we also say at this juncture that only a group of young adults raised in a time of such rapid change could assimilate into this new world culture and thrive, work, and raise families? What kind of guidance can educators provide to build on their strengths associated with openness to change? Levine and Dean (2012) write: "For the United States, this has been a time of dramatic demographic, economic, technological, and global change, which has in a very few years substantially altered many aspects of our lives from how we are conceived to when we die and seemingly everything in between—from how we communicate, entertain ourselves, and shop to how we date, bank, and work . . . The implication of this finding is that schools and colleges need to educate these students in the skills and knowledge essential for such an era, which might be called the three C's: critical thinking, creativity, and continual learning" (p. xiv). Although we as educators often have difficulty coping with the pace of societal change, we can provide substantial learning opportunities for creative and critical thinking, and we can help students understand that they will be life-long learners through both academic programs and curricula for learning outside the classroom.

World of Technology

It can be argued that the major driver and product of this velocity of change is technology. The fact is that yesterday's fast laptop is outdated within a period of months; computing technology that the parents of Millennials had in a large $3,000 workstation is outpaced by their small hand-held $100 smart phone. Real-time news reporting from around the world, and real-time conversation, texting, and social networking has put today's youth in an instantaneous virtual crowd of humanity. Events in any part of the world can be posted on web or social networking sites within minutes. Access to online videos and music has presented fashion, cultural and musical images, and marketing that are incredibly varied yet consistently available across national and continental borders. Friendships, romances, and marriages begin or flourish online. Ideals of personal privacy have eroded. Legal concepts of intellectual and artistic property ownership have been challenged by music, video, and document downloads and file sharing. Programs and applications that fail to keep up with current demands fall by the wayside, and other upstart technologies move in to take their place with record speed. Because technology both drives and reflects societal and world transformations, Millennials have spent their childhood and adolescence living this change. It certainly seems that Millennials are immersed in technology (in today's parlance, they are sometimes called "digital natives" and most of the rest of us are "digital immigrants"). Again, as we talk about the descriptors that follow, we must be careful not to assume that all college students are tied so intimately with their technologies, but this characteristic certainly has implications for how we understand and even communicate information with large numbers of students.

The Pew Research study summarizes Millennials as "history's first 'always connected' generation" (Taylor & Keeter, 2010, p. 1). They describe that, as a result of living with technology, Millennials expect technology to serve them; to be available 24 hours a day, 7 days a week, and to be visual, auditory, stimulating, sharable, and, to some degree, sensational. Many Millennials follow the lives of celebrities, view music videos online, and download individual songs from the internet. According to the Pew Research Group, they obtain their news and facts online rather than from newspapers or network news, and they have an unprecedented ability to share their thoughts and reciprocally to be influenced by others via electronic communications. They may be misled by inaccuracies in the short run, but trust that they and others will provide feedback and correction to set the record straight on web sites such as Wikipedia. Each person may choose whether to be highly visible online, but each person does have a voice and an ability to participate in any aspect of the virtual world (Taylor & Keeter, 2010). As educators, we see opportunities as well as the challenges of these findings; many Millennials expect learning to take place in a stimulating and fast-paced world where current technology supports the educational process. As Levine and Dean (2012) lament, "Digital natives are being taught by digital immigrants in analog universities" (p. 49).

We also know the value of scheduled "quiet" time—opportunities for reflection, writing, and exchange of ideas are critical to develop deeper self-understanding. A mix of opportunities and media may provide the variety to keep students interested. Opportunities to slow down a bit and think after a day in the classroom or working online can help lower the focus on "business" and allow time for learning, and many of those opportunities can be created in the residence halls, student organizations, or other student affairs venues. Opportunities to use technology as part of the process of exploring these issues perhaps offers the best combination of techniques—for example, having students take an online assessment and then having conversations and written feedback about their insights.

A World of Learning

Although Millennials are not yet the most educated generation in American history (Gen X'ers still hold that distinction), Taylor and Keeter (2010) project they will achieve that result. Their study reveals that close to 40% are still in high school, trade school, or college as of 2010. Of those who have already completed college, there are slightly more female than male graduates, continuing a trend that began with Gen X'ers. In terms of pursuing what college has to offer, these students are typically pragmatic, career-oriented, and view higher education from a more utilitarian perspective than their predecessors. Current undergraduates want career skills and knowledge from college. In addition to useful course content, these digital natives expect technology to play a role in their education (Levine & Dean, 2012).

Due especially to online technologies, social networking, and access to many "experts" beyond professors and instructors, student affairs professionals in particular know that learning happens outside the classroom as well as inside. The implications for student affairs and academic professionals alike are profound. Students have the potential to learn throughout their days on campus, and both academic and life lessons are the curriculum. The boundary between academic and student affairs educational efforts, if it ever really existed at all, is no longer relevant. We have an unparalleled opportunity to reach students with many types of intentional and experiential development opportunities, but these efforts have to meet students where they are, in the residence halls and student unions, in dining centers and athletic venues, and during paid employment, organizational, and volunteer activities.

A World of Diversity

According to 2010 US Census data, the population of the United States has grown substantially since 1980, increasing by 82 million or 36%. Concurrently, the percentage of minority population groups has risen rapidly, so that as of the Federal Census of 2010, individuals whose heritage traces to Asia, Spanish-speaking countries, Africa, and India collectively make up a greater proportion of the population than Whites (Census Bureau, 2010). Members of these minorities have advanced in politics and government, pop culture, corporate and educational positions, sports, and medicine. Millennial children have lived next door to, gone to school with, befriended, dated, and applied to colleges with a greater diversity of children than ever before in the United States. Millennial children in the United States often do not recognize or respect racial and ethnic boundaries that have existed between groups in the past.

Sexuality and gender roles are similarly evolving. Expressions of gender identity that never would have been tolerated in the earlier history of the country have blossomed since Baby Boomer times, and more liberal gender roles have been accepted by the Millennial generation as a fact of life. Although there is certainly still resistance in society, some conservative causes, such as the antigay movement, are not an issue to the majority of Millennials. The important ingredient is individuals' right to self-expression, whether in terms of gender, sexual orientation, race, religion, nationality, or interests.

Women in the Millennial generation in Western society have stepped forward into areas not conceived in past generations, but they do not view themselves as feminists or radicals in any sense. In general, they neither support women's return to traditional roles nor specified male/female roles in society, and they *expect* progress toward equalization of the genders to continue: "Change will occur—and women will experience greater gender equity at work and at home—because of personal expectations . . . What makes Millennial women different from every other generation preceding them is the expectation that this will happen. It's not a hopeful optimism but a solid 'that's the way it will be' mindset" (Lowen, 2012, p. 1).

Politically, Taylor and Keeter (2010) explain that Millennials are more likely to identify themselves as liberal in their views than older generations, "reflected not just in their partisan identification and voting patterns, but also in their overall views about the role of government and about a range of social and national security issues . . . The distinctiveness of members of the Millennial generation is particularly evident in their social values, where they stand out for their acceptance of homosexuality, interracial dating, expanded roles for women and immigrants" (p. 63).

The unprecedented stirring of gender roles, sexual practices, cultural traditions, religious beliefs, and nationalities makes for a new type of "soup" for society and a different equation for learning in higher education. A homogeneous presentation of information in education, politics, or religion, if it ever truly worked, is now obsolete. The strengths of Millennial students to accept more broadly the benefits of diversity, and the value of those who hold diverse opinions, has the potential to force positive change in these arenas and in society. It is critical that educators personally model and provide opportunities for diverse learning across gender, national, ethnic, and other schisms so that students are in a positive position to actively participate and thrive in the society in which they will live in the coming decades.

A World of Individual Expression

Although they strive to be individuals in the face of the crowd and the blitz of media images and messages, the uniqueness of an individual in the Millennial generation is represented through their personal *expression* of self within society. Neither the traditional, rugged individualism nor isolation portrayed by cowboys and machismo heroes in time-honored Western culture, nor the stereotypes of "normal" homes, gender roles, attire, and automobiles in the mid-1900s seems appropriate to describe them. Millennials have more choices than ever before in how they express their individuality in dress, language, interests, and music, even piercings and tattoos; this freedom, combined with their numbers, further dilutes the idea that a generic description applies across their population.

It is noteworthy, however, that although Millennials strive to express their individuality, they are truly social in nature. First mentioned in *Millennials Rising* as team-oriented, with "strong team instincts and tight peer bonds," they are described as liking group learning, groups of friends, and team sports such as soccer (Howe & Strauss, 2000, p. 180). Loosely, "friends" may be friends in person or online acquaintances they have never met. Despite Millennials having many different mediums to pursue friendships, the number of close friends a student has may actually be lower than one may think. In a 2006 study published in the *American Sociological Review,* McPherson, Smith-Lovin, and Brahears found that Americans reported only having two close personal friends. This number is down from the initial study completed in 1985 in which Americans reported having three close personal friends. Although Millennial students have new avenues to pursue friendship, it can be argued that the quantity of options does not necessarily lead to quality friends.

Shushok (2011) argued that colleges and universities need to use both classroom and out-of-the-classroom experiences to help students intentionally develop meaningful friendships. Shushok continued by utilizing a Prepare-Engage-Reflect Model to offer suggestions of how institutions can facilitate friendship development. At the heart of the model is the idea of students better understanding themselves so that they may better interact with others. The use of positive psychology and focusing on individuals' strengths helps facilitate this model. When our students know themselves better and know the attributes at which they excel, they can better relate to others and engage in relationships by focusing on others' strengths.

By the time the socially engaged and technologically savvy Millennial freshmen arrive at college, they have the knowledge and opportunity to drift from their parents' and communities' religious, social, and cultural traditions. Some may not closely observe time-honored societal taboos such as limits on attire or the use of profanity in public. Many Millennials, as generations before them, use alcohol, either as a new experience for themselves once away from home, or as a continuation of the practice as they had in high school, with their parents' knowledge or consent. Levine & Dean (2012) cite research that indicates alcohol is by far the substance of choice among those who choose to party, and marijuana and tobacco are the second choices. However, there continue to be dangerous incidences of binge drinking, defined as drinking to get drunk or pass out, with the attendant health risks and impacts on decision making. They cite statistics that more than half of students at 4-year institutions believe alcohol is a serious challenge at their school and more than one quarter drank to excess in order to pass out. Approximately one quarter of the students also conceded that their grades on a course or assignment were negatively affected, and more than 20% admitted that alcohol or drug use had resulted in unplanned or unprotected sexual encounters (p. 61).

Peer pressure has always been a challenge for young people to navigate. In their technological world, students now spend a lot of time hooked into technology, replacing the packs of real people with whom students ran with larger groups of acquaintances in the virtual world—the environment that results in what Levine and Dean (2012) term a "New Tribalism . . . what amounts to a virtual tribe, consisting of friends, family, neighbors, acquaintances, and any other significant people in an undergraduate's life, past or present, and [they] stay connected with that tribe twenty-four hours a day, seven days a week, in class and out. Students live in a world of competition between intimacy and isolation" (pp. 53–54).

In terms of intimacy, it is evident that students know the facts but still do not necessarily make educated decisions about their sexual activities, resulting in paradoxes in behavior. For example, Levine and Dean (2012) explain that for many teens, intimate relationships have evolved to what is described as "a culture of casual relationships and casual sex" (p. 64). Many students describe themselves as sexually active: "By the time they graduate from college, approximately half of all undergraduates (47%) have hooked up or had casual sex with someone" (p. 64). They explain a scenario where students know and discuss sex more openly and explicitly, but even with this knowledge nearly 40% of students "never, rarely or only sometimes use a condom during vaginal intercourse" (p. 65). Moreover, although students do not identify themselves as having "dated," nevertheless only a minority of sexually active college students report more than one partner in the prior 12 months (Levine & Dean, pp. 64–65).

These paradoxes again defy generalization. Based on these findings, although casual sex is apparently normal for approximately half the population, the majority continue relationships with one person for 1 year or more. Although students know more about conception and sexually transmitted diseases than any former generation, approximately 40% still engage in risky sexual behavior. Even with unparalleled freedoms, students are still grappling with the same issues around intimacy, or for that matter alcohol and substance abuse, as former generations. The issue of how one explores the world in a liberated environment while still making decisions that do not derail his or her health, life plans, or dreams continues to challenge even the best and brightest of our youth.

As educators, we know that decision-making skills based on self-esteem, self-knowledge, and clear goals can assist students in their life activities. For example, students who know their own strengths and talents can build their core resolve, but we first have to draw them out of their routine in order to do so. Every routine in the life of students is related and has consequences for their chances at life learning. The time spent in front of a computer is time when students are not learning and polishing their social skills. The time spent only with casual relationships is time where students are not cultivating deeper and more meaningful friendships. The time spent "partying" may be adding to the awkwardness students feel in developing their academic skills and confidence in themselves. The time not spent in self-reflection and the establishment of a personal set of values and beliefs may foster poorer decision making in regard to all these aspects of their lives. The struggle between becoming a mature individual and being driven by the crowd, their peers or their "tribe," is the universal journey—one which student affairs can offer some strategies for navigation and success.

Yet, the promise of great social progress also resides with this generation. In terms of the implications for the positive psychology approach in the Millennial culture, the level of tolerance for diversity and the acceptance of individual expression carry the potential for greater levels of acceptance among individuals and groups, who choose to express themselves both individually and as members of a group contributing to society. Attributing negative descriptions to individuals based on their styles of self-expression may become obsolete at some point; individuals who no longer hide their individuality out of fear of ridicule, and who are accepted by others as the unique person they are, will surely have a better chance of developing a healthy and productive sense of self.

Special, Sheltered, and Optimistic Children

As described by Howe and Strauss (2000) in *Millennials Rising*, specialness is the belief held by Millennials, as nurtured by their parents, grandparents, and society, "that they are collectively vital to the nation and to their parents' sense of purpose" (p. 43). Concurrently, they describe the generation as "sheltered," in that adults have taken extreme care in planning for their children, providing safe environments for them, supervising them closely, emphasizing their well-being, guiding their development, and shielding them from harm. Levine and Dean (2012) describe today's college students as "immature, needy, protected, and tethered to their parents, who are their heroes" (p. 162).

Despite the evolving definition of "family," including traditional heterosexual parents, same-sex couples, and divorced or single parents, adolescents arriving at college generally arrive with adoring adults in tow. Howe and Strauss (2010) explain that Millennials' relationship with their parents tends to be built on a perception of their own "specialness" in their parents' eyes. As the most wanted or planned generation of all time, given the widely available birth control and options such as abortion or adoption, parents often made the specific choice to bring these children into the world. Parents may limit the number of children they have to one or two; they spend their child-rearing time and efforts on fewer children than prior generations. Because both parents probably work, they may have more resources to bring to bear on each child, and they provide material and experiential benefits to their children to help their development, including the means to make college a reality for their children.

Despite what would be expected as the normal "generation gap," most apparent when the use of technology is considered, there is no question that many Millennials have a strong, ongoing, even dependent relationship with their parents. The Pew Research Center (2010) reports that Millennials generally get along well with their parents. Many parents, in turn, remain close to their college student children. It is true that some parents have been disparagingly described in various media as "helicopter parents" (or "Chinook," "Blackhawk," "Lawnmower" or "Snowplow" parents, hovering around or rolling over their children, trying to influence their decisions—which in itself is not always different from the past), but more importantly trying to handle their children's challenges for them, even after their children leave home (Levine & Dean, 2012). Much anecdotal evidence, familiar to student and academic affairs professionals alike, points to parents interceding in students' choices among colleges, administrative requirements, student conduct cases, roommate disputes, majors, courses, grades, and job searches.

Recent information confirms that this parental involvement is accelerating. Levine and Dean (2012) cite statistics from Student Affairs Surveys in 2008 and 2011, comparing parental involvement in students' lives. Two thirds of the respondents cited increased parent involvement in their student's lives since 2008, and 60% reported increased parent contact with faculty members and administration. Of course, this is as much a generalization about the Boomer and X generations as it is the Millennials. Cultural norms, family characteristics, economic forces, and even simple logistical factors such as a college's distance from a student's home have always factored into the closeness students maintain with their parents, but unlike the first half of the prior century, when parents had great control over the influences to which their children were exposed, today's parents must compete for their children's attention with the larger society. The striking and universal difference in the Millennials' experience is the constant, public nature of everything that is presented to them about lifestyles and personal options, both by institutional agents (advertisers, media, government, and even educators) and by other Millennials. Never in history have so many young people been presented with the same images, music, icons, and narratives as today's youth, nor has that presentation been so outside the control of parental, religious, or educational influences.

Whereas parents in older generations could present the case for limited options in terms of religion, family, or work, Millennials are aware of many options open to them. They may honor their parents' core beliefs as valid and appropriate for them, while concurrently moving away from the norms of their parents' upbringing. It is not surprising then that, although they may respect the morals and work ethic of the older generations, Millennials may not be particularly concerned about many of the rules and mores of their parents' and grandparents' generations (Taylor & Keeter, 2010). Although they are polite and understanding of others who hold those beliefs, they are aware of many other ways of living. This may take the form of children questioning or diverging from societal rules, religious beliefs, sexual mores, or educational and workplace cultures and expectations.

Once again, a paradox develops that Millennials have to face. Far from rejecting their parents or their beliefs, yet understanding that the future needs a different set of skills and understanding than their parents can bring to bear, they are to a degree in uncharted waters. They have a world of information and the opportunity for innovation, and they are optimistic about their ability to ultimately succeed, but in the meantime there is a lot of work to do individually and for society.

The optimism of Millennials is also a trait described in many resources. For example, Howe and Strauss (2000) described students at the turn of the millennium thus:

> *Confident* is a good word to describe how Millennials feel about life after graduation. . . . Our Class of 2000 Survey showed only 6 percent expecting to make less money than older Gen Xers and 78 percent expecting to make more. At the same time, the teen view of success has become better-rounded and less exclusively focused toward one life goal. Over the last decade, "marriage/family" and "career success" have each declined in importance as "the one thing" in life. What's now more important is the concept of "balance"—especially, balance between family and work. More teens than ever seek to have a good lifelong relationship with parents. A rising share of high school seniors say "making a contribution to society" is "extremely" or "quite" important, while a declining share (though still a majority) say the same for "having lots of money." In a turnabout from Gen X, Millennials have faith that the American Dream will work for them, and for their own children. (p. 179)

Of course, events during the years between 2000 and current times have changed the world—the trauma of September 11, 2001 and the ensuing wars in Iraq and Afghanistan, domestic and international terrorism, the crash of the housing market, the deep recession beginning in 2008, and the impacts of the economic downturns on layoffs and unemployment—often in students' own families. All of these are events are enough to make the most optimistic among us a bit discouraged.

What has been the impact of economic downturns on the Millennials' sense of optimism? We believe the wildly optimistic students of the year 2000 have become more cautious but not pessimistic; they have become somewhat cynical but not jaded. We see around us students who have come to understand that economic recessions occur and cause hardships to the degree their families are prepared to weather the storm, but most of them have seen their families' survive the challenge—although their finances are certainly not unharmed, their lives are still more or less intact. Although their circumstances have changed, their view of the future has not. Citing Pew Research data, Taylor and Keeter (2010) confirm this hopefulness, describing them as "vulnerable yet optimistic." They explain: "Millennials have not escaped the current economic downturn. But even though they're not happy with their current economic circumstances, they remain highly optimistic about their financial future" (p. 20).

Most Millennials cannot escape the fact, however, that the economic situation in the first decade of the millennia has brought negative impacts on the availability of funds for college, the length of time spent in college (because students must work to help pay for their education), and the prospects of good career jobs in the near term—more paradoxes that students must face. Levine and Dean (2012) find continuing high expectations, despite the dramatic economic climate and its impact on their college experience:

> Today's students are graduating from college to enter a job market in which 9.1 percent of recent grads are unemployed. Two-thirds are leaving not only with a diploma, but also with student loan debts averaging $31,050 for a baccalaureate degree. And one in four eighteen—to twenty-nine year olds, previously living on his her own, is moving back with his or her parents (Pew Social Trends Center, 2010). . . . In spite of all this, this is a generation with higher personal and material aspirations than their predecessors. They are counting on the American Dream being available to them as it was for past generations of college students. Current undergraduates want good jobs and are willing to forego their careers of choice to get them. (p. 148)

Other than careers, how optimistic are Millennials after a decade of hard knocks? Levine and Dean (2012) continue:

> They want successful relationships. Eighty-nine percent say it's important to have a good marriage or relationship . . . They want to have children (89 percent). They want money and material goods. . . . They expect to be at least as well off as their parents (73 percent) . . ." (p. 149). They

explain that students hold a contradictory view of their world—they acknowledge the competition, selfishness and unfairness of society's economics, but "they are latter-day Horatio Algers, believing as did the nineteenth-century novelist that with hard work, determination, and character anyone can succeed in America, rising even from poverty to great wealth. Today's undergraduates believe that hard work always pays off (83 percent), if you want something you should have to work to earn it (97 percent) . . ." (p. 149).

However, Levine and Dean (2012) did find evidence of students' growing cynicism about the many societal challenges facing not only the United States, but the world: "It was the raft of issues . . . ranging from social, economic, and global troubles to the inequity and unfairness of the distribution of power and resources, the inability or unwillingness of government to act, and a general sense of national decline" (p. 150). When asked in spite of these concerns why they thought they will personally succeed anyway, "Their answer was basically that 'I am not going to be one of the statistics. I will beat the odds. I have a big future ahead and the support to achieve it'" (p. 152).

Once again, as student affairs educators, a paradox arises, and because we cannot know the future, we must be careful to nurture students' optimism without creating unrealistic expectations. What we do know is that learning about their own strengths and talents best prepares them to weather future challenges and opportunities. Students without top strengths in strategic thinking may need to use financial planning services early in their careers. Students who are skilled at influencing and building relationships may successfully take their career knowledge into the sales arena. Students with a variety of strengths may be able to make a positive impact on the political and regulatory realm that has created such skepticism in their ranks. Based on a mentality of service, as outlined next, knowledge of one's innate talents holds promise for improvements in the nation.

A World of Service

Parents of Millennials face a dilemma of nurturing "self-concern vs. unselfishness" in their children—that is, recognizing the uniqueness and value of each child while helping that child develop a sense of what challenges and responsibilities will be his or hers in the larger world. Some researchers and the media decry that Millennials have an educated superindividuality that has been described as self-centered, narcissistic, and demanding, or perhaps too far toward the "self" end of the "other/self" dichotomy. Every parent must operate in the continuum between nurturing a self-absorbed, dependent, and insecure child or a child that has the security to develop a deep and authentic individuality, knowing there is a strong base of support from adults who have his best interests in mind.

Another characteristic does exist, however, that helps balance out those described tendencies towards self-centeredness. Although the majority of Millennials, as discussed by Levine and Dean (2012), attend church seldom or never (59%) and describe themselves as not politically active or engaged (68%), they do engage in service activities, especially around issues of specific importance to them and with a focus on local efforts. Eighty-one percent of students at 4-year schools report they were involved in service activities an average of 30.4 hours in the prior 12 months. "These students are involved in a cornucopia of different activities, ranging from hospices and pet protections to homelessness and choice and right to life groups . . . The three most popular have remained constant . . . church and religious activities, work for charity organizations such as the United Way, and child and youth work" (p. 142). Thus, we see these young people taking on the problems of their world on their own terms—not necessarily attending church, but reaching out to others through church-coordinated activities, not "political" but issues-oriented, not seeking to change the world through a mass movement, but doing what is logical on a local basis to begin to change the world as an individual.

Again, although some researchers view Millennials as narcissistic and lacking honest and open knowledge about themselves, in truth, they may have never been challenged to honestly view their own particular strengths in a developmental way and in relation to society at large. As such, they may be unduly threatened by their potential weaknesses. As educators, we may be the first ones to challenge students to explore their strengths, confront their limitations, and deal with the complexities of comparison and competition that actually highlight their inherent talents and strengths, and engaging them in service activities is certainly one tried and true method for self-discovery.

Viewed from the perspective of strengths, if Millennials' comfort with their individuality and self-identity can be mentored appropriately, it can serve them well as society becomes ever more populated and complex. If individuals are taught to reflect and act on their own strengths, beliefs, and values, they can become strong self-determining citizens who can rationally assess the life choices they face and make informed judgments about their careers, relationships, religious beliefs, politics, service, and personal ethics.

Relevance and Rules

As Millennials stretch social mores on all fronts, they are not doing so mindlessly. As children and adolescents, they are increasingly insisting that rules applied to them be "relevant" to them and justified by the adults around them. This objection to irrelevancy may be overtly objective or subjective. As educators, we know they are not afraid to challenge the status quo in the classroom or outside if they believe those rules are not germane.

However, whereas their Boomer parents or grandparents may have left home or taken to the streets in protest of rules they considered irrelevant, we have observed that Millennials tend to protest by withdrawing into the many avenues of technology or friendships available. They have the option to respond to boring classes by browsing the internet or texting, and they can retreat from family confrontations with video games or nights out with friends. Instead of viewing television shows where families challenge but ultimately conform to family rules, teens have been raised on reality television where even outrageous challenges against tradition, authority, or civility may not be presented along with consequences. The relaxation of language and other restrictions on television and the internet furthers the appearance of total freedom.

The ability of many Millennials to seek their own agendas and turn to technology also shows itself in the classroom in terms of several trends described by Levine and Dean (2012), including the inappropriate use of technology during class, resistance to doing library research, plagiarism, and cheating. They state:

> There is much more explanation by professors to their students about what constitutes acceptable classroom behavior and what does not. More and more, admonitions and codes of conduct are making their way into syllabi. One dean told us that what we've accepted as normal common sense we now have to spell out for students regarding 'what we expect in terms of their behavior in the classroom' . . . Another senior student affairs officer said today's college students 'are rule followers. They respect authority now. It comes with a twist. They have to be told the rules' . . . This situation is a conundrum. It is on one hand impossible to believe that students do not understand that using digital devices in a classroom is rude . . . On the other hand, it is clear that today's undergraduates, who have grown up in a world dramatically different from their parents, truly do not know the rules by which adults are expected to live their lives and by which their colleges work." (p. 52)

Building one's identity and individuality can be exciting but daunting under these pressures. It takes time and focus to do so, and as educators we apparently have to set clearer expectations than ever before for our students, in and outside of the classroom.

Intelligence and Wisdom

In terms of wide access to the public school system, desegregation, and efforts to improve the quality of education by federal, state, and local governments, Millennials have had access to a more consistent level of education than prior generations. Not surprising given their population numbers, "the share of 18- to 24-year-olds attending U.S. colleges recently hit an all-time high, with nearly all of the recent growth occurring in community college enrollments" (Taylor & Keeter, p. 42). This has led some researchers to declare Millennials as a whole to be the "smartest" generation.

However, there is recognition that education alone does not automatically equal a generation prepared for the adult world. Other factors such as development of a set of values, a rational respect for rules as discussed in the prior section, awareness of others, compassion and empathy, the ability to make sound decisions, and the ability to move self-confidently though challenges are needed. To some degree, the involvement of some parents in making choices for their children may have negatively impacted children's ability to make the decisions required in an adult world. In particular, young adults need the ability to gather input and information and make sound determinations about potential employment, finances, relationships, political, organizational and religious affiliations, leisure time activities, volunteerism, and service to others.

This is an area where the positive psychology movement has direct potential for impact, in helping young people recognize and internalize a healthy and optimistic sense of self. Such self-knowledge—having been guided and corrected but encouraged and celebrated by parents, educators, and institutions—creates a balanced sense of individuality within society. When young people have not iterated and internalized an individual set of values and a realistic understanding of themselves, they do not have the depth of self-knowledge that could enlighten and guide their decision making as adults. Although their academic education has supplied skills, technologies, and facts, this education taken in the context of a personal set of values and beliefs provides the greatest opportunity for success and useful contributions to society.

Spiritual Quest

According to the Spirituality in Higher Education project conducted at UCLA's Higher Education Research Institute, students are interested in spirituality (Astin, Astin, & Lindholm, 2011). Although there is a renewed interest in spirituality, today's students are not necessarily interested in the religions of their parents that encompasses doctrines and traditions (Chickering, Dalton, & Stamm, 2006). Although spirituality is important to students, higher education often shies away from this area. Shushok (2011) argued that spirituality is an important part of personal development and that it is imperative that colleges and universities engage students in meaningful discussions regarding spiritual questions such as the purpose of life, finding meaning, and discovering values. These are all questions that Astin, Astin, and Lindholm (2011) suggested are spiritual in nature.

Engaging students in spiritual conversations not only helps foster their personal development, it can also enhance their ability to enter into stronger relationships with others. As discussed earlier, groups of friends are important to today's students; however, close friendships can be challenging for Millennials. In his discussion of friendship, Shushok (2011) discussed Aristotle's commentary of friendship found in his work *The Nicomachean Ethics*. Aristotle spoke of a deep friendship, one that Shushok coined as a "spiritual friendship." This type of friend may have shared values and a mutual commitment to each other. Helping our students engage in a discovery of their own spirituality and values can only help them in their ability to develop close friendships. This spiritual type of relationship that was recognized as vital as long ago as Aristotle's writings can be a life-affirming influence. It is telling that descriptions of young school shooters in the United States have usually included a lack of positive friendships.

Pressures and Expectations

Along with gaining information and education prior to their high school graduation, we know that today's students are also well aware of the competitive nature of society, and many have faced extreme pressure to perform by achieving superior grades in high school, taking advanced placement classes, and participating in extracurricular and volunteer activities that differentiate them from other college-bound students. The pressure by parents and society to gain access to certain schools and lucrative disciplines is strong. This pressure may have been accompanied by almost no coaching by adults on the art of self-reflection and self-knowledge. There can be a lot of tension riding on adolescents without the tools to deal with it. Under these circumstances, it is not surprising that the incidences of depression and "acting-out" behaviors are escalating.

Although we know that an expectation to excel in each and every college class or life challenge is unrealistic and even impossible, students arriving at colleges and universities are likely frightened by the prospect of failure. Framing this search for one's real abilities in a positive way is necessary in order for students to emerge from the effects of the self-esteem movement with a more aware and objective self-concept. In this way, the introduction of reflection and discourse about strengths can build *genuine* self-esteem. When students sense that failure is possible, they need to have constructive tools to allow them to use their talents and strengths to excel in the areas that will bring them the most success, joy, and fulfillment in all areas of their lives. This exploration may cause students to reconsider their chosen field of study, with or without the support of their parents. Our goal, then, is to help students become more authentic adults whose honest sense of self, strengths, and relative weaknesses is a guide in making these critical types of decisions.

Much has also been made about the tendency of many parents to stay involved in their children's lives; even as students leave home, technology allows parents to call or text at any time. As discussed earlier, many of us can provide numerous anecdotes of parents who are involved in their students' lives to the point of interference. Although listening, advice, and recommendations are positive contributions from parents, sometimes abstaining from participating in all but serious situations allows students to "experience their own experience," learning valuable lessons about the consequences of their actions or inactions and their own determination and resilience.

Tied to this self-esteem dilemma is the view, also discussed earlier, that Millennials are unrealistically optimistic; according to Howe and Strauss (2000), having been praised, rewarded, and sheltered from failure as children, students often have high positive expectations for grades, lucrative careers, and personal success. The argument is that, as parents and society strove to make children's lives as playful and carefree as possible, "allowing children to be children," there is an understandable desire by students to carry that unsustainable optimism and happiness forward into college and life after graduation. Researchers worry that students may lose forward momentum when life throws unexpected obstacles in their way. They may be unprepared for the realities of studying long hours, working during college, or facing an employment search after graduation. If students are unprepared for the reality of how difficult life can be as an adult, anxiety, disappointment, depression, and cynicism can result.

So, at the level of an overview of such complex topics, we have seen the worlds in which our Millennial students have grown up and now live. One is left with the conclusion that nothing seems simple—complexity exists in the very fabric of the environment for most young adults. They have unprecedented choices about careers and lifestyles, and yet they face very real constraints based on economics, access to jobs and technologies, competition from global sources, political and government actions, and a barrage of media and commercial interests. They face the same pressures as their parents to keep themselves and their families healthy and intact, but they operate in what seems to be an increasingly volatile world. They have interest, as did their parents and grandparents, in making the world a better place, but they will have to go about that quest in new ways and with new vision and infrastructures. In many ways, they are better prepared to take on these challenges than the Boomers and X'ers in their ability to adapt and shape change. They will, in turn, hand over the world they are creating to their own children, who will no doubt have both similar and unique, new characteristics as their Millennial parents. More than ever, the world depends on how well they do.

Practical Strategies

After such an extensive discussion of today's students, it is worth discussing practical strategies for expanding opportunities for students to gain insight and learning in all aspects of their educational experiences. We have seen how students have intense pressures from parents, society, and the educational system, in a world of complex challenges with a bewildering array of potentialities. Economic pressures at home and in the world at large may limit their possibilities, at least in the near term. They may or may not have taken the opportunity to reflect upon their own individuality, spirituality, and their role in the larger world, nor developed a specific set of personal values and beliefs to guide their goal setting and decision making. They may have unbridled optimism but a narrow realization of their own gifts and talents. As educators, how do we help them use their time at college to best position them to thrive now and later?

The authors of this chapter, charged with writing about the Milllennial generation, advocate for intentional and structured opportunities for cocurricular learning in higher education and agree with the broad strategies of the positive psychology movement. Students need to learn the importance of developing a scaffolding of self-knowledge, self-understanding, self-determination, and personal values and beliefs, supporting the academic, professional, and personal structure of their lives. Of course, providing these learning opportunities from an administrative viewpoint entails the development of locations, staffing, curricula, financial and educational resources, and assessment.

Many colleges and universities are now moving toward the integration of learning in all aspects of the student experience, in the classroom, residence and dining hall, student union, athletic facility, and through online resources. It may seem counterintuitive that specific, intentional interventions and opportunities can produce spontaneous and informal learning. However, we know that the design and use of facilities, residence hall space in particular, can support rich and lasting lessons for students, especially in the context of a well-designed program of staffing and educational resources.

In terms of an institutional approach, it is important to construct the philosophical and curricular infrastructure on which educational interventions for Millennial students will be based. As we have learned, they want to know the rationale behind what is being asked of them as undergraduates, and as our student affairs graduate students and entry-level employees (also Millennials) come on board, they will also share the same desire for structure. In turn, as educators we know that spelling out expectations and inspiring the imagination of these students can set them free to achieve the positive outcomes that the college experience can offer.

One successful example was developed at the home institution of this chapter's authors, where student affairs and academic faculty and staff, as well as selected students, had input into a succinct set of skills and understanding we believe students should be able to develop during their time at the university. These five goals are called *Aspirations for Student Learning*, and along with the mission statement and guiding principles for service, comprise the destination toward which all programs in the division of student affairs are calibrated. These aspirations include:

1. **Commit to unwavering CURIOSITY**: Virginia Tech students will be inspired to lead lives of curiosity, embracing a life-long commitment to intellectual development.
2. **Pursue SELF-UNDERSTANDING and INTEGRITY**: Virginia Tech students will form a set of affirmative values and develop the self-understanding to integrate these values into their decision-making.
3. **Practice CIVILITY**: Virginia Tech students will understand and commit to civility as a way of life in their interactions with others.
4. **Prepare for a life of COURAGEOUS LEADERSHIP**: Virginia Tech students will be courageous leaders who serve as change agents and make the world more humane and just.
5. **Embrace *UT PROSIM* as a way of life**: Virginia Tech students will enrich their lives through service to others. (*Ut Prosim* is the Virginia Tech motto, which means "That I May Serve." For more information about the Aspirations for Student Learning, please see the web site at: http://www.dsa.vt.edu/aspirations.)

Once the overall philosophical infrastructure is in place, a myriad of opportunities can be created by intentionally preparing all the aspects of an environment in which Millennial students can learn. Again, using Virginia Tech as an example, the university began the creation of residential colleges—first an Honors Residential College, then a residential college not exclusive to honors students. A large-scale renovation project underway was modified to create the apartment, office, and public area space needed for these programs, and staffing and curricula were jointly developed by student affairs and academic faculty to address the *Aspirations for Student Learning*. Throughout this time, knowledge of the needs and desires of the current generation of students were taken into account. Given that there has not yet been a "cutoff time" declared for the Millennial generation, these structures and staffing stand ready to accept the next group of students as they "morph" from Millennial to "post-Millennial," although outcomes are being assessed over time to assure they are still effective.

As routine as it sounds, another specific draw for Millennial students, who have grown up with a large variety of dining options and experience, is partnering with the food service organization, whether self-operated or contracted, to meet student needs and desires—not only in providing familiar types of food and even franchised eateries, but in exposing students to the variety of regional and ethnic foods that represent the diverse origins of the student body, meanwhile working student learning tie-ins into every aspect of the dining experience. Student employees can be recruited and managed better using an understanding of their background in the Millennial generation, and educational opportunities for learning about nutrition and life-long health issues can be cooperatively developed for all students. The authors have found such involvement strengthens the academic tie-in with the dining area, and a proactive and responsive dining program has real benefits in the recruitment, retention, and satisfaction of students in the residence halls and at the university.

Other common ways to spark the interest and involvement of Millennials are already in place nationwide—student organizations, living and learning communities, intramural sports, and service learning opportunities. The important thing as faculty and staff work with these groups of students is to constantly assess whether the activities and inherent learning opportunities are meeting students where they live in their individualized and group-oriented needs. We know that students "vote with their feet," and we must be open to providing new ways to reach them when interest in some programs wanes and other possibilities appear. This requires that we as administrators and student development professionals be nimble and open to change, and we must be able to advocate for students in discussions regarding facilities, staffing, and other types of resources. Often, parents understand their students' needs as well as anyone, and development appeals for financial support for such programs as welcome and move-in assistance, social networking for new students, relaxation breaks during exam time, and purchase of self-assessment tools have all been supported by parents' fund donations at Virginia Tech.

On the subject of self-assessment, one practical approach that has been used successfully at large and small universities to undergird cocurricular learning is the concept of strengths, particularly the assessment tool called *StrengthsQuest*®, managed by the Gallup organization (Clifton, Anderson and Schreiner, 2006). Although the relatively simple act of taking the online *StrengthsQuest* assessment may yield new and informative insight for students, the instrument itself is only a tool in the designed strategy—*not* the strategy itself. As with any self-assessment instrument and any knowledge gained thereby, it must be understood and used in the context of a larger framework in order to survive and serve a useful purpose. Utilizing the *StrengthsQuest* assessment provides a student with his or her "top five" strengths profile, a set of innate talents that can be developed and practiced to help optimize effective choices. Numerous online and printed resources are available to help students interpret what their results mean, and they provide opportunities for them to reflect on their strengths.

Resources for trainers and educators also guide the design of programming that can address the concepts discussed above, such as belief and value development and life planning. For example, some potential exercises using this strengths approach include:

- In residence hall settings, have roommates share with each other their strengths and talents. This can include ways to best communicate to build a better understanding between them and resolve conflict should it arise.
- In small group or one-on-one scenarios (advising, conduct meetings, mentoring, supervision, etc.), have students reflect on how their strengths can positively serve them in overcoming obstacles they may be facing, and conversely how over use of their strengths can result in behavior that is "in the shadow of their strength," such as when confidence can become overconfidence or analysis become failure to act.
- Utilize social media platforms to emphasize aspects of positive psychology and the supporting mechanism of strengths.
- Encourage friendship and create opportunities to help foster a growing pool of acquaintances and potential friendships. In conversations, ask students to reflect on their current relationships and how they may be enriched and developed, using strengths as a conversation-starter.
- Encourage groups of friends and student organizations to create a "Team Talent Map," where individual strengths are plotted on a chart and grouped under the four broad categories of the instrument, to get a visual picture of where each of their strengths fall, and where clusters and the absence of certain talents may impact a group. Benefits can include greater investment in the self-assessment and self-development process, better assignment of group tasks, and a deeper recognition of individual differences and the group dynamics that can result. Information on developing Team Talent maps is available for users at: https://www.strengthsquest.com.
- Encourage spiritual reflection and growth. Provide resources for local places of worship as well as locations that could foster spiritual reflection.
- Have Student Affairs offices and administrators trained on the use of strengths, and establish it as a discussion opportunity for student clients and employees. Learning ones strengths in the context of student employment can be richly reinforcing.

This list is certainly not exhaustive, and it provides a sample of strategies that can be used by educators. Having knowledge about today's students, and coupling it with the positive psychology framework, can help produce strategies that make an important impact on the products, services, practices, and successes of college and universities.

Conclusion

Although the preceding discussion of various aspects of today's students may have exposed some traits that differ from previous generations, at the heart of the conversation, the same issues remain. That is the quest of students trying to explore who they are. Questions such as those stated earlier: Who am I and what do I value? What is the meaning and purpose of life? What are my gifts and talents? Why am I in college and will I be successful? What kind of relationships should I pursue? How can I matter in the world?

As educators, we know that positive and optimistic individuals are more likely to persevere and succeed in school and in life; there is a level of realistic optimism and positivity needed to meet these challenges. The key then becomes how realistic and resilient are students' expectations of what they can accomplish in life? Again, as educators, if we are familiar with myths and realities about the Millennial generation, we can avail ourselves of empirical and practical tools to help students realistically assess their expectations. We can create the environment and interventions that help students capitalize on their possibilities. If students know their strengths and augment that self-knowledge with sound research and exploration, we can help them develop a world view that includes both positive and realistic expectations. We can urge students to methodically investigate their chosen field of study, and we can work with Career Services personnel or counseling experts to help them determine the viability of their career aspirations.

It is doubtful in the view of this chapter's authors, given the extreme economic and social upheavals of their developmental years, that most students still have a picture of the world that is too optimistic. The economy in the last two decades in particular has exposed many families to various financial pressures, and students are most often aware of the struggles that workers and families are facing, even if their own families are not directly affected. This can drive students to concentrate solely on academics or working their way through college for financial reasons rather than spending time on more reflective activities aimed at self-actualization. In fact, it is essential that we get students' attention and make the pursuit of self-discovery, values formation, and decision-making skills as relevant to them as chemistry and mathematics courses. In this way, we can engage them in evaluating the source and priorities of the pressures they face and the expectations they hold for themselves.

As educators, we need to be aware of the characteristics and traits of our students without simply placing them in a generic box. Having this knowledge can help us engage our students in a way in which they can connect and obtain results. We can assist them in their journey as they ask themselves the important questions. Along the way, we can help them understand their strengths and focus on what is right with them. What can result is a successful student who is more self-aware and ultimately has found clarity and purpose for life.

References

Astin, A. W., Astin, H. S., & Lindholm, J. A. (2011). *Cultivating the spirit: How college can enhance students' inner lives*. San Francisco, CA: Jossey-Bass.

Birnbaum, R., & Shushok F., Jr. (2001). The crisis "crisis" in higher education: Is that a wolf or a pussycat at the academy's door? In P. G. Altbach, P. Gumport, & B. Johnstone (Eds.), *The enduring legacies: In defense of American higher education* (59–84). Baltimore, MD: Johns Hopkins University Press.

Census Bureau. (2010). *2010 census data*. Retrieved from http://2010.census.gov/2010census

Chickering, A. W., Dalton, J. C., & Stramm, L. (2006). *Encouraging authenticity and spirituality in higher education*. San Francisco, CA: Jossey-Bass.

Clifton, D. O., Anderson, E., Schreiner, L. (2006) *StrengthsQuest: Discover and develop your strengths in academics, career and beyond*. New York, NY: Gallup Press.

Coates, J. (2007). *Generational learning styles*. River Falls, WI: LERN Books.

Howe, N., & Strauss, W. (2000). *Millennials rising: The next great generation*. New York, NY: Division Books.

Keen, C. H., Keen, J. P., Parks, S. D., & Daloz, L. A. P. (1996). *Common fire: Lives of commitment in a complex world*. Boston, MA: Beacon Press.

Kuh, G. D., Kinzie, J., Schuh, J. H., & Whitt, E. J. (2010). *Student success in college: Creating conditions that matter*. San Francisco, CA: Jossey-Bass.

Kuh, G. D., Schuh, J. H., Whitt, E. J., & Associates. (1991). *Involving colleges: Successful approaches to fostering student learning outside the classroom*. San Francisco, CA: Jossey-Bass.

Levine, A., & Dean, D. (2012). *Generation on a tightrope: A portrait of today's college student*. San Francisco, CA: Jossey-Bass.

Lowen, L. (2012). How Millennials are creating a cultural shift in gender roles. Retrieved from http://womensissues.about.com/od/intheworkplace/a/MillennialsGenderRoles.htm

McPherson, M., Smith-Lovin, L., & Brashears, M. (2006). Social isolation in America: Changes in core discussion networks over two decades. *American Sociological Review, 71*(3), 353–375.

Palmer, P. J. (1999). *Let your life speak: Listening for the voice of vocation*. San Francisco, CA: Jossey-Bass.

Taylor, P., & Keeter, S. (Eds.). (2010). Millennials—A portrait of generation next: confident, connected, open to change. Retrieved from http://www.pewresearch.org/millennials

Shushok F., Jr., & Hulme, E. (2006). What's right with you: Helping students find their extraordinary life. *About Campus, 11*(4), 2–8.

Shushok, F. (2011). Spiritual and moral friendships: How campuses can encourage a search for meaning and purpose. *Journal of College and Character, 12*(4) 1–8.

Stein, J., & Sanburn, J. (2013, May 20). The new greatest generation: Why millennials will save us all. *Time, 181*, 26–32.

Vaillant, G. E. (2002). *Aging well: Surprising guideposts to a happier life from the landmark Harvard study of adult development*. Boston, MA: Little, Brown and Company.

Weick, K. E. (1979). *Social psychology of organizing (2nd ed.)*. Boston, MA: Addison-Wesley.

3

Positive Psychology 101

JEANA L. MAGYAR-MOE

Positive psychology is the scientific study of optimal human functioning, the goals of which are to better understand and apply those factors that help individuals and communities to thrive and flourish. Research in and applications of positive psychology have proliferated since 1998 when then-President of the American Psychological Association (APA), Martin Seligman, challenged applied psychologists to return to their roots and focus not only upon curing mental illness, but also upon making the lives of all people more fulfilling and identifying and nurturing talent (Seligman & Csikszentmihalyi, 2000). In this chapter, a review of the history of positive psychology is presented, followed by information regarding undergirding positive psychological theories such as Strengths Theory (Clifton & Nelson, 1992), the Broaden and Build Theory of Positive Emotions (Fredrickson, 2001), Subjective Well-Being (Ryff & Keyes, 1995), Authentic Happiness/Well-Being Theory (Seligman, 2011), and the Complete State Model of Mental Health. Finally, two key programs of research over the past decade that have produced psychometrically sound measures of strengths are reviewed, followed by a summary of positive psychology applications to date.

History of Positive Psychology

As noted previously, positive psychology took hold amongst applied psychologists in the late 1990s under the leadership of Martin Seligman, who is often referred to as the father of positive psychology. However, a focus on the positive in psychology did not originate with Seligman's APA Presidential proclamation. Indeed, a focus on the positive within applied psychology can be traced back to the early 1900s.

Prior to the late 19th century, people with mental illness were commonly thought to be evil and often were confined to asylums. The public view toward mental illness slowly began to change in the early 1900s with Beer's (1908) publication of *A Mind That Found Itself*. This publication helped the public to realize the potential for recovery from mental illness and to the presence of strengths that all individuals possess to aid in the recovery process. Similarly, within the field of psychiatry, Menninger (Menninger, Mayman, & Pruyser, 1963) encouraged a focus on prevention versus remediation and challenged the standard view of mental illness as progressive and refractory, calling instead for mental health practitioners to view mental illness as amendable to change and improvements. Menninger's (Menninger, Mayman, & Pruyser, 1963) challenge required practitioners and scholars to engage in a reconceptualization of the health-illness continuum and of treatment goals. "These [goals] need no longer be confined to a reinstatement of the status quo ante ('recovery' in the popular sense), but might push forward toward the development of new potentialities and transcendence of previous levels of vital balance to a state of being 'weller than well'" (p. 401). As a result of such developments, the public came to realize that all people could be helped by psychological interventions, not just those who were identified as having mental illness.

During much of the early 20th century, psychologists were devoted to identifying the best in people. For example, popular during that time were Terman's studies of giftedness and marital satisfaction (e.g., Terman, Buttenwieser, Ferguson, Johnson, & Wilson, 1938) and Watson's (1928) work on positive parenting skills. After World War II, however, the founding of the Veterans Administration (VA) in 1946 and the National Institute of Mental Health (NIMH) in 1947 changed the landscape of psychology. Through the development of the VA, psychologists discovered they could make a career of treating pathology, and through the development of the NIMH, psychologists realized they could receive grant funding if they researched pathology (Seligman & Csikzentmihalyi, 2000). Not surprisingly, a focus on mental illness ensued, and the emphasis on repairing damage resulted in a much better understanding of pathology. As a result, many people who experience mental disorders lead more satisfying lives. However, as psychologists became more invested in treating disorders, the missions of improving the human condition and nurturing high talent were somewhat neglected. Nevertheless, strong theoretical work on healthy development (Erikson, 1959) and mental health (Jahoda, 1958) from the 1960s continued to influence the research and practice of psychologists throughout the decades.

In 1973, Leona Tyler, President of the APA, proposed a design for a hopeful psychology, noting that "modern scientific psychology is rooted in hope" (p. 1021). Her expression of hope for the psychology discipline and for those served by psychologists encouraged a generation of professionals to believe that all people have strengths and resources that can be identified, accentuated, and carefully studied. This belief has shaped the research and practice of positive psychology today (Lopez et al., 2006).

Although considerable research and practice addressing positive constructs and theories had been conducted prior to Seligman's APA presidency, he was instrumental in uniting these concepts under the common theme of positive psychology. Seligman believed that sound positive social science, of the past and the future, would illuminate the role of human strengths in leading a better life. Over a decade later, his beliefs have become reality as evidenced throughout this text as well as through a host of other scholarly outlets. Indeed, in 2008, the first issue of the *Journal of Positive Psychology* was published to accommodate much of the research being done on positive emotions, traits, strengths, and well-being. A variety of books devoted exclusively to positive psychology and even textbooks for use in the college classroom are available as well. Positive psychology is now being taught at over 100 colleges and universities in the United States and Britain, and several schools even offer a master's degree in applied positive psychology. Furthermore, there are several professional organizations (i.e., the International Positive Psychology Association [IPPA] and the Positive Psychology Section of the Society of Counseling Psychology within the APA) and conventions (i.e., The Gallup Global Well-Being Forum, the International Positive Psychology Summit, the European Conference on Positive Psychology, and the IPPA World Congress on Positive Psychology) devoted to the study of positive psychology.

Although there is still much to be done to fully understand and implement what positive psychology has to offer, the available literature suggests that positive psychology can play a prominent role within higher education. The rest of this chapter is devoted to addressing some of the core theories from positive psychology that serve as a foundation for many of the applications of positive psychology that will be presented throughout the rest of this book.

Core Positive Psychology Theories

Strengths Theory

The key idea behind strengths theory as conceptualized by Donald Clifton, a "grandfather" of positive psychology (McKay & Greengrass, 2003), is that it is vital to understand and build from one's strengths while managing (rather than focusing on or repairing) weaknesses (Clifton & Nelson, 1992). Although this perspective appeals to common sense, in reality, a focus on repairing weaknesses tends to be more pervasive. According to Clifton and Nelson (1992), many employers, teachers, parents, and leaders work off the following unwritten rule: "Let's fix what's wrong and let the strengths take care of themselves" (p. 9). Indeed, Gallup Polls reveal that 59% of Americans believe that a focus on weaknesses, not strengths, deserve the most attention, and 77% of parents within the United States indicate that they would focus the most upon low grades such as D's and F's even if their child's report card also contained A's, B's, and C's (Buckingham & Clifton, 2000).

Why is a focus upon fixing what is wrong while overlooking what is right so prevalent? According to Clifton and Nelson (1992), it is because of several errors in thinking to which most people fall victim. The first error is the idea that fixing or correcting a weakness will result in making a person or organization stronger. This is not true, because eliminating a weakness does not make one great, at best it will only help the individual or organization become normal or average. Excellence can only be achieved through focusing on strengths while *managing* rather than working to *eliminate* weaknesses. The second error is the notion that there is no need to foster strengths, because they will take care of themselves and develop naturally. Again, this is faulty because taking one's strengths for granted results in just normal or average outcomes, because those strengths do not mature to their full potential. In order to capitalize upon strengths, they must be nurtured and honed. What leads many to take their strengths for granted is that strengths stem from talents that develop naturally at first and that feel automatic or easy to put into action. Many overlook their own talents due to failing to recognize them as special, assuming all people can do what they do with ease. Hence, the talents never fully mature into strengths because they went unrecognized and therefore undeveloped. The third error in thinking is the belief that strengths and weaknesses are opposites. Although many people think that if they shore up their weaknesses, they can turn them into strengths. This assumption is also false. We do not learn about strengths by studying weaknesses. In fact, the study of weaknesses and deficits provides erroneous information about what to work on to improve performance. For example, studying why college students drop out of college will not provide an understanding of the conditions under which college students remain enrolled through graduation. The final error in thinking that keeps people from approaching life from a strengths perspective is the idea that people can do anything they put their minds to. This notion suggests that *anyone* can be successful at *anything* if they are willing to work hard. This obviously is not the case, however, since all people have their own unique set of strengths that will empower them to be successful in certain areas but not others. Clifton and Nelson (1992) state that "the reality is that we can (and should) *try* anything we wish to try, but long-term success will elude us unless we determine early on that we have a basic talent for the endeavor" (p. 16). Indeed, working hard to be successful in an area that fails to capitalize on one's strengths leads to a negative view of oneself and one's abilities.

The Broaden and Build Theory of Positive Emotions

The broaden and build theory of positive emotions is another key theory that undergirds positive psychology. Indeed, this theory provides an explanation of the utility and importance of positive emotions in peoples' lives. Prior to the development of broaden and build just over a decade ago, little to no research existed on the value of positive emotions. In contrast, negative emotions have been studied for many decades, and most people understand that negative emotions are important for a variety of reasons, including survival. For example, without the ability to feel fear, one would not run from danger, and without the ability to feel anger, one would not defend oneself when appropriate. However, most people, including those who have researched negative emotions, conclude that positive emotions have little utility beyond signaling that there are no problems present. The broaden and build theory explains that positive emotions do much more than just signal that there are no problems. In fact, this theory posits that positive emotions are just as important to our survival and our ability to flourish in life as negative emotions (Fredrickson, 1998, 2001).

The broaden and build theory is a multifaceted model of positive emotions, consisting of the broaden hypothesis, the build hypothesis, the undoing hypothesis, the resilience hypothesis, and the flourish hypothesis (Fredrickson, 1998, 2001). Each of these hypotheses is defined in the sections that follow.

The Broaden Hypothesis

According to Fredrickson (1998, 2001), positive emotions broaden momentary thought-action repertoires, resulting in a wider range of thoughts and actions one is likely to pursue. In other words, when one is feeling positive emotions, they are able to see more possibilities. This broadening effect of positive emotions is the opposite of what happens when people experience negative emotions.

According to Frijda (1986), Lazarus (1991), and Levinson (1994), negative emotions narrow momentary thought-action repertoires. In other words, when one experiences negative emotions, it is as if they have tunnel vision and the range of possibilities is narrowed. Very specific action tendencies narrow the action-urges that come to mind and at the same time, prepare the body to take that specific action. For example, when one feels afraid, he has the action-urge to run and the body prepares for taking flight by increasing blood flow to the appropriate muscles. The narrowed action-urges that come to mind when one experiences negative emotions are thought to be adaptive from an evolutionary perspective. Indeed, such fight or flight responses in the face of fear or anger helped to ensure the survival of our ancestors in life-threatening situations (Toobey & Coosmides, 1990).

The broadening effect of positive emotions is also adaptive from an evolutionary perspective, but not in the same way as negative emotions. More specifically, whereas the narrowing of thought-action repertoires helps to ensure survival in specific life-threatening circumstances, the broadened thought-action repertoires that correspond to the experience of positive emotions are adaptive over the long-term (Fredrickson & Branigan, 2005). This is largely a result of the *building* of personal resources that this broadened mindset brings.

Much of the research that supports the broadening hypothesis has been done utilizing video clips that elicit various emotions in the viewers. For example, to induce joy, Fredrickson and Branigan (2005) showed participants a short video of penguins at play; to induce contentment, they saw a video of various nature scenes; a video of a group of men taunting an Amish family was used to elicit anger; a video of a mountain climber who is hanging precariously from the edge of a mountain elicits fear; and a video of a screen-saver consisting of colored sticks piling up on one another was used for the control condition, eliciting virtually no emotion.

Participants viewed one of the five video clips and then completed a series of global-local processing tasks. These tasks consisted of viewing a standard figure and then deciding which of two comparison figures was most like the standard figure. Although these tasks did not consist of correct or incorrect answers, a global response consisted of choosing the comparison figure that was more similar to the standard figure based on the overall shape, whereas the local response consisted of choosing the comparison figure that was more similar to the standard figure based on the individual shapes that make up the total figure. According to Fredrickson and Branigan (2005), the global response option represents more broadened thinking. The results of this study support the broaden hypothesis; participants in the positive emotion conditions chose the global response options more often in comparison to those in the neutral or negative emotion conditions, suggesting a more broadened pattern of thinking (Fredrickson & Branigan, 2005).

A second study supporting the broaden hypothesis was conducted by Fredrickson and Branigan (2005) using the same video clips but asking participants to then imagine being in a situation in which the most powerful emotion they felt while viewing the film clips were occurring. Given that emotion, they were instructed to list as many things as they felt like doing right at that moment. Each participant was given a handout that had 20 blank lines that began with the statement "I would like to _____." The number of sentences completed was tallied. The more sentences completed represented broader thought-action repertoires. The results of this study confirmed that those who felt positive emotions were able to complete more sentences in comparison to those in the neutral and negative emotion conditions, supporting the broaden hypothesis of positive emotions as well as the narrowing hypothesis associated with negative emotions (Fredrickson & Branigan, 2005).

The Build Hypothesis

The broadening of momentary thought-action repertoires results in building a variety of enduring personal resources over time (Fredrickson, 1998, 2001).

These resources are physical (i.e., coordination, cardiovascular health, and muscle strength), social (i.e., friendships, social skills and support), intellectual (i.e., knowledge and problem-solving), and psychological (i.e., creativity, optimism, and resilience). Although the positive emotions that lead to the building of these resources are fleeting, the personal resources acquired are lasting and can be used later when one finds oneself in a potentially life-threatening situation or when experiencing challenging times.

To better understand how positive emotions build durable physical, social, intellectual, and psychological resources, consider children. Play is the work of childhood. When children are at play, they are typically experiencing positive emotions such as joy, happiness, or contentment. While playing and experiencing positive emotions, the children are also gaining physical strength. As they run about, they are building their cardiovascular strength and lung capacity, honing their motor skills, and fine-tuning their coordination. At the same time, they are building social bonds with their playmates and learning the rules of the game and teamwork. These resources are lasting, even after the positive emotional experience is over. Although one hopes this is never the case, should children find themselves in a situation in which their well-being is at stake, for example, being attacked by a bully, they can turn to the reserve of personal resources they have developed to safely navigate through that negative experience. The physical resources they have developed can help them physically fight off their bully, while the friends they made when at play can also come to their aid. Indeed, the very behaviors children engage in while at play are the same behaviors they put into action when under attack. Had the children not learned these skills under a positive emotional state, they would not have the skills necessary to protect themselves in a fight or flight situation. Later in life, these same resources can be called upon to help in other stressful life situations, even if those situations do not involve danger of life or limb (Fredrickson, 2001).

The Undoing Hypothesis

According to Fredrickson (2003), positive emotions have the potential to *undo* lingering negative emotions. More specifically, the idea behind the undoing hypothesis is that thought-action repertoires cannot be both narrowed and broadened at the same time. Hence, inducing positive emotions in the wake of ongoing negative emotions may loosen the grip of the negative emotion, because the broadening qualities of positive emotions begin to widen the lens through which one views the world. This undoing effect occurs not only at the cognitive level, but at the physiological level as well (Fredrickson, 2003).

Fredrickson, Mancuso, Branigan, and Tugade (2000) tested the undoing hypothesis by measuring the baseline heart rates, blood pressure rates, and peripheral vasoconstriction indices of research participants just before inducing the negative emotion of fear or anxiety in them by telling them that they had one minute to develop a speech that they would present in front of a video camera. They were told that the recording of their speeches would then be evaluated by a group of their peers. The participants reported an increase in anxiety and their measures of heart rate, blood pressure, and peripheral vasoconstriction were elevated as well. Instead of actually giving their speeches, participants were randomly assigned to view one of four emotion-inducing film clips. Two of the clips induced the positive emotions of joy and contentment, one was neutral, and the other elicited sadness. The participants' cardiovascular measures were monitored from the time they began viewing the film clips until the point at which their cardiovascular activity had returned to baseline levels. The results of this study support the undoing hypothesis; those who saw the two positive emotion videos returned to their baseline levels of cardiovascular activity significantly more quickly than those in the neutral and negative emotion condition, with those in the negative emotion condition taking the longest to return to baseline functioning (Fredrickson, Mancuso, Branigan, & Tugade, 2000).

The Resilience Hypothesis

The resilience hypothesis suggests that positive emotions, through their broadening affects, trigger upward spirals of well-being (Fredrickson, 2001). The idea of upward spirals of well-being is the conceptual opposite of the common notion of downward spirals of depression. When people have negative experiences and therefore negative affect, they begin to experience tunnel vision that often leads to negative, pessimistic thinking. This negative thinking leads to more negative affect that can spiral downward very quickly. In contrast, positive emotions take the blinders off, allowing people to see more possibilities and to think more optimistically. Those who experience positive emotions more regularly are likely to experience upward spirals of well-being, which is enjoyable in and of itself. However, perhaps more importantly, upward spirals of well-being also serve to build one's toolbox of coping skills. Hence, those who experience positive emotions more often are better able to cope and are more resilient in the face of adversities in life (Fredrickson, 2001).

Research on the resilience hypothesis includes a study of college students who completed self-report measures of affect and coping on two different occasions, five weeks apart. Results showed that positive affect at time one predicted broad-minded coping at time two and broad-minded coping at time one predicted more positive affect at time two. Furthermore, mediational analyses revealed that broad-minded coping and positive affect enhanced each other (Fredrickson & Joiner, 2002). A similar study was conducted in the days after the September 11, 2001 terrorist attacks with a portion of the participants from the previously reported study (Fredrickson, Tugade, Waugh, & Larkin, 2003). The participants were asked to report what emotions they were feeling in the wake of the attacks, what they learned from the attacks, and how they felt about the future. Almost all the participants reported feeling sad, angry, and afraid, yet those that had been identified as resilient in the previous study also reported feeling positive emotions in the wake of the tragedy. More specifically, they reported positive feelings such as gratitude and optimism, finding goodness in people who were helping in the aftermath of the event. Statistical analyses showed that the tendency to feel positive emotions buffered the resilient people against depression (Fredrickson et al., 2003).

The Flourish Hypothesis

The flourish hypothesis indicates that a key predictor of human flourishing is the ratio of positive to negative affect that one experiences (Fredrickson, 2013). More specifically, the greater the ratio of positive feelings or sentiments to negative feelings or sentiments over time is related to flourishing mental health and other positive outcomes.

Subjective Well-Being

Subjective well-being consists of a combination of two broad lines of research on positive emotions and positive functioning (cf. Ryan & Deci, 2001; Waterman, 1993). Those who are high in subjective well-being report both feeling good and functioning well. More specifically, subjective well-being takes into consideration multiple aspects of both the individual and his or her functioning in society. In total, subjective well-being entails emotional well-being, psychological well-being, and social well-being.

Emotional well-being consists of one's perceptions of declared happiness and satisfaction with life, and the ratio of positive to negative affect experienced (Bryant & Veroff, 1982; Lucas, Diener, & Suh, 1996; Shmotkin, 1998). Emotional well-being differs from happiness in that happiness is based upon spontaneous reflections of pleasant and unpleasant feelings in one's *immediate* experience, whereas emotional well-being adds the life satisfaction component that represents a *long-term* assessment of one's life (Keyes & Magyar-Moe, 2003).

Psychological well-being, as conceptualized by Ryff (1989), has been derived from a variety of concepts within personality, developmental, and clinical psychology, which have also been defined as criteria of mental health (Jahoda, 1958). More specifically, Ryff's (1989) six dimensions model of psychological well-being encompasses a breadth of wellness areas inclusive of positive evaluations of oneself and one's past life, a sense of continued growth and development as a person, the belief that one's life is purposeful and meaningful, the experience of quality relations with others, the capacity to manage effectively one's life and surrounding world, and a sense of self-determination (Ryff & Keyes, 1995). Each of the six dimensions of psychological well-being, as defined in Table 3.1, includes challenges that individuals encounter as they strive to function fully and realize their unique talents (see Ryff, 1989; Ryff & Keyes, 1995).

Social wellness is based upon sociological research on anomie and alienation, which indicates a host of problems that can arise when there is a breakdown of social norms and values within a society (Mirowsky & Ross, 1989; Seeman, 1959). Within this scholarship, issues related to the creation and disillusionment of human solidarity and upon social regulation and order are explored. Drawing on these theoretical roots, Keyes (1998) developed a multidimensional model of social well-being inclusive of social integration, social contributions, social coherence, social actualization, and social acceptance. Each of these five dimensions of social well-being, as defined in Table 3.1, includes challenges that people face as social beings. These dimensions provide information about whether and to what degree individuals are functioning well in their social world (e.g., as neighbors, as coworkers, and as citizens; Keyes, 1998; Keyes & Shapiro, 2004).

Authentic Happiness and Well-Being Theory

Mental health has been purported to consist of authentic happiness that can be achieved via three routes, namely, the pleasant life, the engaged life, and the meaningful life (Seligman, 2002). More specifically, the pleasant life is achieved when people are able to experience positive emotions about their past, present, and future lives. The engaged life is felt when one is deeply involved and absorbed in what one is doing in multiple life roles, including, love, work, and play. Such engagement is thought to occur when one knows and regularly utilizes his or her character strengths in daily life. The meaningful life is defined as using one's strengths in the service of something larger than oneself (Seligman, 2002). When taken together, Seligman (2002) has stated that a full life includes pleasure, engagement, and meaning that is achieved via separate activities or a single activity.

More recently, Seligman (2011) has updated his authentic happiness theory to be more inclusive of the many facets of mental health that go beyond happiness or positive feelings. More specifically, in Seligman's (2011) well-being theory, happiness entails just one of five pillars that together make up human flourishing. The five pillars make up the acronym PERMA and include Positive Emotions (or happiness), Engagement, Relationships, Meaning, and Accomplishment. PERMA represents the basic components for a life of fulfillment and are purported to be intrinsically motivating elements that people pursue for their own sake, not as a means to an end. Well-being theory builds upon authentic happiness theory by adding relationships (i.e., positive social connections) and accomplishment (i.e., achievement pursued for its own sake that is not dependent on outcome) to the original three pillars and by changing the overall goal from experiencing

Table 3.1 **Dimensions of Psychological and Social Well-Being**

Dimensions of Ryff's Psychological Well-Being Model	Dimensions of Keyes' Social Well-Being Model
Self-acceptance: The criterion toward which adults must strive in order to feel good about themselves. Such self-acceptance is characterized by a positive attitude toward the self and acknowledging and accepting multiple aspects of self, including unpleasant personal aspects. In addition, self-acceptance includes positive feelings about past life.	**Social integration:** The evaluation of the quality of one's relationship to society and community. Integration is therefore the extent to which people feel they have something in common with others who constitute their social reality (e.g., their neighborhood), as well as the degree to which they feel that they belong to their communities and society.
Positive relations with others: Consists of the ability to cultivate and the presence of warm, trusting, intimate relationships with others. Concern for the welfare of others, and the ability to empathize, cooperate, and compromise all are aspects of this wellness dimension.	**Social contribution:** The evaluation of one's value to society. It includes the belief that one is a vital member of society, with something of value to give to the world.
Autonomy: Reflects the seeking of self-determination and personal authority or independence in a society that sometimes compels obedience and compliance. The abilities to resist social pressures so as to think or behave in certain ways, and to guide and evaluate behavior based on internalized standards and values, are crucial in this domain.	**Social coherence:** The perception of the quality, organization, and operation of the social world, and it includes a concern for knowing about the world. Social coherence is analogous to meaningfulness in life (Mirowsky & Ross 1989; Seeman 1959, 1991), and involves appraisals that society is discernable, sensible, and predictable.
Environmental mastery: Includes the ability to manage everyday affairs, to control a complex array of external activities, to make effective use of surrounding opportunities, and to choose or create contexts suitable to personal needs. A sense of mastery results when individuals recognize personal needs and desires and also feel capable of and permitted to take an active role in getting what they need from their environments.	**Social actualization:** The evaluation of the potential and the trajectory of society. This is the belief in the evolution of society and the sense that society has potential that is being realized through its institutions and citizens.

(continued)

Table 3.1 **Continued**

Dimensions of Ryff's Psychological Well-Being Model	Dimensions of Keyes' Social Well-Being Model
Purpose in life: Consists of one's aims and objectives for living, including the presence of life goals and a sense of directedness. Those with high purpose in life see their daily lives as fulfilling a direction and purpose and therefore view their present and past life as meaningful.	**Social acceptance:** The construal of society through the character and qualities of other people as a generalized category. Individuals must function in a public arena that consists primarily of strangers. Individuals who illustrate social acceptance trust others, think that others are capable of kindness, and believe that people can be industrious. Socially accepting people hold favorable views of human nature and feel comfortable with others.
Personal growth: Reflects the continuous pursuit of existing skills, talents, and opportunities for personal development and for realizing one's potential. In addition, personal growth includes the capacity to remain open to experience and to identify challenges in a variety of circumstances.	

happiness to experiencing flourishing. In addition, capitalizing upon one's character strengths undergirds and leads to each of the five elements of well-being, not just engagement as originally proposed in authentic happiness theory (Seligman, 2011).

The Complete State Model of Mental Health

The complete state model of mental health asserts that the absence of mental illness is not equal to the presence of mental health; therefore, mental health and mental illness are seen as existing on two separate continuums. Mental health assessment is then based upon the degree of symptoms of mental illness experienced (high to low), as well as the degree of symptoms of well-being experienced (high to low; Keyes & Lopez, 2002). Combining these continua together, an individual can be conceptualized as follows: (1) completely mentally healthy/ flourishing (low symptoms of mental illness and high symptoms of well-being); (2) completely mentally ill/floundering (high symptoms of mental illness and low symptoms of well-being); (3) incompletely mentally healthy/languishing (low symptoms of mental illness and low symptoms of well-being); or (4) incompletely mentally ill/struggling (high symptoms of mental illness and high symptoms of well-being; Keyes & Lopez, 2002).

Working to make improvements in mental health functioning based upon the complete state model is dependent upon the category in which a person falls. For example, individuals who are floundering may come to therapy simply hoping to decrease their symptoms of mental illness, thereby leading to a label of languishing. However, reconceptualizing treatment goals based upon the idea that there is more to life than being free of symptoms of pathology, clients may decide that they would like to not only work to decrease symptoms of mental illness but to also purposefully work to increase symptoms of well-being. This would ultimately lead one to fall within the flourishing category. (See Magyar-Moe, 2009, for more information on how to assess where clients fall within the complete state model and how therapy would proceed based upon this assessment.)

Key Positive Psychological Strengths Measures
Values in Action Inventory of Character Strengths

The Values in Action Inventory of Character Strengths (VIA-IS; Peterson & Seligman, 2004) is a popular strengths measure based upon the Values in Action Classification System developed in 2004 by Peterson and Seligman. The VIA Classification System was created to be an adjunct to the *Diagnostic and Statistical Manual of Mental Disorders* (DSM; American Psychiatric Association, 2000). Just as the DSM provides useful information about psychological disorders and a common vocabulary for therapists to use in describing pathology, the VIA Classification System provides important information and a common vocabulary for therapists to use in describing strengths. It is important to note, however, that the VIA Classification has applications to all people, not just those who are attending counseling or therapy.

The VIA Classification consists of 24 strengths of character that fall under six virtue categories. Within the VIA Classification Handbook, one can find information regarding assessment and applications of each strength, interventions that foster the strengths, paragons or examples of the strengths, the theoretical and research underpinnings of the strengths, the known correlates and consequences of the strengths, how the strengths develop and manifest across the life span, gender differences, and cross-cultural aspects of the strengths (Peterson & Seligman, 2004).

The VIA-IS (Peterson & Seligman, 2004) can be taken for no fee online at www.authentichappiness.org or www.viastrengths.org. The measure takes approximately 30–40 minutes to complete, consisting of 240 items that tap each of the 24 different character strengths. Upon completion of this measure, respondents are provided with information about their top five strengths, as well as a rank order listing of all 24. Table 3.2 contains a list and definitions of the 24 strengths measured by this survey. On the VIA Institute on Character Website (www.viastrengths.org), one can find useful information on the psychometric properties of the VIA measure as well as tips for helping people to capitalize on their strengths.

Clifton StrengthsFinder

The Clifton StrengthsFinder 2.0 ([CSF 2.0] Asplund, Lopez, Hodges, & Harter, 2007; Rath, 2007) is a measure of personal talents, originally developed by Donald Clifton of the Gallup Organization. The measure was developed based upon empirically sound, semistructured interviews. Through the interview data, the 34 talent themes found in Table 3.3 were identified. The personal talents identified on the CSF 2.0 (Asplund, Lopez, Hodges, & Harter, 2007; Rath, 2007) can be developed and used to increase success and satisfaction in a number of life roles, including academia and work (Buckingham & Clifton, 2000; Clifton & Anderson, 2002; Clifton & Nelson, 1992).

The CSF 2.0 (Asplund, Lopez, Hodges, & Harter, 2007) is available online at www.strengthsquest.com. A code is required to access the measure; such access codes can be purchased online and are included in the purchase of StrengthsQuest (Clifton, Anderson, Schreiner, 2006), a resource book designed specifically for college students to accompany the CSF 2.0 measure. This text is highly useful for helping students to develop ways to implement their talents in their daily lives and to apply their strengths in college and the world of work. The CSF 2.0 consists of 178 items, takes approximately 30–45 minutes to complete, and is appropriate for use with adolescents and adults with reading levels of 10th grade or higher. The measure is also available in 17 languages (Asplund, Lopez, Hodges, & Harter, 2007; Rath, 2007).

Upon completion of the CSF 2.0 respondents receive a report on their top five talent themes, 10 ideas for putting each of their top five talent themes into action, and a "strength-based action plan" for designing and implementing short- and long-term goals for using talents and building strengths. In addition, a host of other resources related to the CSF 2.0 measure are available online to those who complete the measure.

Other Areas of Focus Within Positive Psychology

It is important to note that in addition to the foundational theories and key strengths measures previously noted, there are a number of other constructs, applications, and

Table 3.2 Definitions of the 24 Strengths Measured by the Values in Action Inventory of Character Strengths (VIA-IS; Peterson & Seligman, 2004)

Strengths of Wisdom and Knowledge—cognitive strengths that entail the acquisition and use of knowledge

1) **Creativity [originality, ingenuity]:** Thinking of novel and productive ways to conceptualize and do things; includes artistic achievement but is not limited to it

2) **Curiosity [interest, novelty-seeking, openness to experience]:** Taking an interest in ongoing experience from its own sake; finding subjects and topics fascinating; exploring and discovering

3) **Open-mindedness [judgment, critical thinking]:** Thinking things through and examining them from all sides; not jumping to conclusions; being able to change one's mind in light of evidence; weighting all evidence fairly

4) **Love of learning:** Mastering new skills, topics, and bodies of knowledge, whether on one's own or formally; obviously related to the strength of curiosity but goes beyond it to describe the tendency to add systematically to what one knows

5) **Perspective [wisdom]:** Being able to provide wise counsel to others; having ways of looking at the world that make sense to oneself and to other people

Strengths of Courage—emotional strengths that involve the exercise of will to accomplish goals in the face of opposition, external or internal

6) **Bravery [valor]:** Not shrinking from threat, challenge, difficulty, or pain; speaking up for what is right even if there is opposition; acting on convictions even if unpopular; includes physical bravery but is not limited to it

7) **Persistence [perseverance, industriousness]:** Finishing what one starts; persisting in a course of action in spite of obstacles; "getting it out the door"; taking pleasure in completing tasks

8) **Integrity [authenticity, honesty]:** Speaking the truth but more broadly presenting oneself in a genuine way and acting in a sincere way; being without pretense; taking responsibility for one's feelings and actions

9) **Vitality [zest, enthusiasm, vigor, energy]:** Approaching life with excitement and energy; not doing things halfway or halfheartedly; living life as an adventure; feeling alive and activated

Strengths of Humanity—interpersonal strengths that involve "tending and befriending" others

10) **Love:** Valuing close relations with others, in particular those in which sharing and caring are reciprocated: being close to people

11) **Kindness [generosity, nurturance, care, compassion, altruistic love, "niceness"]:** Doing favors and good deeds for others; helping them; taking care of them

12) **Social intelligence [emotional intelligence, personal intelligence]:** Being aware of the motives and feelings of other people and oneself; knowing what to do to fit into different social situations; knowing what makes other people tick

(continued)

Table 3.2 **Continued**

Justice—civic strengths that underlie healthy community life

13) **Citizenship [social responsibility, loyalty, teamwork]:** Working well as a member of a group or team; being loyal to the group; doing one's share

14) **Fairness:** Treating all people the same according to notions of fairness and justice; not letting personal feelings bias decisions about others; giving everyone a fair chance

15) **Leadership:** Encouraging a group of which one is a member to get things done and at the same time maintain good relations within the group; organizing group activities and seeing that they happen

Temperance—strengths that protect against excess

16) **Forgiveness and mercy:** Forgiving those who have done wrong; accepting the shortcomings of others; giving people a second chance; not being vengeful

17) **Humility/modesty:** Letting one's accomplishments speak for themselves; not regarding oneself as more special than one is

18) **Prudence:** Being careful about one's choices; not taking undue risks; not saying or doing things that might later be regretted

19) **Self-regulation [self-control]:** Regulating what one feels and does; being disciplined; controlling one's appetites and emotions

Transcendence—strengths that forge connections to the larger universe and provide meaning

20) **Appreciation of beauty and excellence [awe, wonder, elevation]:** Noticing and appreciating beauty, excellence, and/or skilled performance in various domains of life, from nature to art to mathematics to science to everyday experience

21) **Gratitude:** Being aware of and thankful for the good things that happen; taking time to express thanks

22) **Hope [optimism, future-mindedness, future orientation]:** Expecting the best in the future and working to achieve it; believing that a good future is something that can be brought about

23) **Humor [playfulness]:** Liking to laugh and tease; bringing smiles to other people; seeing the light side; making (not necessarily telling) jokes

24) **Spirituality [religiousness, faith, purpose]:** Having coherent beliefs about the higher purpose and meaning of the universe; knowing where one fits within the larger scheme; having beliefs about the meaning of life that shape conduct and provide comfort

Table 3.3 **Definitions of the 34 Talent Themes Measured by the Clifton StrengthsFinder 2.0 ([CSF 2.0] Asplund, Lopez, Hodges, & Harter, 2007; Rath, 2007)**

Achiever: People strong in the achiever theme have a great deal of stamina and work hard. They take great satisfaction from being busy and productive.

Activator: People strong in the activator theme can make things happen by turning thoughts into action. They are often impatient.

Adaptability: People strong in the adaptability theme prefer to "go with the flow." They tend to be "now" people who take things as they come and discover the future one day at a time.

Analytical: People strong in the analytical theme search or reasons and causes. They have the ability to think about all the factors that might affect a situation.

Arranger: People strong in the arranger theme can organize, but they also have a flexibility that complements that ability. They like to figure out how all of the pieces and resources can be arrange for maximum productivity.

Belief: People strong in the belief theme have certain core values that are unchanging. Out of those values emerges a defined purpose for their life.

Command: People strong in the command theme have presence. They can take control of a situation and make decisions.

Communication: People strong in the communication theme generally find it easy to put their thoughts into words. They are good conversationalists and presenters.

Competition: People strong in the competition theme measure their progress against the performance of others. They strive to win first place and revel in contests.

Connectedness: People strong in the connectedness theme have faith in links between all things. They believe there are few coincidences and that almost every event has a reason.

Consistency: People strong in the consistency theme are keenly aware of the need to treat people the same. They try to treat everyone in the world with consistency by setting up clear rules and adhering to them.

Context: People strong in the context theme enjoy thinking about the past. They understand the present by researching its history.

Deliberative: People strong in the deliberative theme are best characterized by the serious care they take in making decisions or choices. They anticipate the obstacles.

Developer: People strong in the developer theme recognize and cultivate the potential in others. They spot the signs of each small improvement and derive satisfaction from those improvements.

Discipline: People strong in the discipline theme enjoy routine and structure. Their world is best described by the order they create.

(continued)

Table 3.3 **Continued**

Empathy: People strong in the empathy theme can sense the feelings of other people by imagining themselves in others' lives and in others' situations.

Focus: People strong in the focus theme can take a direction, follow through, and make the corrections necessary to stay on track.

Futuristic: People strong in the futuristic theme are inspired by the future and what could be. They inspire others with their vision of the future.

Harmony: People strong in the harmony theme look for consensus. They don't enjoy conflict; rather, they seek areas of agreement.

Ideation: People strong in the ideation theme are fascinated by ideas. They are able to find connections between seemingly disparate phenomena.

Includer: People strong in the include theme are accepting of others. They show awareness of those who feel left out and make efforts to include them.

Individualization: People strong in the individualization theme are intrigued with the unique qualities of each person. They have a gift for figuring out how people who are different can work together productively.

Intellection: People strong in the intellection theme are characterized by their intellectual activity. They are introspective and appreciate intellectual discussions.

Input: People strong in the input theme have a craving to know more. Often they like to collect and archive all kinds of information.

Learner: People strong in the learner theme have a great desire to learn and want to improve continuously.

Maximizer: People strong in the maximize theme focus on strengths as a way to stimulate professional and group excellence. They seek to transform strong into something superb.

Positivity: People strong in the positivity theme have an enthusiasm that is contagious. They are upbeat and can get others excited about what they are going to do.

Relator: People strong in the relator theme enjoy close relationships with others. They find deep satisfaction in working hard with friends to achieve a goal.

Responsibility: People strong in the responsibility theme take psychological ownership of what they say they will do. They are committed to stable values such as honesty and loyalty.

Restorative: People strong in the restorative theme are adept at dealing with problems. They are good at figuring out what is wrong and resolving it.

Self-assurance: People strong in the self-assurance theme feel confident in their ability to manage their own lives. They possess an inner compass that gives them confidence that their decisions are right.

Significance: People strong in the significance theme want to be very important in the eyes of others. They are independent and want to be recognized.

(continued)

Table 3.3 **Continued**

Strategic: People strong in the strategic theme create alternative ways to proceed. Faced with any given scenario, they can quickly spot the relevant patterns and issues.

Woo: Woo stands for "winning others over." People strong in the woo theme love the challenge of meeting new people and winning them over. They derive satisfaction from breaking the ice and making a connection with another person.

measures that fall within the purview of positive psychology. For example, perusal of the literature reveals a host of positive psychological research on topics such as learned optimism (Seligman, 1991), forgiveness (Worthington, 1998, 2001; Witvliet, Phipps, Feldman, & Beckham, 2004; Enright & Coyle, 1998; McCullough & Witvliet, 2002), gratitude (Emmons, McCullough, & Tsang, 2003; Emmons & McCullough, 2003), hope (Synder, 1994), savoring (Bryant & Veroff, 2002), flow (Csikszentmihalyi, 1990), altruism (Batson, Ahmad, Lishner, & Tsang, 2002), and active-constructive responding (Gable, Reis, & Impett, 2004) to name just a few.

Positive psychological assessments also include such measures as the Satisfaction with Life Scale (Diener, Emmons, Larsen, & Griffin, 1985), the Fordyce Emotions Questionnaire (Fordyce, 1988), the General Happiness Scale (Lyubomirsky & Lepper, 1999), the Positive and Negative Affect Scale ([PANAS] Watson, Clark, & Tellegan, 1988), and the Attributional Style Questionnaire ([ASQ] Peterson, Semmel et al., 1982).

Applications of positive psychology within the world of work are noted throughout the literature on positive organizational scholarship (Cameron, Dutton, & Quinn, 2003) and gainful employment (Snyder & Lopez, 2007). Similarly, applications to counseling and psychotherapy have been documented (Magyar-Moe, 2009). More specifically, evidence-based approaches to therapy include Strengths-Based Counseling (Smith, 2006), Strengths-Centered Therapy (Wong, 2006), Positive Psychotherapy (Rashid, 2008), Quality of Life Therapy (Frisch, 2006), Well-Being Therapy (Ruini & Fava, 2004), Hope Therapy (Lopez, Floyd, Ulven, & Snyder, 2000), and more. Positive psychology has been applied to such areas as teaching (Fineburg, 2004), schooling (Buskist et al., 2005; Gilman, Huebner, & Buckman, 2008), coaching (Biswas-Diener & Dean, 2007), community development (Linley, Bhaduri, Sharma, & Govindji, 2010), and beyond.

Summary

The field of positive psychology is burgeoning and will likely to continue to do so in the years ahead. At the core of the popularity of positive psychology sits the fact that positive psychology applies to *all people*. Positive psychology is about "just plain folk" and making the lives of ordinary people more enjoyable, meaningful, and rewarding, hence, there is an application to everyone. One does not have to be an aspiring psychologist to see the application of positive psychology to one's future, nor does one need firsthand experience with psychological disorders or pathology to really understand how positive psychology works. No matter what one's past life experiences entailed or what their futures may hold, various topics of positive psychology are applicable to all people who desire to work towards making their lives better. Indeed, the remaining chapters of this text illuminate the multitude of ways in which positive psychology can be applied within a university setting for the betterment of students, faculty, staff, and the overall campus culture.

References

American Psychiatric Association (2000). *Diagnostic and statistical manual of mental disorders, fourth edition, text revision.* Washington, DC: American Psychiatric Association.

Asplund, J., Lopez, S. J., Hodges, T., & Harter, J. (2007). *Technical report: Development and validation of the Clifton StrengthsFinder 2.0.* Princeton, NJ: The Gallup Organization. http://strengths.gallup.com/private/resources/csftechnicalreport031005.pdf

Batson, C. D., Ahmad, N., Lishner, D. A., & Tsang, J. (2002). Empathy and altruism. In C. R. Snyder & S. L. Lopez (Eds.), *Handbook of positive psychology* (pp. 485–498). New York: Oxford University Press.

Beers, C. W. (1908). *A mind that found itself.* New York: Longmans Green.

Biswas-Diener, R., & Dean, B. (2007). Positive psychology coaching: Putting the science of happiness to work for your clients. Hoboken, NJ: Wiley.

Bryant, F. B., & Veroff, J. (1982). The structure of psychological well-being: A sociohistorical analysis. *Journal of Personality and Social Psychology, 43,* 653–673.

Bryant, F. B., & Veroff, J. (2002). *A process model for positive psychology.* Unpublished manuscript.

Buckingham, M., & Clifton, D. O. (2000). *Now, discover your strengths.* New York: Free Press.

Buskist, W., Benson, T., & Sikorski J. F. (2005). The call to teach. *Journal of Social and Clinical Psychology, 24* (1), 111–122.

Cameron, K., Dutton, J., & Quinn, R. (2003). *Positive organizational scholarship.* San Francisco: Berrett-Koehler Publishers.

Clifton, D. O, & Anderson, E. C. (2002). *StrengthsQuest: Discover and develop your strengths in academics, career, and beyond.* Washington, D.C.: The Gallup Organization.

Clifton, D. O., & Nelson, P. (1992). *Soar with your strengths.* New York, NY: Dell Publishing.

Csikszentmihalyi, M. (1990). *Flow: The psychology of optimal experience.* New York: Harper & Row.

Diener, E., Emmons, R. A., Larsen, R. J., & Griffin, S. (1985). The satisfaction with life scale. *Journal of Personality Assessment, 49,* 71–75.

Emmons, R. A., & McCullough, M. E. (2003). Counting blessings versus burdens: Experimental studies of gratitude and subjective well-being. *Journal of Personality and Social Psychology, 84,* 377–389.

Emmons, R. A., McCullough, M. E., & Tsang, J. (2003). The assessment of gratitude. In S. J. Lopez and C. R. Snyder (Eds.). *Handbook of positive psychology assessment* (pp. 327–341). Washington, DC: American Psychological Association.

Enright, R. D., & Coyle, C. T. (1998). Researching the process model of forgiveness within psychological interventions. In E. L. Worthington Jr. (Ed.), *Dimensions of forgiveness: Psychological research and theological perspectives* (pp. 139–161). Philadelphia: Templeton Foundation Press.

Erikson, E. H. (1959). Identity and the life cycle. *Psychological Issues, 1,* Monograph 1.

Fineburg, A. C. (2004) Introducing positive psychology to the introductory psychology student. In P. A. Linley and S. Joseph (Eds), *Positive Psychology in Practice,* Hoboken, NJ: John Wiley & Sons.

Fordyce, M. (1988). A review of research on the happiness measures: A sixty-second index of happiness and mental health. *Social Indicators Research, 20,* 355–381.

Fredrickson, B. L. (1998). What good are positive emotions? *Review of General Psychology, 2,* 300–319.

Fredrickson, B. L. (2001). The role of positive emotions in positive psychology: The broaden-and-build theory of positive emotions. *American Psychologist, 56,* 218–226.

Fredrickson, B. L. (2003). The value of positive emotions. *American Scientist, 91,* 330–335.

Fredrickson, B. L. (2013, July 15). Updated Thinking on Positivity Ratios. *American Psychologist.* Advance online publication. doi:10.1037/a0033584

Fredrickson, B. L., & Branigan, C. (2005). Positive emotions broaden the scope of attention and thought-action repertoires. *Cognition and Emotion, 19,* 313–332.

Fredrickson, B. L., & Joiner, T. (2002). Positive emotions trigger upward spirals toward emotional well-being. Psychological Science, *13,* 172–175.

Fredrickson, B. L., Mancuso, R. A., Branigan, C., & Tugade, M. M. (2000). The undoing effect of positive emotions. *Motivation and Emotion, 24,* 237–258.

Fredrickson, B. L., Tugade, M. M., Waugh, C. E., & Larkin, G. (2003). What good are positive emotions in crises? A prospective study of resilience and emotions following the terrorist attacks on the United States on September 11th, 2001. *Journal of Personality and Social Psychology, 84,* 365–376.

Frijda, N. H. (1986). *The emotions.* England: Cambridge University Press.

Frisch, M. B. (2006). *Quality of life therapy: Applying a life satisfaction approach to positive psychology and cognitive therapy.* Hoboken, New Jersey: John Wiley & Sons, Inc.

Gable, S. L., Reis, H. T., Impett, E. A. (2004). What do you do when things go right? The intrapersonal and interpersonal benefits of sharing positive events. *Journal of Personality and Social Psychology, 87,* 228–245.

Gilman, R., Huebner, S., & Buckman, M. (2008). Postitive schooling. In S. J. Lopez (Ed.), *Positive psychology: Exploring the best in people,* (pp. 87–98). Westport, CT: Greenwood Publishing.

Jahoda, M. (1958). *Current concepts of positive mental health.* New York: Basic Books.

Keyes, C. L. M. (1998). Social well-being. *Social Psychology Quarterly, 61,* 121–140.

Keyes, C. L. M., & Lopez, S. J. (2002). Toward a science of mental health: Positive directions in diagnosis and intervention. In C. R. Snyder & S. J. Lopez (Eds.), *Handbook of positive psychology,* (pp. 45–62). New York: Oxford University Press.

Keyes, C. L. M., & Magyar-Moe, J. L. (2003). The Measurement and utility of adult subjective well-being. In S. J. Lopez & C. R. Snyder (Eds.), *Positive psychological assessment: A handbook of models and measures* (pp. 411–425). Washington DC: American Psychological Association.

Lazarus, R. S. (1991). *Emotion and adaptation.* New York: Oxford University Press.

Linley, P. A., Bhaduri, A., Sen Sharma, D., & Govindji, R. (2010). Strengthening underprivileged communities: Strengths-based approaches as a force for positive social change in community development. In R. Biswas-Diener (Ed.). *Positive psychology as social change* (pp. 141–156). Dordrecht: Springer.

Lopez, S. J., Magyar-Moe, J. L., Petersen, S. E., Ryder, J. A., Krieshok, T. S., O'Byrne, K. K., Lichtenberg, J. W., & Fry, N. (2006). Counseling psychology's focus on positive aspects of human functioning: A major contribution. *The Counseling Psychologist, 34*, 205–227.

Lopez, S. J., Floyd, R. K., Ulven, J. C., & Snyder, C. R. (2000). Hope therapy: Helping clients build a house of hope. In C. R. Snyder (Ed.), *Handbook of hope* (pp. 123–150). New York: Academic Press.

Lucas, R. E., Diener, E., & Suh, E. (1996). Discriminant validity of well-being measures. *Journal of Personality and Social Psychology, 71*, 616–628.

Lyubomirsky, S., & Lepper, H. (1999). A measure of subjective happiness: Preliminary reliability and construct validation. *Social Indicators Research, 46*, 137–155.

Magyar-Moe, J. L. (2009). *Therapist's guide to positive psychological interventions.* San Diego, CA: Elsevier Academic Press.

McCullough, M. E., & Witvliet, C. V. O. (2002). The psychology of forgiveness. In C. R. Snyder & S. J. Lopez (Eds.), *Handbook of positive psychology* (pp. 446–458). London: Oxford University Press.

McKay, J., & Greengrass, M. (2003). People. *Monitor on Psychology, 34*(3), 87.

Menninger, K., Mayman, M., & Pruyser, P. W. (1963). *The vital balance.* New York: Viking Press.

Mirowsky, J., & Ross, C. E. (1989). *Social causes of psychological distress.* New York: Aldine.

Peterson, C., & Seligman, M. E. P. (2004). *Character strengths and virtues: A handbook and classification.* New York: Oxford University Press.

Peterson, C., Semmel, A., von Baeyer, C., Abramson, L., Metalsky, & Seligman, M. (1982). The Attributional Style Questionnaire, *Cognitive Therapy and Research, 6*, 287–300.

Rashid, T. (2008). Positive psychotherapy. In S. J. Lopez (Ed.), *Positive psychology: Exploring the best in people* (Vol 4, pp. 187–217). Westport, CT: Praeger Publishers.

Rath, T. (2007). StrengthsFinder 2.0. New York: Gallup Press.

Ruini, C., & Fava, G. A. (2004). Clinical applications of well-being therapy. In P. A. Linley & S. Joseph (Eds.) *Positive psychology in practice* (pp. 371–387). Hoboken, NJ: John Wiley & Sons.

Ryan, R. M., & Deci, E. L. (2001). On happiness and human potentials: A review of research on hedonic and eudaimonic well-being. *Annual Review of Psychology, 52*, 141–166.

Ryff, C. D., & Keyes, C. L. M. (1995). The structure of psychological well-being revisited. *Journal of Personality and Social Psychology, 69*, 719–727.

Ryff, C. D. (1989). Happiness is everything, or is it? Explorations on the meaning of psychological well-being. *Journal of Personality and Social Psychology, 57*, 1069–1081.

Seeman, M. (1959). On the meaning of alienation. *American Sociological Review, 24*, 783–791.

Seligman, M. E. P. (1991). *Learned optimism.* New York: Knopf.

Seligman, M. E. P. (2002). *Authentic happiness: Using the new positive psychology to realize your potential for lasting fulfillment.* New York: Free Press.

Seligman, M. E. P. (2011) *Flourish: A visionary new understanding of happiness and well-being.* New York: Free Press.

Seligman, M. E. P., & Csikszentmihalyi, M. (2000). Positive psychology: An introduction. *American Psychologist, 55*, 5–14.

Shmotkin, D. (1998). Declarative and differential aspects of subjective well-being and implications for mental health in later life. In J. Lomranz (Ed.), *Handbook of aging and mental health: An integrative approach* (pp. 15–43). New York: Plenum.

Smith, E. (2006). The strengths-based counseling model. *The Counseling Psychologist, 34*, 13–79.

Snyder, C. R. (1994). *The psychology of hope: You can get there from here.* New York: Free Press.

Snyder C. R., & Lopez, S. J. (2007). *Positive psychology: The scientific and practical explorations of human strengths.* Thousand Oaks, CA: Sage.

Terman, L. M., Buttenwieser, P., Ferguson, L. W., Johnson, W. B., & Wilson, D. P. (1938). *Psychological factors in marital happiness.* New York: McGraw Hill.

Toobey, J., & Cosmides, L. (1990). The past explains the present: Emotional adaptations and the structure of ancestral environments. *Ethology and Sociobiology, 11,* 375–424.

Tyler, L. E. (1973). Design for a hopeful psychology. *American Psychologist, 28,* 1021–1029.

Waterman, A. S. (1993). Two conceptions of happiness: Contrasts of personal expressiveness (eudaimonia) and hedonic enjoyment. *Journal of Personality and Social Psychology, 64,* 678–691.

Watson, J. (1928). *Psychological care of infant and adult.* New York: Norton.

Watson, D., Clark, L. A., & Tellegan, A. (1988). Development and validation of brief measures of positive and negative affect: The PANAS scales. *Journal of Personality and Social Psychology, 54,* 1063–1070.

Witvliet, C. V. O., Phipps, K. A., Feldman, M. E., & Beckham, J. C. (2004). Posttraumatic mental and physical health correlates of forgiveness and religious coping in military veterans. *Journal of Traumatic Stress, 17,* 269–273.

Wong, J. (2006). Strengths-centered therapy: A social constructionist, virtue-based psychotherapy. *Psychotherapy: Theory, Research, Practice, and Training, 43,* 133–146.

Worthington, E. L. (2001). *Five steps to forgiveness: The art and science of forgiving.* New York: Crown Publishers.

Worthington, E. L., Jr. (1998). An empathy-humility-commitment model of forgiveness applied within family dyads. *Journal of Family Therapy, 20,* 59–71.

4

Cultural Competence in Positive Psychology

History, Research, and Practice

JENNIFER TERAMOTO PEDROTTI

As our world becomes more and more diverse, and at the same time more closely connected by technology and communication possibilities, the need for a culturally competent approach becomes clear in all work within psychology as a discipline. This same competence is required of the field of positive psychology in considering what behaviors and qualities are to be called "strength" versus "weakness" or "asset" versus "deficit." Because much of the theory and research behind positive psychology was developed within the Western-focused culture of the United States, cultural competence in this area has been rather slow to develop until fairly recent years (Constantine & Sue, 2006). On today's average college campus, diversity is greater than ever before. Thus, discussion of what is to be termed positive versus negative must be couched in terms of cultural context in order for one to (1) fully understand the benefit (or cost) to one's development and (2) for the application of a positive psychology perspective to be relevant to the diverse array of individuals found today on any college campus.

In this chapter, a section on definitions will be given followed by a brief history of the treatment of culture as an important variable in the understanding of individuals from groups of different backgrounds. Next, several exemplars from current literature and research will be given to provide support for the idea that culture influences the identification, understanding, manifestation, and discussions of strengths. Finally, strategies will be offered with the aim of providing more culturally competent strengths-based services to a diverse array of students on college campuses.

Definitions

The term *culture* has many definitions across the field of psychology, and experts do not agree on a single definition (Matsumoto & Yoo, 2006). However, Triandis (1996) has provided a definition that many consider to be a good approximation of the description of this multifaceted word: "shared elements that provide the standards for perceiving, believing, evaluating, communicating, and acting among those who share a language, a historic period and a geographic location" (p. 408). Culture provides the context in which we live our lives, shaping and influencing development, as well as helping us to interpret new stimuli (Triandis, 2001).

In addition, both broad and narrow parameters exist regarding what factors and characteristics are to be labeled as part of one's individual cultural experience. In the past, many have used the more narrow parameter of including only race, ethnicity, and potentially nation of origin in describing personal culture (American Psychological Association, 2003; Mio, Barker, & Tumambing, 2011). Today, however, more researchers and practitioners are using an increasingly broad definition of culture that includes race, ethnicity, and nation of origin, but also discusses the relevance of generation, sexual orientation, socioeconomic status or social class, religion, disability, and gender in fully understanding the cultural experience of an individual (Hays, 2008). In truly understanding research that discusses culture, these definitions must be understood to appropriately apply their findings in practice. In addition, this broad understanding may be preferable to many college students who are often still in the process of culturally defining themselves as individuals and as adults.

It previous literature, the terms *multicultural* and *cross-cultural* have sometimes been used interchangeably; however, these terms denote two separate experiences. Multiculturalism refers to study of different groups that exist with one another within one context; the United States is a good exemplar of this particular environment because many racial and ethnic groups reside alongside one another in this context (Mio et al., 2012), as is any university campus with its diverse array of individuals within one context. Cross-cultural study refers to comparisons made across two or more contexts, such as studying college students in the United States and in China (Mio et al., 2012). This second type of study also involves groups who are ethnically similar but different in terms of their context (e.g., Japanese college students residing in Japan and Japanese American college students residing in the United States). Cross-cultural research acknowledges that context is an influencing factor in the experiences of these two different groups. In conducting both multicultural and cross-cultural research and practice on campus, one must keep these distinguishing factors in mind in order to understand the complexity involved in studying groups in these two different ways.

Scholars of both multicultural and cross-cultural research, as well as practitioners who use this research to form practical applications, must also consider issues of equivalence in order to appropriately use the tenets described. Mio et al. (2012) discuss three sources of equivalence that must be established before making comparisons between various groups. *Conceptual equivalence* is referred to by these authors as ensuring that constructs have definitional similarity across cultural groups. For example, positive psychology constructs such as optimism, hope, or courage may have different definitions in different cultural groups. Although one group may describe hope as a process of individual goal attainment (e.g., Snyder et al., 1991), this definition is more consistent with a Western focus and may not be as relevant in more collectivist cultural groups. Various positive characteristics may also have different correlates in different cultural groups (see Chang & Banks, 2008; Diener & Suh, 2000; Pedrotti, 2014). In addition to conceptual equivalence, *linguistic* and *metric equivalence* must also be established (Mio et al., 2012). The former concept requires that measures are appropriately translated for use with culturally different populations, after conceptual equivalence has been established; merely translating a measure before conceptual equivalence has been established may result in faulty findings. Metric equivalence refers to the notion that uniformity must be established with regard to understanding of metric increments; in risk-averse cultures, for example, Likert scale endpoints may not be used due to aversion to extremes found in these types of cultures (Mio et al., 2012). In a case such as this, a 1–10 scale may become shortened to a 2–9 scale, and, thus, a score of any number along the 1–10 continuum may not mean the same thing in all groups. Lack of one or another of these equivalences could be cause for misidentification and/or mismeasurement of strengths and weakness in an individual.

The Necessity of Consideration of Culture

Within the field of positive psychology, many agree that a consideration of culture is necessary today in terms of discussing strengths and weaknesses (Pedrotti, Edwards, & Lopez, 2009; Lopez, Pedrotti, & Snyder, 2015). In the past, some researchers have posited that the strength of our science (e.g., measures, research methods, etc.) allows us to be objective and thus allows us to "transcend particular cultures and politics and approach universality" (Seligman & Csikszentmihalyi, 2000, p. 5). Along these lines, some researchers have hypothesized that certain characteristics (often described as "virtues") can be found to exist across multiple cultures and can be called universal strengths (Peterson & Seligman, 2004).

In current literature, however, several studies are beginning examine the cultural applicability of a number of positive traits (Benedikovičova & Ardelt, 2008;

Leu, Wang, & Koo, 2011; Lu & Gilmour, 2004; Uchida & Kitayama, 2009; Uchida, Norasakkunkit, & Kitayama, 2004). Thus, many note today that it is impossible to keep personal values separate from the research process (Constantine & Sue, 2003; Pedrotti & Edwards, 2009). Personal culture plays a role in deciding which constructs to study, the direction of hypotheses about relationships between constructs, and processes that would be beneficial to investigate; in short, our own interests, values, and cultural beliefs permeate the science in which we seek to engage (Leong & Wong, 2003; Pedrotti, 2007; Lopez et al., 2015). Although, it seems evident that positive traits exist in all cultures, the designation of which characteristics are determined to be "strength" versus "weakness" is something that must be viewed within a cultural context (Christopher, 2005; Constantine & Sue, 2006; Pedrotti & Edwards, 2009, 2014). For example, in a college environment, consider the contstuct of competition versus cooperation as it relates to success. In Western individualistic cultures, there is a positive association with competition and with working alone to achieve the top spot; this same connotation is not expressed by cultures that are more collectivist. In these more cooperative-based cultures, assisting others on their pursuit toward success and achieving success as a group may be more valued. In a university setting where student success is based on individual achievement, this type of cooperative effort may be frowned upon unless it is viewed through a cultural lens.

With the development of their "Guidelines on Multicultural Education, Training, Research, Practice, and Organizational Change for Psychologists," the American Psychological Association (2003) asserts that culture is a factor to be considered in all psychological activities. In these publications, the American Psychological Association endorses the culturally embedded view of psychology as a whole (Pedrotti et al., 2009).

In addition, as others have noted in previous research and literature (Seligman & Csikszentmihalyi, 2000), psychology as a discipline has often overlooked the strengths of individuals and groups and has instead focused primarily on weakness. Similarly, the study of psychological topics in specific relation to racial and ethnic minorities has often been neglected. Moreover, when this topic is addressed, it often leads to overpathologization of these minority groups (Sue & Sue, 2003). As such, underrepresented minorities (racial, ethnic, gender, sexual, etc.) are "exposed to 'double jeopardy'—branded as pathological in comparison to the majority group, and within a system that only acknowledges weakness and leaves no room for a balanced description of behavior" (Pedrotti & Edwards, 2009, p. 166). Positive psychology may be particularly poised to assist in creating more healthy and positive views of cultural groups who have been unjustly stigmatized by faulty or prejudicial theories from the past (Pedrotti, 2013). In taking a culturally sensitive and competent approach, the field of positive psychology could potentially undo some of the damage done to these populations. For example, stereotypes exist about academic abilities within different cultural groups;

in these scenarios, racial and ethnic minorities are sometimes stereotyped as less intelligent or as having fewer resources overall, compared with majority groups. Knowledge of Steele's (1994) concept of stereotype threat, and the anxiety that a reminder of these negative stereotypes may cause, as a potential influence on academic testing may help campus workers to understand that the testing process may be a qualitatively different experience for an African American student versus a White student or a male student versus a female student (also see Aronson, Lustina, Good, & Keough, 1999). Thus, potentially normal reactions are not seen as pathological.

From Inferiority to Source of Strength: A Brief History

As mentioned previously, members of nonmajority culture have often been pathologized due to lack of attention given to cultural context in research. Prior to investigating current usage of cultural context in discussing positive psychological constructs, a brief history of the discussion of culture in relation to strength and weakness is required.

Early psychological theories and research discussed cultural differences as "deviances," and they decried any behavior that differed from the norms of majority culture (i.e., European or European American) as a sign of a group's inferiority. These *inferiority models* found their bases in eugenics and in Social Darwinism, and they used the claim of genetic differences between the races to posit that certain racial groups were not capable of success without help from the White majority (Pedrotti et al., 2009). Thus, these models described inherent weakness and pathology in certain cultural groups (i.e., any culture outside of European American culture), although current genetic research has disproved the existence of major biological differences between the races (see Jackson, 1992). Recommendations on how to "civilize" or humanize were often prescribed as necessary in guiding individuals in these groups toward "healthy" development. A clear although troubling example of this time period is the saying often used by educators of American Indians that the job of these teachers was to "Kill the Indian, save the child," that is, to eradicate all vestiges of the "inferior" American Indian culture to "save" the child from these practices and beliefs (Barker, 1997). These different religious practices, customs, language, and rituals were deemed inferior, "savage," or backwards when viewed from the dominant cultural lens, and were used to explain why assimilation was the only option for these groups.

In the 1950s, Allport (1954) and others began to take the viewpoint that these racial differences may not be biological in nature but were determined by environment instead. In this *deficit model*, racial and ethnic minorities were thought to lack certain strengths because of a deficient environment as a result of their sociocultural status as nonmajority individuals. Prejudice, racism, and poor living conditions due to lower socioeconomic status were cited as reasons why racial and ethnic minorities developed fewer strengths or positive coping practices compared with majority groups (Carter, 1994; Sue, 1983). Thus, racial and ethnic minorities were still in need of assistance, according to these models, but the reasons for these deficits were not internal. Although this change in perspective shows some progress in the sense that the reasons for weaknesses were moved outside the individual to the environment, these models still recognize racial and ethnic minority groups as inferior to majority groups (Kaplan & Sue, 1997; Pedrotti et al., 2009; Pedrotti & Edwards, 2014). These models did not fully recognize the complexity of the nonmajority experience. In addition, they ignore the fact that the system of judging which behaviors were strengths and which were weaknesses was set up in one cultural group (the majority) and then used to judge all other cultural groups (Sue & Constantine, 2003). Thus, certain behaviors characterized as weaknesses may not have been viewed as such through a different cultural lens.

Later, models of *cultural pluralism* began to emerge, thus recognizing that different cultural experiences are at the root of the development of different strengths and positive behaviors (Pedrotti et al., 2009). These models began to acknowledge that culture is a key ingredient in determining one's life experiences as a whole, and in this way began to reject the idea that lack of conforming or full assimilation to majority culture was a limiting factor or a source of inferiority. Today, these models have been refined somewhat to include the fact that one's personal cultural experience may be unique; each of us has different cultural facets (e.g., race, ethnicity, gender, socioeconomic status, sexual orientation, etc.) that shape our life experiences. These *human diversity* models state that the dynamic interplay between these facets within the individual and between the individual and his or her environment determine what strengths and weaknesses may be developed and what behaviors and characteristics are viewed as positive or negative (Chin, 1993).

Today, researchers and practitioners in the field of positive psychology are called to actively engage in five main areas:

> (a) presenting a positive presentation of values, potentials, and lifestyle of the culturally different client; (b) shifting from a deficit hypothesis to a difference hypothesis; (c) recognizing that cultural differences exist; (d) examining frameworks that are biased against these differences; and (e) acknowledging that cultural behaviors are adaptive and have withstood the test of time. (Pedrotti et al., 2009, p. 52)

Finally, it is important to recognize that cultural facets may also be a source of strength in and of themselves (Pedrotti, 2011; Lopez et al., 2015).

Cross-Cultural and Multicultural Exemplars in the Field of Positive Psychology

Research in all areas of the field is still emerging because cultural facets have only been more of a focus in relatively recent times. Still, researchers have begun to investigate culture as an influencing factor with regard to the discussion of strength and weakness (Pedrotti & Edwards, 2014). Moreover, several studies provide evidence that culture must be examined in studying different behaviors and characteristics in culturally different groups. First, the notion of universal value of a particular characteristic happiness is challenged by ideas about the construct of happiness from Ahuvia (2001) and others. Second, a close study of Hmong American culture shows that variation in manifestations across cultural groups exist of the concept of forgiveness. Third, studies from Chang (1996), Shaw et al. (1997), and Chang and Banks (2007) show that different correlates are found with various characteristics denoted as "strengths" in Western culture (e.g., optimism, coping, and hope) provide evidence for the idea that we must be careful in ascribing the label of "strength" or "weakness" to any one characteristic. Finally, a discussion of *culturally relevant strengths* is offered with the goal of showing that some positive characteristics might be inherent to certain cultural contexts.

Everybody Wants to Be Happy?

The construct of happiness is one that is often touted as a universal experience, and valued at the top of one's list in a ranking of positive characteristics (Ahuvia, 2001; Myers, 1993; Peterson & Seligman, 2004; Lopez et al., 2015). Ahuvia recounts several experiences regarding this topic including personal conversations with students in which several noted to him that other factors (including social expectations, honor, and monetary rewards) are valued above happiness in other cultures, perhaps particularly those that emphasize obedience to parents and family honor (e.g., Asian cultures). Ahuvia states, "Cross-cultural research shows that values like 'enjoying life' are stronger in affluent Western societies, whereas 'social recognition' and 'honoring parents and elders' are particularly strong in collectivist societies" (p. 77). These data are corroborated by the fact that cross-cultural research (e.g., Diener, Oishi, & Lucas, 2003) finds that Asian research participants from the Pacific Rim of Asia rank happiness as less important than participants from Latin America. In addition, individualist countries (i.e., those that value personal achievement and competition over group achievement and cooperation) have been shown to have higher levels of subjective well-being and life satisfaction and to value these as more important, compared to contries with collectivist cultural values (Diener & Suh, 2000). Suh (2002) hypothesizes that a focus on subjective well-being might be more relevant for individualists, whereas not as salient for collectivistically minded individuals. Thus, even a construct that seems to be universally desirable, may have a different level of value among diverse cultural groups.

It is also possible that less linearly oriented cultures (such as Eastern cultures as compared to Western cultures) may place a value for *balance* above a construct (such as happiness) because of their differences in common thought processes (Lopez et al., 2015). Although individuals in Western cultures may think in a more linear fashion (e.g., thinking toward the future), individuals in Asian cultures may have a more circular thought process. As Lopez et al. posit, Western culture places achievement of goals as the endpoint of the process, whereas an individual from an Eastern culture may think of life as more of a circular process (e.g., the yin and yang). If the Western individual wishes for extreme happiness, he or she stays in that state if the wish is fulfilled (linear goal process). In contrast, however, if an Eastern individual wishes for extreme happiness, he or she does so with the belief that life may also bring the opposite state of extreme unhappiness to maintain balance; as such, this Eastern individual may value overall balance in life over extremes on either side (Lopez et al., 2015). Thus, although the virtue of happiness might be something valued in different cultural groups, it seems likely that cultural differences exist in the importance or ranking of this state.

Manifestations of Forgiveness in Hmong Americans

Culture may also determine how a particular construct is manifested. Sandage, Hill, and Vang (2003) completed an in-depth investigation of practices of forgiveness in an Hmong American sample. In this research, Sandage et al. found that although this construct was valued as a positive characteristic or strength in this cultural group (similarly to majority culture value of this construct), its manifestation was very different. In samples of majority-population individuals within the United States, forgiveness is usually touted as a personal experience, one that takes the victim of a transgression to a benevolent (McCullough, Worthington, & Rachal, 1997) or neutral (Thompson & Snyder, 2003) disposition toward the transgressor. In Sandage and colleagues' investigation of this construct among the Hmong American sample, forgiveness was found to incorporate a specific spiritual component and to emphasize repair of the relationship above personal benefits of forgiveness. In addition, the facilitation of forgiveness was most commonly handled by a third party, who was unrelated to the infraction. This need for a third party as a part of the process of forgiveness is not something noted in many other cultural groups (Lopez et al., 2015), and as such it appears to be a unique facet of the Hmong culture. Thus, although this construct is valued as a strength across cultures, the way in which it is carried out is very different in this cultural group. This may be the case with regard to other traits as well, although all may use the same name (e.g., forgiveness). As such, careful attention to proper operationalization as a trait is dependent on culture is necessary and valued.

Qualitative Differences in Connections Between Constructs

Several works show that looking carefully at qualitative differences between various constructs can provide invaluable information about the benefits (or lack thereof) of usefulness of these characteristics in culturally different populations.

Chang (1996) investigated optimism and pessimism (using the Extended Life Orientation Test; Chang, Maydeu-Oliveras, & D'Zurrilla, 1997) in two culturally different samples: a group of Asian American college students and a group of Caucasian American college students. The purpose of this study was to determine the role of optimism and pessimism in terms of effects on problem solving, depressive symptoms, general psychological, and physical health. Findings showed that significant differences were not found between these culturally different samples in levels of optimism nor in expression of depressive symptoms (Chang, 1996). Upon closer look, however, data revealed significant differences in pessimism were noted between the Asian American and Caucasian American groups, with Asian Americans scoring higher in pessimism. In previous research conducted primarily with Caucasian American samples (e.g., Carver & Gaines, 1987), scores associated with a pessimistic outlook were found to be correlated with higher scores on depression inventories. As such, it would be expected that if pessimism scores were found to be different, so too should depression scores, in keeping in line with the previously found positive correlation. However, this hypothesis was not supported because no significant differences were found between the two groups with regard to the presence of depressive symptomatology (Chang, 1996). Looking deeper, Chang found that *negative* correlations existed between optimism and general psychological and physical health in the Asian American sample, whereas *positive* correlations were found between these variables in their Caucasian American counterparts. In addition, a positive correlation existed between pessimism and increased problem solving in the Asian American sample, although the reverse was found in the Caucasian sample (Chang, 1996).

Chang's (1996) research provides us with a clear example of the importance of valuing cultural influences in positive psychological research and its application. If assumptions were made that the same correlations existed in all samples here, a potential benefiting characteristic could have been missed. It is possible that pessimism, with its positive correlation to problem solving in the Asian American sample, may be viewed as a strength within this cultural group, although it is usually touted as a weakness in majority culture. This type of research can assist college student personnel in myriad ways. For example, a college advisor who noted that a particular advisee was fairly pessimistic in his or her beliefs might do their best to increase optimism in this student, with the aim of it benefitting the student overall in their academic pursuits. Although this may make sense for a Caucasian American student, this well-intentioned act neglects the fact that pessimism may be serving a functional role for a student of Asian American descent. Similar situations could occur within the roles of college counselor or career counselor in which a risk for pathologizing a nonpathological trait in a certain cultural group may occur.

Shaw et al. (1997) provide a second example in this section regarding the importance of looking at intercorrelations between various characteristics across culturally different samples. In their study, these researchers conducted a cross-cultural investigation of various coping strategies used by caretakers of family members with Alzheimer's disease in Shanghai, China and in San Diego, California. Four distinct coping strategies appeared to be viewed as valuable across the two distinct cultural groups (Shaw et al., 1997). Upon closer investigation of these strategies, however, it became clear that the benefits of these particular strategies did not extend to both groups. For example, "cognitive confronting" (described as a cognitive reframing of the situation with the loved one) was found to promote the greatest distress psychologically in the San Diego sample, but this strategy was unrelated to psychological distress in the Shanghai sample. Another of the coping strategies, "behavioral confrontation" (described as taking problem-focused action toward assisting their loved one), was found to be significantly and positively correlated with depression in the San Diego sample, but exactly the reverse correlation (significant and negative) in the Shanghai sample. Similar results were found across the other two common coping strategies, showing differential benefits between the groups. Again, upon first investigation, the factor structure of the coping process appeared to be the same across these two groups. It was only in looking qualitatively at the correlations that the cross-cultural differences were found.

Finally, Chang and Banks (2007) investigated correlations Snyder and colleagues' (1991) concept of hope and a number of other constructs in separate samples of Asian Americans, Latino Americans, African Americans, and Caucasian Americans. Findings in this study showed that in addition to different cultural populations having significantly different mean scores on measures of hope and its two components of pathways and agency, correlations between these components and various other positive constructs were significantly different (Chang & Banks, 2007). For example, these researchers found that links to agentic thinking (i.e., ability to maintain motivation toward moving toward various goals) depended heavily on cultural group, with the best predictor being life satisfaction (Caucasian sample), positive affect (Asian American and African American samples), or rational problem solving (Latino Americans). In addition, the construct with the best predictive power for agentic thinking for some cultural groups was often not related at all to agentic thinking in other groups (Chang & Banks, 2007).

Thus, culture plays a significant role in determining the benefit, and potentially utility, of various constructs.

Culturally Relevant Strengths

In addition to noting that different characteristics may be valued and manifested in different ways in various cultural groups, it is also possible that some positive characteristics are inherent to certain cultural frameworks (Pedrotti et al., 2009).[1] For example, the concept of *familism*, i.e., a strong value for family often found in Latino cultural groups, has been shown to be related to subjective well-being in Mexican American samples (Edwards & Lopez, 2006). It may be that the support and structure inherent in a traditional Latino family is information that could be of use toward assisting a student to achieve their potential. For example, an advisor working with a Latino student struggling with an issue may ask how this student's family could assist them in making the best decision, or the advisor could suggest that the student seek advice from an older sibling. These types of suggestions may resonate more strongly with individuals with a strong concept of familism.

Similarly, situations that arise more commonly for certain individuals as a result of their being a part of a group may help to develop certain strengths as well. Researchers have found that racial and ethnic minorities often develop better coping strategies than individuals from nonminority groups, potentially as a result of the necessity of finding a way to deal with the occurrence of discrimination and prejudice in their lives (Ong & Edwards, 2008; Sue & Constantine, 2003). For example, a college counselor using hope therapy (Lopez, Floyd, Ulven, & Snyder, 2000) might ask a client about past experiences in which he or she has coped with discrimination and then help the client to use these skills in other situations in their life. Although the situation that breeds this strength in coping is not a positive one, it nevertheless represents a skill that is cultivated in a specific cultural group due to their inherent experiences.

In addition, Utsey, Hook, Fischer, and Belvet (2008) show that strong connections with certain cultural identity facets may also influence the development and recognition of various strengths (Lopez et al., 2015). In their 2008 study, Utsey et al. investigated links between levels of optimism, ego resilience, and cultural identification, with the construct of subjective well-being in a sample of African American individuals. Findings from this research showed that the level of adherence participants had to what was described as a traditional African American

---

[1] It is noted that these strengths might not exist or be valued by an individual solely because she or he is a member of a particular cultural group. Thus, assessment of cultural identity, and "checking-in" with students about their cultural background is always appropriate as a first step.

worldview (Utsey et al., 2008) could be used to predict higher well-being and better psychological functioning overall. In addition, those participants who had higher levels of racial pride were also found to be more resilient (Utsey et al., 2008). On a university campus, this type of pride might be increased and culti-vated through culturally based graduation ceremonies, clubs for various cultural groups, and recognition of holidays of multiple groups. Support and presence from administration in events and functions that breed this sort of pride and give voice to it may go a long way toward ensuring that different groups feel comfort-able when expressing these cultural facets in a larger group. In this way, adminis-trators set the example for students in general, modeling for them celebration of cultural identity. Findings such as these point to the fact that there may be specific strengths that are cultivated as a function of certain cultural norms and beliefs (Lopez et al., 2015), and understanding of the processes by which these positive characteristics are developed may be useful in cultivating them in other popula-tions as well.

One final point is the suggestion by Ponterotto and Pedersen (1993) that being an individual who is multiculturally competent may be a strength in and of itself; one that allows an individual to navigate successfully across many cultural groups. These researchers define a *multicultural personality* as "a strength-based cluster of personality dispositions or traits that [is hypoth-esized to predict] quality of life outcomes" (Ponterotto, Mendelowitz, & Collabolletta, 2008, p. 95) within culturally diverse societies. Having the development of such a personality style might be listed as a "University Learning Objectives" alongside other goals such as "knowledge of the major field of study" or "effective communication." University presidents, provosts, chancellors, and others might consider gaining knowledge about the benefits of such a style in order to work toward creation of a future culturally compe-tent workforce.

Strategies for Strength-Based, Culturally Competent Practice on the College Campus

As stated here, attending to positive characteristics in members of any cultural group, can broaden conceptualizations of all individuals. In addition, this knowl-edge can be used to inform faculty and staff's practice and application of these concepts with the goal of offering both positive psychology-based and multicultur-ally competent services on the college campus. Following are several suggestions that may increase the likelihood of offering multiculturally and cross-culturally competent strength-based services to a diverse array of individuals on the college campus.

Use of Broad Definitions of Culture and Understanding Oneself

As described above, researchers have used both broad and narrow definitions of the term culture in times past. In using a broad definition as a practitioner, one opens the door to having a more complex understanding of the individual or group with whom they are working (Hays, 2008). Pamela Hays has developed a framework called ADDRESSING that brings attention to 10 cultural facets that may be viewed as more or less salient for varying individuals. In this framework, each of the letters of the word ADDRESSING stand for a different facet (**A**ge, **D**isability [acquired], **D**isability [developmental], **R**eligion, **E**thnicity, **S**exual orientation, **S**ocioeconomic status, **I**ndigenous heritage, **N**ation of origin, and **G**ender). With this model, Hays is speaking of the differences that may exist between different generations, genders, races, or other cultural facets of individuals. Each of these facets may govern thoughts of any group of individuals with regard to what should be viewed as a strength or a weakness. As a practitioner, faculty, staff person, or other campus worker, use of this framework offers an opportunity to gain a closer look at a student's personal salient cultural characteristics, interpersonal supports, and environmental situations and can then be used to further a better understanding of the potentially different worldviews from which different students operate (Hays, 2008). This information might assist with self-knowledge as well, which can then lead to better skills at avoiding acting on personal bias in cross-cultural or multicultural interactions with others in the campus environment.

Those who work in student services such as campus counseling centers may also use the ADDRESSING framework with their student clients to assess importance of these factors to these individuals and to help individuals recognize these strengths in themselves as well. Different cultural groups may have easier or more difficult times naming personal strengths in a way that feels "normal" within their cultural framework (Hays, 2008). Hays suggests that therapists, in particular, might challenge themselves to attend to strengths in their assessments (both formal and informal) of their clients so that they can assist individuals with naming areas of strength for themselves in this way. Having a more full and complex understanding of the dynamic interplay of personal culture and its effect on the life of these students may help the practitioner to enhance treatment in the therapy setting.

Staying Abreast of Positive Psychology Cultural Research

In some positions in the college campus environment, staying abreast of research related to cross-cultural and multicultural issues may be extremely beneficial in obtaining more positive interactions with a diverse array of individuals.

Faculty, for example, might include multicultural and cross-cultural research in relation to their particular disciplines as a core part of a course as opposed to a special topic. In a positive psychology course, for example, instructors should introduce the idea of culture as a factor in the development, identification, and manifestation of various behaviors and characteristics and offer relevant research to support this supposition throughout the course (Pedrotti, 2012). An individual teaching any course involving research might preface their instruction by discussing bias toward both weakness and personal cultural norms as a function of the researcher(s)' personal worldview and caution students to take a strengths-based, and culturally embedded approach to research. Even in non-psychological disciplines, culture and strengths can be a relevant part of a course. In a course on Urban Planning, for example, individual and group well-being may be differentially influenced by placement of housing in connection with various services. For example, if a community is more collectivist in orientation (e.g., contains within its population a large number of Latino or Asian individuals), offering more communal access to services or locating churches, mosques, or temples in close proximity to housing in a community that places a strong value on religion or spirituality might be preferable. Culture and strengths thus become relevant pieces of the discussion across disciplines.

College counselors may also benefit from staying abreast of culturally oriented research within positive psychological areas for the same reasons as mentioned above but also so that they are adhering to the guidelines developed by the American Psychological Association (2003) with regard to culturally competent practice. Because the area of culture and positive psychology is relatively new, additional research abounds and many findings are just emerging. College counselors will also benefit from having a clear understanding of the aforementioned concepts of conceptual, linguistic, and metric equivalence (Mio et al., 2012) in using assessments within a culturally diverse clientele as well. These types of campus workers are in an ideal position to use culturally competent positive psychological practices to undo some of the past damage done to minorities (racial, ethnic, sexual, etc.) as a result of use of deficit models and biased hypotheses. Knowledge of these concepts may also assist individuals within administrative roles in making good decisions and practices regarding services for students of varying cultural backgrounds. For example, understanding that traditional standardized tests can appear to show false evidence for the superiority of intelligence in males and or majority culture individuals (Steele, 1994), might help administrators to forgo reliance on stereotypes and see nonmajority individuals in a more positive light. In a third example, individuals involved in the advising of students may be able to use this information to augment the type of assessments they use with their advisees.

Attending to the Environmental Factors of
Oppression and Discrimination

Lastly, understanding the effects of oppression on college students who do not have majority status on any number of cultural facets (e.g., sexual minorities, racial and ethnic minorities, women, individuals dealing with disability, and others) may assist any campus worker (Howard-Hamilton & Hinton, 2011; Howard-Hamilton, Cuyjet, & Cooper, 2011). For example, an individual who works in residence life may need to work to cultivate a culturally competent and hate-free living space for all individuals so that they are able to achieve the well-being so crucial to success in college.

This may be especially helpful as these campus workers make efforts to find, cultivate, and enhance strengths within a diverse array of students. As mentioned above, it may be that dealing with oppression and/or discrimination and prejudice may inherently help some individuals to develop strengths within the form of positive coping responses (Edwards & Lopez, 2006; Sue & Constantine, 2003). Staff at the campus Multicultural Center or Pride Center who have this knowledge may be able to assist minority group students in reauthoring experiences with discrimination as negative but strengthening experiences. This type of information could be presented to students one-on-one, but it may also have a large impact in being presented as a seminar or discussion to a larger group. Administrators in high-level positions on campuses may have a different view of students who deal with discrimination and oppression through this type of information as well, which may in turn affect priority level for measures toward creating an inclusive campus climate. Having a clear understanding of these as external influences, i.e., not assigning blame to students for "cultural deficiencies", may assist any campus worker in viewing all students as strength-filled despite cultural differences.

Conclusion

With the increase of global communication as well as the increase in diversity within the United States, and on the college campus, we find a new need for strong skills in cross-cultural and multicultural competence across a wide variety of disciplines (American Psychological Association, 2003). In addition, the importance of being able to recognize the identification, manifestation, and appreciation of strengths embedded within a cultural context is clear (Christopher, 2005; Pedrotti et al., 2009). In cultivating broad-minded and successful students, campus workers of all disciplines must make efforts to have a clear understanding of the influence of cultural context. Incorporating this multiculturally competent mindset with an aim toward looking at human functioning in a more balanced way that includes both strengths and weaknesses can help us to further positive views of all cultural groups and broader application of research in this area of the field.

References

Ahuvia, A. (2001). Well-being in cultures of choice: A cross-cultural perspective. *American Psychologist, 56,* 77–78.

Allport, G. (1954). *The nature of prejudice.* Reading, MA: Addison-Wesley.

American Psychological Association (2003). Guidelines on multicultural education, training, research, practice, and organizational change for psychologists. Washington, DC: Author.

Aronson, J., Lustina, M. J., Good, C., & Keough, K. (1999). When White men can't do math: Necessary and sufficient factors in stereotype threat. *Journal of Experimental Social Psychology, 35,* 29–46.

Barker, D. K. S. (1997). Kill the Indian, save the child: Cultural genocide and the boarding school. In D. Morrison (Ed.) *American Indian Studies: An Interdisciplinary Approach to Contemporary Issues.* (pp. 47–68). New York: Peter Lang Publishing, Inc.

Benedikovičová, J., & Ardelt, M. (2008). The three dimensional wisdom scale in cross-cultural context: A comparison between American and Slovak college students. *Studia Psychologica, 50,* 179–190.

Carter, J. H. (1994). Racism's impact on mental health. *Journal of the National Medical Association, 86,* 543–547.

Carver, C. S., & Gaines, J. G. (1987). Optimism, pessimism, and postpartum depression. *Cognitive Therapy and Research, 11,* 449–462.

Chang, E. C. (1996). Cultural differences in optimism, pessimism, and coping: Predictors of subsequent adjustment in Asian American and Caucasian American college students. *Journal of Counseling Psychology, 43,* 113–123.

Chang, E. C., & Banks, K. H. (2007). The color and texture of hope: Some preliminary findings and implications for hope theory and counseling among diverse racial/ethnic groups. *Cultural Diversity and Ethnic Minority Psychology, 13,* 94–103.

Chang, E. C., Maydeu-Oliveras, A., & D'Zurrilla, T. J. (1997). Optimism and pessimism as partially independent constructs: Relationship to positive and negative affectivity and psychological well-being. *Personality and Individual Difference, 23,* 433–440.

Chin, J. L. (1993). Toward a psychology of difference: Psychotherapy for a culturally diverse population. In J. L. Chin, V. De La Cancela, & Y. M. Jenkins (Eds.), *Diversity in psychotherapy. The politics of race, ethnicity, and gender* (pp. 69–91). Westport, CN: Praeger.

Christopher, J. C. (2005). Situating positive psychology. *Naming and Nurturing: The E-Newsletter of the Positive Psychology Section of the American Psychological Association's Counseling Psychology Division, 17,* 3–4.

Constantine, M. G., & Sue, D. W. (2006). Factors contributing to optimal human functioning of people of color in the United States. *The Counseling Psychologist, 34,* 228–244.

Diener, E., Oishi, S., & Lucas, R. (2003). Personality, culture and subjective well-being: Emotional and cognitive evaluations of life. *Annual Review of Psychology, 54,* 403–425.

Diener, E., & Suh, E. M. (2000). *Culture and subjective well-being.* Cambridge: The MIT Press.

Edwards, L. M., & Lopez, S. J. (2006). Perceived family support, acculturation, and life satisfaction in Mexican American youth: A mixed methods exploration. *Journal of Counseling Psychology, 53,* 279–287.

Hays, P. (2008). *Addressing cultural complexities in practice.* Washington, DC: American Psychological Association.

Howard-Hamilton, M. F., Cuyjet, M. J., & Cooper, D. L. (2011). Understanding multiculturalism and multicultural competence among college students. In M. J. Cuyjet, M. F. Howard-Hamilton, & D. L. Cooper (Eds.) *Multiculturalism on campus: Theories, models, and practices for understanding diversity an creating inclusion* (pp. 11–18). Sterling, VA: Stylus Publishing.

Howard-Hamilton, M. F., & Hinton, K. G. (2011). Oppression and its effect on college student identity development. In M. J. Cuyjet, M. F. Howard-Hamilton, & D. L. Cooper (Eds.) *Multiculturalism on campus: Theories, models, and practices for understanding diversity an creating inclusion* (pp. 19–36). Sterling, VA: Stylus Publishing.

Jackson, F. L. C. (1992). Race and ethnicity as biological constructs. *Race and Ethnicity, 2*, 120–125.

Kaplan, J. S., & Sue, S. (1997). Ethnic psychology in the United Sates. In D. F. Halpern, & A. E. Voiskounsky (Eds.), *States of mind: American and post-Soviet perspectives on contemporary issues in psychotherapy* (pp. 349–369). New York: Oxford University Press.

Leong, F. T. L., & Wong, P. T. P. (2003). Optimal human functioning from cross-cultural perspectives: Cultural competence as an organizing framework. In W. B. Walsh (Ed.), *Counseling psychology and optimal human functioning* (pp. 123–150). Mahwah, NJ: Lawrence Erlbaum.

Leu, J., Wang, J., & Koo, K. (2011). Are positive emotions just as "positive" across cultures? *Cognition and Emotion, 11*, 994–999. doi:10.1037/a0021332.

Lopez, S. J., Floyd, R. K., Ulven, J. C., & Snyder, C. R. (2000). Hope therapy: Helping clients build a house of hope. In C. R. Snyder (Ed.), *Handbook of hope: Theory, measures, and application* (pp. 123–150). San Diego, CA: Academic Press.

Lopez, S. J., Pedrotti, J. T., & Snyder, C. R. (2015). *Positive psychology: The scientific and practical explorations of human strengths.* Thousand Oaks, CA: Sage.

Lu, L., & Gilmour, R. (2004). Culture and conceptions of happiness: Individual oriented and social oriented SWB. *Journal of Happiness Studies, 5*, 269–291.

Matsumoto, D., & Yoo, S. H. (2006). Toward a new generation of cross-cultural research. *Perspectives on Psychological Science, 1*, 234–250.

McCullough, M. E., Worthington, E. L., Jr., & Rachal, K. C. (1997). Interpersonal forgiving in close relationships. *Journal of Personality and Social Psychology, 73*, 321–336.

Mio, J. S., Barker, L., Tumambing, J. (2012). *Multicultural psychology: Understanding our diverse communities.* New York: Oxford.

Myers, D. G. (1993). *The pursuit of happiness.* New York: Avon Books.

Ong, A. D., & Edwards, L. M. (2008). Positive affect and adjustment to perceived racism. *Journal of Social and Clinical Psychology, 27*, 105–126.

Pedrotti, J. T. (2011). Broadening perspectives: strategies to infuse multiculturalism into a positive psychology course. *Journal of Positive Psychology, 6*, 506–513.

Pedrotti, J. T. (2013). Positive psychology, social class, and counseling. In W. M. Liu (Ed.), *The Oxford handbook of social class and counseling* (pp. 131–143). New York: Oxford.

Pedrotti, J. T. (2014, January). Shifting the lens: Including cultural context in discussions of positive psychology. Keynote address presented at the meeting of the Asian Pacific Conference on Applied Positive Psychology. Hong Kong.

Pedrotti, J. T., & Edwards, L. M. (2009). The intersection of positive psychology and multiculturalism in counseling. In J. G. Ponterotto, M. Casas, L. Suzuki, & C. Alexander (Eds.), *Handbook of multicultural counseling.* Thousand Oaks, CA: Sage.

Pedrotti, J. T., & Edwards, L. M. (2014). *Perspectives on the intersection of multiculturalism and positive psychology.* New York: Springer Science + Business Media.

Pedrotti, J. T., Edwards, L. M., & Lopez, S. J. (2009). Positive psychology within a cultural context. In S. J. Lopez (Ed.), *The Oxford handbook of positive psychology* (pp. 49–57). New York: Oxford University Press.

Peterson, C., & Seligman, M. E. P. (2004). *Character strengths and virtues: A handbook and classification.* Washington, DC: American Psychological Association.

Ponterotto, J. G., Mendelowitz, D., & Collabolletta, E. (2008). Promoting multicultural personality development: A strengths-based positive psychology worldview for schools. *Professional School Counseling, 12*, 93–99.

Ponterotto, J. G., & Pedersen, P. (1993). *Preventing prejudice: A guide for counselors and educators.* Thousand Oaks, CA: Sage.

Sandage, S., Hill, P. C., & Vang, H. C. (2003). Toward a multicultural positive psychology: Indigenous forgiveness and Hmong culture. *The Counseling Psychologist, 31,* 564–592.

Seligman, M. E. P., & Csikszentmihalyi, M. (2000). Positive psychology: An introduction. *American Psychologist, 55,* 5–14.

Shaw, W. S., Patterson, T. L., Semple, S. J., Grant, I., Yu, E. S. H., Zhang, M. Y., et al. (1997). A cross-cultural validation of coping strategies and their associations with caregiving distress. *The Gerontologist, 37,* 490–504.

Snyder, C. R., Harris, C., Anderson, J. R., Holleran, S. A., Irving, L. M., Sigmon, S. T., . . . Wu, W. Y. (1991). The will and the ways: Development and validation of an individual-differences measure of hope. *Journal of Personality and Social Psychology, 60,* 570–585.

Sue, S. (1983). Ethnic minority issues in psychology: A reexamination. *American Psychologist, 38,* 583–592.

Sue, D. W., & Sue, D. (2003). *Counseling the culturally diverse: Theory and practice.* New York: Wiley.

Suh, E. M. (2002). Culture, identity consistency, and subjective well-being. *Journal of Personality and Social Psychology, 83,* 1378–1391.

Thompson, L. Y., & Snyder, C. R. (2003). Measuring forgiveness. In S. J. Lopez, & C. R. Snyder (Eds.), *Positive psychological assessment* (pp. 301–312). Washington, DC: American Psychological Association.

Triandis, H. C. (1996). The psychological measurement of cultural syndromes. *American Psychologist, 51,* 407–415.

Triandis, H. C. (2001). Cultural syndromes and subjective well-being. In E. Diener, & E. M. Suh (Eds.), *Culture and subjective well-being* (pp. 13–36). Cambridge, MA: The MIT Press.

Uchida, Y., & Kitayama, S. (2009). Happiness and unhappiness in east and west: Themes and variations. *Emotion, 9,* 441–456. doi:10.1037/a0015634

Uchida, Y., Norasakkunkit, V., & Kitayama, S. (2004). Cultural constructions of happiness: Theory and empirical evidence. *Journal of Happiness Studies, 5,* 223–239.

Utsey, S. O., Hook, J. N., Fischer, N., & Belvet, B. (2008). Cultural orientation, ego resilience, and optimism as predictors of subjective well-being in African Americans. *The Journal of Positive Psychology, 3,* 202–210.

5

Enhancing Intellectual Development and Academic Success in College

Insights and Strategies from Positive Psychology

MICHELLE C. LOUIS

From the perspective of positive psychology, postsecondary educators are entrusted with the vital task of promoting healthy campus communities where students are encouraged to realize their full potential. Among other things, this endeavor prompts educators to "nurture genius, to identify our most precious resource—talented young people—and find the conditions under which they will flourish" (Seligman, 2003, p. xv). In this sense, the purposes inherent to the disciplines of higher education and positive psychology converge on the aim of discovering how to best promote student success and growth during the college years and beyond.

A body of research indicates that the greatest single predictor of college student development and learning is the time and effort that students commit to activities that are educationally enriching (Astin, 1993; Pascarella & Terenzini, 2005; Pace, 1980). Institutional leaders can proactively adopt policies and practices that foster student engagement in these meaningful educational pursuits (Kuh, Kinzie, Schuh, Whitt, & Associates, 2005) as a way of stimulating student development. However, creating a campus climate that encourages students to thrive academically requires that educational leaders consider much more than the logistical aspects of implementing or maintaining various curricular initiatives. It also demands an examination of the psychological factors that influence how students engage with the curriculum, how they view the learning process, and how they perceive themselves as learners. These are important considerations because they shape how and whether students invest themselves in the educational opportunities they encounter on campus. As one author notes, "the beliefs that individuals hold about their abilities and about the outcome of their efforts powerfully influence they ways in which they will behave" (Pajares, 1996, p. 543).

This book describes how positive psychology offers insight into enriching students' collegiate experience, and this chapter contributes to that effort by highlighting several *psychological* factors that are associated with intellectual development and academic success. The chapter provides an overview of how positive psychology is relevant to students' growth as learners by discussing the theory and research that relate student learning and achievement to psychological constructs such as hope, academic self-efficacy, engaged learning, curiosity, implicit self-theory, and perceived academic control. It also provides practical ideas for university personnel seeking to nurture the intellectual development of students with diverse strengths and learning styles.

Key Concepts and Research Support

One definition for student success is that it encompasses satisfaction, persistence, and high levels of learning and personal development" (Kuh et al., 2005, p. xiv). According to this perspective, successful students are not merely distinguished by their academic achievements or their degree attainment; they enjoy the college experience and invest themselves in their education to the extent that it becomes personally transformative and produces significant learning gains. Schreiner (2010) uses the term *thriving* to denote this broader understanding of student success, stating that it is a multifaceted construct that cannot be fully captured through the exclusive use of some of the traditionally cited objective outcome measures such as grade point averages or graduation rates. This understanding of success offers a more holistic perspective, thereby expanding the dialog regarding what academic success and intellectual development might entail. This more comprehensive description of student success is offered as a backdrop to the following summary of linkages that exist in the literature between academic achievement or intellectual development and various psychological variables. Although some of the studies featured construe academic success primarily in terms of the more traditionally used objective measures, this chapter conceptualizes academic success broadly and describes several psychological factors that are related to it.

This review is not intended to present an exhaustive description of all of the contributors to student development and performance. It may be helpful to instead consider the psychological constructs discussed in this chapter as being akin to pieces of a puzzle in that they are merely aspects of a much broader and more complex picture of student success. Although these elements may be interconnected, each makes a distinct contribution. The first set of constructs reviewed here are those that are related to students' beliefs about themselves, including academic self-efficacy, implicit self-theories, and achievement goal orientation. In a basic sense, these constructs provide the psychological underpinnings of how students might answer questions such as: *Do I possess the ability to be academically successful in college?* (a question related to one's academic self-efficacy) and *If I currently lack the skills or abilities required for success, am I capable of developing them?* (a question related to implicit self-theory). The section on self-beliefs is followed by a description of constructs that represent an interaction between the self and the learning environment. The topics described in this second section encompass students' personal beliefs about their abilities to control or direct their educational outcomes in desired ways; the concepts addressed include hope and perceived academic control. Student questions related to these constructs include *Do I have viable strategies for pursuing valued goals and sufficient motivation to use those strategies?* (hope) and *Do I believe that my efforts influence my academic outcomes?* (perceived academic control). The final portion of this review describes constructs that relate to students' beliefs about learning and the nature of the academic experience, and these include engaged learning and curiosity. Relevant student questions associated with these constructs include *Am I energized by and psychologically present to what I am learning, and am I deliberately taking action to enhance my intellectual development?* (engaged learning), and *Am I interested in exploring new information and experiences and do I embrace the unknown?* (curiosity).

Implicit Self-Theory

Collegiate academic performance cannot be accurately predicted by objective measures of aptitude alone (Baron & Norman, 1992), because the beliefs and goals that students bring into the learning context are crucial factors in determining their success (Strage et al., 2002). Implicit self-theories—unstated ideas that people have about the nature of their own abilities and attributes—provide a lens through which students view themselves and their academic experiences, because information from the social environment is organized into a meaning system that determines subsequent thoughts, feelings, and behaviors (Dweck, 1999). Dweck (1999) describes two types of self-theories: the *entity theory* and the *incremental theory*. Entity theorists believe that personal attributes are immutable, trait-like qualities that are not responsive to change, and people who ascribe to this belief have what is called a *fixed mindset*. In contrast, incremental theorists view personal attributes as dynamic characteristics that can be changed and cultivated through experience and effort; individuals with this perspective have a *growth mindset*. For example, within the domain of intelligence, an entity theorist has the conviction that individuals have a certain set amount of innate intelligence and that although people can learn new things, their basic amount of intellectual ability remains unaltered. An incremental theorist, however, asserts that individuals can actually become more intelligent through their efforts because of the belief that intellectual ability is a malleable quality. Implicit self-theories can be broadly pervasive or domain-specific. For example, it is possible for an individual to adopt an incremental theory of personality while believing that intelligence is a fixed trait (Dweck, 1999).

These two types of implicit self-theories create a climate for different psychological realities and different behavioral outcomes. For example, students with a growth mindset believe that effort plays a critical role in developing their abilities, whereas students with a fixed mindset regard having to work hard as indicative of a lack of innate ability. Students who have a fixed mindset are therefore more likely to avoid tasks that require prolonged effort and have a greater propensity to abandon challenging situations when encountering obstacles (Blackwell, Trzesniewski, & Dweck, 2007). Individuals who believe that ability exists at a set level tend to develop a preoccupation with proving their competence. This concern is not particularly relevant for students with a growth mindset because having the opinion that ability can be cultivated allows such individuals to attach greater importance to developing their skills instead of primarily being focused on demonstrating them (Dweck & Leggett, 1988).

Implicit self-theories create a psychological template that helps determine the nature of the goals that students believe are most relevant in achievement situations. The work of Dweck and Elliott (1988) suggests that individuals with a fixed mindset believe that performance situations are occasions for measuring their trait-like capacities, and this assumption leads them to pursue *performance goals* primarily aimed at demonstrating competence. Students with a growth mindset instead view performance situations as opportunities to gain valuable feedback that could help them in their endeavors to expand their existing abilities. Such students therefore tend to adopt *learning goals*, focused on increasing competence (Dweck & Leggett, 1988). Although both goal types can be useful (Harackiewicz, Barron, Tauer, & Elliot, 2002), maladaptive thought and behavior patterns can arise when the two goal types are in conflict and an individual chooses to habitually overemphasize a performance goal orientation even when this goal type precludes engagement in a critical learning opportunity (Dweck, 1999). The need for individuals with a fixed mindset to appear intelligent or capable will often lead them to avoid pursuing challenging goals or participating in learning opportunities that would require the use of skills that they have not yet mastered (Hong, Chiu, Dweck, Lin, & Wan, 1999). As a result, they deprive themselves of many experiences that could prove to be valuable in promoting personal growth.

In addition, implicit self-theories establish cognitive patterns that cause people to have markedly different responses to failure. Building upon the literature on learned helplessness, Dweck and associates (Dweck, 1975; Diener & Dweck, 1978; Dweck & Reppucci, 1973) have identified two distinct reactions that individuals exhibit in response to a challenging situation or a failure: the *helpless response* and the *mastery-oriented response*. A helpless response pattern occurs when a student reacts to a setback by assuming that failure is inevitable and uncontrollable and that the exertion of additional effort would therefore be useless (Dweck,

1975; Dweck & Reppucci, 1973). The helpless response is associated with an entity theory and typically manifests in a withdrawal of effort, negative emotions, decreased expectations, denigration of personal ability, and deteriorating performance (Diener & Dweck, 1978, 1980). In contrast, the mastery-oriented response is characterized by continued effort in the face of a challenge and the use of proactive behaviors to overcome the problem. As might be expected, this type of response is associated with an incremental theory and results in increased effort, positive affect, heightened responsiveness to feedback, and higher levels of performance (Diener & Dweck, 1978, 1980). When students with a mastery orientation encounter difficulties in the academic realm, they do not attribute their struggles to a lack of ability but instead view their problems as challenges that demand ongoing effort and steadfast persistence (Dweck & Sorich, 1999). In a study examining college students' response to performance feedback, grades on an initial course assignment enhanced motivation in all students with learning goal orientations, regardless of their performance. However, for students with performance goal orientations, a more complex pattern emerged in that those who performed well reported a subsequent boost in motivation, whereas those who received negative feedback demonstrated declining motivation (Shim & Ryan, 2005).

As a whole, students who espouse a growth-oriented view of intelligence have greater motivation to learn and are more likely to use the kind of self-regulated learning strategies associated with academic success than are students who believe that their intelligence is fixed (Dweck & Master, 2008). Students with a growth mindset do not deny that differences in ability exist between individuals. They emphasize that regardless of one's current level of skill on a given task, competence can be improved through hard work. Adopting this growth-oriented perspective ultimately results in higher levels of self-esteem and academic performance than does the belief that one's abilities and skills are fixed (Blackwell et al., 2007; Robins & Pals, 2002).

Academic Self-Efficacy

In addition to beliefs about whether abilities can be developed, engagement and performance in academic settings can be influenced by students' beliefs regarding whether they have the capacity to be successful. These beliefs are encapsulated in a construct known as self-efficacy, which is the belief in one's capabilities to take the action required to attain a desired outcome (Bandura, 1977). Self-efficacy is positively associated with an individual's likelihood of engaging in challenging tasks, persisting at them with sustained effort, and performing them successfully, such that perceived self-efficacy is a better predictor of performance than are actual skill level or task difficulty (Bandura, 1997, 1982).

Not surprisingly, task- or domain-specific measures of self-efficacy are more accurate predictors of behavior and performance than are global measures of this construct (Pajares, 1996). For this reason, most research on self-efficacy has been focused within a particular domain, such as academics, or even within a specific type of academic work. Academic self-efficacy refers to the judgments about one's personal ability to succeed in academic pursuits, and several studies highlight its relevance to college outcomes. A longitudinal study of first-year university students found that academic self-efficacy was associated with adjustment, overall satisfaction, and commitment to remain in school (Astin, 1993; Chemers, Hu, & Garcia, 2001). Academic self-efficacy has been linked to cognitive engagement (Pintrich & Degroot, 1990), and self-efficacy beliefs have been found to determine how much effort students expend on an activity, how long they will persevere in the face of difficulties, and the amount of self-regulatory strategies they will use in completing academic tasks (Pajares, 1996). A meta-analytic study examining the predictive value of several psychosocial constructs on college persistence and academic performance found that students' confidence in their academic abilities was the best predictor of both outcomes (Robbins, Lauver, Le, Davis, Langley, & Carlstrom, 2004). In short, individuals have greater willingness to engage in an activity when they feel confident and competent, and these attitudes subsequently influence objective performance (Pajares, 1996).

Perceived Academic Control

This section describes the association between students' sense of control over their academic outcomes and the kinds of behaviors they tend to use in learning situations. Perceived control is "a person's subjective estimate of his or her capacity to manipulate, influence, or predict some aspect of the environment" (Perry, Hall, & Ruthig, p. 369), and it entails two major elements. The first component of perceived control is *self-efficacy*; as previously noted, this refers to people's convictions regarding whether they have the ability to do what is required to obtain desired outcomes. The second component of perceived control is *locus of control*, which refers to an individual's beliefs about whether outcomes are predominantly influenced by personal actions (internal) or by other people or forces (external) (Thompson, 2009). Perceived academic control is a form of perceived control that exists in an educational setting and encompasses "students' perceived influence over and responsibility for their academic performance that involves a perceived contingency between the student's actions (e.g., studying) and subsequent academic outcomes (i.e., success or failure)" (Perry et al., 2005, p. 376).

Although perceived academic control is considered to be a relatively stable psychological disposition, research indicates that it is amenable to change through targeted interventions (Hall, Perry, Chipperfield, Clifton, & Haynes, 2006; Perry et al., 2005). Perhaps most well-known among these are programs involving attributional retraining (AR), which focuses on helping students reconsider maladaptive attributions that they may have for undesirable academic outcomes (such as having "bad luck"). AR encourages students to adopt explanations for events that are more within the realm of their control to change in the future (such as insufficient effort or inappropriate use of strategies). Research has demonstrated that exposing students to even relatively brief interventions that help modify their attributions to become more adaptive can produce notable results in terms of increased effort and higher resulting grades (Haynes, Perry, Stupinsky, & Daniels, 2009).

A large body of literature indicates that perceived academic control is an important contributor to college student success because it is predictive of academic outcomes such as course grades and overall semester grade point averages (Hall, Perry, Ruthig, et al., 2006; Ruthig, Hladkyj, Perry, Clifton, & Pekrun, 2001), even after pre-existing academic performance is statistically controlled. Some researchers claim that perceived academic control contributes to college students' grade point averages in even greater measure than do their critical thinking skills (Stupinsky, Renaud, Daniels, Haynes, & Perry, 2008). These findings may be explained by research indicating that when students believe that they can influence their academic outcomes (i.e., when they have high levels of perceived academic control), they are more likely to invest greater effort in academic tasks and to remain enrolled in their courses. Perceptions of academic control foster a mastery orientation to challenges, whereas low academic control is associated with a helpless response to stressful or challenging situations (Perry, 2003). Studies reveal that students high in perceived academic control tend to work harder, report lower levels of anxiety and boredom, react to setbacks with greater resilience, and use more effective cognitive strategies than do their low-control classmates (Cassidy & Eachus, 2000; DasGupta, 1992; Perry et al., 2001, 2005; Stupinsky et al., 2008), all of which may create a climate for intellectual development and academic success. It is likely that students' perceptions of control within the academic domain and their actual academic achievement exist in a reciprocal relationship, because perceived academic control promotes subsequent academic achievement, and achievement is in turn predictive of enhanced perceptions of control over future academic outcomes.

Hope

Emerging literature has offered a succinct definition of hope that has been helpful in researchers' ongoing efforts to study and measure this construct and to differentiate it from common understandings of this term as simply a positive expectation for the future. Specifically, hope can be defined as "a positive motivational state that is based on an interactively derived sense of successful (a) agency (goal directed energy) and (b) pathways (planning to meet goals)" (Snyder, Irving, &

Anderson, 1991, p. 287). *Agency* is the willpower or motivational energy needed to pursue a goal; *pathways* are multiple strategies for accomplishing the goal (Snyder, Rand, & Sigmon, 2002). These two essential components of hope are "additive, reciprocal, and positively related, but not synonymous" (Edwards et al., 2007, p. 83), and they form the basis of instruments designed to assess individuals' levels of hopefulness, such as the *Adult Dispositional Hope Scale* (Snyder, Harris, et al., 1991). Hope and self-efficacy research both suggest that personal agency is the main determinant of goal attainment, but hope theory places greater emphasis on creating specific pathways for achieving goals (Snyder, 2002).

A wellspring of research has demonstrated the relationship between hope and numerous positive outcomes, such as academic achievement (Barlow, 2002; Curry et al., 1997; Snyder, Shorey, et al., 2002), mental health (Gallagher & Lopez, 2009; Snyder, Feldman, Taylor, Schroeder, & Adams, 2000), and psychological adjustment (Snyder, Cheavens, & Sympson, 1997). People with higher levels of hope outperform low-hope individuals on objectives measures of academic achievement such as semester grades, graduation rates, and standardized tests (Curry et al., 1997; Snyder, Harris, et al., 1991), even after controlling for pre-existing levels of intelligence and ability. A longitudinal study indicated that assessments of hope taken during students' first semester of college were predictive of subsequent cumulative grade point averages and graduation rates, because students with higher levels of hope performed more favorably than did low-hope individuals on both of these measures, even after the effects of prior grades and self-esteem were statistically removed (Snyder, Wiklund, & Cheavens, 1999). Additional studies have also demonstrated a positive correlation between hope and college students' semester and cumulative grade point averages (Barlow, 2002; Chang, 1998; Curry et al., 1997). Empirical measures of hope are positively related to indicators of perceived academic competence (Onwuegbuzie & Daley, 1999), as well as to increased problem-solving ability, greater academic satisfaction, and fewer incidents of disengagement in academic settings (Chang, 1998).

There are several possible reasons for the observed hope-related differences in academic achievement. One possibility is related to the observation that high- and low-hope individuals experience stressful situations in notably distinct ways. Specifically, low-hope individuals may tend to worry that they will perform poorly (Michael, 2000), whereas high-hope students tend to view examinations as challenges to be conquered (Snyder, Shorey, et al., 2002). These differences have practical consequences in that students with high levels of hope report less test-taking anxiety than do their low-hope counterparts, who are more likely to be distracted during tests by self-deprecatory and task-irrelevant thoughts that impede the realization of their goals (Onwuegbuzie, 1998; Snyder, 1999). Students low in hope often exhibit problem-avoidance patterns of self-criticism or social withdrawal when faced with academically challenging situations, whereas individuals high in hope tend to adopt these behaviors with significantly less frequency, opting instead for rational problem-solving approaches (Chang, 1998). People high in hope tend to be more attentive to positive messages and demonstrate a heightened ability to block out negative messages compared with low-hope individuals (Snyder, Lapointe, Crowson, & Early, 1998), a difference that may influence the environmental cues to which students attend. Other researchers note that high-hope individuals' ability to generate a greater number of possible responses to stressors may lead to more effective coping strategies than those evidenced in people low in hope (Snyder, Harris, et al., 1991; Snyder & Pulvers, 2001).

Another possible reason for the reported link between hope and academic achievement is found in research that examines the frequency and type of goal setting that occurs in high- versus low-hope individuals. Specifically, compared with people low in hope, high-hope people tend to set a greater number of goals (Langelle, 1989, as cited in Snyder, 2002) that are more specific as opposed to vague or general (Snyder, 1994). In addition, people high in hope often establish more difficult personal performance standards that result in more optimally challenging goals than those adopted by individuals who are low in hope (Luthans, Youssef, & Avolio, 2007; Snyder et al., 2000). People with high levels of hope tend to construct intermediate targets that help them track their progress in the pursuit of a larger goal, whereas students low in hope are not as focused on internal goals, opting instead to judge personal performance based upon academic comparisons (Snyder, Shorey, et al., 2002). These authors also note that students with high levels of hope are more likely to set personally meaningful goals than are their low-hope counterparts who rely primarily on external cues or expectations in goal determination. Each of these factors offer plausible explanations as to why hope is associated with academic success.

Curiosity

In recent years, curiosity is beginning to emerge as a focus of increased scientific inquiry after having been a relatively understudied construct within psychology (Silvia & Kashdan, 2009). This progress can be attributed to its differentiation from related constructs in the literature (such as intrinsic motivation and openness to experience), as well as to the development of reliable, valid instruments to measure curiosity (e.g., the Curiosity and Exploration Inventory-II, Kashdan et al., 2009). Although several operational definitions still exist within various theoretical traditions regarding what curiosity entails, there is a consensus that curiosity is a an approach-oriented motivational state that prompts exploration, learning, and a psychological focus on something of interest that commands one's attention (Kashdan & Silvia, 2009). There is empirical support for the idea that curiosity consists of two distinct elements. These include *stretching*, which is the drive to regularly pursue new experiences and abilities, and *embracing*, which denotes an eager acceptance of the uncertain or unpredictable features of daily life (Kashdan et al., 2009). Earlier writing also proposed two ways that curiosity can manifest: as *specific curiosity*, which is focused on seeking greater depth of knowledge or skill in a particular area of interest, or as *diversive curiosity*, which is the tendency to pursue a more general or broad range of ideas, experiences, and challenges (Berlyne, 1960).

Heightened curiosity is associated with deeper information processing and better recall of that information, a greater tendency to persevere in the pursuit of goals, and an inquisitive and open-minded approach to novel information or events (Sanstone & Smith, 2000; Silvia, 2006), and it is therefore believed to play a pivotal role in intellectual development and other desired outcomes (for reviews, Kashdan, 2009; Silvia, 2006). Curious individuals explore new information and deliberately strive to challenge themselves by engaging in unfamiliar tasks, a stance that stimulates personal growth by prompting ongoing exposure to new ideas and the development of additional skills (Ainley, Hidi, & Berndorff, 2002). When immersed in a stimulating learning environment, students with high levels of curiosity tend to be more academically successful than their less curious peers (Schiefele, Krapp, & Winteler, 1992). These findings may be attributed to the observed correlation between curiosity and with psychological characteristics that support learning, such as enjoyment of cognitive activities, positive self-appraisals and future expectancies, confidence in one's ability to overcome obstacles, and openness to novel ideas and experiences (Kashdan, Rose, & Fincham, 2004). A study of academically successful and thriving college seniors highlighted curiosity as one of this group's most pervasive distinguishing features (Louis & Hulme, 2012). Individuals with high levels of trait curiosity report more frequent participation in growth-oriented activities and also an elevated sense of well-being and meaning in life during the times when they feel especially curious (Kashdan & Steger, 2007).

Engaged Learning

Active engagement in the learning process positions students to optimize their college experience. When students are self-regulated learners who monitor their own comprehension of material, ask questions or initiate conversations with faculty about course topics, and exceed minimal academic expectations, they are exhibiting the kind of engagement that is associated with meaningful learning and persistence to graduation (Astin, 1993; Carini, Kuh, & Klein, 2006; Fredricks, Blumenfeld, & Paris, 2004; Svanum & Bigatti, 2009). Engagement has been positioned at the foundation of one author's learning taxonomy out of the conviction that "learning begins with student engagement" (Shulman, 2002, p. 37). Although a clear relationship exists between engagement and positive learning outcomes, several authors note that there is some ambiguity as to whether engagement precedes or follows achievement, because these may be mutually reinforcing constructs (Furrer & Skinner, 2003). Therefore, engagement has been described as "both an end and a means" (Edgerton & Shulman, 2003, p. 4) as it relates to effective learning and high levels of achievement. The study of engagement is further complicated because this term is often used synonymously with related terms such as *involvement* and *integration*, even though these concepts are unique (Wolf-Wendel, Ward, & Kinzie, 2009). For this reason, engagement can be "theoretically messy" because it "suffers from being everything to everybody" (Fredricks et al., 2004). There is not a consensus regarding whether engagement is primarily behavioral or psychological (or some combination of the two), or whether it refers to what an individual student does or instead to the interplay between institutional practices and student behaviors.

To clarify the meaning of engagement within this chapter, the term *engaged learning* will be used. Engaged learning is defined as "a positive energy invested in one's own learning, evidenced by meaningful processing, attention to what is happening in the moment, and involvement in learning activities" (Schreiner & Louis, 2006, p. 9). This definition encompasses behaviors that are educationally beneficial and a psychological investment or attentiveness to learning because both are critical determinants of how much a student will derive from a learning activity. One author notes that engagement is a "product of motivation *and* active learning. It is a product rather than a sum because it will not occur if either element is missing" (Barkley, 2010, p. 6).

Engaged learning is included in this review of psychological constructs because research indicates that the psychological components of engaged learning—including *meaningful processing* and *focused attention*—are significantly more predictive of reported gains in critical thinking skills, academic performance, and student satisfaction with learning and the college experience as a whole than are the behavioral aspects of engagement (such as active participation in class discussions or asking questions during a class session) (Schreiner & Louis, 2011). Students exemplify meaningful processing when they are engaged in the kind of mindful, deep learning that results from making personally relevant connections to new material or formulating connections between previous knowledge and unfamiliar information (Langer, 1997; Tagg, 2003). Although engaged learning is not represented in some of the most frequently used outcome measures of academic success, few would argue the importance of developing habits of the mind that will prepare students to become lifelong learners.

Application and Practice

Taken together, the following recommendations address many of the core psychological contributors to academic success among college students. The practices outlined here are intended to serve as a catalyst for further dialog among faculty, administrators, and support staff regarding how to promote optimal student learning on their particular campuses. These suggestions should be modified and supplemented according to student needs and situational factors to cultivate a learning environment in which all students can experience success.

Encourage the Development of Curiosity Through Valuing Exploration, Modeling Ongoing Inquiry, and Cultivating Critical Learning Environments

Some suggest that curiosity may be cultivated despite its trait-like features (Kashdan, Rose, & Fincham, 2004), a notion that raises the question of how educators can encourage its growth among their students. Catalyzing students' curiosity may have long-term benefits. This is because curiosity is hypothesized to form a positive feedback loop in which the exploration and pursuit of challenges inherent to curiosity catalyzes knowledge acquisition or skill enhancement, and using new information or skills promotes feelings of competence or pleasure, which reinforce the desire for further learning and exploration.

One study (Kashdan & Yuen, 2007) underscored the importance of faculty and administrators providing adequate challenge to students and sending students a clear message that their educational environment is one in which academic effort and rigor are held in high regard. These researchers found that when students perceive their school to be a place that values academic success and offers rigorous learning opportunities, curiosity is positively associated with performance on objective measures of academic achievement. However, students with high levels of curiosity had the worst academic outcomes in schools that they perceived to be less challenging, a finding that highlights how critical it is for curious students to learn in an environment that they perceive as being supportive of their value for growth and exploration.

Faculty can serve as powerful models of curiosity for their students when they present course topics in ways that invite dialog and questions as opposed to outlining prescriptive or definitive conclusions. When faculty regularly prompt students to ask questions, encourage them to develop and articulate their own perspectives and to value those of others, give students opportunities to explore topics of personal interest in course assignments, and model an inquisitive spirit in their own interaction with course topics, they create a climate for curiosity in their classrooms. Although faculty may define the questions that a particular course will seek to address, they also play a critical role in stimulating students to develop their own set of questions about the subject matter. A specific practice that encourages questioning as a normative activity could be asking students to bring a question to class related to a particular topic or assigned reading, or to take a few minutes at the end of a class session to ask students to write about what questions remain for them about the topic at hand, a technique sometimes referred to as the *minute paper* (Angelo & Cross, 1993). Another possibility might be to assign students to write a reflective essay sometime near the end of the semester describing the most important unanswered question they have about course topics and why they believe that particular question is such a compelling one.

Bain (2004) notes that students learn best when they are trying to solve a problem they believe is important or to answer a question that they find intriguing. His research on highly effective college teachers indicates that they generate curiosity among their students by creating what he calls a *natural critical learning environment* in which students "encounter the skills, habits, and information they are trying to learn embedded in questions and tasks that arouse curiosity and become intrinsically interesting" (p. 99). Instead of structuring class sessions around a series of facts to communicate to students, an intriguing or provocative question is the main focus within a natural critical learning environment. In these classrooms, a compelling question is presented, and then subsequent dialog and learning are centered on that question, which involves helping students to grasp the significance of the question, to use evidence to formulate and defend possible answers, and to generate new questions that result from their learning (Cialdini, 2005).

Shape Students' Self-Theories Through the Use of Process Praise, by Sending Explicit Messages About the Value of Effort, and by Encouraging Learning-Focused Goals

Self-theories are believed to be such influential belief systems that efforts to impact them may result in a "cascade of effects, altering [students'] meaning systems and their academic outcomes" (Dweck & Molden, 2005, p. 123). This bold assertion is based upon an extensive body of evidence suggesting that implicit self-theories exert a kind of "domino effect" on human thought and behavior such that modifications to self-theory have a profound effect on a multitude of other attitudinal and performance variables. Given these assertions, it is advisable for educators to more fully consider how students view their own abilities by integrating practices designed to promote a growth mindset into their broader strategies designed to promote student success.

Although longitudinal research with college students has demonstrated that self-theories are relatively stable belief systems (Robins & Pals, 2002), many studies have also revealed that targeted interventions designed to alter self-theory can be effective. Researchers have been able to manipulate implicit self-theories by simply exposing students to printed articles containing information supportive of entity or incremental theories (Levy, Stroessner, & Dweck, 1998). Other research has successfully used other brief means to influence mindset. One such study prompted African American college students to view intelligence as a malleable quality through the use of film clips and brief writing exercises, and the study found that these students reported greater engagement with and enjoyment of their academics and obtained higher grade point averages than did their counterparts in control groups who received no targeted messages related to the nature of intelligence (Aronson, Fried, & Good, 2002). Another study demonstrated that describing students' personal talents and strengths in terms of potentialities as opposed to as fixed entities that are either present or absent helped such students to approach the process of developing their strengths from a more growth-oriented perspective (Louis, 2011).

In addition, students' self-theories can be influenced by the kind of feedback offered by their instructors (Kamins & Dweck, 1999), a finding that has implications for how faculty or administrators might best offer feedback to students during the learning process. Specifically, Dweck (2002) suggests that when educators comment on students' successes, they should be mindful to emphasize the effort and strategies that supported this achievement (*effort praise* or *process praise*) as opposed to simply attributing students' achievements to their innate intelligence or talent (*person praise*). This recommendation is based upon the finding that affirming students' traits alone leads to a fixed mindset and a tendency to set goals related to performance as opposed to pursuing learning, as well as to an ultimate decline in motivation (Mueller & Dweck, 1998).

Dweck and Master (2008) also caution that educators should be careful not to praise students for completing work quickly or easily, because this behavior might convey the false message that being intelligent is related to performing tasks with minimal effort. Finally, these authors suggest that educators also consider how to help students consider establishing goals related to the kind of learning they hope to do, skills they would like to gain, and effort they would like to invest in college instead of exclusively those which are achievement-focused. An example of a practical strategy for doing so might occur when faculty present a course syllabus to students, and engage them in a thoughtful consideration of what they hope to learn throughout the class, as opposed to simply describing the course's associated academic requirements.

Other educational efforts to cultivate a growth mindset might also be readily integrated into classrooms, academic support services, or advising sessions, explicitly teaching students that their intellectual abilities can be developed and that success is a result of perseverance and effort as opposed to innate ability. For example, Sriram (2010) suggests preceding study skills training with curriculum that promotes a growth mindset by helping students understand the ways in which their effort can improve their outcomes, supporting these claims with evidence from neuroscientific studies on brain plasticity. Barkley (2010) describes the practice of inviting successful former students to visit a class and share their tips for success with the current students. Faculty can request that the visiting group describe specific behaviors they implemented or strategies they used in the course, reinforcing the idea that success is a result of effortful actions as opposed to innate ability. Alternatively, at the end of each semester, a professor might consider spending a few minutes asking students to record their strategies for success on notecards, and then synthesize the advice these students offered into a typed document to distribute to future students as a part of the course syllabus (Barkley, 2010). This practice creates a framework for beginning the semester with a discussion of how success results from hard work and effective strategy use.

Reinforce the Value of Career Planning and Academic Support Services and Normalize Their Use for Incoming Students

Implicit self-theory is also particularly relevant to consider when planning support services, programs, and curriculum for first-year students or those new to the campus community. Although programs designed for this population seek to help students develop effective coping strategies for navigating the college environment (Barefoot, 2000), research on self-theories suggests that these efforts may be ineffective without first addressing students' underlying self-theories. Specifically, research suggests that if students have a fixed mindset of intelligence or ability, they are likely to remain unwilling to access academic support services or to take remedial action because of a belief that doing so would expose their deficiencies (Hong, Chiu, Dweck, & Wan, 1999). Although the tendency of some well-meaning educators may be to approach such students with more information about the nature of available support services and how to access them, this effort may be fruitless if students' self-theories preclude their willingness to take advantage of the opportunities made available to them. This reality underscores the importance of not only heightening students' awareness of the support services that are available on campus in the form of academic tutoring, career planning, advising, mentoring, study skills workshops, and other related opportunities but also in seeking to help them cultivate a growth mindset about their learning. The research linking self-theories to coping styles provides a compelling argument for including curriculum within a first-year seminar that seeks to promote a growth mindset, as "educators interested in fostering adaptive coping with adversity among students should consider working directly with students' implicit theories" (Hong, Chiu, & Dweck, 1995, p. 211). Faculty and student development personnel can also be intentional in conveying the message that it is adaptive to seek help during times of challenge or uncertainty and that successful students are those who proactively use the support services available on campus. Testimonies from other students related to how the use of these services enhanced their learning experience and academic performance may be especially useful in normalizing and promoting help-seeking behaviors.

Use Evaluation and Assessment Practices That Reinforce Students' Active Role in Learning

Some students feel as though evaluation of their academic work is not in their purview because it is something that simply "happens to them." For many, this attitude might result in powerlessness, passivity, and decreased academic control. One way to combat these undesirable outcomes is for faculty to simultaneously give students assignments and the grading rubrics that will be used to evaluate them, thereby clarifying exactly what constitutes quality work. As appropriate, students may be able to participate in creating rubrics or criteria for evaluating their work, which can be a powerful learning activity. Rubrics vary in complexity, but Stevens and Levi (2005) suggest that the most helpful rubrics contain four basic components: a description of the task, components of the task, a scale to rate how students performed on each component—whether numerical or categorical—and written descriptions of what kind of performance characterizes each position along the scale.

Feedback is ideally a regular feature built into the teaching process, not merely a summative assessment of performance. From this perspective, evaluating student progress is an iterative process that represents an ongoing dialog between a professor and a student. Prompt, regular feedback that occurs before a final grade is assigned, highlighting what the student is doing well and offering practical suggestions for improvement is the type of information that is likely to help nurture students' perceptions of academic control. To teach students the skill of self-assessment and to reinforce the idea that they are active agents in their learning process, faculty and academic support staff can also provide multiple opportunities for students to gauge their own learning progress and performance. As a part of these assessments, students are prompted to reflect on what remains unclear or confusing to them and to brainstorm specific practical steps that they might be able to take to gain clarity.

Integrate Attributional Retraining or Developmentally Oriented Strengths-Based Approaches

Entering college is a transition in which students are adjusting to a new physical and social environment as well as increasingly rigorous academic standards. For some, this adjustment is accompanied by unexpected academic failure and feelings that their academic outcomes are determined by factors beyond their control—circumstances that can often make the first year of college feel like a "prototypic low-control situation" (Perry, 2003, p. 216). For this reason, it is especially important to consider ways to help students who are new to campus maintain a sense of control during their transition into the college community.

Research indicates that when exposed to high-quality instruction, students with a strong sense of perceived academic control demonstrate heightened levels of academic performance, but students with low control do not derive achievement benefits in these learning situations (Perry & Dickens, 1984; Perry & Magnusson, 1989). These findings suggest that improving instructional quality or simply offering additional programs are insufficient solutions to boost academic achievement in low-control students. Many of the current approaches in higher education may not address the core reasons why some intellectually capable students underperform in academic settings. Failing to attend to issues related to students' perceptions of control is particularly problematic in that "those students who are most in need of effective teaching are least likely to benefit from it" (Perry et al., 2001, p. 777).

Perry et al. (2001) have developed a series of theory-based interventions targeted at enhancing perceived academic control among college student populations (see Haynes, et al., 2009 for a review). Their program of *attributional retraining* (AR) involves teaching students to use controllable and modifiable explanations for their academic performance as opposed to viewing their academic outcomes as being due to permanent, external, uncontrollable factors. AR could be integrated into classroom, academic support, or advising settings with relative ease because research indicates that even very brief interventions can be effective in helping to reformulate students' attributional styles. For example, research has demonstrated that exposing students to printed materials or videotapes that emphasize the importance of effort and study strategies in shaping academic outcomes can exert a measurable effect on their perceived academic control (Haynes et al., 2009). Haynes et al. (2009) provide an AR protocol and emphasize that the efficacy of AR to modify attributions, enhance perceived control, and improve academic performance among college students is supported by three decades of research.

Another strategy for helping college students maintain a sense of perceived academic control during the transition into college is known as a *strengths approach to education* (Louis & Schreiner, 2012). Strengths-oriented education has been described as a process of designing learning activities to help students "identify, develop, and apply their strengths and talents in the process of learning, intellectual development, and academic achievement to levels of personal excellence" (Anderson, 2004, p. 5). One of its core principles is that students' positive attributes need to be deliberately nurtured and that the collegiate environment can provide myriad opportunities for strengths development (Lopez & Louis, 2009). This idea relates to a study of highly effective postsecondary institutions, which recognize that "student success starts with an institutional mission that espouses the importance of talent development and then enacts this vision" (Kuh et al., 2005, p. 266) by structuring learning experiences according to a consideration of what students do well (Kuh, Kinzie, Buckley, Bridges, & Hayek, 2006).

Many contemporary strengths-focused initiatives use one of several possible strengths inventories to give participants individualized feedback, although effective strengths interventions can be conducted without the use of a specific assessment tool (e.g., Seligman, Steen, Park, & Peterson, 2005). The most commonly used strengths measure for undergraduate populations is the *Clifton StrengthsFinder* (Gallup, 1999), a web-based instrument that can be paired with a resource called *StrengthsQuest* (Clifton, Anderson, & Schreiner, 2006) that offers additional information and learning activities for college students. In this model, a *strength* is revealed in "consistent, near-perfect performance in a given activity" (Buckingham & Clifton, 2001, p. 25) and is cultivated when knowledge and skill are added to existing talent.

Educational leaders on campuses across the country have used this inventory as a part of strengths-based programs within the spheres of academics, leadership development, and advising (Louis & Schreiner, 2012; Shushok & Hulme, 2006). Research reveals that compared with students who do not receive strengths training, those who are exposed to a strengths intervention demonstrate greater levels of engagement and better academic performance (Cantwell, 2005; Williamson, 2002), and that they also report higher levels of perceived academic control (Louis, 2008). College students who are able to capitalize on their strengths are also better able to mobilize social support and to build upon past successes (Bowers & Lopez, 2010). Those individuals who develop the habit of seeking to understand the strengths of others may be more well-positioned to engage in perspective-taking (Louis, 2013), which is the ability to imagine a situation from another person's point of view—a skill that is critical for managing interpersonal conflict and developing positive social relationships (Galinsky, Ku, & Wang, 2005).

However, some strengths approaches are more beneficial than others in terms of the outcomes they generate. For example, when teaching students about their strengths, it is important to use a developmental approach. Describing strengths as malleable qualities that can be increased through awareness and effort is critical. Research indicates that likening strengths to fixed traits that one either possesses or lacks can cause students to assume a fixed mindset (Louis, 2011), which is predictive of long-term underperformance relative to ability among undergraduates (Robins & Pals, 2002). A developmental approach to strengths programs might require a consideration of how strengths can be applied to new situations or emerging challenges, how various strengths work together within an individual to produce desired outcomes (Biswas-Diener, Kashdan, & Minhas, 2011), a discussion of "strength-environment fit," and whether particular strengths have the potential for associated liabilities if misused (Louis, 2011). Strengths development may also include encouragement to understand and appreciate the diverse strengths of others, as well as an analysis of how to modulate the use of a particular strength in accordance with situational demands by using it more or less frequently (Kaplan & Kaiser, 2010), with greater insight, or in accordance with personal values.

Consider Differences in How Students Learn and Demonstrate Knowledge

A related discussion emerges in the area of learning styles. The literature on this topic is vast and complex in that there are divergent opinions on how learning styles should be defined and understood and how they differ from similar terms such as cognitive styles, intellectual styles, thinking styles, and learning preferences (Evans, Cools, & Charlesworth, 2010; Zhang & Sternberg, 2006). A detailed description of this topic and some of the practical and theoretical debates within the styles literature is beyond the scope of this chapter (for a review, see Zhang & Sternberg, 2006). In summary, although there is support for the usefulness of style as a construct (Sternberg, 1996), some authors contend that there is no evidence to support the widespread idea that the most effective learning occurs when educators match their teaching practice with students' predominant learning modalities (Riener & Willingham, 2010). These authors emphasize that it is perhaps most beneficial to avoid grouping students into broad learning preference typologies (such as auditory vs. kinesthetic; linear vs. holistic, etc.), suggesting instead that educators appraise the knowledge, interests, and abilities of their students and design learning experiences accordingly.

However, the underlying message is that regardless of whether one resonates with the concept of learning styles as it is described in the literature, most would agree that students do tend to approach the learning process somewhat differently and with unique preferences related to how they acquire, use, and demonstrate knowledge. Learning is a complex endeavor, particularly because individual differences exist between students in terms of their interest for various scholarly pursuits, background knowledge, and capacity to learn specific areas of content.

To validate the differences that exist among students, it is advisable for educators to communicate that there are multiple ways of approaching the learning process and that all are useful if they produce the required outcome (Pritchard, 2009). Aside from explicit messages of this nature, the valuing of various approaches to learning can also take more implicit forms in the classroom. Signaling to students that various ways of thinking or learning about a topic can be useful occurs when faculty intentionally vary their teaching modalities throughout a given course. For example, this variation might assume the form of using many different types of teaching materials such as film clips, survey or assessment results, music, images, quotations, webpages, or podcasts. Moreover, as appropriate to the subject matter, faculty might simply plan to involve several different activity types within a particular class session, such as large group dialog, brief written reflections, engaging in a task or discussion with a partner or a small group, brief experiments, brainstorming possible solutions to a particular problem, building a model to illustrate a concept, or conducting a structured debate, among other possibilities.

Another way of demonstrating value for different learning preferences is to give students choices in how they will engage with course topics by providing a set of possible learning activities from which they select one or two to complete within the course of a semester, such as reflective journaling, visiting an exhibit, creating a blog or short film, independent research, writing an essay, interviewing professionals in the field, or others as relevant to the course (Barkley, 2010). A related approach might be to provide several options for how student learning can be demonstrated and assessed, allowing students enrolled in the course to select or propose the project or assessment type that is most compatible with their own learning styles, preferences, and strengths—even though the learning outcomes remain the same for all students. This strategy supports the acceptance of varied learning styles; it is also consonant with a strengths-focused approach and with helping students feel a sense of control within the academic realm.

Infuse a Positive Perspective into the Advising Process through Strengths-Based Advising, Appreciative Advising, or Academic Coaching

Advising relationships have the potential to function as a central activity in the educational experience because meaningful advising relationships often span the entirety of students' undergraduate years, thereby offering students an ongoing relationship with someone invested in their success and familiar with institutional policies and opportunities. To provide optimal benefit, advising relationships aid students in far more than course planning and selection by helping them to also consider the unique talents they have as resources that can be mobilized in the academic environment.

Advising conducted within this framework assesses the personal assets or positive qualities that the student possesses and considers how the student can use and build upon these qualities to realize personal aspirations.

Three similar methods for advising from a strengths perspective appear in the literature: *strengths-based advising* (Schreiner & Anderson, 2005), *appreciative advising* (Bloom, Hutson, & He, 2008), and *academic coaching* (Robinson & Gahagan, 2010). These approaches focus on potential-building instead of problem solving and begin with the use of open-ended questions or assessments to help students identify their strengths and interests. Advisors or coaches using these models then prompt students to generate specific goals and help them to create a detailed plan for achieving them. For example, academic coaches work with individuals to create academic and student engagement plans that specify how a student hopes to approach the learning process within the classroom and through other opportunities for involvement (Robinson & Gahagan, 2010). Optimal action planning includes integrating an individual's strengths and values in the process of articulating concrete and measurable goals that help students establish high personal standards for achievement. Finally, strengths-oriented advising practices teach students to anticipate challenges they might encounter in the college setting and to consider how they might mobilize their strengths or use alternate strategies in the face of obstacles (Louis & Schreiner, 2012; Schreiner & Anderson, 2005).

Offer Learning Communities That Are Organized Around a Wide Variety of Interests and Intellectual Topics

Learning communities use active and collaborative learning approaches and prompt participants to engage in complementary academic and social activities that extend their learning beyond a traditional classroom setting, providing an interactive environment that challenges students to construct knowledge collaboratively. Research indicates that participation in a learning community is associated with several desirable outcomes. These include increased academic effort, greater openness to diverse perspectives, positive interpersonal development (Zhao & Kuh, 2004), heightened persistence and academic performance (Lindblad, 2000), and intellectual and emotional growth (Stassen, 2003). Learning communities can provide an immersive experience in which students are challenged to engage with topics of personal interest, to explore curiosities in an interactive setting, and to integrate their academic and social learning. The nature of learning communities promotes contextual learning and enhances student engagement and overall satisfaction with the college experience (Zhao & Kuh, 2004). Such climates foster regular involvement with a supportive group of peers outside of the traditional classroom, which is an important contributor to increased retention and personal development during college (Pascarella & Terenzini, 2005).

Multicultural Considerations

Some prevalent themes in the literature indicate that at present, many institutions have not yet been able to create a learning environment that promotes a uniformly positive experience for all students. Race and ethnicity combined with other descriptors such as gender, age, sexual orientation, ability, and socioeconomic status contribute to a complex picture of oppression and privilege (Ladson-Billings, 2000; Solórzano, Ceja, & Yosso, 2000) that can influence academic success. Subtle and implicit forms of racist norms or beliefs, also called *microaggressions*, are often embedded into the structures and policies of postsecondary institutions, even though they may be difficult for some to detect (Solórzano et al., 2000). It is critical to challenge microaggressions and draw attention to any features of educational communities that devalue their members in order to promote campus climates that are responsive to racial and ethnic differences (Harper & Hurtado, 2007; Solórzano et al., 2000; Villalpando, 2004). One author notes that it is important to "encourage practitioners to reflect on practices—their own and the institution's—[that] are implicated in producing unequal educational outcomes" (Bensimon, 2007, p. 456).

Several of these detrimental practices are evident when students describe their experiences within the academic environment. For example, students of color report that they are often expected to educate others about their racial or ethnic group or to speak on behalf of their entire race or ethnicity (Bourke, 2010; Jones, 1999). They may also feel that others doubt their scholarly abilities (Davis et al., 2004; Fries-Britt & Turner, 2001). Steele (1999) suggests that negative stereotypes exert a powerful and subconscious influence on students' thoughts and behaviors, even when students themselves reject them on a conscious level. *Stereotype threat* occurs when students feel pressure to perform well in a domain for which a negative stereotype about their ability exists (based on gender, race, ethnicity, etc.) and the resulting anxiety distracts students and leads to impaired performance. Steele's (1999) work can help educators develop an awareness of the extra academic pressures that some students encounter based upon stereotypes that exist related to a group of which they are a member. Research indicates that a mindset intervention can be a useful strategy for addressing stereotype threat by helping students develop a greater awareness of the importance of their own effort and strategy use in shaping their academic outcomes (Aronson, Fried, & Good, 2002). Bain (2004) suggests that highly effective faculty address this concern by regularly and deliberately communicating positive expectations to all students about their abilities to succeed in academic pursuits and helping them understand the kinds of strategies that will enable desired outcomes. Across racial groups, engaging in enjoyable relationships with faculty members and maintaining regular student-faculty interaction are both strong predictors of student learning, an effect that is strongest for students of color (Lundberg & Schreiner, 2004).

As a field, positive psychology is only in the beginning phases of addressing some of the cultural factors that influence the development and maintenance of optimal human functioning (Lopez et al., 2005). One of the areas requiring further investigation is whether psychological constructs such as those described in this chapter are equivalent across cultures, because much of the existing research has been conducted with predominantly Western participant samples. Some researchers highlight the importance of cultural context and differentiate between individualistic and collectivist cultures when exploring psychological or behavioral processes (Chang, 2001). For example, an individualistic construct such as academic self-efficacy or hope might be influenced by cultural values such that members of one culture might be primarily interested in personal goals and beliefs related to individual capabilities, whereas another culture may be more concerned with group goals and communal definitions and determinants of success. From the perspective of positive psychology, it is important to magnify strengths wherever they exist, and future research in this field may broaden the lens to be more inclusive of the qualities and perspectives offered by cultures across the globe.

Case Example

You are the long-time instructor of an introductory statistics course offered on your liberal arts campus. Your class is a prerequisite for ongoing study in math and science-related fields, and yet it also attracts students who do not intend to pursue continued coursework in these areas because they are able to fulfill their mathematics course requirement through the completion of your class. In recent years, you have noticed that an increasing number of students enter your course in the latter group and that they commonly express a high level of anxiety about their ability to be successful in learning statistics.

In past semesters, you have sought to support your students' efforts to learn through offering extended office hours and detailed review sessions before exams, hoping to increase students' sense that help is available and to bolster their confidence in their ability to do well in your course. Although some students do participate in these academic support initiatives, you notice that most do not—even when their performance in your course would warrant additional assistance or tutoring. During your informal interactions with students who do not seek help when they are struggling, they often report to you that they have not done well in previous mathematics courses, and they describe feeling afraid of taking yet another course in a discipline that presents seemingly insurmountable challenges for them. Many students tell you that they just "don't have a math brain," and they often readily admit that their highest aspiration when enrolling in your course has been to do well enough to simply earn a passing grade.

Although you recognize that these students do often need help in mastering and learning to apply course concepts, you have begun to wonder whether the most significant barrier that they experience is actually psychological as opposed to primarily academic. Specifically, you hypothesize that perhaps students' performance in your statistics course is determined in large part by their idea that they are unable to learn or understand statistics, their fear for the course itself based on past experiences, their diminished confidence and perceived lack of control over their academic outcomes, and the reduced effort that often accompanies these beliefs. You realize that in offering additional support for learning course material, you have been presenting solutions that address some of the academic concerns that these students may have, but perhaps you have not adequately addressed the psychological dynamics that are exerting a powerful influence on students' behavior and performance in your course.

As you plan for the semester ahead, you decide that although the primary learning objectives will remain the same, you will change some aspects of how you structure your statistics course to allow you to be more proactive in addressing students' self-beliefs and the sense of control they perceive that they have over their course performance. You also hope to help your students establish positive course goals and develop tangible strategies for attaining those goals. Although teaching students to understand and apply statistics will remain the primary emphasis in your course, you will also seek to empower students to cultivate a growth mindset, to establish a sense of self-efficacy and academic control, to become more hopeful about their course performance, and to engage course topics with greater curiosity.

You begin by restructuring the course syllabus. To engage students' curiosity and establish a tone of inquiry in your course, you write a two-paragraph case study to add to the early portion of the syllabus. The case study presents a problem designed to pique students' interest, and it also requires the acquisition of statistical knowledge offered in your course to solve. Although in previous semesters you have included a description of the learning outcomes associated with the course, you decide this semester to rephrase each learning outcome as a question to be answered. You add a more thorough, gripping written description of the kind of problems that statistics can help people understand or solve so that your students can better understand the course's real-world application. You plan to model your own ongoing process of inquiry and curiosity by telling students the story of how you personally became interested in mathematics, noting the things you find most intriguing about statistics, and describing the kinds of statistical questions that you are currently interested in exploring.

You also become more strategic as you plan for the initial class session with the students. Although your traditional description of course expectations, assignments, and topics to be addressed will still be a part of what you discuss, you decide to add some elements that are designed to help your students approach the course from the perspective of a growth mindset. To that end, you devote some time during the first class session to debunking the myth of a "math brain," explaining to students that success in mathematics is related not to some inborn quality but instead to the acquisition of a set of skills that can be learned and practiced over time. You emphasize that *all* students have the capacity to learn statistics and to excel in the course if they learn and apply the correct strategies. You indicate that it is your role as their professor to teach your students those skills, and it is their role to practice and hone them throughout the semester and beyond. Seeking to speak to students who have low self-efficacy and who have made internal, permanent attributions for past failure in math courses, you begin discussing the reality that students who have struggled with math in the past can learn new strategies for success in your course that will lead to positive outcomes. You assert that the best mathematicians are most accurately described as individuals who work persistently at solving problems, even in the face of difficulties—and you offer some historical examples to illustrate your point.

To continue to cultivate a growth mindset climate in your classroom and to promote students' perceived academic control, you think of those students you have had in class during recent semesters who have done well in the course because of their hard work or their willingness to seek assistance. You invite several such students to visit your class during the first week as positive role models who spend some time talking to your current students about the strategies they used that helped them be successful in your course and the resources (academic support services, for example) they utilized in the process. You also speak about the specific strategies you have used to overcome the challenges you encountered during your own course of study. Throughout these conversations, you work to normalize struggle and highlight the benefits that are associated with seeking help.

During the first week of class, you also engage in a hope-building activity in which you ask students to write at least two specific goals they have for the course. You emphasize that although the students may have goals for their performance, at least one of these goals they write should be related to something specific that the student wants to learn—a new skill he or she would like to acquire or a particular kind of problem that the student hopes to learn how to solve. Then, you prompt students to break their overarching goals into smaller subgoals and to proactively imagine which specific course of action they might take if they encounter barriers along the way.

You also consider how you might adjust the methods you use to teach the course content so that you can more effectively prompt students' curiosity and engagement and tap into a wider range of learning preferences. In past semesters, you planned that each class session would address a particular discrete topic and you constructed an accompanying lecture containing the facts or concepts that were necessary to communicate to students during that class period. Now, instead of beginning each session by telling students what topic will be covered that day and following that announcement with a lecture, you instead decide to frame each class period around a real-life problem that involves the use of statistics. To do so, you use a variety of resources including news articles that contain statistics, case studies of actual problems that require the application of statistical concepts, and you also invite some professionals who use statistics in their occupations to visit your class and share briefly with students about the nature of their work. To engage various learning preferences, you vary the style of your course so that what was previously exclusively a lecture format now also includes activities in which students build physical models to illustrate statistical concepts, use computers to solve problems, teach each other in small groups, play educational games that use statistics, and engage in other diverse learning activities. This means that your course now consists of independent work time, class discussion, activities in small groups, and other types of learning. You also work to heighten students' curiosity by prompting them to develop their own questions about the subject matter. As a part of that effort, you end each class period by inviting students to write remaining questions or curiosities on note cards and you then spend some time during the subsequent class session addressing these issues.

You also modify the way that you conduct assessment and offer feedback. In the past, students' performance and progress has been assessed through a series of five written statistics exams throughout the semester and your feedback consisted of providing their exam score and perhaps a remark or two. This semester, as you give feedback on students' work, you are careful to offer more detailed information to them than simply their final score on an examination. To help students develop a growth mindset about their work and a sense that they control their academic outcomes, you integrate more "process praise" that focuses on the skills, strategies, and effort students are demonstrating as opposed to merely commenting on their overall performance or their innate abilities. Your feedback is more nuanced than it has previously been because you take the time to indicate to students what they are doing well and how they can draw on those strengths to ensure ongoing learning in the future. You also decide that you will now conduct more frequent, informal, and abbreviated assessment throughout the semester during class that merely offers students feedback about their comprehension of various concepts without impacting their course grade. You also adopt a more strengths-oriented approach to assessment that also promises to help students feel a greater sense of control in shaping their academic outcomes. Specifically, you provide an assignment that invites students to select one of several project types according to their personal interests. In addition, your concluding assignment for the course allows students to demonstrate their understanding of course concepts through selecting one of two possible options according to their strengths and preferences: a traditional written examination or a portfolio that documents their mastery of learning outcomes.

Although you currently teach the same statistical concepts to students as in previous semesters, you find that this semester's students seem to be more engaged in your course, are demonstrating greater effort, and have higher performance on objective measures of learning. Making several small adjustments to your teaching methodologies, the messages you convey through the type of feedback and autonomy you offer students in your classroom, and the explicit statements you make to students about their potential as learners all seem to have a positive collective impact. Attending to the psychological aspects of students' experience is associated with notably enhanced academic performance in your statistics course.

Conclusion

As described in this chapter, positive psychological constructs are vital contributors to intellectual development and academic achievement among college students. Therefore, it is important to consider how to address these factors and to develop strategies that capitalize upon relevant research findings when designing and implementing student success initiatives. The ideas presented here will hopefully provide impetus for educators to continue the dialog regarding how to help all students learn effectively and maximize the educational opportunities presented on campus in the process of realizing their full potential.

References

Ainley, M., Hidi, S., & Berndorff, D. (2002). Interest, learning, and the psychological processes that mediate their relationship. *Journal of Educational Psychology, 94*(3), 545–561.

Anderson, E. C. (2004). *What is strengths-based education? A tentative answer by someone who strives to be a strengths-based educator.* Unpublished manuscript.

Angelo, T. A., & Cross, K. P. (1993). *Classroom assessment techniques: A handbook for college teachers* (2nd ed.). San Francisco, CA: Jossey-Bass.

Aronson, J., Fried, C., & Good, C. (2002). Reducing the effects of stereotype threat on African American college students by shaping theories of intelligence. *Journal of Experimental Social Psychology, 38*(2), 113–125.

Astin, A. W. (1993). *What matters in college? Four critical years revisited.* San Francisco, CA: Jossey-Bass.

Bain, K. (2004). *What the best college teachers do.* Cambridge, MA: Harvard University Press.

Bandura, A. (1977). Self-efficacy: Toward a unifying theory of behavioral change. *Psychological Review, 84*(2), 191–215.

Bandura, A. (1982). Self-efficacy mechanism in human agency. *American Psychologist, 37*(2), 122–147.

Bandura. A. (1997). *Self-efficacy: The exercise of control.* New York, NY: Freeman.

Barefoot, B. O. (2000). The first-year experience: Are we making it any better? *About Campus, 4*(6), 12–18.

Barkley, E. F. (2010). *Student engagement techniques: A handbook for college faculty.* San Francisco, CA: Jossey-Bass.

Barlow, J. (2002). The measurement of optimism and hope in relation to college student retention and academic success. *Dissertation Abstracts International, 63*(08B), 3969–4051. (UMI No. AAT3061812)

Baron, J., & Norman, M. F. (1992). SATs, achievement tests, and high school class rank as predictors of college performance. *Educational and Psychological Measurement, 52*(4), 1047–1055.

Bensimon, E. M. (2007). The underestimated significance of practitioner knowledge in the scholarship on student success. *The Review of Higher Education, 30*(4), 441–469.

Berlyne, D. E. (1960). *Conflict, arousal, and curiosity.* New York, NY: McGraw-Hill.

Biswas-Diener, R., Kashdan, T., & Minhas, G. (2011). A dynamic approach to psychological strength development and intervention. *The Journal of Positive Psychology, 6*(2), 106–118.

Blackwell, L. S., Trzesniewski, K. H., & Dweck, C. S. (2007). Implicit theories of intelligence predict achievement across an adolescent transition: A longitudinal study and an intervention. *Child Development, 78*(1), 246–263.

Bloom, J., Hutson, B., & He, Y. (2008). *The appreciative advising revolution*. Champaign, IL: Stipes Publishing.

Bourke, B. (2010). Experiences of black students in multiple cultural spaces at a predominantly white institution. *Journal of Diversity in Higher Education, 3*(2), 126–135.

Bowers, K. M., & Lopez, S. J. (2010). Capitalizing on personal strengths in college. *Journal of College and Character, 11*(1), 1–11.

Buckingham, M., & Clifton, D. O. (2001). *Now, discover your strengths*. New York, NY: The Free Press.

Cantwell, L. (2005). A comparative analysis of strengths-based versus traditional teaching methods in a freshman public speaking course: Impacts on student learning and engagement. *Dissertation Abstracts International, 67*(02A), 478–700. (UMI No. AAT3207574)

Carini, R. M., Kuh, G. D., & Klein, S. P. (2006). Student engagement and student learning: Testing the linkage. *Research in Higher Education, 47*(1), 1–32.

Cassidy, S., & Eachus, P. (2000). Learning style, academic belief systems, self-report student proficiency, and academic achievement in higher education. *Educational Psychology: An International Journal of Experimental Educational Psychology, 20*(3), 307–322.

Chang, E. C. (1998). Hope, problem-solving ability, and coping in a college student population: Some implications for theory and practice. *Journal of Clinical Psychology, 54*(7), 953–962.

Chang, E. C. (2001). A look at the coping strategies and styles of Asian Americans: Similar and different? In C. R. Snyder (Ed.), *Coping and copers: Adaptive processes and people* (pp. 222–239). New York, NY: Oxford University Press.

Chemers, M. M., Hu, L., & Garcia, B. F. (2001). Academic self-efficacy and first-year college student performance and adjustment. *Journal of Educational Psychology, 93*(1), 55–64.

Cialdini, R. (2005). What's the best secret device for engaging student interest? The answer is in the title. *Journal of Social and Clinical Psychology, 24*(1), 22–29.

Clifton, D. O., Anderson, C. E., & Schreiner, L. A. (2006). *StrengthsQuest: Discover and develop your strengths in academics, career, and beyond* (2nd ed.). New York, NY: Gallup Press.

Curry, L. A., Snyder, C. R., Cook, D. L., Ruby, B. C., & Rehm, M. (1997). Role of hope in academic and sport achievement. *Journal of Personality and Social Psychology, 73*(6), 1257–1267.

Davis, M., Dias-Bowie, Y., Greenberg, K., Klukken, G., Pollio, H. K., Thomas, S. P., & Thompson, C. L. (2004). "A fly in the buttermilk": Descriptions of university life by successful Black undergraduate students at a predominantly White southeastern university. *Journal of Higher Education, 75*(4), 420–445.

DasGupta, B. (1992). Perceived control and examination stress. *Psychology: A Journal of Human Behavior, 29*(1), 31–34.

Diener, C. I., & Dweck, C. S. (1978). An analysis of learned helplessness: Continuous changes in performance, strategy, and achievement cognitions following failure. *Journal of Personality and Social Psychology, 36*(5), 451–462.

Diener, C. I., & Dweck, C. S. (1980). An analysis of learned helplessness (II): The processing of success. *Journal of Personality and Social Psychology, 39*(5), 940–952.

Dweck, C. S. (1975). The role of expectations and attributions in the alleviation of learned helplessness. *Journal of Personality and Social Psychology, 31*(4), 674–685.

Dweck, C. S. (1999). *Self-theories: Their role in motivation, personality, and development*. Philadelphia, PA: Psychology Press.

Dweck, C. S. (2002). Messages that motivate: How praise molds students' beliefs, motivation, and performance (in surprising ways). In J. Aronson (Ed.), *Improving academic achievement: Impact of psychological factors on education* (pp. 37–60). San Diego, CA: Academic Press.

Dweck, C. S., & Elliott, E. S. (1988). Goals: An approach to motivation and achievement. *Journal of Personality and Social Psychology, 54*(1), 5–12.

Dweck, C. S., & Leggett, E. L. (1988). A social-cognitive approach to motivation and personality. *Psychological Review, 95*(2), 256–273.

Dweck, C. S., & Master, A. (2008). Self-theories motivate self-regulated learning. In D. H. Schunk & B. J. Zimmerman (Eds.), *Motivation and self-regulated learning: Theory, research and applications* (pp. 31–51).

Dweck, C. S., & Molden, D. C. (2005). Self-theories: Their impact on competence motivation and acquisition. In A. J. Elliott & C. S. Dweck (Eds.), *Handbook of competence and motivation* (pp. 122–140). New York, NY: Guilford.

Dweck, C. S., & Reppucci, N. (1973). Learned helplessness and reinforcement responsibility in children. *Journal of Personality and Social Psychology, 25*(1), 109–116.

Dweck, C. S., & Sorich, L. A. (1999). Mastery-oriented thinking. In C. R. Snyder (Ed.), *Coping: The psychology of what works* (pp. 232–251). New York, NY: Oxford University Press.

Edgerton, R., & Shulman, L. S. (2003). *Foreward to the National Survey of Student Engagement Annual Report.* Bloomington, IN: Indiana University Center for Postsecondary Research.

Edwards, L. M., Rand, K. L., Lopez, S. J., & Snyder, C. R. (2007). Understanding hope: A review of measurement and construct validity research. In A. D. Ong & M. H. M. VanDulmen (Eds.), *Oxford handbook of methods in positive psychology* (pp. 83–95). New York, NY: Oxford University Press.

Evans, C., Cools, E., & Charlesworth, Z. M. (2010). Learning in higher education—how cognitive and learning styles matter. *Teaching in Higher Education, 15*(4), 467–478.

Fredricks, J. A., Blumenfeld, P. C., & Paris, A. H. (2004). School engagement: Potential of the concept, state of the evidence. *Review of Educational Research, 74*(1), 59–109.

Fries-Britt, S. L., & Turner, B. (2001). Facing stereotypes: A case study of black students on a white campus. *Journal of College Student Development, 42*(5), 420–29.

Furrer, C., & Skinner, E. (2003). Sense of relatedness as a factor in children's academic engagement and performance. *Journal of Educational Psychology, 95*(1), 148–162.

Galinsky, A. D., Ku, G., & Wang, C. S. (2005). Perspective-taking and self-other overlap: Fostering social bonds and facilitating social coordination. *Group Processes & Intergroup Relations, 8*(2), 109–124.

Gallagher, M. W., & Lopez, S. J. (2009). Positive expectancies and mental health: Identifying the unique contributions of hope and optimism. *The Journal of Positive Psychology, 4*(6), 548–556.

Gallup. (1999). *Clifton StrengthsFinder.* Washington, DC: Author.

Hall, N. C., Perry, R. P., Ruthig, J. C., Hladkyj, S., & Chipperfield, J. G. (2006). Primary and secondary control in achievement settings: A longitudinal field study of academic motivation, emotions, and performance. *Journal of Applied Social Psychology, 36*(6), 1430–1470.

Harackiewicz, J. M., Barron, K. E., Tauer, J. M., & Elliot, A. J. (2002). Predicting success in college: A longitudinal study of achievement goals and ability measures as predictors of interest and performance from freshman year through graduation. *Journal of Educational Psychology, 94*(3), 562–575.

Haynes, T. L., Perry, R. P., Stupinsky, R., & Daniels, L. M. (2009). A review of attribution retraining treatments: Fostering engagement and persistence in vulnerable college students. In J. C. Smart (Ed.), *Higher education: Handbook of theory and research* (Vol. 24, pp. 227–272). Norwell, MA: Springer.

Hong, Y., Chiu, C., & Dweck, C. S. (1995). Implicit theories of intelligence: Reconsidering the role of confidence in achievement motivation. In M. H. Kernis (Ed.), *Efficacy, agency, and self-esteem* (pp. 197–216). New York, NY: Plenum.

Hong, Y., Chiu, C., Dweck, C. S., Lin, D., & Wan, W. (1999). Implicit theories, attributions, and coping: A meaning system approach. *Journal of Personality and Social Psychology, 77*(3), 588–599.

Harper, S. R., & Hurtado, S. (2007). Nine themes in campus racial climates and implications for institutional transformation. *New Directions for Student Services, 120,* 7–24.

Jones, A. (1999). The limits of cross-cultural dialogue: Pedagogy, desire, and absolution in the classroom. *Educational Theory, 49*(3), 299–316.

Kamins, M., & Dweck, C. S. (1999). Person versus process praise and criticism: Implications for contingent self-worth and coping. *Developmental Psychology, 35*(3), 835–847.

Kaplan, R. E., & Kaiser, R. B. (2010). Toward a positive psychology for leaders. In P. A. Linley, S. Harrington, & N. Garcea (Eds.), *Oxford handbook of positive psychology and work* (pp. 107–117). New York, NY: Oxford University Press.

Kashdan, T. B. (2009). *Curious? Discover the missing ingredient to a fulfilling life.* New York, NY: William Morrow.

Kashdan, T. B., Gallagher, M. W., Silvia, P. J., Winterstein, B. P., Breen, W. E., Terhar, D., & Steger, M. F. (2009). The curiosity and exploration inventory-II: Development, factor structure, and psychometrics. *Journal of Research in Personality, 43*(6), 987–998.

Kashdan, T. B., & Yuen, M. (2007). Whether highly curious students thrive academically depends on perceptions about the school learning environment: A study of Hong Kong adolescents. *Motivation and Emotion, 31*(4), 260–270.

Kashdan, T. B., Rose, P., & Fincham, F. D. (2004). Curiosity and exploration: Facilitating positive subjective experiences and personal growth opportunities. *Journal of Personality Assessment, 82*(3), 291–305.

Kashdan, T. B., & Silvia, P. J. (2009). Curiosity and interest: The benefits of thriving on novelty and challenge. In S. J. Lopez & C. R. Snyder (Eds.), *Oxford handbook of positive psychology* (2nd ed., pp. 367–374). New York, NY: Oxford University Press.

Kashdan, T. B., & Steger, M. F. (2007). Curiosity and pathways to well-being and meaning in life: Traits, states, and everyday behaviors. *Motivation and Emotion, 31*(3), 159–173.

Kuh, G. D., Kinzie, J., Buckley, J. A., Bridges, B., & Hayek, J. C. (2006, July). *What matters to student success: A review of the literature.* Paper presented at the National Symposium on Postsecondary Student Success, Washington, DC.

Kuh, G. D., Kinzie, J., Schuh, J. H., Whitt, E. J., & Associates (2005). *Student success in college: Creating conditions that matter.* San Francisco, CA: Jossey-Bass.

Ladson-Billings, G. (2000). Racialized discourses and ethnic epistemologies. In N. K. Denzin & Y. S. Lincoln (Eds.), *Handbook of qualitative research* (2nd ed., pp. 257–277). Thousand Oaks, CA: Sage.

Langelle, C. (1989). *An assessment of hope in a community sample.* Unpublished master's thesis, Department of Psychology, University of Kansas, Lawrence, KS.

Langer, E. J. (1997). *The power of mindful learning.* Reading, MA: Addison Wesley.

Levy, S. R., Stroessner, S. J., & Dweck, C. S. (1998). Stereotype formation and endorsement: The role of implicit theories. *Journal of Personality and Social Psychology, 74*(6), 1421–1436.

Lindblad, J. (Spring 2000). Learning community assessment studies: What the Washing- ton Center resources show. *Washington Center News.*

Lopez, S. J., & Louis, M. C. (2009). The principles of strengths-based education. *Journal of College and Character, 10*(4), 1–8.

Lopez, S. J., Prosser, E. C., Edwards, L. M., Magyar-Moe, J. L., Neufeld, J. E., & Rasmussen, H. N. (2005). Putting positive psychology in a multicultural context. In C. R. Snyder & S. J. Lopez (Eds.), *Handbook of positive psychology* (pp.700–714). New York, NY: Oxford University Press.

Louis, M. C. (2008). A comparative analysis of the effectiveness of strengths-based curricula in promoting first-year college student success. *Dissertation Abstracts International,69*(06A). (UMI No. AAT 3321378)

Louis, M. C. (2011). Strengths interventions in higher education: The effect of identification versus development approaches on implicit self-theory. *The Journal of Positive Psychology, 6*(3), 204–215.

Louis, M. C., & Hulme, E. E. (2012). Thriving in the senior-year transition. In L. A. Schreiner, M. C. Louis, & D. D. Nelson (Eds.). *Thriving in transitions: A research-based approach to college student success* (pp. 167–189). Monograph for the National Resource Center for the First-Year Experience and Students in Transition. Columbia, SC: University of South Carolina Press.

Louis, M. C., & Schreiner, L. A. (2012). Helping students thrive: A strengths development model. In L. A. Schreiner, M. C. Louis, & D. D. Nelson (Eds.). *Thriving in transitions: A research-based approach to college student success* (pp. 19–40). Monograph for the National Resource Center for the First-Year Experience and Students in Transition. Columbia, SC: University of South Carolina Press.

Louis, M. C. (2013). Using a strengths approach to build perspective-taking capacity. In J. J. Froh & A. C. Parks (Eds.), *Activities for teaching positive psychology: A guide for instructors* (pp. 23–28). Washington DC: American Psychological Association.

Lundberg, C. A., & Schreiner, L. A. (2004). Quality and frequency of faculty-student interaction as predictors of learning: An analysis by student race/ethnicity. *Journal of College Student Development, 45*(5), 549–565.

Luthans, F., Youssef, C. M., & Avolio, B. J. (2007). *Psychological capital: Developing the human competitive edge.* New York, NY: Oxford University Press.

Michael, S. T. (2000). Hope conquers fear: Overcoming anxiety and panic attacks. In C. R. Snyder (Ed.), *Handbook of hope: Theory, measures, and applications* (pp. 355–378). San Diego, CA: Academic Press.

Mueller, C. M., & Dweck, C. S. (1998). Intelligence praise can undermine motivation and performance. *Journal of Personality and Social Psychology, 75*(1), 33–52.

Onwuegbuzie, A. J. (1998). Role of hope in predicting anxiety about statistics. *Psychological Reports, 82,* 1315–1320.

Onwuegbuzie, A. J., & Daley, C. (1999). Relation of hope to self-perception. *Perceptual and Motor Skills, 88*(2), 535–540.

Pace, C. R. (1980). Measuring the quality of student effort. *Current Issues in Higher Education, 2,* 10–16.

Pascarella, E. T., & Terenzini, P. T. (2005). *How college affects students: A third decade of research* (Vol. 2). San Francisco, CA: Jossey-Bass.

Pajares, F. (1996). Self-efficacy beliefs in academic settings. *Review of Educational Research, 66*(4), 543–578.

Perry, R. P. (2003). Perceived (academic) control and causal thinking in achievement settings. *Canadian Psychology, 44*(4), 312–331.

Perry, R. P., & Dickens, W. J. (1984). Perceived control in the college classroom: Response-outcome contingency training and instructor expressiveness effects on student achievement and causal attributions. *Journal of Educational Psychology, 76*(5), 966–981.

Perry, R. P., Hall, N. C., & Ruthig, J. C. (2005). Perceived (academic) control and scholastic attainment in higher education. In J. C. Smart (Ed.), *Higher education: Handbook of theory and research* (Vol. 20, pp. 363–436). Norwell, MA: Springer.

Perry, R. P., Hladkyj, S., Pekrun, R., & Pelletier, S. (2001). Academic control and action control in the achievement of college students: A longitudinal field study. *Journal of Educational Psychology, 93*(4), 776–789.

Perry, R. P., & Magnusson, J. (1989). Causal attributions and perceived performance: Consequences for college students' achievement and perceived control in different instructional conditions. *Journal of Educational Psychology, 81*(2), 164–172.

Pintrich, P. R., & De Groot, E. V. (1990). Motivational and self-regulated learning components of classroom academic performance. *Journal of Educational Psychology, 82*(1), 33–40.

Pritchard, A. (2009). *Ways of learning: Learning theories and learning styles in the classroom* (2nd ed.). New York, NY: Routledge.

Riener, C., & Willingham, D. (2010). The myth of learning styles. *Change, 42*(5), 32–35.

Robbins, S. B., Lauver, K., Le, H., Davis, D., Langley, R., & Carlstrom, A. (2004). Do psychosocial and study skill factors predict college outcomes? A meta-analysis. *Psychological Bulletin, 130*(2), 261–288.

Robins, R. W., & Pals, J. L. (2002). Implicit self-theories in the academic domain: Implications for goal orientation, attributions, affect, and self-esteem change. *Self and Identity, 1*(4), 313–336.

Robinson, C., & Gahagan, J. (2010). Coaching students to academic success and engagement on campus. *About Campus, 15*(4), 26–29.

Ruthig, J. C., Hladkyj, S., Perry, R. P., Clifton, R. A., & Pekrun, R. (2001, April). *Academic emotions and perceived control: Effects on achievement and voluntary course withdrawal.* Paper presented at the annual meeting of the American Educational Research Association, Seattle, WA.

Sanstone, C., & Smith, J. L. (2000). Interest and self-regulation: The relation between having to and wanting to. In C. Sanstone & J. M. Harackiewicz (Eds.), *Intrinsic and extrinsic motivation* (pp. 341–372). San Diego, CA: Academic.

Schiefele, U., Krapp, A., & Winteler, A. (1992). Interest as a predictor of academic achievement: A meta-analysis of research. In K. A. Renninger, S. Hidi, & A. Krapp (Eds.), *The role of interest in learning and development* (pp. 183–212). Hillsdale, NJ: Erlbaum.

Schreiner, L. A. (2010). The thriving quotient: A new vision for student success. *About Campus, 15*(2), 2–10.

Schreiner, L. A., & Anderson, E. C. (2005). Strengths-based advising: A new lens for higher education. *NACADA Journal, 25*(2), 20–29.

Schreiner, L. A., & Louis, M. C. (2006, November). *Measuring engaged learning in college students: Beyond the borders of NSSE.* Paper presented at the annual meeting of the Association for the Study of Higher Education, Anaheim, CA.

Schreiner, L. A., & Louis, M. C. (2011). The Engaged Learning Index: Implications for faculty development. *Journal on Excellence in College Teaching, 22*(1), 5–28.

Seligman, M. E. P. (2003). Foreword: The past and future of positive psychology. In C. L. M. Keyes & J. Haidt (Eds.), *Flourishing: Positive psychology and the life well-lived* (pp. xi-xx). Washington, DC: American Psychological Association.

Seligman, M. E. P., Steen, T. A., Park, N., & Peterson, C. (2005). Positive psychology progress: Empirical validation of interventions. *American Psychologist, 60*(5), 410–421.

Shim, S., & Ryan, A. (2005). Changes in self-efficacy, challenge avoidance, and intrinsic value in response to grades: The role of achievement goals. *The Journal of Experimental Education, 73*(4), 333–349.

Shulman, L. S. (2002). Making differences: A table of learning. *Change, 34*(6), 36–44.

Shushok, F., & Hulme, E. (2006). What's right with you: Helping students find and use their personal strengths. *About Campus, 11*(4), 2–8.

Silvia, P. J. (2006). *Exploring the psychology of interest.* New York, NY: Oxford University Press.

Silvia, P. J., & Kashdan, T. B. (2009). Interesting things and curious people: Exploration and engagement as transient states and enduring strengths. *Social and Personality Psychology Compass, 3*(5), 785–797.

Snyder, C. R. (1994). *The psychology of hope: You can get there from here.* New York, NY: Free Press.

Snyder, C. R. (1999). Hope, goal-blocking thoughts, and test-related anxieties. *Psychological Reports, 84*(1), 206–208.

Snyder, C. R. (2002). Hope theory: Rainbows in the mind. *Psychological Inquiry, 13*(4), 249–275.

Snyder, C. R., Cheavens, J., & Sympson, S. C. (1997). Hope: An individual motive for social commerce. *Group Dynamics: Theory, Research, and Practice, 1*(2), 107–118.

Snyder, C. R., Feldman, D. B., Taylor, J. D., Schroeder, L. L., & Adams, V., III. (2000). The roles of hopeful thinking in preventing problems and enhancing strengths. *Applied and Preventative Psychology, 9*(4), 249–269.

Snyder, C. R., Harris, C., Anderson, J. R., Holleran, S. A., Irving, L. M., Sigmon, S. T., Yoshinobu, L., Gibb, J., Langelle, C., & Harney, P. (1991). The will and the ways: Development and validation of an individual-differences measure of hope. *Journal of Personality and Social Psychology, 60*(4), 570–585.

Snyder, C. R., Irving, L., & Anderson, J. R. (1991). Hope and health: Measuring the will and the ways. In C. R. Snyder & D. R. Forsyth (Eds.), *Handbook of social and clinical psychology: The health perspective* (pp. 285–305). Elmsford, NY: Pergamon.

Snyder, C. R., Lapointe, A. B., Crowson, J., & Early, S. (1998). Preferences of high- and low-hope people for self-referential input. *Cognition and Emotion, 12*(6), 807–823.

Snyder, C. R., & Pulvers, K. (2001). Dr. Seuss, the coping machine, and "Oh, the places you will go." In C. R. Snyder (Ed.), *Coping and copers: Adaptive processes and people* (pp. 3–29). New York, NY: Oxford University Press.

Snyder, C. R., Rand, K. L., & Sigmon, D. R. (2002). Hope theory: A member of the positive psychology family. In C. R. Snyder & S. J. Lopez (Eds.), *Handbook of positive psychology* (pp. 257–276). New York, NY: Oxford University Press.

Snyder, C. R., Shorey, H. S., Cheavens, J., Pulvers, K. M., Adams, V. H., III, & Wiklund, C. (2002). Hope and academic success in college. *Journal of Educational Psychology, 94*(4), 820–826.

Snyder, C. R., Wiklund, C., & Cheavens, J. (1999, August). *Hope and success in college.* Paper presented at the annual meeting of the American Psychological Association, Boston, MA.

Solórzano, D. G., Ceja, M., & Yosso, T. (2000). Critical race theory, racial microaggressions, and campus racial climate: The experiences of African American college students. *The Journal of Negro Education, 69*(1–2), 60–73.

Sriram, R. (2010). *Rethinking intelligence: The role of mindset in promoting success for academically high-risk college students.* Unpublished doctoral dissertation, Azusa Pacific University, Azusa, CA.

Strage, A., Baba, Y., Millner, S., Scharberg, M., Walker, E., Williamson, R., & Yoder, M. (2002). What every student affairs professional should know: Student study activities and beliefs associated with academic success. *Journal of College Student Development, 43*(2), 246–266.

Stassen, M. L. A. (2003). Student outcomes: The impact of varying living-learning community models. *Research in Higher Education, 44*(5), 581–613.

Steele, C. M. (1999). A threat in the air: How stereotypes shape intellectual identity. In Y. E. Lowe (Ed.), *Promise and dilemma: Perspectives on racial diversity and higher education* (pp. 116–118). Princeton, NJ: Princeton University Press.

Sternberg, R. J. (1996). Styles of thinking. In B. P. Baltes & U. M. Staudinger (Eds.), *Interactive minds* (pp. 347–365). New York, NY: Cambridge University Press.

Stevens, D. D., & Levi, A. (2005). *Introduction to rubrics: An assessment tool to save grading time, convey effective feedback, and promote student learning.* Sterling, VA: Stylus.

Stupinsky, R. H., Renaud, R. D., Daniels, L. M., Haynes, T. L., & Perry, R. P. (2008). The interrelation of first-year college students' crucial thinking disposition, perceived academic control, and academic achievement. *Research in Higher Education, 49*(6), 513–530.

Svanum, S., & Bigatti, S. M. (2009). Academic course engagement during one semester forecasts college success: Engaged students are more likely to earn a degree, do it faster, do it better. *Journal of College Student Development, 50*(1), 120–132.

Tagg, J. (2003). *The learning paradigm college.* Bolton, MA: Anker Publishing.

Thompson, S. C. (2009). The role of personal control in adaptive functioning. In S. J. Lopez & C. R. Snyder (Eds.), *Oxford handbook of positive psychology* (2nd ed., pp. 271–278). New York, NY: Oxford University Press.

Villalpando, O. (2004). Practical considerations of critical race theory and Latino critical theory for Latino college students. In A. M. Ortiz (Ed.), *Addressing the unique needs of Latino students: New directions for student services, 105* (pp. 41–50). San Francisco, CA: Jossey-Bass.

Williamson, J. S. (2002). *Assessing student strengths: Academic performance and persistence of first-time college students at a private church-affiliated college.* Unpublished doctoral dissertation, University of Sarasota, New York, NY.

Wolf-Wendel, L., Ward, K., & Kinzie, J. (2009). A tangled web of terms: The overlap and unique contribution of involvement, engagement, and integration to understanding college student success. *Journal of College Student Development, 50*(4), 407–428.

Zhang, L., & Sternberg, R. J. (2006). *The nature of intellectual styles.* Mahwah, NJ: Lawrence Erlbaum Associates.

Zhao, C. M., & Kuh, G. D. (2004). Adding value: Learning communities and student engagement. *Research in Higher Education, 45*(2), 115–138.

6

Positive Psychology in the Classroom

JEANA L. MAGYAR-MOE

Positive psychology can be applied in a variety of ways in the college classroom for enhancing teaching and learning. This chapter addresses how instructors can capitalize upon foundational positive psychological theories and research findings in terms of recognizing, nurturing, and capitalizing upon their own strengths as well as the strengths of their students, how to communicate with and provide feedback to students in ways that make them feel respected and cared for and that serves to increase motivation to work hard, how to assign group projects and conduct course exams that allow students to build their intellectual and social resources, and strategies for instilling hope and enhancing student engagement.

Identifying and Nurturing Strengths

Perhaps the most well-documented and theoretically sound applications of positive psychology to the classroom surround the topic of strengths-based education. Although there are multiple operational definitions of strengths-based education, the commonality among them is that those who practice this approach take a philosophical stance combined with ongoing practices that emphasize strengths (of both themselves and their students) and the positive aspects of student effort and achievement. According to Lopez and Louis (2009), strengths-based educational models exemplify basic educational principles that were in place sporadically throughout history, but that have been largely replaced over time by more deficit-based approaches. Indeed, Froebel designed the first kindergarten to elicit the active power or strengths of children in 1830. In the early 1900s, Binet and Simon (1916) were dedicated to enhancing the skills of students and to managing (versus solely focusing upon) weaknesses, and Hurlock (1925) published important information regarding the powerful effects of praise of student work in relation to performance in comparison with the negative effects of criticism of students' efforts. Terman (Terman & Oden, 1947) spent his entire career studying gifted students for the purpose of identifying characteristics of success, and Chickering's (1969; Chickering & Reisser, 1993) theory of college student development emphasized the development of students' broad-based talents. Famous educational philosophers such as Dewey (1938) also emphasized the importance of enhancement of the best qualities of students within academic settings, more specifically, noting that "the purpose of education is to allow each individual to come into full possession of his or her personal power" (p. 10).

According to Lopez and Louis (2009), strengths-based education builds upon these historical foundations and is combined with more contemporary research related to the measurement of strengths, achievement, and determinants of positive student outcomes (Carey, 2004; Lopez, 2004; Rettew & Lopez, 2009; U.S. Department of Education, 2004), individualization of teaching methods to student needs and interests (Gallup, 2003; Levitz & Noel, 2000), networking with people who affirm strengths (Bowers, 2009), deliberate application of strengths inside and outside of the classroom (Rath, 2007; Seligman, Steen, Park, & Peterson, 2005), and intentional development of strengths through new applications and specific practices throughout a semester, academic year, or college career (Louis, 2008).

Strengths-based educators work from the perspective that *all* students have strengths and resources that can be put into action for the purposes of achieving success in many life roles (Anderson, 2000; Saleebey, 2001) and adhere to Strengths Theory (Clifton & Nelson, 1992), which asserts that nurturing and capitalizing upon talents and strengths while managing weaknesses results in better outcomes and more opportunities for flourishing than does a sole focus upon repairing personal weaknesses or deficiencies. (See Chapter 3 for more information regarding Strengths Theory.) Strengths-based educators participate in assessing, teaching, and designing experiential learning activities to help students identify their talents and develop such talents into strengths in the process of learning substantive knowledge, acquiring academic skills, developing thinking and problem-solving skills, and demonstrating such learning in educational settings to levels of excellence (Anderson, 2004). Similarly, strengths-based educators intentionally work to discover their own talents and to develop those talents into strengths that can be utilized to help them remain current in their fields, to design and implement their curricula, and to improve their teaching (Anderson, 2004; Lopez & Louis, 2009; Louis, 2010; 2011). Lopez and Louis (2009) summarize strengths-based education as a process that "begins with educators discovering what they do best and developing and applying their strengths as they help students identify and apply their strengths in the learning process so that they can reach previously unattained levels of personal excellence" (p. 2).

Teacher Strengths

The best professionals in any field are those who have found a way to utilize their strengths, and teachers are no exception. Although it is common for aspiring teachers to be given the advice to emulate their own best teachers from their own educational histories, the reality is that such advice can be erroneous. There is no check-list or cookie-cutter approach to good teaching. Indeed, the only rule that applies universally is that all great teachers are alike in that "they use their natural talents to the utmost, whether they are aware of it or not" (Liesveld & Miller, 2005, p.11). Similarly, Palmer (1998) notes that "whoever our students may be, whatever the subject we teach, ultimately we teach who we are" (p. 9), and Anderson (2004) advises that the best avenue to achieving teaching excellence is to avoid trying to be someone else; instead, strive to be oneself fully and completely. As teachers bring themselves to the classroom, they are role models for their students, hence, teaching from one's strengths is crucial to strengths-based education. Indeed, when a strengths-based approach is not intentionally utilized, a deficit-based model is more likely to prevail, resulting in definitions of self and others by personal weaknesses that represent what we are not, rather than being defined by talents and strengths that represent who we are (Anderson, Cave, & McDowell, 2001).

The first step in learning to teach with one's strengths is to identify one's talents. A talent is defined as a naturally recurring pattern of thought, feeling, or behavior that can be productively applied in a variety of settings (Clifton & Anderson, 2002). Anderson (2004) reports that talents cannot be acquired, however, "all people have talents that naturally exist within them—and because those talents represent the best of their natural selves, they are the crucial component of strengths and our best opportunities to perform at levels of excellence" (p. 1). Talents that are developed result in strengths. A strength is defined as "the ability to provide consistent, near-perfect performance in a given activity . . . strengths are produced when talents are refined with knowledge and skill" (Clifton & Anderson, 2002, p. 8).

Teachers can discover their talents through attending to their own behavioral and thinking patterns that lead to effectiveness and efficiency, empowering beliefs, and energizing motivations that push them to take and sustain goal-focused action (Anderson, 2004). Similarly, Liesveld (2013) reports that individuals can attend to the following five clues in the process of discovering their talent themes: (1) yearnings or internal forces that repeatedly attract one to certain activities or environments; (2) rapid learning in the context of new challenges or environments.; (3) flow or complete engrossment in an activity to the point that one loses track of time; (4) feelings of satisfaction from experiences where the emotional and psychological rewards are great; and (5) glimpses of excellence or flashes of past outstanding performances.

A more formal strategy for talent identification is via completion of the Clifton StrengthsFinder 2.0 ([CSF 2.0] Asplund, Lopez, Hodges, & Harter, 2007; Rath, 2007), an online measure of personal talents (available at www.strengthsfinder. com), originally developed by Donald Clifton of the Gallup Organization. The CSF 2.0 consists of 178 items, takes approximately 30–45 minutes to complete, and results in feedback regarding one's top five talent themes of 34 possible themes assessed on this measure (See Chapter 3 for definitions of all 34 Talent Themes).

White (2013) suggests that once educators are aware of their top talent themes, they deliberately think through all of the ways in which they can utilize (and have likely already been utilizing) each theme in overall course design, individual class preparations, development of instructional activities and assignments, involving students in the learning process, relating to students inside and outside the classroom, establishing expectations, and assessing learning. For example, a teacher high in the Achiever talent theme is one who works hard and gets a lot of things done. This theme will likely be evident within the classroom in terms of the teacher's expectations that students work hard for the course and via provision of checklists and progressive due dates to encourage a sense of achievement for students. Taking the time to explain the personal motivations behind these teaching approaches may serve to inspire the students to put forth more effort. Teachers high in Woo (winning others over) talent will strive to win their students over to their course content and subject matter, assignments, activities, and even to themselves. The means by which this is done will vary based upon the teacher's other talent themes, with some winning their students over via being actors or entertainers, whereas others will be more quiet influencers. Students are likely to learn how to sell an idea or be more persuasive when taught by educators high in Woo talent. All 34 Talent Themes can be developed into strengths that can be implemented regularly in the classroom. For more examples of how each of the themes can be applied to good teaching, see Table 6.1.

The VIA Survey is another popular measure of strengths based upon the Values in Action Character Strengths Classification System developed by Peterson and Seligman (2004). Perusal of the *VIA Classification Handbook* reveals that in addition to defining the 24 strengths that make up the classification, the handbook also provides readers with a host of other information such as ways to assess and apply each strength, interventions that foster the strengths, paragons or examples of the strengths (many of whom are teachers), the theoretical and research underpinnings of the strengths, the known correlates and consequences of the strengths, how the strengths develop and manifest across the life span, gender differences, and cross-cultural aspects of the strengths (Peterson & Seligman, 2004). The VIA Survey can be completed online (at www.viastrengths.org) in approximately 30–40 minutes. The measure consists of 240 items that tap the 24 character strengths of this model. Upon completion of this measure, respondents are

Table 6.1 **Possibilities for Good Teaching That Emerge from Each of the 34 StrengthsFinder Themes (White, 2013)**

1. **Achiever**—Because you work hard and get a lot of things done, you expect this of your students. You set high standards and high expectations and encourage them to work hard for your class. You may provide checklists and progressive due dates to encourage a sense of accomplishment. As you explain your personal motivations, you can inspire students to put forth more effort.

2. **Activator**—Active learning has always made sense to you. You move your students from theory to practice as you expect them to act on what they are learning. You turn concepts into, "What are we going to DO about it?" You expect active participation in your classes. You show that action is an important part of learning.

3. **Adaptability**—Your "adjustable" teaching style allows you to go with the flow and capture that teachable moment, even if it wasn't in the plan for the day. You also adapt to diverse learners and enjoy the newness of each classroom experience. You have a well-planned syllabus, but you don't mind making adjustments to the plan as you respond to the learning needs and interests of your students. You model for your students a relaxed and flexible approach to the surprises and complexities that each day may bring.

4. **Analytical**—You teach students how to think. You model this way of thinking in the way you have designed the course and the way you present the material. You ask questions, lead discussions, and design assignments to spur their analytical thinking. You help students grasp this process when you take time to explain your way of thinking and when you give specific feedback in your grading.

5. **Arranger**—You enjoy planning the course syllabus and arranging the content and sequence for the semester. You give attention to the physical environment of the classroom and the seating arrangement for the students. You optimize learning by arranging teams or partners who will benefit from working together. You will arrange and rearrange to get the best outcome.

6. **Belief**—You teach out of your passion for the subject, for the students, and for the teaching/learning process. You really believe in what you are doing or you wouldn't be doing it. This passion translates into enthusiasm in the classroom. Whatever matters to you comes through in your teaching, and the students know where you stand, and that clarity engenders respect. You also encourage students to discover and express their own passions.

(continued)

Table 6.1 **Continued**

7. **Command**—You bring a strong presence to the classroom. The students know that you are in charge, and they learn to trust your judgment. Classroom management issues are rare, but when they occur, you handle them quickly and with authority. When questions arise or when situations need resolution, you have an ability to speak decisively and move everyone forward. From your example, students may be encouraged to take charge of their learning, their opinions, their time management, etc.

8. **Communication**—You find it easy to convey the course content choosing whatever medium is best to get the point across. The classroom energizes you, because you have a ready audience. You bring learning alive with great examples, stories, photos, quotes, etc., using the appropriate means to engage your audience and get your point across. This style helps you connect with your students, because you take time to get to know them so that you know how best to reach them. Through assignments and classroom interaction, you also encourage your students to communicate well.

9. **Competition**—You want to "win" at teaching. You want your course evaluations to be the best. You want students in your classes to work hard and do well. You bring that competitive spirit into your encouragement for them to do their best.

10. **Connectedness**—You help students see the larger picture. You connect the topics and units of the current course into a cohesive whole. You help students connect what they are learning in your class to what they have learned or will be learning in other classes within the discipline and across disciplines as well. You make connections to current events, to spiritual matters, to their future careers.

11. **Consistency**—Your students know what is expected of them. The syllabus is very clear. They know that you will be fair in your grading and in your dealings with each of them. You model for them the importance of saying what you mean and meaning what you say. You expect for them to be consistent in their attendance, in their study, and in their completion of the course.

12. **Context**—You develop a good rapport with your students because you remember what it was like to be a student, and you prepare to teach with that reality in mind. You model the importance of the past, of how we got to where we are, of why the subject matter has evolved as it has. You are likely to share your own personal context and why you teach. You do not teach in the vacuum of the present, but you give meaning to the present by exploring and learning from the past.

(continued)

Table 6.1 **Continued**

13. **Deliberative**—You give a lot of thought to what you are going to teach and how you are going to teach it, to the textbook you will use and the assignments you will require. You give a lot of thought as to how to relate to your students. You model this deliberative style by telling your students that you value their questions, but you need time to think before you give them an answer. Your students learn from you that it is ok to take time to think things through before responding.

14. **Developer**—You are a patient encourager and your students benefit from that approach. Your recognition of their potential can cause them to grow in areas that they might never have considered. Your enthusiasm for their progress ignites their motivation for further learning. From your supportive approach with them, students learn to be more patient and encouraging of their own learning.

15. **Discipline**—You bring order, structure, and routine to the classroom. You model self-discipline when you share how you operate or suggest how they might approach a certain assignment. You teach a disciplined approach to learning when your assignments don't just focus on the content outcome, but also focus on the process and the attention to detail.

16. **Empathy**—Your personal care and concern for your students is evident. You sense when the class is "getting it" and when they are not. You model for your students that learning isn't just about the cognitive, but it also involves the affective. Both domains of development are important in your classroom as you strive to teach the whole person.

17. **Focus**—You plan your course with clear intentions, and you bring that perspective to every class. Goals and objectives matter. When you lead discussions, you are able to bring attention back to the most important concept. When you grade assignments, you are able to attend to the key element. You help your students to remain focused on their priorities, whether that is completing the next assignment or staying focused on finishing their degree.

18. **Futuristic**—You help students envision the future. How does the content of this class fit into their future? How will their behavior in this class affect their future? By asking questions about the future, you teach students to think beyond the present and give consideration to where they are going and how are they going to get there.

19. **Harmony**—Learning is a collaborative venture. That is why the classroom is so important to you. Your role as a peacemaker promotes careful listening, better understanding of another's views, and a more magnanimous approach to living in our diverse world. The way you handle conflict in the classroom, or the way you process divergent opinions speaks volumes to your students about respect, kindness, and peace.

(continued)

Table 6.1 **Continued**

20. **Ideation**—You bring new ideas to your curriculum and to your teaching. You are willing to try something new or engage in a discussion of a new possibility. You ask questions and invite brainstorming. In loving ideas, you model an openness to thinking broadly, considering multiple perspectives, and allowing new thoughts to be respected and given consideration.

21. **Includer**—Through your approach to the students in your class, you model the idea that everyone matters, that everyone belongs, that everyone has contributions to make to the larger group. This mindset enriches the learning environment and teaches others to be more socially sensitive.

22. **Individualization**—You get to know students by name. Each person matters. You don't just teach a class, you teach each student in that class. You provide choices and options for completing certain aspects of the course, allowing for individual preference. Through that personal motivation, you encourage individual learners to put forth their best effort.

23. **Input**—Your teaching is enriched by the resources that you share. You bring a wealth of knowledge to your subject matter that has been gleaned from your years of experience and your curiosity about the topic. Your input may come from the gathering of books, anecdotes, photos, cartoons, quotes, etc. Your attention to resources may inspire your students to be more aware of the related artifacts in their surroundings.

24. **Intellection**—You bring a reflective mindset to the classroom, and you encourage that in your students. Your classroom questions show that you expect students to have been thinking about the subject matter before they come to class. Your discussion questions will promote good thinking about the topic and encourage the students to think as they read, think about the meaning connected to an assignment, think about what they learned from taking that exam or writing that paper.

25. **Learner**—Your curiosity is contagious. You bring a fresh learning mindset to every class that you teach. You join your students as learners each semester as you explore the topic together. You teach sound principles of learning as you prepare assignments and guide students in their approach to learning. You care about teaching the process of learning as well as the content of your curriculum.

(continued)

Table 6.1 **Continued**

26. **Maximizer**—Excellence matters to you. You set high expectations for your students and expect them to maximize their time and effort for your class. Shoddy work is unacceptable; incomplete work is unacceptable. Your standards raise the bar and give students an opportunity to expect excellence of themselves. In grading you comment on the most excellent components. You also talk to students about making the most of this educational opportunity. These are important years of their lives that should not be wasted.

27. **Positivity**—You bring a smile to your classroom. Learning together is fun and exciting. Your positive energy is contagious. Students enjoy coming to class because the experience is so uplifting. You can find the good in most circumstances, and you encourage students to look for what's good and be more hopeful about what they are able to do.

28. **Relator**—Relationships matter to you. The teacher–student relationship is a very important one and you encourage students to establish that connection. You take time to build relationships with the class and encourage the students to take advantage of your office hours to get better acquainted.

29. **Responsibility**—You take your role as a teacher very seriously. You prepare well, begin class on time, grade promptly, etc. You let your students know that you accept your responsibilities to teach and that you expect them to accept their responsibilities to learn. These high expectations can encourage and motivate students to grow in this important area.

30. **Restorative**—You enjoy fixing things, restoring order, or bringing wholeness. In your teaching you may bring a restorative process to problem solving—showing students how to approach a problem, decide on a solution, and follow through to completion. This theme may have a more personal bent as you seek out individuals who need restoration of some sort. You might be that teacher who works to correct past hurts, or resolve test or learning anxieties. Whatever the application, you do not leave well enough alone, but you model the approach of improving on the current situation or finding a solution to solve the problem.

31. **Self–Assurance**—You approach your teaching and your knowledge of the subject matter with a sense of confidence. Students trust your judgment and find it easy to believe what you are saying. You help encourage your students to develop their own sense of self. You teach this self-confidence by probing their thoughts during discussions or by challenging the ideas in their writing.

(continued)

Table 6.1 **Continued**

32. **Significance**—Through your teaching you want to make a difference in the lives of your students. You approach your teaching with a certain sense of gravity, because you know that these educational years involve moments of significance for each person. By your actions and your words, you model your regard for the significance of each person and even each class period that is shared.

33. **Strategic**—You bring careful thought and planning to the content of the course, to the sequence of the material, and to the specific teaching strategies and assignments, but you are always open to Plan B. You love contingency options and alternative ways of proceeding. When you explain your reasoning process and your resulting decisions, students are able to see strategic thinking in action.

34. **Woo**—You love to win students over to your subject matter, to yourself as their teacher, to the current assignment, etc. You may be the actor, entertainer, or perhaps the quiet influencer, but your style will have an impact on the learners. You will have opportunity through classroom activities or assignments to teach "woo," by helping students learn how to sell an idea or be more persuasive with an argument.

provided with information about their top five strengths, as well as a rank-order listing of all 24. (See Chapter 3 for definitions of all 24 VIA strengths.)

Research to date supports connections between identifying and nurturing VIA Character Strengths and workplace enjoyment and success. More specifically, Harzer and Ruch (2012, 2013) found that employees who reported regularly using at least four of their top five VIA strengths at work also reported more positive work experiences and viewing their work as a calling in comparison to their colleagues who reported regular use of less than four of their highest strengths. Similarly, when strengths were aligned with work activities, employees reported higher levels of job satisfaction and pleasure, engagement, and meaning in the workplace. Finally, Crabb (2011) reports that focusing on character strengths in the workplace is one of the three most critical components that drive employee engagement, and, as such, it is important for employees to purposefully work to identify and utilize their strengths at work while also informing others in the workplace of their signature strengths.

Research specific to teaching excellence and the VIA Strengths combines use of the VIA Survey and The Teacher Behaviors Checklist (Keeley, Smith, & Buskist, 2006), a measure of target teaching behaviors amenable to modification that was derived from qualitative descriptors associated with teaching exemplars. McGovern and Miller (2008) offer an approach to faculty development that assists faculty in becoming more reflective and deliberate about their teaching and learning strategies through connecting the 24 VIA character strengths to the

28 behavioral qualities most often reported as being enacted by master teachers as reported in Table 6.2.

Regardless of how talents and strengths are identified, a key factor in strengths-based teaching is making explicit the connections between the personal talents of teachers and their teaching philosophies and methods so as to inspire students to engage in talent development and strengths applications in their lives as well.

Student Strengths

The information in the previous section on teacher strengths is also highly relevant to the process of identifying and nurturing student strengths. Indeed, the informal strategies regarding talent identification for teachers are also applicable to talent identification for students. In fact, such strategies can be harnessed by strengths educators in the development of class activities and course assignments. For example, assigning Positive Introductions (Rashid, 2008; Magyar-Moe, 2009) on day one can serve as a great ice-breaker activity and opportunity to teach about Strengths Theory that can help students to identify potential talent themes via attending to past glimpses of excellence or flashes of outstanding performance. More specifically, students are asked to write a one-page positive introduction of themselves in which they tell a story about a time when they were at their best and to read that story to a small group of classmates who are instructed to listen for and provide feedback upon the strengths they identify in the introduction story. In order for students to be able to recognize the strengths revealed in the positive introductions of their peers, it is useful to provide handouts containing the definitions of the 34 strengths from the CSF 2.0 and the 24 strengths from the VIA Survey. Once familiar with these strength definitions, students (and educators) are often amazed at how many talent and strengths themes can be inferred from just one positive introduction story. Astute teachers are also able to pick up on and point out talent themes and strengths by intentionally listening for such clues even within very brief conversations they may have with students before, during, and after class. Helping students to realize when they have used their talents to experience a sense of engagement or to achieve some level of success in life is the key.

Asking students to reflect upon the talents identified and to consider how to more fully develop those talents into strengths are useful next steps that should be combined with other course learning outcomes. For example, students in a public speaking course might be asked to prepare and deliver a speech about their talent themes, those in an English composition course could be assigned to complete a written paper on this topic, and students in a music composition course might be asked to create an original song that represents their own talent themes. Similarly, those in a career development course could be assigned to find matches between

Table 6.2 **Virtues and Character Strengths Applied to Teaching and Learning (McGovern & Miller, 2008)**

1. Wisdom and knowledge: Cognitive strengths used to acquire and create knowledge

- Creativity and ingenuity: Constructs novel and innovative conceptualizations of student learning and pedagogy
- Curiosity and openness to experience: Examines processes as well as outcomes of teaching and learning; finds gratification even in the mundane phenomenology of required tasks
- Open-mindedness and critical thinking: Seeks and evaluates evidence that may be contrary to personal beliefs, perspectives, prior decisions
- Love of learning: Pursues new discoveries systematically and appreciates serendipity in the world of ideas
- Perspective and wisdom: Provides wise counsel to students and other teachers, grounded in reflected experience and with empathy for ways of seeing and being in the world

2. Courage: Emotional strengths that involve the exercise of will to accomplish goals despite external or internal opposition

- Integrity and authenticity: Truthfully presents one's self and declares clear principles or values; models consistently how this quality is essential for trusting relationships
- Bravery and valor: Takes actions deliberately despite potentially great risks and dangers; affirms "bearing witness"
- Persistence and perseverance Sustains effort despite obstacles, boredom, or frustration, and often without apparent rewards
- Zest and vitality Demonstrates a passion for teaching and learning that is grounded in reflective practices for deliberate well-being; having a sense of priorities

3. Humanity Interpersonal strengths that involve tending and befriending others

- Kindness and caring: Ethically and responsibly contributes to the teaching and learning of others despite a breadth or depth of differences
- Love: Creates a safe haven in the classroom to foster interpersonal relationships of support and respect, with demonstrated cognitive and affective acceptance
- Social intelligence: Tries to be attentive to subtle cues in teacher and student relationships and group dynamics; uses emotions as part of reasoning and problem solving

(continued)

Table 6.2 **Continued**

4. Justice Civic strengths for a healthy community life

- Citizenship and teamwork: Builds collaborative communities of learners rather than solely rewarding individual achievements
- Fairness: Nuanced capacity to identify biases in one's perspectives; reasons, makes judgments, and implements ethical actions
- Leadership: Adroitly facilitates the task demands and interpersonal dynamics of learning environments

5. Temperance Strengths that protect against excess

- Forgiveness and mercy: Diminishes anger with empathy to sustain and renew relationships and build more collaborative learning opportunities
- Humility and modesty: Communicates a consistent self-assessment of strengths and limitations; values multiple perspectives and potential outcomes
- Prudence: Takes care in daily choices; promotes balance and harmony in the pursuit of intended goals for teaching and learning
- Self-regulation and self-control: Reflectively tries to override initial reactions to consider and implement alternative responses, especially in difficult, "no-win" classroom and professional situations

6. Transcendence Strengths that forge connections to the larger universe and its meanings

- Awe, appreciation of beauty and excellence: Recognizes and takes pleasure in the talents and creativity of others and oneself, but especially in the splendid discoveries made by one's students
- Gratitude: Appreciates and responds to being graced by profound and simple gifts found in the classroom and its diverse participants
- Hope, optimism, future orientation: Responds to the successes and adversities inherent in teaching and learning with an open-minded perspective; expects the best and works to achieve it
- Humor and playfulness: Approaches education with a playful recognition of incongruities and circumstances beyond one's control
- Spirituality or religiousness" Fosters learning environments where inquiry about higher purposes and meanings becomes one accepted means to develop a mature narrative identity

their talent themes and several potential careers of interest, whereas first-year seminar students could be asked to make connections among utilizing their talent themes in the process of navigating both the academic and extracurricular aspects of their college careers.

Like their teachers, students who are interested in more formal analyses of their talents and strengths can complete the CSF 2.0 and the VIA Survey. Students will likely find completion of the CSF 2.0 measure under the StrengthsQuest (Clifton & Anderson 2002) label to be more appealing and useful (versus completion of the measure under the more general StrengthsFinder label), given the specificity of feedback and resources provided relevant to their lives as college students. Indeed, StrengthsQuest was designed specifically for use with a college population to help students discover and develop their talents into strengths in academia, career, and beyond, whereas StrengthsFinder is more focused upon applications of strengths specific to the world of work. In addition to receiving information regarding their top five talent themes, students who participate in the StrengthsQuest program gain access to a wealth of online resources (available at www.strengthsquest.com) to help them to more fully explore and develop their talent themes. Furthermore, educators can also access numerous resources for implementing strengths development in their classrooms (available at www.strengthsquest.com/content/141365/Resources.aspx). Braskamp (2006) reports 10 potential benefits of utilizing the StrengthsQuest program, including helping students to develop greater awareness and acceptance of self and others, enhancement of academic self-efficacy and learning, achievement of greater clarity regarding vocational callings and purpose, development of better leaders and team members, enhancement of expectations of staying in school through graduation, improvement in interpersonal relationship functioning, and helping students to more readily experience a meaningful sense of membership in the campus community.

Multiple research studies designed to assess the impact of strengths-based classrooms on college student outcomes further support the benefits of a strengths approach as previously noted by Braskamp (2006). More specifically, using a sample of over 600 college students enrolled in a first-year seminar course, Anderson, Schreiner, and Shahbaz (2003) found that completion of the CSF and six 1-hour class sessions regarding strengths theory and strengths development resulted in significant increases in optimism, personal strengths awareness and awareness of the strengths of others, self-acceptance, goal directedness, self-confidence, and realistic expectations utilizing pre- and postclass administrations of the Self-Reflection Survey (Clifton, 1997). A second study of first-year seminar students revealed similar findings, with those enrolled in courses that included a strengths intervention (i.e., completion of the CSF and use of the *StrengthsQuest Curriculum Guide and Learning Activities* by Anderson, 2003) scoring significantly higher on all outcomes measured by the Self-Reflection Survey (Clifton,

1997) versus those in a control group who were not exposed to the strengths activities (Anderson, Schreiner, & Shanbaz, 2004). Estévez (2005) used qualitative research methods to assess the effects of a strengths-based first-year seminar course for students who had been identified as underprepared for college work. Students in the course completed the CSF, and the *StrengthsQuest* text (Clifton & Anderson, 2002) was used in addition to the existing curriculum during four class periods. Several themes that emerged in the course of the individual student interviews and focus group interviews support a connection between strengths approaches and student success. Estévez (2005) reported that "students who engaged courses on the premises of their strengths more readily engaged the academic demands of the course" (p. 72). The students also reported elevated levels of academic motivation after learning about their personal strengths, a better understanding of how to apply their strengths to meet academic challenges, and a positive impact on their ability to form social networks. Finally, Louis (2008) studied the effects of a first-year seminar class in which the focus was primarily upon talent identification versus a course in which students were assisted in learning how to develop their talents versus simply identifying them. She also compared outcomes for students in these courses with outcomes for students in a first year seminar that did not contain any information regarding strengths identification or development. Students in the strengths development group reported the highest levels of perceived academic control, defined as their perceived influence over and responsibility for their academic performance, which is predictive of their likelihood to work harder on academic tasks, to obtain better grades, and to remain enrolled in classes (Hall, Perry, Ruthig, Hladkyj, & Chipperfield, 2006; Perry, Hladkyj, Pekrun, & Pelletier, 2001). Louis (2008) concludes that although strengths-based approaches help first-year students maintain a sense of academic control, teaching students about their talents without providing instruction related to how to develop them may unintentionally promote fixed mindsets and the cultivation of performance goal orientations that are correlated with less positive outcomes. Hence, including a developmental component in strengths-based initiatives is highly recommended.

Cantwell (2005) compared the effects of a strengths-based approach versus a traditional method of teaching a college-level public speaking course on student levels of academic engagement and proficiency in course-specific learning outcomes. Students in the strengths-based condition completed the CSF and used the *StrengthsQuest* text (Clifton & Anderson, 2002). In addition, the course instructor used a strengths-based approach when offering feedback to students on their coursework, whereby emphasis was on what students were doing well and reminders were provided for students to consider how to capitalize on their strengths in order to complete the coursework. Students in the control group were not exposed to any of the strengths materials or feedback, rather, they were taught according to a traditional public speaking curriculum that had been used in previous semesters. Students in the experimental condition reported significantly higher levels of academic engagement at the end of the semester and attained higher levels of proficiency in course-relevant outcomes, as evidenced by significantly higher scores on objective examinations and independent evaluations of their public speaking skill.

Research to date also supports connections between identifying and nurturing VIA Character Strengths and positive educational outcomes. More specifically, Proctor et al. (2011) found that students who participated in strengths-building activities and challenges with the school curriculum experienced increased life satisfaction in comparison to their peers who did not participate in strengths-building activities. Similarly, Seligman et al. (2009) found that positive educational programming that was inclusive of character strengths assessment and intervention led to improved school performance and greater student enjoyment and engagement.

Potential Obstacles to Implementation of Strengths-Based Teaching

Within most higher education settings exists a foundational assumption that deficit remediation is the most effective strategy for helping students to complete their college degrees (Schreiner & Anderson, 2005). Although they are likely well-intentioned, faculty and staff who engage in deficit-based remediation programming are actually working within a system that interferes with academic achievement and excellence. Anderson (2004) provides a comparison of the deficit-based remediation and the strengths-based developmental educational approaches outlined in Table 6.3. Anderson (2004) also notes the potential negative effects of the deficit-based model in terms of decreases in student morale, motivation, and confidence, reminding students of past failures and frustrations, setting up negative expectations by students and lowering expectations of faculty towards students, increasing stigmatizing, and stereotyping. As these negative effects accumulate, students become less active on campus because they feel as if they do not really belong, and the more detached they feel and become, the less effort they will put into achieving, which leads faculty and staff to invest less time and energy into the students. Indeed, faculty and staff who are steeped in the deficit-based model will often assume that students who are not putting in effort are students who should not have been admitted in the first place or are students who will not succeed even if they invest time in them (Anderson, 2004). In contrast, the potential positive effects of strengths-based education include increased awareness of talents, heightened personal and academic confidence, positive expectations about academic potential and abilities to achieve, increased

Table 6.3 Comparison of Deficit-Based and Strengths-Based Education

Approach	Methods/Foundations	Outcomes Sought	Approach with New Students	Approach After Entry
Deficit-Based Remediation	• Sensitivity to student needs, problems, & concerns • Create programs & services to remediate student problems & deficiencies	• Increase student persistence • Increase student achievement	• Diagnose student defects, deficiencies, ignorances, needs, problems, & concerns. • Immediately place students in classes & programs to remediate deficiencies.	• Required participation in remedial programs based on diagnosis • Monitor for progress • Guide to available services • Set expectation that remediation will be completed by a certain time
Strengths-Based Development	• Awareness that every student has talents through which he/she can achieve excellence • Create programs & services to develop talent awareness & promote strengths development	• Maximize college experience & student confidence • Achievement of levels of excellence • Fulfillment of potential • Character development in addition to learning knowledge, skills, & learning how to learn • Personal integrity & excellence in academics, Careers, & service	• Assess student strengths, talents, interests, & previous achievements • Build student awareness of talents & potential for excellence • Guide students to courses & opportunities that capitalize on talents & build strengths. Train students in applying strengths to manage weaknesses	• Monitor development of strengths & building on talents • Reinforce involvement around strengths & affirm progress • Stimulate the application of strengths to academics & areas of needed improvement • Create ways to apply developed strengths to academic, personal & career excellence • Apply strengths to help others achieve excellence & reinforce personal integrity.

Adapted from Anderson (2004).

motivation for studying and working hard toward other academic and career goals, increased use of talents in academics and personal life, enhanced communication, improved relationships, and understanding of others (Anderson, 2004).

Despite the many potential benefits of strengths-based teaching and learning, faculty, staff, and students may resist implementation of this approach due to past experiences in which they have been taught to believe that success is achieved through focusing on fixing weaknesses. Individuals may also shy away from a strengths-based approach if they fear that they do not have any talents or strengths or if they suspect that following their talents would lead to conflict with important others in their lives. This is especially likely for students whose parents may expect them to enter a certain profession despite having talents more aligned in a different area. Resistance to identification and implementation of talents and strengths may also stem from a fear that such efforts will lead to arrogance or laziness or that exercise of one's strengths may threaten others, leading to unwanted conflict or rejection. Some resist learning about their talents because they do not believe that there is anything special about their abilities. Indeed, such beliefs are common, especially when one has a very powerful talent. Due to the talent, the individual is able to do certain things with ease and, as a result, inaccurately concludes that anyone can do what they do and that there is nothing special about them or their talents (Anderson, 2004). In order to decrease such resistance, accurate information regarding strengths theory must be provided to faculty, staff, students, and others within the students' primary social networks. In addition, direct discussion of the typical sources of resistance should be addressed early within this educational process. Doing so may normalize such resistance, allowing individuals to more readily open their minds to the possibility of a new way of (1) understanding themselves and others and (2) approaching the classroom and related educational settings.

Faculty and staff may further resist a strengths-based approach due to their own beliefs that universities are places where high standards are to be maintained; thus, a system that accommodates who students are as opposed to where the standards lie is automatically rejected. Some believe that identifying students' weaknesses is exactly what should happen because they erroneously believe that the process of overcoming deficiencies builds character. Some reject a strengths-based approach because they believe that one purpose of higher education is to weed out those students that are not "fit" for advanced training in graduate and professional schools. As a result of such views, faculty and staff propose that the best thing to do for those who "are not college material" is to remove them from higher education as soon as possible. Others resist a strengths-based approach simply because it is different and it may require more work, at least initially. Some faculty and staff reject a strengths-based approach because of the power they feel they have when focusing upon students' needs, problems, weaknesses, defects, and deficits (Anderson, 2004). Finally, some faculty members who have adopted a strengths-based approach may find that their colleagues who do not subscribe to a strengths-based approach reject or look down upon their methods, which can be difficult to navigate, especially if those colleagues are members of their retention and promotion committees.

Although the process may be slow, it is recommended that those within settings in which resistance to strengths-based education may be high begin implementation within the contexts where one has more control (e.g., individual classes taught, student organizations advised, direct student advisees or mentees, and departmental or university committees chaired) and with the assistance of any and all others (colleagues, students, administrators) who also value a strengths-based approach. Garnering support from colleagues at other colleges and universities in which a strengths-based perspective has been adopted is also recommended. Over time, as more people within the university come to see the value of a strengths-based approach, the overall resistance levels are likely to diminish.

Understanding the aforementioned potential obstacles and intentionally working to help others to overcome such resistance by debunking the myths regarding the merits of a deficit-based approach are key to successful implementation of the strengths-based developmental model of education. Indeed, working within an entire school system that has adopted the strength-based perspective is ideal although challenging to develop. Such a system is led by administrators who work as strengths-based educational leaders, applying their talents and strengths in the process of keeping the overall focus upon student learning and academic achievement via hiring, retaining, and promoting faculty and staff based upon their talents and strengths to be true educators and providing funding for programmatic activities that can best help students identify their talents and develop and apply strengths (Anderson, 2004).

Classroom Applications of Positive Psychology Theories

It is important to note that a key factor in strengths-based education is to extend beyond student talent identification and strengths development to a perspective where such information simply serves as the foundation for teaching any subject matter from a strengths-based perspective. Louis (2010) reports that the best outcomes have been associated with strengths-based teaching and learning that is integrated throughout a course versus being presented as a distinct topic within a given course. Hence, regardless of subject matter, strengths-based teachers consider strengths theory in determining how they teach to include the type of feedback provided to students, options they offer to students to demonstrate their mastery of learning objectives, and in terms of how they model their own use of personal strengths in teaching and other life roles. To this end, teachers can utilize findings from other positive psychological scholarship through applications of the broaden-and-build theory of positive emotions (Fredrickson, 1998), active-constructive responding (Gable, Reis, & Impett, 2004), positive empathy (Conoley & Conoley, 2009), and hope (Snyder, 1994). Brief explanations of these theories and examples of theory applications when interacting with students, providing student feedback, designing course assignments, and conducting course exams follow.

Broaden-and-Build Theory of Positive Emotions

The broaden-and-build theory of positive emotions (Fredrickson, 1998) contends that positive emotions broaden one's awareness, attention, and thinking and encourage more complete and creative examinations of potential actions one can take in a particular situation or circumstance. Over time, broadened mindsets stemming from positive emotional states lead to the building of enduring personal resources in the social, intellectual, psychological, and physical realms. Positive emotions have also been found to have the capacity to undo the lingering effects of negative emotions (Fredrickson, 2003), to be key ingredients in resilience (Fredrickson, 2001), and to seed human flourishing (Fredrickson, 2013). Indeed, research has shown that within limits, the higher the ratio of positive feelings or sentiments to negative feelings or sentiments over time is related to flourishing mental health and other positive outcomes. (See Chapter 3 of this text for more details on the broaden-and-build theory.)

Applications of the broaden-and-build theory within the college classroom are abundant, given that any activities, methods, or assignments that serve to induce positive emotional experiences help to fuel student well-being and enhance learning via broadened attention (Fredrickson & Branigan, 2005; Rowe, Hirsh, & Anderson, 2007), more creative thinking (Estrada, Isen, & Young, 1994; Isen, Daubman, & Nowiski, 1987), and more holistic thinking (Isen, Niedenthal, & Cantor, 1992). For example, infusing each class period with the use of appropriate humor, music, video content, or interesting literature that helps breathe life into the subject matter for that day may all serve to get students into a positive and more broadened mindset. Similarly, starting each class period with a brief mindfulness exercise whereby students are asked to engage in focused breathing or body scans can help them to release any negativity they brought into the room, clearing the way for a mindset that is more conducive to learning (Oades, Robinson, Green, & Spence, 2011). Consistent attention to and recognition of student positive actions and strength deployment in relation to classroom discussions, activities, and assignments also fosters positive emotions as does participating in a classroom atmosphere in which affirming instructor and peer feedback is the norm (Louise, 2010). The flourish hypothesis becomes especially relevant to the classroom in relation to the valance of feedback received. Given the power of the negative, teachers must be alert to the need to point out and highlight multiple positives for each criticism shared with their students. For example, in providing a class with test feedback, many instructors are inclined to point out what students did wrong and to focus on their concerns about those who scored low or failed. Based on the flourish hypothesis, such deficit-based feedback is not likely to motivate students to work harder; in fact, it is likely to demotivate them. Instead, instructors should craft their feedback to highlight those aspects of the exam with which the students were most successful and to work together with the students to devise a plan for how to improve performance on those areas of the test with which they struggled. Similarly, teachers should subscribe to the flourish hypothesis when providing written feedback on student papers and projects and when working with them during mentoring or advising sessions.

Positive emotions are also more likely to develop when teachers provide options for how student learning is demonstrated and assessed; hence, designing courses with such flexibility is recommended. Guiding students to select from the options provided based upon the best alignment with their talents, strengths, and interests is also suggested (Louis, 2010). Relatedly, Linley and Harrington (2006) report that understanding and using strengths can have a positive effect on team-work and team outcomes; therefore, teachers who implement group assignments or projects are advised to do so based upon helping students to understand which strengths might be most usefully applied during group work. Finally, allowing students to complete course exams with a partner has been shown to facilitate learning and result in more positive attitudes toward the testing experience (Zimbardo, Butler, & Wolfe, 2003; Magyar-Moe, Clemins, & Krueger, 2004; Magyar-Moe, Hoffman, & Kline, 2006). More specifically, evidence suggests that the positive outcomes of team-testing may be the result of social and intellectual broadening due to increases in positive emotions felt by students before exams completed with partners of their choice (Magyar-Moe et al., 2008).

The examples of applications of the broaden-and-build theory provided in this section are just a sampling of the limitless ways in which teachers can promote positive emotions in the classroom. As such, instructors are encouraged to use these ideas as springboards for positive emotion enhancement in their own class-room spaces based upon their own talents and strengths as educators.

Active-Constructive Responding

According to Gable et al. (2004), there are four possible ways in which one can respond to the good events in the lives of those with whom they interact. The responding styles include *passive-destructive* (lacking interest, displaying little to no eye contact, turning away, or leaving the room), *active-destructive* (pointing out the downside and displaying negative nonverbal cues), *passive-constructive* (happy, but lacking enthusiasm or downplaying; showing little to no active emotional expression), and active-constructive (responding enthusiastically; maintaining eye contact, smiling, and displaying positive emotions). Of the four styles, only the active-constructive style benefits both the individual with whom one is interacting as well as the relationship between the two parties. Indeed, research supports that those who participate in active-constructive interactions experience higher levels of daily happiness, more satisfaction, more trust and intimacy within their relationships, and less conflicts (Gable, Reis, & Impett, 2004). In contrast, the other three response styles are negatively related to well-being for both the person with the good news and one's relationship with that individual.

Applications of this research in the college classroom are abundant, given the many opportunities that faculty have to engage with students before, during, and after class begins. Teachers are encouraged to respond in the active-constructive manner to the good news, positive experiences, and victories that they hear in the stories that their students tell. Faculty are encouraged to not only listen for the good events in the lives of their students but to purposefully work to elicit discussion of such positive events by prompting them with such questions as "what went well for you yesterday" rather than the more generic, "how was your day", to which most people respond with the negatives (Magyar-Moe, 2009).

Positive Empathy

Students commonly share their frustrations and struggles with their teachers, and how faculty respond to such information affects student motivation, morale, and sense of belonging in the classroom and, more generally, on campus. Some faculty have a basic understanding of empathy and how to respond to students in empathic ways. However, many are not aware of positive empathy and the value of positive empathy responses when assisting students with their struggles.

Empathy is typically defined as the ability to understand and enter into another's feelings, emotions, and experiences, and is a hallmark of therapy processes. Rogers (1957) notes that traditional empathy typically focuses on experiences of pain, fear, or anger. For instance, an empathic response to a student who says "I have tried, and tried, and tried to figure out a way to complete this project but nothing works" might be "I can see that you are feeling frustrated and worn out because nothing you try seems to be working." Although this response may be validating and help the student to feel understood, it emphasizes the negative and has the potential to increase a sense of hopelessness. In contrast, a positive empathy response would entail validation of the experience while also attending to the positive aspects of the story, with the focus being on the student's experiences of hope and desire (Conoley & Conoley, 2009). In this case, a positive empathic response would be "although you are feeling some frustration, it is apparent that you are really committed to your studies. Your persistence is a strength that will help you to reach your academic goals." Pointing out the commitment of this student as well as his or her personal strength of perseverance versus emphasizing the struggle can make a world of difference in terms of the student's levels of hope and motivation, as well as how the student views him or herself.

Hope

Hope consists of one's perceptions of his or her abilities to create clear goals, develop plans for reaching those goals (pathways thinking), and find and maintain the energy and motivation necessary for following through with goal pursuits (agency thinking; Snyder, 1994). Goals can be anything people desire to experience, create, get, do, or become; therefore, they may be major, lifelong goals or more minor, short-term goals. In order for individuals to achieve their goals, both pathways and agency thinking are necessary (Lopez et al., 2004).

Hope within educational contexts has been studied extensively over the past two decades, with findings suggesting that hope is malleable and is not related to intelligence (Snyder, McDermott, Cook, & Rapoff, 2002; Feldman & Dreher, 2012) or income (Gallup, 2009). Students who are higher in hope earn better grades in core subjects (Marques, Pais-Ribeiro, & Lopez, 2011), score higher on achievement tests (Snyder et al., 1997), and have higher overall grade point averages (Gallup 2009; Snyder et al., 1991; Worrell & Hale, 2001; Gallagher & Lopez, 2008; Snyder, Shorey, et al., 2002). In addition, the predictive power of hope in relation to a host of positive educational outcomes remains even when controlling for intelligence (Snyder et al., 1997), prior grades (Gallagher & Lopez, 2008; Snyder, Harris, et al., 1991; Snyder, McDermott, Cook, & Rapoff, 2002), self-esteem (Snyder, McDermott, et al., 2002), and college entrance examination scores (Gallagher & Lopez, 2008; Snyder, McDermott, et al., 2002). More specifically, high hope positively correlates with higher semester and overall grade point averages (Chang, 1998; Curry, Snyder, Cook, Ruby, & Rehm, 1997), and student hope levels measured at college entrance significantly predicted academic progress over the course of six years. High hope scores significantly predicted higher cumulative grade point averages (the high-hope students averaged a B compared to a C for the low-hope students), higher likelihoods of graduating, and lower likelihoods of dropping out (Snyder, Shorey, Cheavens, Pulvers, Adams, & Wiklund, 2002). Snyder (2005) contends that the high-hope students excel because they set lucid goals, have well-defined strategies for learning and studying, and put in the effort needed to put those strategies into action without getting off task while studying and taking exams. Furthermore, high-hope students are not as distracted by self-deprecating thoughts and negative emotions compared with their lower-hope peers (Onwuegbuzie & Snyder, 2000).

Being a hope-focused educator benefits both students and faculty alike. Indeed, high-hope people perform better at work (Peterson & Byron, 2008), have higher well-being (Gallagher & Lopez, 2009), and live longer (Stern, Dhanda, & Hazuda, 2001). Teachers can help their students to be more hopeful by modeling a hopeful lifestyle, working to create excitement about the future, and teaching students strategies for doing well in school and solving problems (Lopez, 2009).

In order to help foster student excitement about the future and motivation to work towards goals, faculty are encouraged to help students to set goals that are emotionally important to them, to encourage them to track the progress they make toward their goals in tangible ways, and to celebrate progress towards goal attainment (Lopez, 2009). Educators are also advised to be very aware of the everyday communications they have with students and colleagues so that their communications inspire rather than frustrate. Indeed, the words of educators have the power to make students enthusiastic about the future and, in turn, foster hope and engagement; the words of educators can also undermine the excitement that others feel about their day, week, or even the semester or academic year (Lopez, 2009). Indeed, the faculty at Chaffey College in Rancho Cucamonga, California, learned this lesson firsthand during a summer institute training in which the professors were in the student role and being taught by instructors who demonstrated low-hope teaching: they called the participants out on not doing homework, predicted that many would drop out or perform poorly, and were neglected when they asked questions or needed help. They were also provided with a "low-hope syllabus" packed with challenging assignments but with no suggestions for how to complete the work or offers to provide assistance in the future. When the institute trainers switched over to a high-hope syllabus and hope-focused talk, the effect on morale was clear. Faculty members took from this training the importance and value of designing courses around pathways and agency thinking and speaking in the language of hope (Grasgreen, 2012). For example, a comment from a student such as "I will never be able to do this" or "I knew I wouldn't do well on this assignment" might prompt a hope-based response such as "although this feels challenging right now, if we break this down into a series of smaller steps it will likely feel more do-able" or "let's work together to figure out what you need to do to do better next time."

Snyder (2005) offered five lessons of hope for teachers who strive to be purveyors of hope within their classrooms based upon observations of and interviews with master teachers, interviews with students regarding what they think teachers can do to foster hope, and upon his own research on hope for almost two decades. The five hope lessons include: (1) spending time on and caring about students; (2) setting goals for students that are clear and cooperative in nature; (3) creating routes for learning that involve interacting with fellow students; (4) helping students to become motivated in joint learning activities; and (5) imparting an atmosphere whereby students are concerned about their welfares and the welfares of their classmates. Each of these lessons is briefly described in the sections that follow.

Spending Time and Caring

When asked to describe their childhoods, young adults who scored high on hope versus those scoring low on hope reported that during childhood, they had adult caregivers, including teachers, who had spent large amounts of time mentoring them. Their low-hope counterparts, on the other hand, reported receiving very little attention during childhood from the adults in their lives, including their teachers (Snyder, 1994). Bjornesen (2000) reports that undergraduate students view the most important activity of a college professor to be spending time interacting with students. These studies suggest that what is important to college students and their future success is that they feel that their instructors care about them and about what happens to them. Hence, hopeful teaching is built upon spending time with and caring about one's students (Snyder, 2005).

Setting Goals for the Class

Establishing a sense of order in the classroom is necessary for learning. Related to order is the establishment of an atmosphere in which students and teachers are accountable for their actions, leading to a level of reciprocal respect. Teachers play a key role in establishing such respect and also in cultivating an atmosphere of trust in the classroom. Educators who are cynical of students instantly undermine the trust that is critical for building hope. Therefore, teachers must interact with students in ways that make them look good and that promote growth-inducing, stretch goals tailored to each individual student (Snyder, 2005).

Faculty should also model hope thinking via being as clear as possible about their learning objectives, including how students will attain grades and how they will go about mastering the material in each learning unit. High-hope teachers are very clear about their objectives, and they take care to convey these objectives to the class and to individual students. They also make the goals of the class concrete and understandable and break larger tasks into smaller subgoals that students can accomplish at each stage (Snyder, 2005).

Creating Pathways to Class Goals

High-hope teachers plan their courses by setting up step-by-step course sequences so that both within a single class period and across a full semester, the information unfolds in a clear, comprehensible manner. Snyder (2005) suggests that instructors create alternate exercises they can use should a given approach not work. To determine whether the pathways used are working or whether there might be alternative pathways that could be implemented for greater learning, consulting with present and past students about approaches that work, as well as talking with other teachers about their favorite techniques is recommended. Snyder (2005) suggests that among such pathways-related teaching techniques, high-hope teachers should set up learning experiences so that a maximal number of students can participate cooperatively versus setting up a highly competitive atmosphere focused upon the pursuit of grades and potentially vicious social comparisons and competitions among students. Too many failures result within this latter course format, resulting in diminished hope levels. The "jigsaw" classroom approach where students are divided into work groups in which each student is given only a portion of the information required to complete an assignment (Aronson & Patnoe, 1997) helps to establish an atmosphere in which students share their particular information, and this then becomes a pathway for success at learning the material. All of these pathways-related teaching activities rest upon a willingness to interact with and listen to one's students (Snyder, 2005).

Raising Agency to Pursue Class Goals

Snyder (2005) reports that modeling enthusiasm for one's course material is a crucial avenue for teachers who desire to increase student motivation in their courses. Teachers are models of hope for their students; therefore, setting up one's courses so that the instructor is interested is crucial. Students readily adopt their teacher's enthusiasm and also hone in quickly on lack of enthusiasm and respond accordingly. Snyder (2005) asserts that instructors must do whatever it takes to be enthused when entering the classroom. Hopeful teachers also listen well and are responsive to and flexible in interacting with students. Educators can further raise student agency via praising and encouraging student efforts and improvements.

Teach Hope and Self-Esteem Will Follow

There has been a movement to increase student self-esteem, defined as the level of one's perceived worth. Accomplishing this goal proves to be a challenge, however, because teachers have largely been told to rely on simply telling students that they are worthwhile or putting "smiley faces" on their papers. Most students are very adept at seeing through the façade of such feedback and may not know how to learn because they have been given superficial feedback about their efforts and skills. Snyder's (2002) research shows that students feel good about themselves (i.e., have elevated self-esteem) when they perceive that they have successfully learned how to pursue a desired learning goal; therefore, teachers are encouraged to reward students for efforts expended at learning how to learn and how to become effective problem solvers in a variety of content areas. "Such genuine feedback will lead students to experience levels of self-esteem that are based on efforts expended, along with the knowledge and skills that can be used and built upon across a lifetime . . . self-esteem is a by-product, albeit an important one, of an ever-evolving skill-based, hopeful thought process" (Snyder, 2005, p. 80).

Overall, at the core of the role of hope within education for students is "learning how to learn" (pathways) and development of the "I can" motivation to continue to learn (agency). Therefore, effective instructors teach the content of their particular subjects while also engendering hope in the students' thinking. Many college students have the will to pursue a future they desire; however, they often lack the ways or necessary strategies to reach the big goals of graduation and employment. Given the intense commitment faculty give to teaching content and students put into learning content, the *process* of getting good grades and solving daily problems may remain a mystery for some because the process is not explicitly taught in most courses. Student hope may be enhanced by educators who take the time to teach students ways to study for tests, prepare for examinations and final exam periods, track grades over time, navigate interpersonal disputes, pursue career interests, and interview for jobs (Lopez, 2009). "Long after our students have forgotten the content of what we have taught, and long after that content may have been supplanted by new and different content, we still can be assured of one enduring lesson—hope can guide and empower a lifetime of learning." (Snyder, 2005, p. 81).

Case Study

Dr. Anita Davis, Associate Professor of Communication, has just completed her first year of teaching at a liberal arts college. She is somewhat dissatisfied with her experiences in the classroom because she did not get as much positive feedback on her course evaluations as she had hoped, and she felt like she was not fully connecting to her students. Dr. Davis enrolls in a professional development course on teaching and learning in which she is informed about strengths-based education. As she reflects upon her first year of teaching, she quickly realizes that she had been focused much more on student weaknesses and problems than upon the strengths and efforts put forth by her class members. She also realized that she had not been implementing her own strengths as a teacher—in fact, she was not even sure what her strengths were because she had never stopped to analyze this about herself. She had simply been trying to emulate her own favorite college professor and was struggling to do so because her favorite professor was very extraverted and demonstrative and she, by nature, was more introverted and reserved.

Dr. Davis took the VIA Strengths Survey and the CSF to determine her highest strengths of character and her greatest talent themes. She began to recall times in the past when she had capitalized upon her strengths and how this often resulted in positive outcomes as a student and as a graduate teaching assistant.

For example, she had gotten excellent feedback as a graduate assistant from students who noted that her calm and quiet demeanor made them feel very comfortable asking questions and approaching her with problems and that her ability to mediate conflict, to find ways to include everyone, and to promote harmony was especially useful during heated classroom discussions. Dr. Davis realized that teaching from her strengths was not only much more enjoyable for her, but it was also more appealing to students. She included information about her own strengths on her syllabus and drafted a teaching statement of her teaching philosophy for inclusion on her syllabi as well.

Dr. Davis decided that in the upcoming term, she would require all students in her courses to learn and share with her their highest strengths and talents, and she would include several lectures and discussions on Strengths Theory in the early part of the term to be sure that her students also understood what she was learning about the power of strengths-based education. Dr. Davis then utilized the information regarding the strengths of each of her students to guide how she designed her classroom lessons and activities throughout the rest of the new semester. For example, in her interpersonal communication class, a number of students had VIA Strengths of Humanity such as Social Intelligence and Genuineness and Influencing StrengthsFinder Talent Themes such as Winning Others Over and Maximizer. Given this, Dr. Davis structured the course to include an abundance of discussion time and assigned group projects so that students could hone their strengths and achieve success in the course as a result. In contrast, her public speaking course included students with a wide array of strengths and talent themes; hence, she taught using a combination of lecture and discussion strategies, individual and group projects, and included a number of possible assignments that students could choose to complete based upon their own strengths and talents. For example, rather than assigning all of the students to do a persuasive speech, she gave them the option of choosing between a persuasive speech or an informative speech. Hence, students with high Influencing Talent Themes could choose to do persuasive speeches, whereas those higher in Strategic Thinking Talent Themes could choose to complete informative speeches. She also assigned an introductory speech in which students shared their highest strengths and examples of their strengths in action after having interviewed their closest friends and family members about this topic.

Dr. Davis also changed the way she provided feedback to students such that she no longer only shared with them areas for improvement or aspects of assignments that they did not do correctly. Instead, she shared with them what they did well and then encouraged them to consider how they might use their strengths and talents to better manage those aspects they struggled with. For example, one student came to realize that she could use her strength of humor and playfulness within the introduction of her speeches as a way to overcome her anxiety about speaking in front of her peers. Dr. Davis also made a conscious effort to consistently respond to the good news and experiences of her students using active-constructive responding and to respond to their struggles and problems using positive empathy. She also made a point to start each class with a short story, quotation, or student interaction exercise to set a positive tone for the remainder of the class session, to capitalize upon the broadening and building aspects of positive emotions.

Finally, Dr. Davis created and offered to her students handouts that would help them to structure their work load in her courses, to clarify their goals, and to track their goal progress on a weekly basis so as to enhance hope and increase the likelihood of positive outcomes. She was also very careful to model a hopeful outlook through her approach to teaching and via her responses to her students both inside and outside of the classroom. For example, she responded in a timely manner to student questions and requests for help and reassured them that she was there to support them and help them to break down challenging tasks into more manageable components.

Dr. Davis was delighted by how much more connected she felt to her students during her second year of college teaching, how much better she felt about herself as a teacher, and by the much higher course evaluations she earned via implementation of a strengths-based educational approach. Indeed, at the end of year two, she was honored with an early-career teaching award, after being nominated by a host of students who reported that they found her courses to be among the most interesting and engaging. The students also felt that she was truly dedicated to them as students and concerned about them as individuals.

Conclusion

Strengths-based educators aim to teach the whole person by engaging students personally and emotionally in the process of understanding and honing their unique talents and strengths. Strengths-based educators serve as role models via application of their own strengths to their teaching methods and engaging in hopeful thinking inclusive of excitement for their subject matter and for their students. Furthermore, they are intentional in their approaches to fostering positive emotions in the classroom and adhering to the greater ratio of positive to negative experiences needed in order to seed flourishing for those that they teach. Finally, emphasizing student positive experiences through responding actively and constructively and validating their negative experiences and struggles without contributing to feelings of hopelessness via using positive empathy are commonplace for those who teach from a positive psychology perspective. Although the information and strategies provided in this chapter are not exhaustive of all possible applications of positive psychology in the classroom, educators who begin with these strategies and adapt or expand upon them in ways that best fit their unique talents, strengths, subject matter, course formats, and student populations are likely to experience work in more positive ways and to have students who also benefit greatly in terms of both academic achievement and personal growth and development.

References

Anderson, E. C. (2000, February). *Affirming students' strengths in the critical years.* Paper presented at the National Conference on the First Year Experience, Columbia, SC.

Anderson, E. C. (2003). *StrengthsQuest: Curriculum outline and learning activities.* Princeton, NJ: Gallup.

Anderson, E. C. (2004). *What is strengths-based education? A tentative answer by someone who strives to be a strengths-based educator.* Unpublished manuscript.

Anderson, E. C., Cave, S., & McDowell, S. (2001, October). *Why become strengths-based? An academic and theological context for strengths programming.* Paper presented at Eastern College, National Conference on Identifying and Developing Student Strengths, St. Davids, PA.

Anderson, E. C., Schreiner, L. A., & Shahbaz, P. (2003). *Research and evaluation of strengths counselors in a New Beginnings course.* Unpublished raw data, Azusa Pacific University, Azusa, CA.

Anderson, E. C., Schreiner, L. A., & Shahbaz, P. (2004). *Research and evaluation of strengths counselors in a New Beginnings course.* Unpublished raw data, Azusa Pacific University, Azusa, CA.

Aronson, E., & Patnoe, S. (1997). The jigsaw classroom: Building cooperation in the classroom (2nd ed.). New York: Addison Wesley Longman.

Asplund, J., Lopez, S. J., Hodges, T., & Harter, J. (2007). *The Clifton StrengthsFinder 2.0 technical report: Development and validation.* Princeton, NJ: Gallup.

Binet, A., & Simon, T. (1916). *The development of intelligence in children* (E. S. Kit, Trans.). Baltimore: Williams & Wilkins.

Bjornesen, C. A. (2000). Undergraduate student perceptions of the impact of faculty in activities in education. *Teaching of Psychology, 27*(3), 205–208.

Bowers, K. (2009). Making the most of human strengths. In S. J. Lopez (Ed.) *Positive psychology: Exploring the best in people: Discovering human strengths* (pp. 23–36). Westport, CT: Praeger.

Braskamp, L. (2006). *The StrengthsQuest guidebook: Introducing strengths-based development and StrengthsQuest to higher education leaders.* Princeton, NJ: Gallup Organization.

Cantwell, L. (2005). A comparative analysis of strengths-based versus traditional teaching methods in a freshman public speaking course: Impacts on student learning and engagement. *Dissertation Abstracts International, 67*(02A), 478–700. (UMI No. AAT3207574)

Carey, K. (2004). *A matter of degrees: Improving graduation rates in four-year colleges and universities.* Washington, DC: Education Trust.

Chang, E. C. (1998). Hope, problem-solving ability, and coping in a college student population: Some implications for theory and practice. *Journal of Clinical Psychology, 54,* 953–962.

Chickering, A. W. (1969). *Education and identity.* San Francisco: Jossey-Bass.

Chickering, A. W., & Reisser, L. (1993). *Education and identity.* San Francisco: Jossey-Bass.

Clifton, D. O. (1997). *The Self-Reflection Survey.* Princeton, NJ: Gallup.

Clifton, D. O., & Anderson, C. E. (2002). *StrengthsQuest.* Washington, DC: Gallup.

Clifton, D. O., & Nelson, P. (1992). *Soar With Your Strengths.* New York, NY: Dell.

Conoley, C. W., & Conoley, J. C. (2009). Positive psychology & family therapy: Creative techniques and practical tools for guiding change and enhancing growth. Hoboken, NJ: Wiley.

Crabb, S. (2011). The use of coaching principles to foster employee engagement. *The Coaching Psychologist, 7*(1), 27–34.

Curry, L. A., Snyder, C. R., Cook, D. L., Ruby, B. C., & Rehm, M. (1997). The role of hope in student-athlete academic and sport achievement. *Journal of Personality and Social Psychology, 73*, 1257–1267.

Dewey, J. (1938). *Experience in education.* New York: Collier.

Estévez, E. F. (2005). The role of strengths-based case management strategies in the promotion of social capital and academic success of underprepared students. *Dissertation Abstracts International, 66*(08A), 2852–2975. (UMI No. AAT3185052)

Estrada, C. A., Isen, A. M., & Young, M. J. (1994). Positive affect improves creative problem solving and influences reported source of practice satisfaction in physicians. *Motivation and Emotion, 18*, 285–299.

Feldman, D. B., & Dreher, D. E. (2012). Can hope be changed in 90 minutes? Testing the efficacy of a single-session goal-pursuit intervention for college students. *Journal of Happiness Studies, 13*, 745–759.

Fredrickson, B. L. (1998). What good are positive emotions? *Review of General Psychology, 2*(3), 300–319.

Fredrickson, B. L. (2001). The role of positive emotions in positive psychology: The broaden-and-build theory of positive emotions. *American Psychologist, 56*(3), 218–26.

Fredrickson, B. L. (2003). Positive emotions and upward spirals in organizations. In K. S. Cameron, J. E. Dutton, & R. E. Quinn (Eds.), *Positive organizational scholarship: Foundations of a new discipline* (pp. 163–75). San Francisco: Berrett-Koehler.

Fredrickson, B. L., & Branigan, C. (2005). Positive emotions broaden the scope of attention and thought-action repertoires. *Cognition and Emotion, 19*, 313–332.

Fredrickson B. L., & Losada M. F. (2005). Positive affect and the complex dynamics of human flourishing. *American Psychologist, 60*, 678–686.

Gable, S. L., Reis, H. T., Impett, E. A., & Asher, E. R. (2004). What do you do when things go right? The intrapersonal and interpersonal benefits of sharing positive events. *Journal of Personality and Social Psychology, 87*, 228–245.

Gallagher, M. W., & Lopez, S. J. (2009). Positive expectancies and mental health: Identifying the unique contributions of hope and optimism. *Journal of Positive Psychology, 4*, 548–556.

Gallagher, M. W., & Lopez, S. J. (2008). *Hope, self-efficacy, and academic success in college students.* Poster presented at the annual convention of the American Psychological Association. Boston, MA.

Gallup Organization. (2003). Teaching and leading with individualization. June 26, 2007

Gallup. (2009). Hope, Engagement, and Well-Being as Predictors of Attendance, Credits Earned, and GPA in High School Freshmen. Unpublished data. Omaha, NE.

Grasgreen, A. (2012, July 6). Researchers apply hope theory to boost college student success. *Inside Higher Ed.*

Hall, N. C., Perry, R. P., Ruthig, J. C., Hladkyj, S., & Chipperfield, J. G. (2006). Primary and secondary control in achievement settings: A longitudinal field study of academic motivation, emotions, and performance. *Journal of Applied Social Psychology, 36*, 1430–1470.

Harzer, C., & Ruch, W. (2012). When the job is a calling: The role of applying one's signature strengths at work. *Journal of Positive Psychology, 7*, 362–371. doi:10.1080/17439760.2012.702784

Harzer, C., & Ruch, W. (2013). The application of signature character strengths and positive experiences at work. *Journal of Happiness Studies, 14*(3), 965–983.

Hurlock, E. B. (1925). An evaluation of certain incentives used in school work. *Journal of Educational Psychology, 16*, 145–159.

Isen, A. M., Daubman, K. A., & Nowicki, G. P. (1987). Positive affect facilitates creative problem solving. *Journal of Personality and Social Psychology, 52,* 1122–1131.

Isen, A. M., Niedenthal, P. M., & Cantor, N. (1992). An influence of positive affect on social categorization. *Motivation and Emotion, 16,* 65–78.

Keeley, J., Smith, D., & Buskist, W. (2006). The Teacher Behaviors Checklist: Factor analysis of its utility for evaluating teaching. *Teaching of Psychology, 33,* 84–91.

Levitz, R., & Noel, L. (2000). *The earth-shaking, but quiet revolution, in retention management.* Retrieved from www.noellevitz.com

Liesveld, R. (2013). Inspiring your students by being you. *Go Teach (Online) ISSN 2163-8225.* Retrieved from www.futureeducators.org/goteach/2013/03/15/inspiring-your-students-by-being-you

Liesveld, R., & Miller, J. A. (2005). *Teach With Your Strengths.* New York, NY: Gallup Press.

Linley, P. A., & Harrington, S. (2006). Strengths coaching: A potential-guided approach to coaching psychology. *International Coaching Psychology Review, 1,* 37–46.

Lopez, S. J. (2004). *Naming, nurturing, and navigating: Capitalizing on strengths in daily life.* National Conference on Building a Strengths-Based Campus: Best Practices in Maximizing Student Performance: Omaha, NE.

Lopez, S. (2009). *Hope, academic success, and the Gallup Student Poll.* Gallup Inc.

Lopez, S. J., & Louis, M. C. (2009). The principles of strengths-based education. *Journal of College and Character, 10*(4), 1–8.

Lopez, S. J., Snyder, C. R., Magyar-Moe, J. L., Edwards, L. M., Pedrotti, J. T., Janowski, K., Turner, J. L., & Pressgrove, C. (2004). Strategies for accentuating hope. In P. A. Linley & S. Joseph (Eds.), *Positive Psychology in Practice* (pp. 388–404). Hoboken, New Jersey: John Wiley & Sons, Inc.

Louis, M. C. (2008). A comparative analysis of the effectiveness of strengths-based curricula in promoting first-year college student success. *Dissertation Abstracts International, 69*(06A). (UMI No. AAT 3321378)

Louis, M. C. (2010). Optimizing strengths development initiatives in the classroom. Princeton, New Jersey: Gallup. Found on-line at http://www1.uwindsor.ca/sia/sites/uwindsor.ca.sas/files/students-strengths-development-programming-Louis-3pgs(brief).pdf

Louis, M. C. (2011). Strengths interventions in higher education: The effect of identification versus development approaches on implicit self-theory. *The Journal of Positive Psychology, 6*(3), 204–215.

Magyar-Moe, J. L. (2009). *Therapist's guide to positive psychological interventions.* San Diego, CA: Elsevier Academic Press.

Magyar-Moe, J. L., Becker, K., Burek, C., McDougal, A., & McKeel, A. (2008, August). *Team-testing: Does it increase positive emotions which broaden and build?* Poster presented at the 116th Annual Convention of the American Psychological Association, Boston, MA.

Magyar-Moe, J. L., Hoffman, S., & Kline, A. (2006, August). *Outcomes for college students choosing team testing: A follow-up study.* Poster presented at the 2006 meeting of the American Psychological Association, New Orleans, LA.

Magyar-Moe, J. L., Clemins, J., & Krueger, M. (2004, August). *Outcomes for and characteristics of college students who choose team testing.* Poster presented at the 2004 annual meeting of the American Psychological Association, Honolulu, HI.

Marques, S. C., Pais-Ribeiro, J. L., & Lopez, S. J. (2011). The role of positive psychology constructs in predicting mental health and academic achievement in children and adolescents: A two-year longitudinal study. *Journal of Happiness Studies.* doi:10.1007/s10902-010-9244-4.

McGovern, T. V., & Miller, S. L. (2008). Integrating teacher behaviors with character strengths and virtues for faculty development. *Teaching of Psychology, 35,* 278–285.

Oades, L. G., Robinson, P., Green, S., & Spence, G. B. (2011). Towards a positive university. *The Journal of Positive Psychology, 6,* 432–439.

Onwuegbuzie, A. J., & Snyder, C. R. (2000). Relations between hope and graduate students' studying and test-taking strategies. *Psychological Reports, 86*, 803–806.

Palmer, P. (1998). *The courage to teach: Exploring the inner landscape of a teacher's life.* San Francisco: Jossey–Bass.

Perry, R. P., Hladkyj, S., Pekrun, R., & Pelletier, S. (2001). Academic control and action control in the achievement of college students: A longitudinal field study. *Journal of Educational Psychology, 93*, 776–789.

Peterson, S. J., & Byron, K. (2008). Exploring the role of hope in job performance: Results from four studies. *Journal of Organizational Behavior, 29*, 785–803.

Peterson, C., & Seligman, M. (2004). *Character strengths and virtues: A handbook and classification.* New York, NY: Oxford University Press; Washington, D.C.: American Psychological Association. http://www.amazon.com/Character-Strengths-Virtues-Handbook-Classification/dp/0195167015#reader_0195167015

Proctor, C., Tsukayama, E., Wood, A., M., Maltby, J., Fox Eades, J., & Linley, P. A. (2011). Strengths gym: The impact of a character strengths-based intervention on the life satisfaction and well-being of adolescents. *Journal of Positive Psychology, 6*(5), 377–388.

Rashid, T. (2008). Positive psychotherapy. In S. J. Lopez (Ed.), *Positive psychology: Exploring the best in people* (Vol 4, pp. 187–217). Westport, CT: Praeger Publishers.

Rath, T. (2007). *StrengthsFinder 2.0.* New York: Gallup Press.

Rettew, J. G., & Lopez, S. J. (2009). Discovering your strengths. In S. J. Lopez (Ed.) Positive psychology: Exploring the best in people: Discovering human strengths (pp. 1–21). Westport, CT: Praeger.

Rogers, C. (1957) The necessary and sufficient conditions of therapeutic personality change. *Journal of Consulting Psychology, 21*(2), 95–103

Rowe, G., Hirsh, J. B., & Anderson, A. K. (2007). Positive affect increases the breadth of attentional selection. *Proceedings of the National Academy of Sciences, U S A, 104*, 383–388.

Saleebey, D. (2001). *Human behavior and social environments: A biopsychosocial approach.* New York, NY: Columbia University Press.

Schreiner, L. A., & Anderson, E. C. (2005). Strengths-based advising: A new lens for higher education. *NACADA Journal, 25*(2), 20–27.

Seligman, M. E. P., Steen, T., Park, N., & Peterson, C. (2005). Positive psychology progress: Empirical validation of interventions. *American Psychologist, 60*, 410–421.

Seligman, M. E. P., Ernst, R. M., Gillham, J., Reivich, K., & Linkins, M. (2009). Positive education: Positive psychology and classroom interventions. *Oxford Review of Education, 35*, 293–311.

Snyder, C. R. (1994). *The psychology of hope: You can get there from here.* New York: Free Press.

Snyder, C. R. (2002). Hope theory: Rainbows in the mind. *Psychological Inquiry, 13*, 249–275.

Snyder, C. R. (2005). Teaching: The lessons of hope. *Journal of Social and Clinical Psychology, 24*, 72–84.

Snyder, C. R., Harris, C., Anderson, J. R., Holleran, S. A., Irving, L. M., Sigmon, S. T., Yoshinobu, L., Gibb, J., Langelle, C., & Harney, P. (1991). The will and the ways: Development and validation of an individual-differences measure of hope. *Journal of Personality and Social Psychology, 60*(4), 570–585.

Snyder, C. R., McDermott, D., Cook, W., & Rapoff, M. (2002). *Hope for the journey* (revised ed.). Clinton Corners, NY: Percheron Press.

Snyder, C. R., Hoza, B., Pelham, W. E., Rapoff, M., Ware, L., Danovsky, M., Highberger, L., Ribinstein, H., & Stahl, K. J. (1997). The development and validation of the Children's Hope Scale. *Journal of Pediatric Psychology, 22*, 399–421.

Snyder, C. R., Shorey, H. S., Cheavens, J., Pulvers, K. M., Adams, V. H., III, & Wiklund, C. (2002). Hope and academic success in college. *Journal of Educational Psychology, 94*, 820–826.

Stern, S. L., Dhanda, R., & Hazuda, H. P. (2001). Hopelessness predicts mortality in older mexican and european americans. *Psychosomatic Medicine, 63*, 344–351.

Terman, L. M., & Oden, M. H. (1947). *The gifted child grows up: Twenty-five years' follow-up of a superior group.* Stanford, CA: Stanford University Press.

United States Department of Education. (2004). *Performance measure and accountability.* Retrieved from http://www.ed.gov/about/offices/list/ovae/pi/cte/perfmeas.html

White, D. L (2013). Teaching with your strengths. Retrieved from http://oldsite.leeuniversity.edu/Media/6446f89a-f3f5-4807-8609-653ba062bb92/dwhite-teaching-with-strengths.pdf

Worrell, F. C., & Hale, R. L. (2001). The relationship of hope in the future and perceived school climate to school completion. *School Psychology Quarterly, 16*, 370–388.

Zimbardo, P. G., Butler, L. D., & Wolfe, V. A. (2003) Cooperative college examinations: More gain, less pain when students share information and grades. *Journal of Experimental Education 71*(2), 101–25.

7

Positive Career Counseling

JOHN C. WADE

Many college students understandably tend to approach the process of considering life after college with much trepidation and uncertainty. Students often feel internal and, at times, external pressure to find the "right answer" and to choose the "right career." Confusion feels uncomfortable, but, developmentally speaking, confusion is a fertile state because it means the student is allowing himself or herself to remain open to possibilities.

Positive psychology is ideally suited for the task of considering one's future identity, exploring career possibilities, and deciding how to use and direct one's strengths and passions. However, although several career theories and models contain elements that resonate with the tenets and research findings of positive psychology, and some more recent models identify themselves based on positive psychology constructs such as hope (Niles, Amundson, & Neault, 2011) or strengths (Schutt, 2007), to date there is no explicitly identified "positive career counseling model." This chapter will attempt to create and describe such a model, drawing upon relevant positive psychology-based research and constructs in the current career counseling literature. The following premises will serve as the foundation of the positive career counseling model, and they will be described more fully in the chapter:

- Expectations for the counseling process need to be reframed from trying to quickly find the "right" career or the "right" fit, to exploring and better understanding one's self and the world, and from this understanding will flow the information, both intuitive and rational, to guide the career decision making process.
- Career exploration is grounded in listening to and honoring one's "calling," which is a multifaceted process, with clues given by being attentive to one's excitements, interests, strengths, and passions.

- Identifying and utilizing strengths is central to career decision making and future career success.
- Information is the basis of decision making, and engagement is vital to increasing the fund of knowledge and awareness from which to understand the self and the world and to make well-grounded and informed career decisions.
- Positively focused questions serve as the foundation of the career counseling process, both in identifying interests and "callings" and also identifying the steps and processes to begin to bring the aspirational into reality.
- Career decision making is viewed as a life-long skill to be practiced, not just a one-time process to be completed and put to rest.

Reframe Expectations

Within the framework of positive career counseling, career indecision should be regarded as a normal process, not as a problem to be overcome, but rather as an expectant pause because the individual is about to enter a new stage of life and forge a new identity. After all, big decisions should not be taken lightly or made quickly. Savickas (1995) asserts that career indecision is natural if the student has not yet recognized her talents or calling or contemplated her life purpose and work. Savickas (1995) also states that career counselors can help resolve career indecision by assisting students to clarify their life themes and discuss the steps involved in moving toward their goals. If the counselor responds skillfully, this uncertainty presents an impetus for exploration and growth. "A client's indecision becomes an opportunity for making meaning of one's life when a counselor concentrates on how that career indecision fits into the pattern of larger meanings being lived by the client" (Savickas, 1995, p. 366). Exploring the client's story can help illuminate her ongoing life narrative and pattern of living and serve as a springboard for helping her to articulate her career ambitions.

Reframing the discomfort of uncertainty and ambiguity can be very powerful. As William James, the father of American psychology told us over one hundred years ago, happiness is found by reducing the discrepancy between expectations and reality. The importance of narrowing the gap between expectations and reality firmly applies to career counseling as well. If uncertainly is framed to be an expected part of the career exploration process, it may still be uncomfortable at times, but it will likely feel much more manageable. It is important that career counselors explicitly reframe career uncertainty as a positive indicator, a sign of open-mindedness and receptiveness to possibility, because discomfort is often interpreted as a sign of a problem or something to be avoided. Gelatt (1989) coined the term "positive uncertainty" to note that focusing on the positive aspects of uncertainty helps clients deal more effectively with change and ambiguity, be more accepting of uncertainty and inconsistency, and to use their nonrational and intuitive side of thinking and choosing. Cochran (1991) normalizes the process of career indecision and captures the affirmative potential with the term "wavering." Indecision is viewed as part of the normal experience that occurs when individuals are in the process of losing their current place and making a new place in the world as they transform themselves and forge a new identity. The indecision is the understandable and reasonable hesitation before embarking in a new direction. "Wavering" reflects movement toward meaning rather than toward a more limited goal, and it provides the opportunity for clients to review their lives and focus on understanding the direction and themes of their lives so far. This process of gaining greater understanding and awareness can eventually lead to resuming forward movement with greater clarity (Savickas, 1995, p. 365).

Honoring Callings: Helping Students Listen to Their Life

Callings, those yearnings to pursue a certain career because it would feel inauthentic and untrue to ourselves not to, are intertwined with positive psychology because they "capture the most positive and generative manifestation of the connection between people and their work that scholars have studied" (Wrzesniewski, 2011, p. 45). A calling can be thought of as the force that summons a person to pursue a career for the fulfillment that the work itself brings, not focusing on financial gains or other external incentives. It is experienced as the enactment of personally significant beliefs and values, the reflection of one's identity (Wrzesniewski et al., 1997), and the expression of one's purpose in life and true self (e.g., Hall & Chandler, 2005; Levoy, 1997). Approaching work as a calling is associated with positive personal and professional outcomes, and those who view their work as a calling are less likely to suffer from stress and depression (Bunderson & Thompson, 2009).

So how does a student ascertain his or her calling, addressing the most fundamental human question, "What should I do with my life?" Palmer (2000) suggests that determining one's vocation is not an act of will focused on establishing goals and plans, but rather an ongoing act of listening to the calling of one's life. He emphasizes the importance of trying to understand one's life apart from both perceived external expectations and from internal expectations of what one might like to be, as opposed to who one really is. Palmer notes that "vocation" is rooted in the Latin word for "voice." The real question of vocation is not "What should I do with my life?" but rather, the questions are more fundamental, such as "Who am I?" and "What is my nature?" One's vocation is not a goal to pursue but a calling to be heard through becoming clearer about one's identity, standards, yearnings, and values (Palmer, 2000, pp. 4–5). It is important to listen not only to strengths and virtues but also to liabilities and limitations, which provide valuable information.

Palmer (2000) likens the process of listening for one's calling to an ancient pilgrimage, which is a difficult journey involving hardships and fear but ultimately has transformative and growthful outcomes. Understanding ourselves and the patterns of our life history is the true foundation of career decision making. Our lives give clues to our identity and vocation, which can be difficult to decipher, but trying to interpret these clues can yield meaningful information that can help guide both our personal and career journey. Research indicates that viewing one's career as a calling is correlated with desirable outcomes related to both career and general well-being (Dik, Duffy, & Eldridge, 2009).

Levoy (1997) also delves into the dilemma of finding one's calling, advising that it must be grounded in the habit of self-reflection, or more simply, talking to oneself. This is often an angst-ridden process, filled with stress and confusion. College students often experience great anxiety trying to determining whether their thoughts, feelings, and interests signify a true calling or simply fool's gold or a mistaken passing fancy. Levoy (1997) suggests that a calling is likely to be true if it keeps coming back and does not go away. In spite of ambiguity or mixed emotions, at a deeper level it feels "right." The mundane tasks are not dreaded, and the person looks forward to and feels energized by the tasks of the work. Callings are generally questions that often rock the boat because they tend to be unexpected. For Levoy (1997), the most fundamental question is "What do you love?" (p. 31). He observes that the word *passion* derives from the Latin *passio* for suffering. Callings do not always feel welcome, for example, the student who feels pulled to teach even though accounting would better support the life style she wants. They also tend to keep resurfacing until they are addressed. Engagement is key—callings cannot transform into careers without action being taken. This is often a scary process—by attempting nothing, there is no chance of failure. However, as Levoy (1997) notes, without action, nightmares will not occur, but neither will our dreams.

The anxiety surrounding this process is the prospect of getting it wrong and of investing time, effort, and part of one's life in something that may not be right. How do we know whether we are responding to a "true" calling? Our energy level is another good clue, which can be ascertained by questions such as the following: "How did it *feel* to act on a calling? Did you feel more awake? Was there a kind of rightness to your actions? Did you experience a flood of energy? . . . Did you feel gratitude? . . . Did your friends declare that they haven't seen you so excited in a long time?" (Levoy, 1997, p. 38).

Wisdom and perspective can often be broadened through looking at the practices and traditions of other cultures. The Quakers have a tradition of providing what they call "clearness committees" to any member struggling for clarity in discerning a call and responding to it. The individual invites up of half a dozen friends, colleagues, mentors, even strangers to gather at the meeting. The committee first observes a period of meaningful silence. The rules of the clearness committee are simply to ask questions only. No advice, storytelling, windy narratives, problem solving, or challenging is allowed. "Simply pose questions in a spirit of caring rather than even curiosity, evocation rather than imposition. The goal is not so much to comprehend as to apprehend." (Levoy, 1997, p. 41). In essence, the framework is to ask questions designed to tap the wisdom and prompt clarity within the individual. The Western tendency is frequently toward being proactive and action oriented, and when confronted with career uncertainty, it is very tempting to try to problem-solve and reduce the anxiety inherent to the process. However, by assuming that the answers reside within the person seeking clarity, asking questions designed to elicit strengths and tightly held values seems to engage the focus of the person in a way that makes hearing his or her own inner guidance more possible.

Career Flow

The metaphor of navigating a white water river, which evokes both excitement and fear and requires using adaptive strategies and skills to navigate successfully, is used to describe the approach of "career flow" (Niles, Amundson, and Neault, 2011). The framework strives to provide practical, grounded steps for both listening to and acting upon callings. Career flow competencies to be nurtured and developed include: (1) hope, (2) self-reflection, (3) self-clarity, (4) visioning, (5) goal setting and planning, and (6) implementing/adapting. These competencies are derived from human agency theory (Bandura, 2001), and they emphasize understanding oneself and developing, implementing, and adjusting plans based on new learning. Each of these components will be more fully described:

> *Hopefulness*—relates to envisioning a meaningful goal and believing that positive outcomes are likely to occur when action is taken. Having a sense of hope enables considering the possibilities of situations and propels action. The focus of this competency is to identify meaningful goals toward which the client is motivated and enhancing the client's capacity to develop specific strategies for achieving these goals.
>
> *Self-reflection*—is the awareness and examination of one's thoughts, beliefs, and circumstances. Related to career counseling, it involves taking time to consider one's identity, current life, and the life hoped for. Career clients can be prompted to consider and explore many possible questions, such as: What is important to me? What skills do I enjoy using? What skills would I like to develop? What sort of lifestyle would I like to live? How

effectively am I using the talents I want to use, engaging in activities that I enjoy, and participating in activities that are important to me? Do I have a vision for my future?

Self-Clarity—is the foundation of self-reflection and self-awareness. Human nature tends to desire certainty over ambiguity; however, denying uncertainty can give a false sense of control over our lives, and it can cause us to avoid taking on the challenge of defining who we are and what we want from life. The basic starting point of developing self-clarity is for the client to give himself permission to remain uncertain while exploring and determining what he wants to experience in his career.

Visioning—is the process of thinking about future career possibilities and identifying desired future outcomes. Niles et al. (2011) suggest thinking of admired qualities of role models and also journaling and looking for recurring themes. Visioning can also be guided by reflecting upon "flow" experiences experienced while working various jobs or volunteer activities.

Goal setting and planning—follows visioning and involves creating action steps to transform visions into goals by creating both short- and long-term goals. Hope can be engendered during this process by developing pathways to begin to bring the vision into reality.

Implementing/adapting—focuses on the practical skills necessary to respond to a calling by taking the steps to secure a job and start on a career. This stage involves resume writing, networking, etc. Students can conduct "culture audits" to identify some of the subtle indicators of what it will be like to work within the professions being considered.

Putting Student Strengths to Work

Part of listening to our calling involves becoming more deeply aware of our strengths. Our strengths are an expression of our talents and passions, and they reflect our life story of what we have chosen to invest in and develop. Our callings are often embodied in our strengths and in the activities we do well and feel compelled to learn more about and to improve. Strengths can be identified in many ways, both formal and informal. Formal methods include measures such as the Clifton StrengthsFinder (Lopez, Hodges, & Harter, 2005), which is a web-based assessment instrument that identifies an individual's top five strengths or "themes" from among 34 possibilities. However, good assessment also involves triangulation of methods, meaning that more sources of information yield more comprehensive and better information, and different sources used in combination create "triangles" by their different sources and perspectives. Asking directly about a person's strengths typically is of limited value. Although this may be changing in the age of Facebook, we are typically taught to be humble, and it can feel uncomfortable to directly articulate our strengths. However, indirect questions can be very useful:

- What talents were you surprised to discover that you had at your last part time job?
- How would your friends describe you?
- When your girlfriend brags about you, what does she say?

Paying attention to flow experiences (Csikszentmihalyi, 1990) can also serve as a clue to our strengths. Flow experiences are those in which we feel "in the zone," when we are totally immersed in the activity, when we lose awareness of ourselves, and time seems to stand still. We are most likely to experience flow when we are using our strengths in activities that are challenging yet within our ability range. Surprisingly, we are also most likely to experience flow at work, because if our job is well-suited, we have many opportunities to use our strengths through our work (Csikszentmihalyi, 1990). Other clues for strengths include consistently good performance, the desire to learn more, the feeling of satisfaction, and a feeling of energy that arises from using the strength.

Shushok and Hulme (2006) reflect that a strengths approach helps shape a student's sense of identity through the emergence of possible selves. By knowing our strengths, we know ourselves. "Intentionally enabling students to identify, understand, and leverage their talents, passions, and strengths allows their unique genius to emerge and sets them on a course for success" (Shushok & Hulme, 2006, p. 4). The process of learning what is right about themselves and identifying their strengths helps students begin the process of learning how their talents and interests can be used for both career and personal opportunities.

Experiencing positive emotions can help augment the benefit of an individual's strengths. Research on the Broaden-and-Build model (Fredrickson, 1998, 2001; Fredrickson & Branigan, 2001) suggests that experiencing positive emotions tends to increase creative problem-solving strategies, the awareness of personal resources, and task persistence. The positive emotions prompted by the identification of strengths may enable the utilization of these strengths in a more enthusiastic manner (Bowers & Lopez, 2010). College students who feel supported and encouraged by parents, friends, or their career counselor will likely feel a more positive affect, which can translate to being open to new ideas, activities, and increased engagement. Career exploration discussion groups can also be very helpful in this process.

Bowers and Lopez (2010) note the importance of creating opportunities for success, which can help students capitalize or leverage their strengths. Successful goal pursuits may increase the likelihood for generating a greater number of pathways to future goals and increasing the sense of personal agency, ultimately facilitating greater goal achievement. Moreover, when people share news of a positive event with others or celebrate accomplishments, the positive emotion they experience is magnified beyond the increases associated with the positive event itself. A possible mechanism for this increased benefit is that sharing with others requires retelling the event, which creates an opportunity for reliving and re-experiencing the event, and may build social resources by fostering positive social interactions, which are reinforcing in and of themselves (Gable, Reis, Impett, & Asher, 2004). Career exploration support groups and regular check-in and sharing time in career and life-planning classes offer a possible means of facilitating social support and opportunities to reinforce the usage of strengths.

Planned Happenstance: Increased Opportunities and Knowledge Through Engagement

Career counseling is often based in the logical but ungrounded framework that self-awareness + career awareness = a satisfying career decision (Miller, 1983, p. 16). The traditional career counseling approach assumes that the career process is linear, straightforward, and rational, and that good information equals good decision making (Mitchell, Levin, & Krumboltz, 1999). However, in all likelihood, reflecting upon your own career path, and those of friends and family, reveals that career paths are seldom straight forward and predictable. Krumboltz (2009) noted that he has asked hundreds of people in career counseling workshops if they had decided to be a career counselor when they were 18, and no one has ever said yes. The focus of career counseling should not be on trying to predict occupational goals but on preparing career clients to better take advantage of opportunities (for both career exploration and career development) as they present themselves.

Miller (1983) encourages career counselors to view happenstance as normal, natural, and an unavoidable aspect of career choice and to emphasize to clients that they learn about both their career interests and aptitudes through the plethora of everyday activities. Within a planned happenstance perspective, learning and adaptability are the primary goals, and the attributes of willingness to change plans, take risks, work hard to overcome obstacles, and be actively engaged in pursuing their interests are encouraged and cultivated (Mitchell, Levin, & Krumboltz, 1999, p. 118). Thomas Edison advised that "opportunity is missed by most people because it is dressed in overalls and looks like work" (as quoted in Mason, 1990, p. 55).

The planned happenstance theory consists of two premises: (1) exploration generates chance opportunities, and (2) skills enable people to better seize opportunities. Responses to chance opportunities depend upon preparedness and openness to possibilities. The greater the sense of personal agency an individual has, the more likely he or she is to capitalize on opportunities and realize desired futures, especially given plentiful social support (Bandura, 1982). A sense of personal agency can be strengthened by the development of skills and competencies, increasing the percept of self-efficacy, and self-regulatory capacities for exercising self-directedness. "Mastering the tools of personal agency does not necessarily assure desired futures. But with such skills people are better able to provide supports and direction for their actions, to capitalize on planned or fortuitous opportunities, to resist social traps that lead down detrimental paths, and to disengage themselves from such predicaments should they become enmeshed in them" (Bandura, 1982, p. 754). Therefore, helping to strengthen the client's sense of personal agency is an essential component of the career counseling process.

Gelatt (1989) expands upon planned happenstance by positing the concept of "positive uncertainty" to help career clients deal with ambiguity, accept inconsistency, and use the intuitive side of decision making. This paradigm seems especially appropriate because the world of work is becoming ever more rapidly changing and unstable. The goal of career counseling is not the singular focus of making an occupational decision, but the goal is "to facilitate the learning of skills, interests, beliefs, values, work habits, and personal qualities that enable each client to create a satisfying life within a constantly changing work environment" (Krumboltz, 1996, p. 61).

However, for opportunities to be realized, action must be taken. Career counselors are encouraged to raise awareness of and cultivate the following positive personal characteristics that are correlated with creating and using chance opportunities:

- Curiosity: exploring new learning opportunities
- Persistence: exerting effort despite setbacks
- Flexibility: change attitudes and circumstances
- Optimism: viewing new opportunities as possible and attainable
- Risk Taking: taking action in the face of uncertainty (Mitchell, Levin, & Krumboltz, 1999, p. 118)

Krumboltz (2009) details the process of career counseling from a planned happenstance orientation (pp. 147–149):

1. *Orient client expectations.* Prepare clients for a counseling process in which unexpected events are regarded as normal and necessary. Helpful statements might include:
   - Anxiety about planning the future is normal and can be replaced by a sense of adventure.
   - Naming your future occupation is only one possible starting point for exploring career opportunities.

2. *Identify the client's concern as the starting place.* Help clients identify what would make their lives more satisfying.
   - Can you describe activities in your life where you feel energized?
   - How did you happen to discover these energizing activities?
3. *Empower clients to see that their past successes contain lessons for present actions.* Ask clients for stories of how unplanned events have influenced their lives or careers.
   - What have you done in the past that put you in a position to be influenced by it?
   - How did you recognize the opportunity?
   - After the event, what did you do to capitalize on it?
4. *Sensitize clients to recognize potential opportunities.* Help them to learn to reframe unplanned events as career opportunities.
   - Tell me a chance event you wish would happen to you.
   - How can you act now to increase the likelihood of that desirable event?
   - How would your life change if you acted?
   - How would your life change if you did nothing?
5. *Overcome blocks to action.* Help clients to overcome dysfunctional beliefs that block constructive action.
   - What do you believe is stopping you from doing what you really want to do?
   - What do you believe is a first step you could take now to move one step closer to what you want?
   - What do you believe is stopping you from taking that first step?

The ultimate goal of career counseling from a planned happenstance perspective is to help clients become actively engaged in seeking, recognizing, and capitalizing on opportunities. If personal agency is nurtured and developed, the individual will be able to learn and benefit from everyday interactions with the world. Similar to teaching a child how to ride a bicycle, the learning occurs through experience, not through "a lecture on the importance of adjusting the balance and manipulating the steering" (Krumboltz, 2009, p. 150). The career counselor guides the client through the process, recognizing that the occasional skinned knee is a necessary part of the learning process.

Eliciting Client Wisdom Through Positively Focused Questions

To a large degree, the effectiveness of career counseling depends on artfully and skillfully asking questions that prompt the client to consider herself and her future from a new and richer perspective. Two counseling and exploration approaches, Appreciative Inquiry (AI) and Narrative/Constructivist Therapy, as adapted to career counseling, will be described in detail, with examples of questions to pose. Both of these models are very well suited for a positive psychology-based career counseling approach because they aim to elicit client strengths and possibilities.

Appreciative Inquiry

AI (e.g., Cooperrider & Whitney, 2000; Whitney & Trosten-Bloom, 2003) was originally developed as a model to facilitate organizational change; however, the principles also apply to promoting change and growth in individuals. AI is grounded in the premise that identifying and appreciating the strengths already present in an organization or an individual can cause them to amplify. Positively oriented questions are carefully and intentionally used to illuminate and build upon strengths. Many of AIs' guiding philosophies and techniques can be recognized as a blending of positive psychology and solution-focused therapy.

The 4-D model (e.g., Cooperrider, Whitney, & Stavros, 2005), consisting of the four stages of Discovery, Dream, Design, and Destiny, operationalizes the guiding principles of AI into a pragmatic coaching approach. Each stage will be described along with practical applications to career counseling. As the name AI suggests, AI emphasizes appreciating the best of what is already present. This includes asking about strengths, accomplishments, values, virtues, dreams, and aspirations. Change is regarded as occurring the moment a question is asked, captured in the tenet, "inquiry is intervention" (Whitney & Trosten-Bloom, 2002). Growth-facilitating questions need to be positively focused, asking about what the individual wants more of or wants to expand, versus asking about problems or what needs to be fixed. A foundational premise of AI is that the focus of inquiry is on a *topic,* not a *goal,* because a goal-focused mentality can tend to shut down the exploration process, whereas focusing on a topic allows for perusal and "wiggle room." In *Letters to a Young Poet,* Rainer Marie Rilke (1987) recommended that we embrace questions that engage us to think about our best selves, without trying to figure out too quickly what the answers might be. As career considerations are explored, the counselor will help the client to begin to reflect more expansively on what he or she wants to create and become, and to flesh out his or her picture of success. Good AI questions are meant to express curiosity, not judgment, and to invite multiple answers rather than the "right" one, and to serve as thought starters (Orem, Binkert, & Clancy, 2007).

Stage 1: Discovery

In career counseling, both the client and the counselor, not uncommonly, feel pressure to quickly get something done, and move from the uncomfortable state of uncertainty or ambiguity to the more comfortable and secure state of decidedness. The initial stage of AI, the Discovery Stage, is focused on reflecting and appreciating, and it sets the tone for viewing the task of career exploration as a process. By asking about high-point experiences and times when the client felt particularly energized and excited about an activity or her work, counselors can provide fertile ground for helping the client to reflect on and appreciate her strengths and values (Orem, Binkert, & Clancy, 2007). As with all counseling, the more specific the client is in describing these details, the more powerful the experience becomes, especially because attention is paid to the details that made the experience significant for the client.

Possible Discovery Stage questions include:

- Describe your three greatest accomplishments to date.
- What made these accomplishments stand out for you?
- Who are your role models?
- What attributes of these role models do you admire or appreciate?
- What would you like to contribute to the world?
- What are you most wanting to achieve in the next three years? (adapted from Orem, Binkert, & Clancy, 2007).

Stage 2: Dream

The purpose of the Dream Stage is to build upon the exploration of the Discovery Stage and to start thinking about the possibilities. This phase is identified with the question "what might be?" (Cooperrider, Whitney, & Stavos, 2005, p. 417). The career counselor supports the client in articulating a meaningful picture of the future, which is regarded as an intentional, deliberate process. Clients are encouraged to describe their dream in an active voice and in the present tense so that it feels as if it were already manifest. The dream for the future is encouraged to be expansive and not constrained by pragmatic limitations or obstacles. It is also expected to be grounded in the client's history and personal characteristics, so that it is aspirational but not mere fantasy.

Possible Dream Stage questions include:

- What is the world calling for you to be?
- What are the most enlivening and exciting possibilities for you?
- What is the inspiration for your life?
- Thinking about the times you were most happy, what about those times would you want to carry into the future?
- What do you notice about yourself as you dream into the future?

- If you could communicate with yourself into the future, what questions would you want to ask yourself? What would you like others to ask you?
- What would your mentor (mom, dad, grandmother, best friend) wish for you for your future? (Orem, Binkert, & Clancy, 2007, pp. 140 & 147)

As clients reflect on their successes and high-point experiences, they are encouraged to consider what factors accounted for their success and to note vital life themes or values contained in their reflections to help guide their aspirations (Schutt, 2007). The following prompts are suggested to help students begin to picture themselves in their preferred career:

- The best work situation for me is one where I . . .
- The most important life giving forces that I need to carry forward are . . .
- My ideal work-life scenario would be . . .
- My ideal position gives me energy and a feeling of purpose because . . . (Schutt, 2007, p. 29).

Stage 3: Design

The purpose of the Design Stage is to direct attention and action and to help the client begin to bring the dream into reality. However, an overly detailed plan should be avoided because that can restrict the client from taking advantage of opportunities that may naturally emerge and overly narrow the focus (Orem, Binkert, and Clancy, 2007, p. 150). The counselor assists the client to focus on compelling priorities, reflect on ways she is already living her dream, and begin to take actions to incorporate elements of the dream into the everyday present. Asking the client to picture the dream fully realized and what the daily activities and behaviors would look like can be very helpful. Asking what activity or step would have the most leverage can help clients get the process started. Schutt (2007) suggests encouraging clients to break through their self-imposed limitations by asking questions such as, "If you were to be ten times more bold in the pursuit of your ideal work-life scenario, what would you do?" (p. 30).

Stage 4: Destiny

This final stage emphasizes the process of making plans to bring the dream to fruition. Schutt (2007) outlines a process for developing an action plan:

1. For each of the goals, identify two or three action steps necessary to get the goal moving and headed in the right direction.
2. Identify the goals and action steps that draw on strengths, life-giving forces, and wishes.

3. Identify which of the goals and action steps that something can be done about and that are within the participant's ability to influence the outcome.

4. What is the smallest step that could be taken that would have the largest impact? (p. 31)

In addition, it can be beneficial to identify any possible obstacles and ways they can be effectively managed.

Narrative and Constructivist Counseling

Narrative counseling (e.g., White & Epston, 1990) posits that our identity and therefore our choices are shaped by the accounts we hold of our lives as filtered through our stories or narratives. The narrative approach emphasizes trying to expand the client's usually narrow perspective of himself or herself and asking the client to envision different possible narratives and future directions. Narrative counseling is grounded in social constructionism, which emphasizes the postmodern tenets of collaboration, nondirectiveness, and multiple perspectives (Whiting, 2007), which fits perfectly with the exploratory nature of career counseling.

From the Narrative perspective, career counseling is viewed as a meaning-making endeavor, a process for making the client's life patterns intelligible to him or her and for modifying the client's narratives about the self from a constructivist perspective (Savickas, 1995). This model focuses on clarifying life themes, which enhances the ability of clients to decide and ease into forward movement. This is combined with attention to the practical skills and steps needed to attain a job in the desired profession.

Similar to Levoy's (1997) conceptualization of a true calling as a knocking that cannot be ignored and will not go away, the constructivist career counselor seeks to elicit stories that reveal the client's *preoccupation* or central life concern and stories that reveal what they plan to do about their preoccupation (Savickas, 1995). The counselor seeks to elicit and understand the client's identity, often starting at the beginning of the client's life, by asking for stories about his family and being alert to hints of struggle or imbalance in the story that can often point to the preoccupation or thematic problem around which the client organizes his life. For example, the student who had to care for a sick parent may express their thematic problem through the desire to become a nurse or a researcher trying to find a cure. Questions about role models while growing up, favorite books and movies (asking the client to elaborate on the plot), favorite motto or saying, and favorite subjects during junior high and high school can also be used to help elucidate the client's "career story" (Savickas, 1998). Similar to Murray's (1938) thesis of the "life press" that serves as the foundation for the Thematic Apperception

Test, constructivist counseling posits that the type of stories that may be most useful in recognizing life project are stories about the client's heroes and heroines because these role models illustrate narratives for problem solving that the client has intentionally adopted.

Savikas (1998) suggests directly addressing the client's indecision before stepping into the future:

- How does it feel to be undecided?
- Of what does this feeling remind you?
- Tell me an incident in which you had this same feeling.
- Do you have any idea of what haunts you?
- What part of your life story is most important to your current indecision? (p. 369)

Clarifying the indecision prepares the client to extend the imaginative plot lines into the future. Particular attention should be given to stories that reveal life patterns, indicate meaning, and hint at future solutions to old problems. "Narratives that situate career indecision in the context of a life theme, with its central preoccupation and corresponding plot, serve to clarify choices and enhance the ability to decide. When clients envision the future as a continuation of their stories, they can overcome their hesitation and author the next chapter." (Savikas, 1998, p. 371)

Savikas (1998) asserts five steps for Constructivist Counseling for Career Indecision:

1) Counselor collects from the client stories that reveal the client's life theme.
2) Counselor narrates the theme to the client.
3) Client and counselor discuss the meaning of the current indecision by relating it to the life theme.
4) Client and counselor extend the theme into the future by naming interests and occupations that address the preoccupation and project that define the life theme.
5) Client and counselor rehearse behavioral skills needed to specify and implement a career choice. (p. 367)

Pressures that interfere with hearing or acting upon callings need to be illuminated and addressed. Successful narrative career counseling can help clients to connect with their dreams and passions, which provides energy and focus to the career decision and pursuing process. This can serve as momentum-building way to lay the foundation for transitioning to the action stage of combining goals with the practical steps necessary to bring them to fruition.

Career Decision Making: A Life Long Journey of the Head and the Heart

Traditional career counseling focuses on attempting to identify interests, aptitudes, and the person-environment fit to provide clients with information from which to make informed and logical career decisions. In contrast, the goal of positive career counseling is to identify strengths and "callings" and to help clients to create situations to utilize and leverage their talents and passions. This is seen as a life-long process involving logic, emotions, and values.

Most of us overly identify with the rational aspect of our personality and tend to think that we make choices based mainly on reason. (We also tend to struggle to understand the logic of those who make different choices than we do.) In their study of problem solving, Heppner and Krauskopf (1987) note that contrary to what we want to believe, "people are often quite unsystematic and irrational" (p. 376). Jonathan Haidt, author of *The Happiness Hypothesis* (2006), aptly notes that neither reason nor intuition/emotion is better or worse than the other, but it is imperative that we listen to the information from both "sides." He brilliantly describes this with the metaphor of the self as an elephant and a rider, with the rider representing reason and logic and the much larger elephant representing everything else—our emotions, family history, genetics, habits, etc. It is clear which part is bigger and stronger, and we ignore or underestimate the elephant only at our peril. Haidt (2006) goes on to observe that we often confabulate, meaning that we find reasons to believe what we want to believe, but that reason usually comes after emotion. In fact, observations of patients who have brain impairments and are physically incapable of feeling emotions are functionally debilitated, because without the guiding force of emotions they are incapable of making even the simplest of decisions such as what to have for lunch.

Similar to Plato's analogy of the self as the chariot driver of two horses, one guided by reason and the other by wild instinct, the key is to emphasize the importance of both logic and intuition without overemphasizing either and have them both work together as a team. Both provide very valuable information, but the key is that the knowledge base of both is increased through interaction with the world. Knowledge of work is gained through extracurricular activities, internships, summer jobs, volunteer activities, etc.

Career counselors, in addition to helping clients with the systematic and rational aspects of career decision making, just as importantly also need to assist with the unsystematic and nonrational aspects of choosing. Decision making is a nonsequential, nonsystematic, nonscientific human process. The assumption that goals precede action is often mistaken, and starting with clear objectives in career counseling can often discourage people from making choices that lead to new experiences (Gelatt, 1989). Helping people create satisfying lives for themselves is a far more complex and important goal than merely declaring an occupational aspiration (Krumboltz, 1998). Therefore, the purpose of career counseling is "to facilitate the learning of skills, interests, beliefs, values, work habits, and personal qualities that enable each client to create a satisfying life within a constantly changing work environment" (Krumboltz, 1996, p. 61).

Career counseling is gradually moving away from the focus on "the match" of person with job to that of focusing on adapting to change. This mirrors the increased need for adaptability within the current employment milieu, which is likely to become even more transitory and unstable, and to further value the employee skills of flexibility and comfort with change. The trilateral model of adaptive career decision making (Krieshok, Black, & McKay, 2009) includes rational and intuitive mechanisms of career decision making, which are both grounded and kept in check by engagement. Rational and intuitive processes for decision making are both important, providing different but equally useful sets of information, but engagement (testing the ideas through real-life experiences) is critical for the process to be truly effective. This model is explicitly adaptive, emphasizing the important nature of consistently re-evaluating the fluid person-environment career fit, and implicitly encourages the career client to learn a process to become their own career counselor.

It is easy to prize reason and rationality when making choices; however, closer examination reveals that we tend to utilize both reason and experience when faced with decisions. Engagement leads to having a greater wealth of experiences and therefore a greater source of information from which to draw. "Through occupational engagement, vocational and self-schemas evolve and vocational judgments and decisions are more informed, as are judgments about the larger host of life matters" (Krieshok et al., 2009, p. 284). The ability to adapt career decision making, based on the accumulation of information and experience, is made possible by occupational engagement. Engagement becomes the basis for recognizing patterns in one's life and increasing awareness of the self in the world through experiences with the world, and, in a sense, become an expert on one's life. Activities that create engagement serve to "fund the bank of information that the individual can draw upon" (Krieshok et al., 2009, p. 284) when making career decisions. Krieshok et al. (2009) note that career counselors can never go wrong by prescribing the gathering of varied experiences. Schreiner (2010) notes that when engaged learning is blended with such factors as academic determination, a positive perspective, and social connectedness, that thriving tends to be the outcome. This also helps students to move from the question of "Who am I?" to the more goal directed question of "Who do I want to become?"

Both rationality and intuition become richer through more and varied experiences, and this is especially so if the client is asked to think and feel about experiential information in an intentional way. An adaptive career decision maker will view career decision making as a life-long process, and he or she will be open to change as needed or as beneficial, which is becoming increasingly more important as the employment world is changing at ever more breathtaking speeds. Effective career counseling is not a one-time activity of helping a student to decide on a career path before graduating, but rather it is helping the person to learn a process to use continuously throughout life as they need to adapt to workplace changes and re-evaluate and alter their career trajectory periodically on an ongoing basis.

Multicultural Considerations

The population of the United States is becoming increasingly diverse, and it is projected that people of color will become the majority in the not so distant future. However, many of the pre-eminent career theories were developed based on European American expectations and values, such as individualism and opportunity being available to all. Flores and Heppner (2002) posit that "career counselors are in the unique position to serve as social justice advocates in help-ing racial and ethnic minorities move into the schools and workplaces that have long discriminated against and marginalized them" (p. 181). It is important for career counselors to be mindful of the impact of cultural and ethnic background on perceptions of career opportunities and the career process, such as the pres-sure an international student may feel to get a high-paying job to make the family sacrifice worthwhile, and to regard career development as a dynamic interaction between the person and his or her environment. Flores and Heppner (2002) advise that career counselors need to help ethnic or racial minority clients exam-ine and understand how their ideas about different careers have been formed. Minority groups may perceive that only a shortened list of possible careers is available to them, whether through lack of exposure to various professions or lack of role modeling by family or friends. Exploring how racism, sexism, and poverty may have influenced the client's self-efficacy beliefs can be very valuable and help the client to increase their personal sense of agency as well as help to broaden the realm of perceived possibilities. Encouraging the use of social networks and role models can be of particular benefit to racial and ethnic minority clients. Bandura (1986) suggests that role models that are considered similar to oneself are the most powerful for changing self-efficacy beliefs.

Practitioners of this positive psychology-based career counseling model need to fully appreciate the challenges that can be presented by the employ-ment environment and also by internal negative self-expectations grounded in historical inequalities. Positive career counseling, focusing on the identification and amplification of dreams, values, and aspirations and incorporating the narra-tive perspective of re-visioning one's life story is inherently well-suited for work-ing with clients from all backgrounds. Reflecting on the hidden potential of a strength-based perspective, Shushok and Hulme (2006) note that the identification of strengths enables the person to understand both himself, but also to recognize that he needs others with complementary strengths. Thus, a strength-based perspective can serve as a vehicle or perspective through which to appreciate diversity in the real world.

Case Example

Jacob is a 21-year-old White college junior. In some ways, he is the model college student. He is very bright and has made good grades in all of his classes. However, because he has abilities in many areas, he has already switched majors three times, and he is frustrated with himself that he does not have a clear career direction, especially because it seems to him that most of his friends do, and his parents are pressuring to choose a high-paying profession and be focused in his efforts so that he does not become a 6th-year senior.

He comes to the career center and meets with you for the initial session experiencing a mixture of emotions—hopefulness to get resolution for his uncertainty and also some urgency because he is already a semester behind as a result of having a history of "major switching." As you listen to what he is looking for from you and the career counseling process, you acknowledge the difficulty with decision making that he faces as a student who has the ability to be successful in many different areas, and you commend him for his willingness to have tried several different directions already. You discuss with him the strength of character that he has shown not to quickly make a decision just to "get the process over with." He seems to experience noticeable relief at hearing this, and he mumbles that he has been "beating himself up a lot" for being behind schedule. Jacob asks you about the instruments that he has heard you will administer to him. He says he knows that an assessment or two will not magically tell him what to do with the rest of his life, but he does want something to help him figure out what career path he should be attempting, something better than his own efforts have produced so far.

You explain to him that you will be working from a positive career counseling model and will discuss the basics of the framework and the rationale for the approach. You explain that although you will be utilizing some assessment instruments to provide additional information and providing some information and suggestions, that this endeavor will be a collaborative effort, and that he is the expert on his life and his goals and dreams. Ultimately, the goal will be for him to achieve greater career decision and direction and be equipped with practical steps to take to translate these goals into career success. He will also learn a process that he can utilize periodically as his desires or work changes and he wants or needs to revise his career path.

You ask Jacob to tell you about how he chose the three majors he has pursued. As he explains his choices and reasons, you listen for hints of passion and energy and also for obstacles and pressures he has felt. You ask about his high-point experiences, events or times throughout his life when it felt like he was in flow, and wanted to learn more about what he was doing. Jacob details that he has tried biology, pre-med, and graphic design as majors because he likes science and has an aptitude for it, and he wants to somehow combine his interest in art for his career. He reflected that he often spends hours just drawing sketches, and he even shows you the sketch pad he keeps in his backpack. Although he has liked various aspects of the three majors he attempted, he never felt like he fit in well with the other students who seemed committed to the fields they had chosen. You prompt him to envision different career futures, and you also stress to him the importance of engagement. Then, you give him the assignment of conducting informational interviews with 2–3 people who have careers that look appealing to him.

You also continue to help him reframe the career exploration process, empowering him to see that his past successes likely contain the plan for present actions. You emphasize that the path may continue to be nonlinear but that it is important for him to recognize the often disguised opportunities that will be knocking. As you explain the concept of planned happenstance, he understands that it is important for him to increase the likelihood for positive opportunities to occur. He continues to check in with you periodically during his next two years until graduation, because he decides to stick with biology but also to take computer-assisted design and graphic design classes to help him pursue his dream of becoming a medical illustrator. He is also becoming more comfortable allowing himself to be immersed in both the biology and medical field and also the illustration and design realms, and he has become active in school organizations in both. You assisted him to find an internship later in his junior year, and during his senior year, given your good relationship, he has come to your office several times for help with his resume and to do mock interviews. You have stressed to him that he seems to have developed the vitally important skill of willingness to investigate and to use the resources available to him.

Conclusion

In personal counseling, specific concerns such as anxiety, depression, adjustment issues, etc. almost always serve as the impetus that compels the person to seek psychotherapy. The ultimate goal of therapy, although not usually identified as such by the client until late in the process, is not merely to resolve the presenting concern but to also give the client the tools to effectively "become their own therapist" and to be able to effectively manage similar difficulties should they arise in the future. A similar process occurs with career counseling. Clients invariably arrive at the career center anxiously wanting to know what career they should pick, what job the aptitude tests say is right for them, and how to get a job. Personal counseling stresses that discomfort is not to be avoided but embraced and understood. Career anxiety for the client is not to be pushed through, but rather the client is encouraged to give herself permission to be with the process for a while and swim around in the uncertainty and to be open to the possibilities that might be present. Adept career counselors will be able to tease out and amplify the energy and excitement as clients begin to draw upon both their reason and intuition and identify career possibilities that seem to call to them. Career counselors also can help give clients practical tools to help to leverage opportunities, e.g., encouraging networking, creating an "elevator speech," etc. The idea of teaching the client to fish versus telling them which fish is the right fish and handing it to them is especially important because the world of work is becoming increasing competitive and rapidly changing, and the attributes of flexibility and adaptability are paramount.

The focus on identifying and using strengths serves as the foundation for the development of a firmly grounded positive psychology perspective that will have benefits beyond the career exploration and decision-making stage. Understanding and appreciating one's strengths leads to increased personal agency, which can provide confidence and motivation to attempt more challenges and to better weather the inevitable storms in both personal and professional realms. Intentionally strengthening one's individual positive psychology constructs, such as hope, self-efficacy, and curiosity can serve as the bedrock of future, ongoing career self-exploration and decision making. Moreover, focusing on possibilities and having a positive perspective has also been found to be associated with higher salaries and greater career advancement, as well as a myriad of emotional of health benefits (Seligman, 2002).

The career counselor of the past was a person who provided information. The positive career counselor of the future will be a person who guides the client through the process of creating greater understanding of the self, the world, and the interaction between the two. The counselor also fosters the development of the life-long skills of engagement and learning to adeptly use both the intuitive and rational information gained from experience to guide ongoing career decision making.

References

Bandura, A. (1982). The psychology of chance encounters and life paths. *American Psychologist*, 37(7), 747–755.

Bandura, A. (1986). *Social foundations of thought and action*. Englewood Cliffs, NJ.

Bandura, A. (2001). Social cognitive theory: An agentic perspective. *Annual Review of Psychology,* 52(1), 1–26

Bowers, K. M., & Lopez, S. J. (2010). Capitalizing on personal strengths in college. *Journal of College and Character,* 11(1), 1–11.

Bunderson, J. S., & Thompson, J. A. (2009). The call of the wild: Zookeepers, callings, and the dual edges of deeply meaningful work. *Administrative Science Quarterly,* 54(1), 32–57.

Cochran, L. (1991). *Life-shaping decisions.* New York: Peter Lang.

Cooperrider, D. L., Whitney, D., & Stavros, J. M. (2005). *Appreciative Inquiry handbook.* San Fransisco: Berrett-Koehler.

Cooperrider, D. L., & Whitney, D. (2000). A positive revolution in change: Appreciative Inquiry. In D. L. Cooperrider, P. F. Sorensen, Jr., D. Whitney, & T. F. Yaeger (Eds.), *Appreciative Inquiry: Rethinking human organization toward a positive theory of change.* Champaign, IL: Stipes Publishing, L.L.C.

Csikszentmihalyi, M. (1990). *Flow.* New York: Harper & Row, Publishers, Inc.

Dik, B. J., Duffy, R. D., & Eldridge, B. M. (2009). Calling and vocation in career counseling: Recommendations for promoting meaningful work. *Professional Psychology: Research And Practice,* 40(6), 625–632.

Flores, L. Y., & Heppner, M. J. (2002). Multicultural career counseling: Ten essentials for training. *Journal of Career Development,* 28(3), 181–2002.

Fredrickson, B. L. (1998). What good are positive emotions? *Review of General Psychology,* 2(3), 300–319.

Fredrickson, B. (2001). The role of positive emotions in positive psychology: The Broaden-and-Build theory of positive emotions. *American Psychologist,* 56(3), 218–226.

Fredrickson, B. L., & Branigan, C. A. (2001). Positive emotions. In T. J. Mayne & G. A. Bonnano (Eds.) *Emotion: Current issues and future developments* (pp. 123–151). New York: Guilford Press.

Gable, S. L., Reis, H. T., Impett, E., & Asher, E. A. (2004). What do you do when things go right? The intrapersonal and interpersonal benefits of sharing positive events. *Journal of Personality and Social Psychology,* 87(2), 228–245.

Gelatt, H. B. (1989). Positive uncertainty: A new decision-making framework for counseling. *Journal of Counseling Psychology,* 36(2), 252–256.

Haidt, J. (2006). *The happiness hypothesis: Finding modern truth in ancient wisdom.* New York: Basic Books.

Hall, D., & Chandler, D. (2005). Psychological success: When the career is a calling. *Journal of Organizational Behavior,* 26(2), 155–176.

Heppner, P. P., & Krauskopf, C. J. (1987). An information-processing approach to personal problem solving. *The Counseling Psychologist,* 15(3), 371–447.

Krieshok, T. S., Black, M. D., & McKay, R. A. (2009). Career decision making: The limits of rationality and the abundance of non-conscious processes. *Journal of Vocational Behavior,* 75(3), 275–290.

Krumboltz, J. D. (1996). A learning theory of career counseling. In M. L. Savickas &W. Bruce Walsh (Eds.), *Handbook of career counseling theory and practice* (pp. 55–80). Palo Alta, CA: Davies-Black.

Krumboltz, J. D. (1998). Serendipity is not serendipitous. *Journal of Counseling Psychology,* 45(4), 390–392.

Krumboltz, J. D. (2009). The happenstance learning theory. *Journal of Career Assessment,* 17(2), 135–154.

Levoy, G. (1997). *Callings: Finding and following an authentic life.* New York: Harmony Books.

Lopez, S. J., Hodges, T., & Harter, J. (2005). *The Clifton StrengthsFinder technical report: Development and validation.* Washington, DC: The Gallup Organization.

Mason, J. L. (1990). *An enemy called average.* Insight Publishing, Inc.

Miller, M. J. (1983). The role of happenstance in career choice. *Vocational Guidance Quarterly*, 32(1), 16–20.

Mitchell, K. E., Levin, A. S., Krumboltz, J. D. (1999). Planned happenstance: Constructing unexpected career opportunities. *Journal of Counseling and Development*, 77(2), 115–125.

Murray, H. A. (1938). *Explorations in personality*. New York: Oxford University Press.

Niles, S. G., Amundson, N. E., & Neault, R. A. (2011). *Career flow: A hope-centered approach to career development*. Boston, MA: Pearson Education, Inc.

Orem, S. L., Binkert, J., & Clancy, A. L. (2007). *Appreciative coaching: A positive process for change*. San Francisco: Jossey-Bass.

Palmer, P. J. (2000). *Let your life speak*. Hoboken, NJ: John Wiley & Sons.

Rilke, R. M. (1987). *Letters to a young poet*. New York: Vintage Books.

Savickas, M. L. (1995). Constructivist counseling for career indecision. *Career Development Quarterly*, 43(4), 363–374.

Savickas, M. L. (1998). Career style assessment and counseling. InT. Sweeney (Ed.), *Adlerian counseling: A practitioner's approach* (4th ed., pp. 329–360). Philadelphia, PA: Accelerated Development.

Schreiner, L. A. (2010). The "Thriving Quotient": A new vision for student success. *About Campus*, May–June, 2–10. doi:10.1002/abc.20016.

Schutt, D. (2007). A strength-based approach to career development using appreciative inquiry.

Seligman, M. E. P. (2002). *Authentic happiness*. New York: Free Press.

Shushok, F., Jr., & Hulme, E. (2006). What's right with you: Helping students find and use their personal strengths. *About Campus*, September–October, 2–8. doi:10.1002/abc.173

White, M., & Epston, D. (1990). *Narrative means to therapeutic ends*. New York: WW Norton.

Whiting, J. B. (2007). Authors, artists, and social constructionism: A case study of narrative supervision. *The American Journal of Family Therapy*, 35(2), 139–150.

Whitney, D., & Trosten-Bloom, A. (2003). *The power of Appreciative Inquiry: A practical guide to positive change*. San Francisco: Barrett-Koehler.

Wrzesniewski, A. (2011). Callings. InK. Cameron &G. Spreitzer (Eds.), *Oxford Handbook of Positive Organizational Scholarship* (pp. 45–55). New York: Oxford.

Wrzesniewski, A., McCauley, C., Rozin, P., & Schwartz, B. (1997). Jobs, careers, and callings: People's relations to their work. *Journal of research in personality*, 31(1), 21–33.

8

Positive Supervision and Training

JANICE E. JONES AND JOHN C. WADE

Supervision and training can provide a perfect opportunity to utilize positive psychology constructs. A broad definition of supervision can be thought of as overseeing and assuming responsibility for both the development of the supervisee or employee and the quality of the work performed. It typically involves observation, evaluation, the fostering of supervisee self-assessment, and the acquisition of knowledge and skills by instructing, modeling, and mutual problem solving (Falender & Shafranske, 2004, p. 3). A review of the literature on the common factors of supervision suggests that four primary supervisory roles are commonly utilized: coach, teacher, mentor, and administrator (Morgan & Sprenkle, 2007, pp. 11–12). Effective supervision depends upon flexibility and the ability to utilize different supervision roles depending upon the needs of the situation. The focus of this chapter is intended to look at supervision and training broadly, because it can apply to various settings and functions on campus, ranging from a housing director supervising her staff to a faculty member working with his research assistants to more clinically focused supervision such as in professional training programs.

Holloway (1995) calls supervision the "the critical teaching method," and she writes that "professional education depends on the supervisory process to facilitate the development of the students from the novice to the autonomously functioning individual" (Holloway, 1995, p. 177). Given that this chapter is about training and supervision, it is helpful to define the two terms. Lambert and Ogles (1997) define training as when supervisees are learning new skills, whereas supervision occurs when supervisees practice their developing skills with the guidance and support of a seasoned professional.

The Wade and Jones (2014) model of strengths-based supervision was inspired by Smith's (2006) strengths-based counseling model, but it adds an intentional focus of applying empirically supported positive psychology constructs. Although the Wade and Jones (2014) model originally focused on clinical and mental health supervision, the model has been expanded in this chapter to address broader areas of student affairs and campus functioning. The factors of the model that will be discussed in detail in this chapter are as follows:

- Perspective on supervision
- Creating hope and fostering growth
- Setting the stage for effective supervision
- Uncovering potential
- Evaluation and feedback
- Diversity: Searching for higher ground, not just common ground
- Addressing problems and framing solutions
- Beyond competence: Fostering excellence

Perspective on Supervision

Our model has been influenced by several theoretical conceptualizations of supervision, but it was most heavily influenced by the developmental perspective of supervision, which will be described here. Developmental models of supervision are based on the assumption that trainees and supervisees progress through predictable stages of development as they gain increased knowledge and skill. The task of the supervisor is to identify the stage of the supervisee or employee and to tailor the focus and approach of supervision in accordance, with the general assumption that novices need more structure and guidance, whereas more advanced supervisees tend to benefit from a more collaborative and conceptual focus. The stages of growth and learning are qualitatively different from each other, and each stage of development requires different approaches and emphases in supervision.

The influential developmental psychologist Lev Vygotsky (1978) asserted that maximal growth occurs when tools and support are provided through carefully "scaffolding" training experiences to meet developmental needs. He coined the term "zone of proximal development" to describe the difference between what the learner can do on her own and what she can do with assistance. Development occurs through the use of scaffolding offered by someone with more knowledge and experience by providing increasing challenging experiences as the learner acquires greater mastery. The supervisor helps to elicit and clarify what the supervisee already knows, building upon these strengths and drawing out the supervisee's understanding. Milne (2009) likens the scaffolding process to the metaphor of taking a journey with a guide. The supervisee must exert effort and take some chances, thereby contributing to what is undertaken and achieved, but the process works best with a supervisor who behaves like an experienced guide, who can draw upon his or her experience of already having traveled the path (Milne, 2009, p. 131). Developmental models such as the influential Integrated Developmental Model (IDM) (Stoltenberg, 1981; Stoltenberg & Delworth, 1987; Stoltenberg, & Delworth, 1998; Stoltenberg & McNeil, 2010) focus on tailoring the supervision process to meet the supervisees' current level of development, based on the premise that trainees go through predictable stages of development. As the supervisee develops competence or mastery, the supervisor gradually moves the scaffolding to encourage the supervisee to apply the learning to the next stage. The IDM categorizes three levels of development:

- Level 1—beginning trainees who are generally eager and motivated but anxious and fearful of evaluation. The focus is on acquiring rudimentary knowledge and skills.
- Level 2—midlevel range of experience, with fluctuating confidence and motivation.
- Level 3—supervisees feel more secure in their abilities, are more efficient and effective, and are able to be more self-reliant and creative in their work.

Hess (1987) offers another developmental model, utilizing a four-stage framework, that also provides a helpful understanding of the common developmental sequence:

1. Inception stage—supervisees tend to feel insecure, and value basic skill building, role definitions, and setting of boundaries.
2. Skill Development stage—supervisees become more adept with fundamental skills and strategies. This stage involves a shift to the apprenticeship model, with supervisees developing greater autonomy.
3. Consolidation stage—supervisees (and observers) begin to recognize individual skills and talents. The previously acquired building blocks are integrated. The role of the supervisee's personality more fully emerges, and skill refinement and competence more fully develop.
4. Mutuality stage—the supervisee role in supervision becomes more of an autonomous professional seeking consultation, similar to peer consultation. The supervisee becomes more comfortable and proficient problem solving and creating solutions. (pp. 251–252)

Although numerous developmental models of supervision exist, the common shared premise is to match learning characteristics with the optimal learning environment. In other words, supervision should be designed to optimize the supervisee's learning at each stage of development.

Creating Hope and Fostering Growth

Creating hope is essential for the training process to be effective. Hope serves as the springboard for growth, providing the energy and momentum to power the work required for change. New supervisees frequently feel anxious about their abilities and are overly self-conscious and doubtful. Hope is an empirically supported construct explained by Snyder (2000) as a positive motivational state that is based on agency (goal-directed energy) and pathways (plans to meet goals). In other words, meaningful hope is achieved by having goals and a belief that with work one can make a difference in the outcome, combined with achievable pathways to achieve the goals (Lopez, Snyder, Magyar-Moe, Edwards, Pedrotti, Janowski, Turner, & Pressgrove, 2004). In addition, Lopez et al. (2004) suggest that it is important to set developmentally appropriate goals, because realistic hope is also correlated with successfully meeting developmental tasks. Goals that are easy to meet will become mundane. Snyder (2000) instructs us to include goals that challenge us or require us to "stretch" out of our comfort level and subsequently grow in our abilities. These he calls "stretch goals." Successful attainment of stretch goals will lead to growth.

The task of the supervisor is to both elicit his or her supervisee's goals (and perhaps offer some guidance) and to conjointly develop a roadmap with the supervisee that will serve as a path to the achievement of those goals. Typically, hope increases as we successfully meet developmental tasks (Snyder, Rand, & Sigmon, 2005). The acronym of SMART goals has become widely known in both business and education, and conjointly developing these goals with our trainees can be an easy, manageable task for supervision. The acronym SMART (Doran, 1981) stands for: Specific, Measurable, Attainable, Realistic, and Time-bound. These parameters help to ensure that agreed-upon goals will have a greater likelihood of being achieved and that progress toward the goals can be more easily and meaningfully tracked.

Setting the Stage

Many factors are important in "setting the stage" for effective supervision and training, but for the sake of brevity, only a couple will be explored in this section.

The broaden-and-build model (Fredrickson, 1998; Fredrickson, 2001; Fredrickson & Branigan, 2001) posits that positive emotions are contagious and create a more fertile ground for learning.

Borders (1994) observed that good supervisors, not surprisingly, tend to enjoy supervision and transmit their comfort and enthusiasm to their supervisees throughout the process. Good supervisors share the characteristics of being committed to helping the supervisee grow, demonstrate commitment to supervision by being prepared for and involved in supervision and training, have a clear sense of their own strengths and limitations as a supervisor and can identify how their personal traits and interpersonal style may affect the supervision process, and, very importantly, have a sense of humor that helps both the supervisor and supervisee get through rough spots and achieve a healthy perspective (p. 1).

An investigation of "good" supervision events from the supervisee perspective (Worthen & McNeill, 1996) revealed that positive supervision experiences are characterized by a supervisory relationship experienced as empathic, nonjudgmental, and validating, with encouragement from the supervisor to explore and experiment. Struggle is normalized, resulting in nondefensive analysis, re-examination of assumptions, acquisition of a metaperspective, and a sense of "freeing" consisting of reduced self-protectiveness and receptivity to supervisory input. "Good" supervision resulted in strengthened confidence, refined professional identity, expanded ability to conceptualize and execute, and a strengthened supervisory alliance (Worthen & McNeill, p. 28).

Getting the most from supervision depends upon both the supervisor and supervisee having the right expectations. The "Pygmalion effect" refers to the finding that leader expectations for subordinate performance can subconsciously affect leader behavior and consequently impact the performance of subordinates (Rosenthal & Jacobson, 1968). The self-fulfilling prophecy of the Pygmalion effect has largely been explained in terms of the mediating variables of leadership behavior and self-expectations (White & Locke, 2000). For example, teachers' expectations for students who were believed to have differing ability levels were subconsciously translated into differential behavior, such as smiling more and creating a warmer and friendlier environment for students thought to have greater ability or potential. Teachers have also been found to give high-expectancy students more challenging assignments, as well as more positive, constructive feedback (White & Locke, 2000). Those believed to have higher potential typically receive more of the following behaviors from their trainers or supervisors:

- Coaching on effective work habits
- Stimulating enthusiasm for meeting a goal or achieving excellent performance
- Enhancing others' feelings of importance and self-worth
- Encouraging members to form relationships and work together as a team (Eden, 1990)

These leadership traits were dubbed the "Pygmalion Leadership Style," which appears to include both deliberate and unconscious elements. Eden (1990) described that the Pygmalion Leadership Style involves:

". . . consistent encouraging, supporting, and reinforcing of high expectations resulting in the adoption, acceptance, or internalization of high expectations on the part of the subordinates. In the simplest and most straightforward instance, it is a manager reassuringly telling a subordinate 'I know you can do this well.' This message can be transmitted in an endless variety of ways. The hallmark of an effective leader is his ability to get this message across convincingly and to inspire high self-confidence among the other persons around him" (1990, p. 125).

The Pygmalion effect depends upon the self-expectations of the leaders being transmitted to their subordinates, leading them to raise their own expectations for how well they can perform (White & Locke, 2000). Noting that the increased performance occurred as a result of increased external expectations being internalized as an increased sense of internal self-efficacy, White and Locke (2000) recommend focusing on increasing self-efficacy using the four learning techniques identified by Bandura (1986, 1997):

(1) Enacting mastery or building skills through practice. Supervisors can focus on guided mastery, achieved through breaking down complex tasks into simpler components, practicing the elements one at a time with instruction, and gradually reintegrating them into a whole. The goal is to set the stage for success by building the trainee's sense of self-efficacy through a series of "small wins."

(2) Role modeling or observing the performance of competent others with whom one can identify. Supervisors can emphasize to supervisees how to derive maximum benefit from observing models, such as mentally organizing what they observe (i.e., identifying principles) and planning opportunities to incorporate components of what they have observed.

(3) Verbal persuasion or expressions of encouragement. Persuasive communication becomes more powerful when supervisors can share why and how they believe supervisees can succeed.

(4) Interpreting ambiguous states of arousal in positive terms (e.g., encouraging someone to interpret butterflies in the stomach as excitement rather than fear). (pp. 405–408)

White and Locke (2000) also encourage supervisors to adopt a "learning orientation" versus a "performance orientation" with trainees to enhance the benefits of Pygmalion training. They explain that a learning orientation reflects the attitude that the pursuit of a goal is a learning process, and those with a learning orientation tend to devote time to determine what skills are necessary for performing a task, or what task strategies are most beneficial for reaching a goal. In addition, mistakes or setbacks are regarded as opportunities for learning and development. In contrast, supervisees with a performance orientation typically are averse to failure and try to work on easy tasks to ensure success and recognition rather than working on challenging tasks for the pleasure of learning and mastery. Mistakes are viewed in terms of slowing down progress rather than as mechanisms for learning (White & Locke, 2000, pp. 408–409).

Both supervisors and supervisees know the fundamental tension of supervision—the defensive, protective stance focused on "saving face," versus the open stance of accepting the vulnerability of making mistakes during the learning process. Carol Dweck's (1986) research has carefully examined this duality. Learning goals emphasize progress and mastery through effort. This creates the tendency to be energized by the challenge, whereas a focus on ability judgments can result in a tendency to avoid and withdraw from challenge (Dweck, 1986, p. 1041). In contrast, those with performance goals are more likely to interpret negative outcomes in terms of their ability and become discouraged (Dweck, 1986, p. 1042). Workers with learning goals use obstacles as a cue to increase their effort or to analyze and vary their strategies, which increases their likelihood of maintaining or improving their strategies under difficulty or failure. Effort is regarded as a means of using or activating their ability, surmounting obstacles, and of increasing their ability.

Learning, by definition, includes failure and times of realizing that the current path is not working (Peterson & Seligman, 2004, p. 166). Drawing upon Dweck's (1986) research, Schreiner (2010) asserts that students who thrive know that it is the investment of effort on a regular basis that will help them succeed. They are motivated to do well and have educational goals that are important to them, and they have strategies for reaching those goals. Most importantly, when things get tough or confusing, they do not give up, but rather they try new strategies or ask for assistance (Schreiner, 2010, pp. 4–5). Supervisors who can help to prompt and instill a growth mindset or learning orientation can greatly help their supervisees manage difficulties more effectively and be more open to learning from their experiences.

Uncovering Potential

Within a strengths-based supervision model, identifying and nurturing strengths is a crucial element. Interestingly, one of the key reasons it is so important to intentionally focus on strengths is that *bad is stronger than good* (Baumeister, Bratslavsky, Finkenauer, & Vohs, 2001). It seems that from an evolutionary perspective, it is adaptive to give more weight and urgency to the negative than to the positive.

Baumeister et al. (2001) further explain that from an evolutionary perspective, organisms that were better attuned to the negative would have been more likely to survive threats, and consequently, would have increased the probability of carrying on their genes. Survival requires urgent attention to possible bad outcomes, but it is less urgent with regard to good ones, making it biologically advantageous to be negatively oriented (Baumeister et al., 2001, p. 325). Bad emotions, bad parents, and bad feedback all have more impact than good ones, and bad information tends to be processed more quickly and less reflectively than the good. This seems especially noteworthy in the initial impression-forming stage of the supervisory relationship, when bad impressions and bad stereotypes can form quickly and are more resistant to disconfirmation than good ones. The importance of intentionally focusing on strengths is underscored by Seligman (2002) who observed that learned helplessness can develop from just a few failures, and it is hard to undo this perception even with numerous positive successes.

Jones-Smith (2014) succinctly summarized that the mind predominantly has a negativity bias that causes most people not to recognize their strengths (p. 34). We tend to focus most on what captures our attention, which given our evolutionary tendencies, means that we will often be drawn to the negative. This works well for survival, but it is not very helpful for learning and growth. Although identifying and working from strengths can be very useful to the supervision process, it is important to first recognize that although a strengths perspective may have intuitive appeal, that given our human tendencies, it will likely require conscious and intentional attention from both supervisors and supervisees. We are drawn to operating from a deficit mindset, in which we tend to focus weaknesses, such as our low grades or mistakes, without giving enough weight to our successes. Utilizing strengths causes them to more fully develop, making strengths development a process of internal talent and ability combined with awareness and practice (Jones-Smith, 2014, pp. 50–51). Instead of trying to change weaknesses into strengths, which is often a frustrating and counter-productive process, we should attempt to bring areas of weakness into "functional competence", even though we are unlikely to become exceptional in these areas, because trying to fix weaknesses generally leads to merely average performance (Jones-Smith, 2014, p. 23).

If building upon strengths is a key component of the strength-based supervision approach, helping our supervisees recognize and acknowledge, claim ownership, and intentionally practice their strengths is critical. Strengths can be identified through using formal measures and also informally, through less structured, more conversational methods. Listening attentively to our supervisees for expressions of high energy and enthusiasm, stories of success, and challenges successfully navigated can give us clues as to our supervisee's strengths. Summarizing research from Donald Clifton and colleagues, Compton and Hoffman (2013) state that strengths can be recognized as sharing the following characteristics:

1) Yearnings—we feel a strong psychological pull toward interests, goals, and activities that connect to our strengths. These can serve as an internal compass.

2) Satisfaction—when we utilize or fulfill a strength, we experience intrinsic satisfaction, and we feel good about ourselves and the activity.

3) Learning—we tend to learn more easily in areas of our strengths, and we are drawn to want to learn more. If we have a talent for golf or computer science or ballet, we likely enjoy reading books and magazines about these topics. If these are not areas of strength, probably nothing could be more boring than reading about these topics.

4) Excellence or flow—when we activate a strength, we can exhibit consistently good performance, and at times will experience a flow state while engaged in the activity.

5) Less effort—we tend to both learn and execute more easily within our areas of strength. (p. 264)

These are all tell-tale indicators to be attuned to. We can also ask our supervisees about their strengths, through indirect questions such as the following:

- How would your friends describe you?
- What skills were you surprised to learn that you had at your last job?
- When your partner brags about you, what does he or she say?
- What seems to come easily for you?
- Did you experience some moments when things seems to be "clicking?" Tell me about these.
- Tell me about the parts of your work that have seemed easy for you?

Two empirically supported formal strengths identification instruments are widely used, which can provide an objective and efficient way to ascertain our supervisee's strengths, as well as providing a common language to talk about them further. The Values Inventory of Strengths (VIA-IS; Peterson & Seligman, 2004) is a 240-item instrument that measures 24 character strengths (10 items for each strength) and can be completed in approximately 30 min. The other major strengths inventory, which is designed to more readily translate to organizational setting than the VIA-IS (and is consequently frequently used in business and academic settings) is the Clifton StrengthsFinder (Buckingham & Clifton, 2000), now in its' second rendition, the Clifton StrengthsFinder 2.0 (Asplund, Lopez, Hodges, & Harter, 2007).

Identifying strengths is important, but it is only meaningful if followed by an intentional focus on strengths development. For strengths to truly exist, they must be applied into action, otherwise they are merely potentials, not actual strengths. Strengths do not develop merely through time and experience, but they require conscious practice and repetition. Growth, and the transformation of potential into realized strengths, requires intentionally focusing conscious attention and effort on areas of high ability (Jones-Smith, 2014, p. 64). Lopez and Edwards

(2008, pp. 96–97) summarized that intentionally integrating the wise application of strengths with goals and motivation has also been found to enhance the ability to reach goals.

Although it is important to identify and build upon strengths, for strengths to be effectively applied also involves discernment and wise application. Schwartz and Sharpe (2006) suggest that practical wisdom is necessary to discern when it is best to use particular strengths, and they state that relevance, conflict, and specificity must be considered. One needs to consider what bearing a strength may or may not have on a situation, how different strengths may be in conflict with one another, and how they might be tailored to the specific situation at hand. Too much (overuse) and too little (underuse) of character strengths has been shown to have a negative impact on well-being (e.g., Grant and Schwartz, 2011) and goal achievement. When I (J. C. W.) give workshops on strengths, I will often use the adaptability we naturally use as we communicate to illustrate this principle. We typically talk a certain way at work, a slightly different way with our friends, another way still in the locker room, and a decidedly different way at church. For most of us, if we were to talk the same way in church as we do in the locker room it would cause problems, or at the very least embarrassment. The same principle operates with the application of strengths—although operating from strengths is generally good, effective application typically involves nuance, flexibility, and awareness of the context and situation. Even though utilizing our strengths is typically advantageous, more is not always better. For instance, the overutilization of the strength of leadership or reliance upon it in the wrong situations will result in being regarded as bossy or controlling. Curiosity carried too far or used unwisely can morph into intrusiveness.

In addition to the importance of judiciously utilizing strengths, Wright and Lopez (2002) advocate for a balanced focus on both strengths and weaknesses, as well as the recognition of environmental resources and stressors. Supervisors must be committed to examining all four areas, which serves to counterbalance the tendency to focus on pathology or weaknesses. Wright and Lopez (2002) urge us to "remain on guard lest positives in the person and situation remain overlooked because of the intrusion of the fundamental negative bias and environmental neglect" (p. 38).

Niemiec (2013) describes a three-step model of strengths development, termed the Aware-Explore-Apply model. It was created for working with the VIA character strengths, but its' principles seem to broadly apply to working with strengths in general. The three steps involve:

1. Aware: strengths-spotting, combating strengths blindness, and cultivating strengths awareness
2. Explore: exploring strengths overuse, underuse, use across contexts, past use with problems and successes

3. Apply: taking action with goal-setting, deploying and aligning strengths, and valuing strengths in others (Niemiec, 2013).

Evaluation and Feedback

Saptya, Riemer, and Bickman (2005) use the analogy of trying to learn archery without being able to see if you have hit the target to describe the importance of feedback to the learning process. Feedback is central to learning. Without feedback, mistakes can go uncorrected, bad habits can develop, effective behaviors are not recognized, and inaccurate assumptions about performance can be made (Westberg & Jason, 1993). Supervisees seem to intuitively recognize the importance of feedback, ranking receiving supervisor observation and feedback as the most effective factor contributing to their skill development (Smith, 1984). Effective evaluation practices also are positively associated with and predictive of a stronger supervisory working alliance (Lehrmann-Waterman & Ladany, 2001).

However, feedback is not uniformly effective and can be counterproductive if not done well. When feedback causes attention to be directed to the self and away from the activity, it can actually detract rather than enhance performance (Kluger & DeNisi, 1996, 1998). Feedback that prompts increased self-consciousness, especially on complex tasks, depletes cognitive resources needed for task performance and redirects some of that energy to self-enhancement and defensiveness. To minimize the potential risks associated with feedback, it is helpful to relate feedback to previously established goals, which are more likely to direct attention to the task at hand and not to the self (Kluger & DeNisi, 1996).

Providing Effective Feedback

The terms feedback and evaluation are often used interchangeably, but they are distinct in both form and function. Feedback is based on observations and presents information, not judgment (Ende, 1983), and helps the trainee remain on course in reaching a goal. Evaluation, on the other hand, is summative. It comes after the fact and presents a judgment about how well or poorly a trainee is meeting a given goal, in relation to established criteria or measured against the performance of peers.

Not all feedback is equally effective, and the quality of feedback is influenced by the timing, nature, and appropriateness of the feedback given. Compilations of standard practices from the fields of personnel management, group dynamics, and education suggest that effective feedback should be founded upon a collaborative supervisory relationship; mutually agreed upon goals; based on first-hand data and limited to behaviors that are changeable; phrased in descriptive, nonevaluative language; and deal with specifics and not generalizations. Subjective data and interpretations can be appropriate at times, but subjective data should be identified as such by the supervisor (Ende, 1983).

Applying Motivational Interviewing Concepts to Feedback

Although it seems very reasonable to assume that that supervisees would want their unsuccessful interventions and misguided efforts illuminated and examined, as human beings with our inherent sensitivities and defenses we often have trouble hearing and accepting feedback even when it is constructively and diplomatically presented. Noticing that many of the factors associated with good supervision (e.g., empathy, respect, normalizing, encouraging the supervision to take an active role) are inherent in *motivational interviewing* ([MI] e.g., Miller & Rollnick, 2002; Rollnick, & Miller, 1995), Sobell, Manor, Sobell, and Dum (2008) created a motivational procedure for facilitating feedback during supervision. MI is defined as a directive, client-centered counseling style for eliciting behavior change by helping clients explore and resolve ambivalence (about both wanting to change and wanting to continue the behavior) (Rollnick & Miller, 1995). It is a therapeutic style developed for discussing sensitive issues with clients who may be at varying levels of openness or receptivity (Miller & Rollnick, 2002). The basic goal of MI is to minimize or decrease resistance and to enhance motivation to change the target behavior. This would certainly seem to transfer well to supervision, in which supervisees, especially when beginning or unsure of themselves, are likely to feel vulnerable and anxious. The spirit of MI, in which the focus is on using careful inquiry to elicit the wisdom of the supervisee and foster ownership, also fits very well within a positive psychology framework. The primary tasks and principles of the supervisor using an MI approach would be to (1) express support, (2) develop the discrepancy between the current behavior and important goals or values, (3) "roll" with resistance, and (4) support self-efficacy and optimism.

The goal of MI-based supervision is for supervisors to use MI techniques to construct a conversation with supervisees that minimizes resistance by being nonconfrontational, nonjudgmental, and empathic. Supervisors encourage trainees to be full collaborators in the feedback discussion process (Sobell et al., 2008, p. 152). Thus, a residence hall director might say to a resident assistant after handling a difficult situation, "As you reflect on the situation, tell me about what seemed to go well and what didn't seem to go so well." This could be followed with open-ended questions to further expand the exploration (e.g., "What things might you do differently in future situations?").

From an MI perspective, getting supervisees to "give voice" to their awareness of the need to make changes would be viewed as more likely to get them to consider making a serious change attempt than the supervisor telling trainees what they must change. MI can be used to increase trainees' motivation for change by giving them personalized feedback in a nonthreatening, nonjudgmental way. For example, a supervisor of student tutors might say, "So, it sounds like you were try-ing to help the student look more carefully at his studying methods. This is very different from when you first started working with him. How were you able to do that?" or "You talked about asking him several back-to-back questions about his studying approach. What do you know about how people typically respond when asked multiple questions in a row?" (adapted from Sobell et al., 2008, p. 152).

Additional questions from an MI perspective could include:

Empathy/Reflective Listening:

"I hear your frustration that your students don't seem to be paying attention well or seem invested in learning the material."

"It seems that you are feeling confused about how to best plan this event."

"It seems really hard to want to listen intently but also share your insights before you forget them."

Develop discrepancy:

"Tell me how you are feeling about your work with the other members on the project"

"Where are you with the idea of trying to empower your student advisees to accept more responsibility to acting on the information you provide them?"

"What do you make of the low return rate of your career counseling clients?"

Rolling with Resistance:

Reflection—simply acknowledge it by reflecting it back

Amplified reflection—overstate it a bit. "I can see that the Sorority house you advise is likely to make some terrible decisions if you hold back some of your advice."

Double-sided reflection—"On the one hand you see the value of helping your students become more independent. On the other hand, it is difficult to trust them to make good decisions."

Enhance Confidence:

"What gives you some confidence that you can make good progress on your proj-ect this week?"

"What is there about you that could help you succeed in making this change?"(adapted from Wade & Jones, 2014).

The Role of Positive Emotions in Feedback

Evaluation and feedback, when viewed from a positive psychology lens, is intended to provide growth experiences for supervisees. The following questions may be helpful to consider frequently when providing strength-based supervision:

- What am I doing to focus the supervisee's attention away from being overly self-conscious to being more fully immersed in learning and challenging herself?
- What am I role modeling for my supervisees?
- Reflecting on the best experiences I have had receiving feedback or evaluation, what made these such good experiences? How can I incorporate some of these elements into the feedback and evaluation I am currently providing?
- Does the time allocation in our supervision sessions roughly mirror the supervisory goals? If not, what changes would be helpful to make?
- What is the one "take home" feedback message I want my supervisee to really hear? How can I convey this most effectively? Are there ways we can work with this concept to (role playing, etc.) to help her incorporate it more fully?
- Is there feedback that would be beneficial but I am hesitant to give? What can I do to make it a more comfortable process? For the supervisee? For myself as the supervisor? (Wade & Jones, 2014)

In addition, it is necessary to seek other growth opportunities as well. Helping supervisees reach outside of familiar territory and develop culturally competent skills will facilitate a search for higher ground, not just common ground.

Diversity: Searching for Higher Ground, Not Just Common Ground

In the book, *Outliers: The Story of Success*, Malcolm Gladwell (2008) grippingly tells the story of an international flight that very avoidably ran out of gas and crashed simply because the pilot and the air traffic controller were attempting to communicate from their own cultural perspective and were unable to cross the cultural divide and understand each other. Although the stakes are not usually quite so high with cross-cultural supervision on campus, appreciating differences of worldview and perspective is nonetheless vitally important. Effective supervision is dependent upon truly appreciating the differences of perspective and worldview that permeate every interpersonal exchange. However, appreciating diversity and effectively navigating differences does not merely mean that potential problems and bad outcomes can be minimized, it also can add richness and increased perspective to interpersonal interactions and supervision. Trevino (2012) eloquently explains, "For me, the blessing of diversity is to experience ourselves as interconnected, integrated in all that lives. We are called to experience the gift that when we stand for each other, greatness can bloom before our eyes . . . how can we reconcile the challenges and blessings of diversity? . . . The blessing is our opportunity to embrace 'what is' without wanting to change it into something else" (p. 38).

The importance of being able to work effectively with issues of diversity is very clear. Referring to the example of personal counseling, Constantine (2002) found that the shared variance between clients' perception of counselors' general counseling competence and clients' perceptions of counselors' multicultural-counseling competence was approximately 60%, indicating that it is not a stretch to say that "multicultural competence is synonymous with general counseling competence" (Coleman, 1998, p. 153). Even if not always explicit, culture is an inevitable silent participant in all human interactions (Das, 1995, p. 50). Being able to bridge cultural differences and establish common understanding is essential to all supervision, regardless of whether it is between a faculty member and graduate teaching assistants or a residence life director supervising the housing staff.

In addition to strengthening understanding and communication, the intentional attunement to and exploration of areas of diversity can often help lead to the identification of strengths. Racial and ethnic minorities have been found to often develop better coping strategies than individuals from nonminority groups, possibly as a result of having to learn to deal with prejudice and discrimination (Ong & Edwards, 2008). Although being a member of any nonmajority group can at times involve prejudice, discrimination, and unique hardships, strengths are often borne through adversity, and they can become resources to utilize. However, it is important to be able to view strengths and weaknesses from the perspective of the trainee, not just our own perspective, because various "strengths" may be perceived or expressed differently depending upon the culture (e.g., Leu, Wang, & Koo, 2011).

It is also important to be attuned to group and cultural differences of the meaning and expression of "strengths" and "weaknesses." For example, Chang (1996) found that Asian Americans scored higher in pessimism than Caucasian Americans; however, no differences were found in levels of depression, which would have been expected from a traditional Western or Caucasian perspective. A closer look at the data revealed that negative correlations were found between optimism and general psychological and physical health in the Asian American sample, whereas positive correlations existed between these variables in the Caucasian American group. However, positive correlations existed between pessimism and increased problem-solving in the Asian American sample, whereas the reverse was found in the Caucasian sample, illustrating that it is important to view strengths and weaknesses from the perspective of the client or supervisee and be attuned to nuances of the expressions of strengths.

However, even if we are well intentioned and the benefits of appreciating and understanding diversity are apparent, it does not necessarily come naturally or easily. Our brains are wired to be "cognitive misers" or, put more bluntly, to be "lazy" (DiSalvo, 2011, p. 80), and we tend to selectively process information in a manner that is consistent with our own worldview (Pitner & Sakamoto, 2005, p. 686). Yamagishi & Mifune (2008) note the strong appeal of perceived in-group trustworthiness. Not surprisingly, people typically judge those perceived to be more like them as nicer, more generous, trustworthy, and fair. People also tend to expect better treatment from in-group members because they are thought to value, and want to further, in-group member interests.

Although the literature is replete with admonitions to examine one's own attitudes and beliefs and discussion of the benefits of doing so (e.g., Anderson & Carter, 2003), the naturally occurring cognitive and affective barriers that can easily arise as part of this process are seldom acknowledged or discussed. Pitner and Sakamoto (2005) encourage engaging in "critical consciousness," moving away from one's own worldview and becoming attentive to the other's worldview, but also acknowledge that it does not come without a cognitive cost and even the risk of backfire. Because critical conscious awareness is not an automatic process, it requires more cognitive expenditure than does automatically processing information from one's own perspective, with a possible end result of the increased cognitive load being the inadvertent automatic use of heuristics to lessen the cognitive drain (Pitner and Sakamoto, 2005, p. 691). In other words, because exercising higher awareness about biases and stereotypes can be so cognitively taxing, it can result in the unwitting default to biases and stereotypes.

So, what to do? As we work with supervisees to try to foster increased multicultural awareness and effectiveness, care needs to be taken to try to normalize the process and help trainees to feel enthusiasm about the possibility of growth in another important area of effectiveness, instead of unwittingly fostering a "fixed" learning perspective (e.g., Dweck, 2006) that causes trainees to focus on trying to convey the impression of instant diversity competence. Gonzalez (1997) emphasizes the need for supervisees to be given permission to be imperfect when it comes to multicultural competency. Supervisees can become resistant during the training process, often brought on by the persistence supervisors use when pushing or challenging supervisees to become more culturally competent (Butler, 2003). Supervisors should model that diversity awareness is always a work in progress and that continuous growth, not perfection, is the standard.

In addition, embracing a phenomenological perspective can be a very useful way to normalize and deshame the process. The phenomenological approach (which is often used with research but certainly seems to fit with supervision as well) starts with acknowledging our biases and filters, recognizing that as humans we all have perceptual filters. The goal is not to free ourselves from our perspective and become totally neutral, which is an impossibility even in the more abstracted arena of research. Rather, the intent is that by acknowledging our limitations of perspective and blind spots, we will be less negatively impacted by them. Acknowledging our biases and the constrictions of our perceptual filters can limit the adverse effects because that of which we have awareness we can manage better, and the powerful impact of unacknowledged or examined preconceptions can be lessened. The phenomenological approach helps to reframe the invitation of diversity awareness from the potentially shame-inducing task of admitting prejudices to simply acknowledging one's pre-existing perceptions and reflecting on how our particular perceptual filters may affect the supervision relationship. For example, acknowledging the challenges of examining one's preconceptions but discussing the benefits of doing so during a work group meeting can go a long way to making the process more inviting.

Addressing Problems and Framing Solutions

Difficulties and problems are inevitable and an intrinsic part of learning. How failures and setbacks are perceived is critical to the learning process of supervision. Failure and difficulties are expected in the process of learning, but ultimately it is an optimistic belief that with practice and effort success will come. Struggle is perceived as part of the learning process, which is crucial because people tend to "persevere only if they perceive falling down as *learning* rather than *failing*" (Heath & Heath, 2010, p. 169). Trainees typically begin new tasks feeling very anxious, and explicitly framing supervision and the learning process from a growth mindset can help to quiet the anxiety. It can also be helpful to address any possible unrealistic expectations that the supervisee may have (Juhnke, 1996).

Strength-based supervision acknowledges both strengths and weaknesses, but it intentionally focuses on and utilizes the supervisee's natural abilities to both further develop areas of strength and also to tackle weaknesses and problems. Wetchler (1990) notes that focusing solely on mistakes or problems in supervision makes it difficult for the supervisee to develop a solid conceptual and practical foundation, which can lead to confusion and ineffectiveness, whereas a solution-focused supervision model is designed to create a greater sense of efficacy (p. 131). The knowledge of what supervisees do correctly is more important to the overall development of personal competency than is a continual focus on mistakes (Wetchler 1990, p. 130). Supervisees are encouraged to identify what they have done well and repeat those behaviors in similar situations.

Traditional supervision can often fall into the well-intentioned trap of being problem focused instead of solution oriented. The Appreciative Inquiry (AI) model of change (e.g., Ludema, Whitney, Mohr, & Griffin, 2003) is premised on the assumption that what we focus on tends to become larger. Consequently, even though well intentioned, the traditional problem-solving approach to addressing problems through greater understanding of the problem (i.e., identifying the key problem, analyzing the root causes of failure, searching for possible solutions, and developing an action plan) often serves to simply further entrench the stuckness of the problem. In contrast, the AI model assumes that what people focus on becomes their reality and that in every individual something works (Orem, Binkert, & Clancy, 2007). The fundamental question shifts from trying to avoid what we want less of, to trying to create more of what is already working and more of what we do want. Intentionally focusing and amplifying the supervisees' strengths and progress will likely increase their sense of agency, which Bandura (1994) notes is associated with seeking more challenges, persisting with difficult tasks longer, and viewing themselves as capable and successful even when they experience failure.

AI, as the name suggests, is fundamentally an approach grounded in appreciating the strengths and talents already present and using questions to illuminate and expand what one wants more of. AI questions are meant to express curiosity, not judgment, and to serve as thought starters that invite multiple answers. *Pivoting* is the conscious act of turning attention away from what the person does not want, away from the failed attempt, to what he or she does want (envisioning what a successful attempt would look like) (Orem et al., 2007). The stance of affirming and appreciating our supervisees pulls them away from self-oriented preoccupation and enlarges their focus (Cooperrider, 1990). An effective tool to do this is simply "being-with." This acknowledges the darkness and difficulty, and it does not reject or minimalize problems, but it also does not give them greater focus (Orem et al., 2007, p. 165).

Part of the task of supervision is to determine, or make an educated guess, regarding whether the supervisee's difficulties are simply the result of a lack of knowledge, and whether a problem can best be addressed through a solution-focused intervention or whether education would be most helpful (Wetchler, 1990). If simple lack of knowledge is an issue, education by the supervisor can often easily remedy the problem while allowing the supervisee to "save face," because focusing on what supervisees have done incorrectly implies inadequacy, but incompetence is not a factor when the difficulty results from a lack of knowledge (Wetchler, 1990, p. 134). When an attempt has gone badly, asking the supervisee about intentions also can help maintain forward focus in supervision, because intentions are almost always good even if the execution was not (Edwards & Chen, 1999), inviting the supervisee and supervisor to consider ways of more effectively eliciting the desired positive outcome. However, it can also be important to be mindful that our first instinct when wanting to change other people's behavior is to teach them something (Heath & Heath, 2010, p. 113), which at best can be ineffective and at worst can raise defenses. As we know from smoking cessation and many other examples, knowledge alone does not change behavior, it needs to be coupled with small, simple steps that "provide a path" and also provide hope (addressing the emotional component of resistance to change).

Thomas (1994) offers some practical questions that a supervisor might ask to facilitate movement and growth:

- "What is the most important thing I need know about your work at this time?"
- "How will you know when things have improved for you?"
- "How have you improved since our last supervision meeting?"
- "What will be the first thing I will notice about a specific work skill when it improves?"
- "When things are better, what are you doing differently?"
- "What is a small step that you could make in this direction (of the goal)?"
- "What is the smallest change you could make that would likely make a difference?"
- "When was the problem just a little bit different?" "How do you account for your ability to do that?"
- "When you are at a (1–2 points higher on a 1–10 scale than the supervisee's current self-identified level), what will you be doing differently?"
- "So it isn't much better—what have you been doing to keep it from getting worse?" (pp. 15–16)

Strength-based supervision encourages the supervisee to assume responsibility and think of multiple solutions (just the act of thinking of multiple solutions can be very helpful with stuckness), with the goal of building the supervisee's ability to generate solutions (Juhnke, 1996).

Beyond Competency: Fostering Excellence

Probably the greatest gift an educator can give her students is to instill the love of learning. Similarly, one of the most important metagoals that good supervisors have is to foster and develop a sense of learning for their supervisees, to help them essentially learn to supervise themselves and to seek and utilize feedback to continue to improve.

Having a learning orientation has been found to be positively associated with performance outcomes (Button, Mathieu, & Zajac, 1996; Phillips & Gully, 1997). A learning orientation reflects the attitude that learning is a process, and mistakes or setbacks are viewed as opportunities for learning and development and a time to re-evaluate strategies. In contrast, the focus for people with a performance orientation is on external reinforcement such as recognition and praise, often resulting in avoiding challenges to ensure success. Within a performance orientation, mistakes are viewed as hindering progress toward a goal rather than as mechanisms for learning (White & Locke, 2000, pp. 408–409).

Dweck (2006) describes the different orientations toward learning as the "fixed" mindset versus a "growth" mindset. Those with a fixed mindset believe that abilities, e.g., intelligence, personality, etc. are unchangeable and consequently the focus is on proving oneself versus learning. This can have a profound effect on supervision, with the supervisee operating from the implicit goal of trying to look good at all times. This is in contrast to the growth mindset, which is based on the belief that our abilities can be nurtured through exercise, namely, that all abilities are like muscles that can be strengthened with practice. This engenders a perspective of wanting to seek challenges in order to grow versus simply trying to prove oneself. Not surprisingly, a growth mindset is associated with more effective problem solving, perseverance, and the desire to work harder. From the process-oriented perspective of a growth mindset, mistakes are perceived as informative, serving as a wake-up call to make modifications. Dweck asserts that great teachers believe in the growth of intellect and talent, set high standards for all students but within a supportive and nurturing atmosphere, and operate from the perspective of teaching, not judging, which would seem to be a wise template for effective strength-based supervision.

Continued Learning and Expert Performance

Learning and growing involves much more than simply acquiring experience. People at any job tend to learn quickly at first, but then once they are able to meet the demands of the job reliably and competently learning often slows or stops (Ericsson & Charness, 1994). In fact, extensive research from a wide range of fields shows that people often fail to become outstandingly good at what they do, and they frequently do not get much better after years of practice. Surgeons are no better at predicting hospital stays after surgery than residents are, and stockbrokers get no better at recommending stocks with experience. In some instances, people actually get worse with experience, more experienced doctors typically score lower on tests of medical knowledge than less experienced doctors (Caamerer & Johnson, 1991).

The ultimate goal for both supervisors and supervisees is obviously not to reach competency and settle, but to strive to maximize one's ability and achieve outstanding performance. Ericcson and Charness (1994) have extensively researched expert performance, and they have identified ways to go beyond simply accruing experience, which tends not to result in increased skill development or performance, but to engage in structured learning and effortful adaptation termed "*deliberate practice.*" This involves monitoring their training and activity with full concentration, which is often in contrast to the automaticity that occurs once competence has been attained. Effective supervisors have to provide frequent and ongoing feedback, and they must also adapt the training situation to provide opportunities to deliberately practice and improve areas of weakness. For example, a tennis player with a weak backhand volley will not likely improve this stroke simply by playing lots of games of tennis, because this situation will likely only be encountered occasionally during each game. To improve, a tennis coach would give the player hundreds of opportunities to practice that shot, with a specific target.

Colvin (2008) notes that deliberate practice is typically designed by teachers who can have a clear, unbiased view of the trainee's performance, and it is one of the reasons that even the best golfers, tennis players, etc., use coaches. Deliberate practice involves identifying specific elements of performance to be improved then working intently on them. This practice should occur in the "learning zone" where the skills and abilities are just slightly out of reach, not in the "comfort zone" where there is no challenge, and not in the "panic zone" where anxiety and lack of competence renders learning impossible.

Self-regulation and self-awareness are key throughout the learning process, involving continually monitoring performance and considering whether modifications need to be made. An active approach to learning also facilitates the building of integrated knowledge bases that lead to understanding and linking new to existing knowledge (Mann, Gordon, & MacLeod, 2009). Mamede and Schmidt (2005) identified a five-factor structure for reflection (especially useful in anticipation of complex or challenging situations) that can serve as a useful template:

- Deliberate induction—taking time to reflect upon an unfamiliar problem
- Deliberate deduction—logically deducing the consequences of a number of possible hypotheses
- Testing—evaluating predictions
- Openness to reflection—willingly engaging in active reflection when faced with unfamiliar situations
- Meta-reasoning—thinking critically about one's own thinking process

Reflective thinking can be facilitated by certain interventions—such as self-appraisal of learning, group discussion and feedback regarding learning strategies, and journal writing (Mamede & Schmidt, 2005). Across diverse settings and methods, it appears that the most influential elements in enabling the development of reflection and reflective practice are a supportive environment, both intellectually and emotionally, accommodation for individual differences in learning style, mentoring, group discussion, and free expression of opinions. Additional enabling factors are perceptions of relevance, organizational climate, including respect between professionals, and time for reflection (Mamede & Schmidt, 2005).

Case Study

Jennifer is a new residence hall director at a large state university. She received much praise during her 3 years as a resident assistant and did well as a Master's student, but she is anxious about the new tasks and significantly increased responsibility.

Her supervisor, Mary, likes to conduct supervision from a strengths-based perspective. During their first supervision meeting, Mary intentionally tries to normalize Jennifer's anxiety, sharing her experiences as a beginning doctoral student and discussing the nervousness that she felt at the time. She also reflected that Jennifer's anxiety probably indicated that she was conscientious and invested in doing a good job. This seemed to reassure Jennifer and to reduce the feeling she had been having of needing to look good to her new supervisor. Mary went beyond the "typical" in her efforts to reduce her initial anxiety, and she also tried to instill a "positive Pygmalion effect" for Jennifer, highlighting specific strengths that Jennifer possesses.

Mary: "I was so glad when you accepted our offer for the position, and was especially pleased knowing that I would be your supervisor. We had the luxury of having an usually high number of applications this year, and were able to be more selective than usual. I was very impressed to see from your recommendation letters that you are poised, even when working with very difficult situations and crisis situations. What do you do to remain calm during these times?"

After Jennifer expanded some on the challenging situations she had successfully handled (she explained that she was usually anxious inside even if it may not have been apparent to others), Mary asked her about other positive qualities and skills that she learned that she had through her previous residence life experience.

Mary: "I'd like to hear your thoughts about some strengths you have that you'd like to further develop and build upon, and also some areas that may be newer to you that you'd like to build more skill and competency."

As Jennifer elaborated upon these, Mary explained to Jennifer that she would probably be more directive and didactic at first with skills she had less familiarity with, but she would also encourage her to branch out and experiment more in the areas she felt more competent. She shared with her the kitchen sink metaphor—that you want to protect a stainless steel sink from getting deep gouges or scratches that will cause lasting damage and cannot be removed, but that a plethora of little nicks and scratches actually enhances the beauty of the sink and creates a patina, which would not exist if the sink was never used and had never been broken in.

During their ongoing meetings, Mary invited Jennifer to share both the situations she felt she was handling well, as well as the inevitable situations that caused her to feel stuck or less capable. Mary would frequently reinforce a learning orientation with Jennifer, often showing more excitement for a mistake that Jennifer was able to identify and then provide a potential solution for than when she simply did good work and everything went smoothly. When occasionally Jennifer felt totally stuck or had tried something with a resident that did not work at all, Mary inquired about her intention, asking her what she was trying to accomplish through her efforts. Invariably, the intended outcome seemed reasonable, and other ways to get to the intended outcome could then be more easily explored. Mary would often ask one of her favorite fall back questions, "What is the smallest change you could make that would likely make a difference?" As the supervision progressed, Jennifer became more adept and more willing to identify both successes and areas to be strengthened, and she made demonstrable progress to the ultimate goal of supervision—that of becoming her own supervisor.

Conclusion

Creating mechanisms to engender a learning orientation and to foster self-reflection and critical thinking seem to be a fundamental task of supervision, across all stages of development. Integrating a factor-based model of strength-based supervision into the training environment helps to create hope and foster growth, allows for diversity to be celebrated and strengths to be identified and shared, encourages supervisees to internalize learning and strive for excellence, and enables positive psychology to flourish in the work being done across all spectrums of the university.

References

Anderson, J., & Carter, R. (2003). *Diversity perspectives for social work practice*. Boston: Allyn & Bacon.

Asplund, J., Lopez, S. J., Hodges, T., & Harter, J. (2007). The Clifton StrengthsFinder®2.0 technical report: Development and validation. The Gallup Organization, Princeton, NJ.

Bandura, A. (1986). *Social foundations of thought and action: A social cognitive theory*. Englewood Cliffs, NJ: Prentice Hall.

Bandura, A. (1994). Self-efficacy. In V. S. Ramachaudran (Ed.). *Encyclopedia of human behavior* (Vol. 4, pp. 71–81). New York: Academic Press.

Bandura, A. (1997) *Self efficacy: The exercise of self control*. New York: Freeman.

Baumeister, R. F., Bratslavsky, E., Finkenauer, C., & Vohs, K. D. (2001). Bad is stronger than good. *Review of General Psychology, 5*(4), 323–370.

Borders, L. D. (1994). The good supervisor. *Eric Digest, 1-2*, EDO-CG-94-18.

Buckingham, M., & Clifton, D. O. (2000). *Now discover your strengths*. New York: Free Press.

Butler, S. K. (2003). Multicultural sensitivity and competence in the clinical supervision of school counselors and school psychologists: A context for providing competent services in a multicultural society. *The Clinical Supervisor, 22*, 125–141.

Button, S. B., Mathieu, J. E., & Zajac, D. M. 1996. Goal orientation in organizational research: A conceptual and empirical foundation. *Organizational Behavior and Human Decision Processes, 67*, 26–48.

Caamerer, C. F., & Johnson, E. J. (1991). The process-performance paradox in expert judgment: How can experts know so much and predict so badly? In K. Anders Ericcson & Jacqui Smith (Eds.), *Toward a general theory of expertise: Prospects and Limits* (pp. 195–217). New York: Cambridge University Press.

Chang, E. C. (1996). Cultural differences in optimism, pessimism, and coping: Predictors of subsequent adjustment in Asian American and Caucasian American college students. *Journal of Counseling Psychology, 43*(1), 113.

Coleman, H. L. K. (1998). General and multicultural counseling competency: Apples and oranges? *Journal of Multicultural Counseling and Development, 26*, 147–156.

Colvin, G. (2008). *Talent is Overrated: What really separates world-class performers from everybody else*. New York: Portfolio-Penguin Group.

Compton, W. C., & Hoffman, E. (2013). *Positive Psychology: The science of happinessand flourishing* (2nd ed.). Belmont, CA: Wadsworth.

Constantine, M. G. (2002). Predictors of satisfaction with counseling: Racial and ethnic minority clients' attitudes toward counseling and ratings of their counselors' general and multicultural counseling competence. *Journal of Counseling Psychology, 49*, 255–263.

Cooperrider, D. L. (1990). Positive image, positive action: The affirmative basis for organizing. In S. Srivastva & D. L. Cooperrider (Eds.). *Appreciative management and leadership: The power of positive thought and action in organizations* (pp. 91–125). San Francisco: Jossey-Bass.

Das, A. K. (1995). Rethinking multicultural counseling: Implications for counselor education. *Journal of Counseling and Development, 74*, 45–52.

DiSalvo, D. (2011). *What makes your brain happy and why you should do the opposite*. New York: Prometheus Books.

Doran, G. T. (1981). There's a SMART way to write management's goals and objectives. *Management Review, 70*(11), 35–36.

Dweck, C. (1986). Motivational processes affecting learning. *American Psychologist, 41*, 1040–1048.

Dweck, C. S. (2006). *Mindset: The new psychology of success*. New York: Random House.

Eden, D. (1990). *Pygmalion in management: Productivity as a self-fulfilling prophecy*. Washington, DC: Lexington.

Edwards, J. K., & Chen, M. (1999). Strengths-based supervision: Frameworks, current practice, and future directions A Wu-wei method. *Family Journal: Counseling and therapy for couples and families, 7*(4), 349–357.

Ende, J. (1983). Feedback in clinical medical education. *Journal of the American Medical Association, 250*(6), 777–781.

Ericsson, K. A., & Charness, N. (1994). Expert performance: Its structure and acquisition. *American Psychologist, 49*, 725–747.

Falender, C. A., & Shafranske, E. P. (2004). *Clinical supervision: A competency-based approach* (pp. 37–58). Washington, DC: American Psychological Association.

Fredrickson, B. L. (1998). What good are positive emotions? *Review of General Psychology, 2*, 300–319.

Fredrickson, B. L. (2001). The role of positive emotions in positive psychology: The Broaden-and-Build of positive emotions. *American Psychologist, 56*, 218–216.

Fredrickson, B. L., & Branigan, C. (2001). Positive emotions. In T. J. Mayne & G. A. Bonnanon (Eds.), *Emotion: Current issues and future directions* (pp. 123–151). Guilford Press: New York, NY.

Gladwell, M. (2008). *Outliers: The story of success.* New York: Little, Brown and Company.

Gonzalez, R. C. (1997). Postmodern supervision: A multicultural perspective. In D. B. Pope-Davis & H. L. K. Coleman (Eds.), *Multicultural counseling competencies: Assessment, education and training, and supervision* (pp. 350–386). Thousand Oaks, CA: Sage.

Grant, A. M., & Schwartz, B. (2011). Too much of a good thing: The challenge and opportunity of the inverted u. *Perspectives on Psychological Science, 6,* 61–76.

Heath, C., & Heath, D. (2010). *Switch: How to change things when change is hard.* New York: Broadway Books.

Hess, A. K. (1987). Psychotherapy supervision: Stages, Buber, and a theory of relationship. *Professional Psychology: Research and Practice, 18*(3), 251–259.

Holloway, E. (1995). *Clinical supervision: A systems approach.* Thousand Oaks, CA: Sage.

Jones-Smith, E. (2014). *Strengths-based therapy: Connecting theory, practice, and skills.* Los Angeles: Sage.

Juhnke, G.A. (1996). Solution-focused supervision: Promoting supervisee skills and confidence through successful solutions. *Counselor Education and Supervision, 1996, 36,* 48–58.

Kluger, A. N., & DeNisi, A. D. (1996). The effects of feedback interventions on performance: A historical review, a meta-analysis, and a preliminary feedback intervention theory. *Psychological Bulletin, 119,* 254–284.

Kluger, A. N., & DeNisi, A. (1998). Feedback interventions: Toward the understanding of a double-edged sword. *Current Directions in Psychological Science, 7,* 67–72.

Lambert, M. J., & Ogles, B. M. (1997). The effectiveness of psychotherapy supervision. In C. E. Watkins, Jr. (Ed.), *Handbook of psychotherapy supervision* (pp. 421–446). New York: Wiley.

Lehrman-Waterman, D., & Ladany, N. (2001). Development and validation of the evaluation process within supervision inventory. *Journal of Counseling Psychology, 48,* 168–177.

Leu, J., Wang, J., & Koo, K. (2011). Are positive emotions just as "positive" across cultures? *Emotion, 11*(4), 994.

Lopez, S. J., & Edwards, L. M. (2008). The interface of counseling psychology and positive psychology: Assessing and promoting strengths. *Handbook of counseling psychology,* 86–99.

Lopez, S. J., Snyder, C. R., Magyar-Moe, J. L., Edwards, L. M., Pedrotti, J., Janowski, K., Turner, J. L., & Pressgrove, C. (2004). Strategies for accentuating hope. In P. A. Linley & S. Joseph (Eds.), *Positive psychology in practice.* John Wiley and Sons: Hoboken, NJ. Doi:10.1002/9780470939338.ch24.

Ludema, J. D., Whitney, D., Mohr, B. J., & Griffin, T. J. (2003). *The Appreciative Inquiry Summit.* San Francisco: Barrett-Koehler Publishers, Inc.

Mamede, S., & Schmidt, H. (2005). The structure of reflective practice in medicine. *Advances in Health Sciences Education, Theory and Practice, 10,* 327–337.

Mann, K., Gordon, K., & MacLeod, A. (2009). Reflection and reflective practice in health professions education: A systemic review. *Advances in Health Science Education, 14,* 595–621.

Miller, W. R., & Rollnick, S. (2002). *Motivational interviewing: Preparing people for change* (2nd ed.). New York: Guilford Press.

Milne, D. (2009). *Evidence-based clinical supervision: principles and practice.* New York: Wiley-Blackwell.

Morgan, M. M., & Sprenkle, D. H. (2007). Toward a common-factors approach to supervision. *Journal of Marital and Family Therapy, 33,* 1–17.

Niemiec, R. M. (2013). VIA character strengths: Research and practice (The first 10 years). In H. H. Knoop & A. Delle Fave (Eds.). *Well-being and cultures: Perspectives on positive psychology* (pp. 11–30). New York: Springer.

Ong, A. D., & Edwards, L. M. (2008). Positive affect and adjustment to perceived racism. *Journal of Social and Clinical Psychology, 27*(2), 105–126.

Orem, S. L., Binkert, J., & Clancy, A. L. (2007). *Appreciative Coaching: A Positive Process for Change*. San Francisco: Jossey-Bass.

Peterson, C., & Seligman, M. E. P. (2004). *Character strength and virtue: A handbook and classification*. New York: Oxford University Press.

Phillips, J. M., & Gully, S. M. (1997). Role of goal orientation, ability, need for achievement, and locus of control in the self-efficacy and goal—setting process. *Journal of Applied Psychology, 82*, 792–802.

Pitner, R. O., & Sakamoto, I. (2005). The role of critical consciousness in multicultural practice: Examining how its strength becomes limitations. *American Journal of Orthopsychiatry, 4*, 684–694.

Rollnick, W., & Miller, W. R. (1995). What is motivational interviewing? *Behavioural & Cognitive Psychotherapy, 23*, 325–334.

Rosenthal, R., & Jacobson, L. (1968). *Pygmalion in the classroom: Teacher expectation and pupils' intellectual development*. New York: Holt, Rinehart, & Winston.

Saptya, J., Riemer, M., & Bickman, L. (2005). Feedback to clinicians: Theory, research, and practice. *Journal of Clinical Psychology, 61*(2), 145–153.

Schreiner, L. A. (2010). The "Thriving Quotient:" A new vision for student success. *About Campus/May-June*, 2–10. Doi:10.1002/abc.20016.

Schwartz, B., & Sharpe, K. E. (2006). Practical wisdom: Aristotle meets positive psychology. *Journal of Happiness Studies, 7*, 377–395.

Seligman, M. E. (2002). *Authentic happiness: Using the new positive psychology to realize your potential for lasting fulfillment*. New York: Simon and Schuster.

Smith, E. J. (2006). The strength-based counseling model. *The Counseling Psychologist, 34*(1), 13–79.

Smith, H. D. (1984). Moment-to-moment counseling process feedback using a dual-channel audiotape recording. *Counselor Education and Supervision*, 346–349.

Snyder, C. R. (2000). *Handbook of hope*. San Diego, CA: Academic Press.

Snyder, C. R., Rand, K. L., & Sigmon, D. R. (2005). Hope theory: A member of the positive psychology family. In C. R. Snyder & S. J. Lopez (Eds.), *Handbook of positive psychology*. New York: Oxford University Press.

Sobell, L. C., Manor, H. L., Sobell, M. B., & Dum, M. (2008). Self-critiques of audiotaped therapy sessions: A motivational procedure for facilitating feedback during supervision. *Training and Education in Professional Psychology, 2*, 151–155.

Stoltenberg, C. (1981). Approaching supervision from a developmental perspective: The counselor complexity model. *Journal of Counseling Psychology, 28*, 59.

Stoltenberg, C. D., & Delworth, U. (1987). *Supervising counselors and therapists: A developmental approach*. San Francisco: Jossey-Bass.

Stoltenberg, C. D., & Delworth, U. (1998). *Supervising counselors and therapists: A developmental approach*. San Francisco: Jossey-Bass.

Stoltenberg, C. D., & McNeill, B. W. (2009). *IDM supervision: An integrative developmental model for supervising counselors and therapists*. New York: Taylor & Francis.

Thomas, F. N. (1994). Solution-oriented supervision: The coaxing of expertise. *The Family Journal: Counseling and Therapy for Couples and Families, 2*, 11–18.

Trevino, Y. (2012). Reconciling the blessings and challenges of diversity through ancestral spiritual values. In K. Schaaf, K. Lindahl, K. S. Hurty, & G. Cheen (Eds.), *Women, spirituality, and transformative leadership* (pp. 36–39). Woodstock, VT: Skylight Paths Publishing.

Vygotsky, L. S. (1978). *Mind in society: The development of higher psychological processes*. Cambride, MA: Harvard University Press.

Wade, J. C., & Jones, J. E. (2014). *Strengths based clinical supervision: A positive psychology approach to clinical training*. New York: Springer.

Westberg, J., & Jason, H. (1993). Providing constructive feedback. In J. Westberg & H. Jason (Eds.), *Collaborative clinical education: The foundation of effective health care* (pp. 297–318). New York: Springer Publishing.

Wetchler, J. L. (1990). Solution-focused supervision. *Family Therapy, 17*, 129–138.

White, S. S., & Locke, E. A. (2000). Problems with the Pygmalion effect and some proposed solutions. *Leadership Quarterly, 11*, 389–415.

Worthen, V., & McNeill, B. W. (1996). A phenomenological investigation of "good" supervision events. *Journal of Counseling Psychology, 43*, 25–34.

Wright, B. A., & Lopez, S. J. (2002). Widening the diagnostic focus: A case for including human strengths and environmental resources. In C. R. Snyder & S. J. Lopez (Eds.), *The handbook of positive psychology* (pp. 26–44). New York: Oxford University Press.

Yamagishi, T., & Mifune, N. (2008). Does shared group membership promote altruism? Fear, greed, and reputation. *Rationality and Society, 20*(1), 5–30.

9

Personal Growth and Development

CHRISTINE ROBITSCHEK AND MEGAN A. THOEN

College students are presented with experiences and challenges that result in a variety of responses and choices, some adaptive and some maladaptive. Personal growth and development are inherent parts of the college experience. Sometimes students make conscious decisions to change and improve themselves during college. At other times, the personal growth process is less intentional. Graduating seniors might be aware that they have changed since they arrived for that first semester on campus but might not be able to identify the specific factors leading to this personal growth. From a positive psychology perspective, this chapter describes the benefits of an intentional personal growth perspective, examples of these behaviors, and how college staff and faculty can help students increase their perspective of personal growth as being intentional and purposeful.

Consider those students who arrive at college having sailed through high school without needing to work hard. Good grades came easily in high school and studying was rare. Sometimes these students do not do well in classes during the first semester of college because the work is substantially more difficult than what they have been used to and requires much more effort. Understandably, students can be confused by this turn of events and initial reactions can vary widely, including blaming poor performance on teaching quality, not being able to understand the accents of international teaching assistants (TAs), unfair grading practices, etc.

Upon further reflection, several scenarios might unfold, demonstrating quite different views of the problem. Some students might try to talk with an instructor or two but not find it helpful. In extreme cases, students may get frustrated, depressed, and even convinced that "college isn't for me." They may fail classes and be forced to leave college. In a more typical scenario, students still get frustrated, might question their intellectual abilities, settle for a lower than expected GPA, and foreclose on career options that require a high college GPA. In these cases, students can lose confidence in their academic abilities, which can negatively impact their mental and physical health (Chemers, Hu, & Garcia, 2001).

In contrast, some students successfully resolve the situation of having to adjust to greater academic demands. These students still experience the initial frustration and negative thoughts that are often unavoidable and also frequently question their intellectual abilities, but the difference for students who successfully adapt is that they view the emotions and cognitions they experience as providing valuable information about the presence of a growth opportunity. They ask themselves, "How can I change myself? What abilities can I acquire to meet the demands of this new situation?" They might ask other students how *they* are making good grades, or might observe other students' study habits and recognize differences from their own habits. These students are likely to ask for guidance from faculty, TAs, academic advisors, and residence hall staff. Just like with the less successful students, there are typical and extreme levels of successful responses. Typical successful students will acquire some new skills and be satisfied with the positive change in their level of success in college. However, extremely successful students will continue to improve their approach to school work, acquiring new study skills, seeking additional resources to help with this process, and applying the new skills to each new class—even if the material comes easily. Although good grades are satisfying to these students, it is the process of personal growth, what we call *Personal Growth Initiative* ([PGI] Robitschek, 1998, 1999) that is most satisfying. Students with high PGI recognize that they have engaged in a process of intentional personal growth. They internalize this process of self-improvement and carry these mechanisms for self-improvement with them into the next situation that calls for changing the self.

Several times we have referred to a *process* of personal growth. The focus of this chapter is the intentional personal growth process, that can have important ramifications for college students. As illustrated above, when students approach the inevitable challenges of college life with a perspective that identifies these challenges as opportunities for personal growth, they can intentionally learn new skills and ways of being in the world that can serve them far into the future. In contrast, if students approach challenges as threats to the self, they are at increased risk of failing to meet their goals and being successful in college.

An important implication of the PGI perspective is that the focus is on the *process* of intentional personal growth, rather than the *outcomes* of these growth processes. This means that the specific goals of growth efforts are not important as long as they are reasonable. Instead, it is the development of a serviceable generic process of personal growth and change that is of critical importance to college students, a process that can be applied across areas of life and across the lifespan. This chapter will focus on the PGI model, which can serve as a pragmatic tool to use in conjunction with and in the service of many of the concepts that will be discussed in the other chapters in this section.

Theory and Research

Personal Growth Initiative

It is important to understand PGI within the context of other models of personal growth and change. Perhaps the most prevalent modern model is the Transtheoretical Model (Prochaska & DiClemente, 1986) which consists of specific, predictable, sequential stages through which a person moves as he or she engages in trying to change a specific behavior. Although this model incorporates processes of change (e.g., consciousness raising and behavioral rewards and punishments; Prochaska & DiClemente, 1982), the focus is on guiding the client through these processes to change specific behaviors (Prochaska & DiClemente, 1982) rather than explicitly teaching the change processes to the client. *Helping* a person engage in a process is importantly different from *teaching* the person to engage in the process. When we help people engage in change processes, the client's focus is on the content (e.g., smoking cessation) rather than the process, itself. In contrast, when behavioral processes are taught, the focus is on training the client to master a specific skill set. This enables the client to view the acquired specific change process as a skill that can be transferred to other situations as needed (Robitschek et al., 2012).

PGI and the corresponding interventions (Thoen & Robitschek, 2013) differ from the transtheoretical model in this important way; they focus on the skill set of the change process so that persons can bring these skills to bear across life domains. More specifically, PGI is a set of self-improvement skills that can be applied in each new life experience (Robitschek et al., 2012). Although people may be born with an inherited set-point for PGI, this skill set of thoughts and behaviors is developed over time, taught to children by their parents and cultures (Whittaker & Robitschek, 2001). More specifically, PGI comprises four components: Readiness for Change, Planfulness, Using Resources, and Intentional Behavior.

- *Readiness for Change* is the ability to identify areas in which we can grow and improve, and the awareness of when the time is right to make these changes. In reality, it is not always a good time to try to improve ourselves. For example, if a student wants to quit smoking, it probably is not a good idea to do this during final exams or just before a Spring Break trip to Daytona Beach.

- *Planfulness* is having a generic plan for how we can improve ourselves when we need or want to do so, and are able to tailor this plan to specific areas in which we want to grow. For example, can we describe how to identify areas in which to improve ourselves, typical steps in this process, and methods for assessing our level of success in enacting our plan?
- *Using Resources* is the awareness of typical types of resources we might access in the process of improving ourselves, such as friends, family, the internet, and professional resources, and the likelihood that we will actually use these resources to help ourselves grow.
- *Intentional Behavior* is following through on our plans for personal growth and actually engage in the self-change process.

The original *Personal Growth Initiative Scale* ([PGIS] Robitschek, 1998, 1999) is a 9-item, single-factor scale that has been used extensively in research with college students. The Personal Growth Initiative Scale—II ([PGIS-II] Ashton, Robitschek, Geiger, & Murray, 2010; Robitschek et al., 2012) is a second-generation measure of PGI, that assesses the four components of PGI, in addition to yielding an over-all score. The PGIS-II remains brief (16 items) and is beginning to be used widely with college students. The full PGIS-II is included at the end of this chapter. Both measures are available free of charge for (noncommercial) applied and research use through the PGI research laboratory website: https://pgilab.wordpress.com. Normative data and scoring procedures for both measures also are available through this website. The PGIS also is available through the University of Pennsylvania Positive Psychology Center Resources for Researchers website: http://www.ppc. sas.upenn.edu/ppquestionnaires.htm#PGIS.

Intentionality

We grow and change throughout our lives, sometimes because we intend to do so, sometimes in spite of our best efforts to remain as we are currently, and some-times when we have no idea we are changing (Robitschek, 1999). For example, students might intentionally try to participate more in class discussions despite being shy; this would be personal growth that is in awareness and intentional. In contrast, European American students might realize that a sociology course reduced their racial bias by teaching them about discrimination experienced by Black Americans in the last 30 years; this would be personal growth that is in their awareness (i.e., they know the event that prompted the growth) but yet is uninten-tional. Still other students might be able to recognize that they have more social skills in their senior year than sophomore year but have no idea how the change occurred; this would be personal growth that is out of their awareness (and, by default, unintentional). It is when college students grow *intentionally* that they are most likely to have other positive psychological outcomes from their personal growth (Robitschek, 1999). In fact, research has suggested that when students grow in any other way, whether it is in their awareness or not, the efforts are likely to have negative, or at least less positive psychological outcomes (Robitschek, 1999), such as decreased psychological well-being, which includes for example, dissatisfaction with one's self, diminished meaning in life, and difficulty managing daily tasks (Ryff, 1989). Although this might seem counterintuitive, perhaps when personal growth is not intentional, it is more difficult to achieve high levels of well-being, to maintain the benefits of unintentional growth experiences, or replicate the growth when new challenges are encountered. Thus, an intentional growth process is of critical importance for college students.

Normative Student Development

There is considerable research demonstrating the importance of PGI for college students. For example, students with high levels of PGI tend to have high GPAs (Robitschek & Anderson, 2011), low levels of psychological distress (Robitschek & Kashubeck, 1999; Weigold & Robitschek, 2011), positive social relationships (Robitschek & Kashubeck, 1999), and high levels of emotional and psychological well-being (Robitschek & Keyes, 2009). In short, these students tend to thrive in the college environment, particularly in contrast to their low PGI colleagues. It is not surprising, then, that PGI is a strong predictor of college student career development. Between college admission and graduation, students are expected to use their academic and work exploration to crystallize vocational choices (Super, 1957), construct a meaningful role for work among their other life-roles (Savickas, 2000), and develop transferable skills for responding to expected and unexpected events in their future careers (Savickas, 1997). Compared with low PGI peers, college students with high PGI engage in more career exploration (Bartley & Robitschek, 2000; Robitschek & Cook, 1999), experience less anxiety about exploring career options and making career decisions (Bartley & Robitschek, 2000), have more self-efficacy for making career decisions (Bartley & Robitschek, 2000), and have a more crystallized vocational identity, namely a clearer sense of who they are in relation to the world of work (Robitschek & Cook, 1999).

In addition, PGI has been theoretically and empirically linked with career adaptability, which is a readiness to handle predictable and unpredictable changes in the career path (Savickas, 1997; Super & Knasel, 1981). Career adaptability is comprised of three core competencies: planfulness (i.e., orientation to the future), exploration (i.e., seeking information), and decision making (i.e., making judgments and acting on those decisions in the world of work) (Savickas, 1997). Ashton and Edwards (2010) theorized that PGI's components of Readiness for Change, Planfulness, Using Resources, and Intentional Behavior map well onto these core competencies, and that college students with high levels of PGI should be more adaptable in their career paths than students with low PGI (Ashton & Edwards, 2010). Recent research in this area has supported these propositions, finding that college students with high PGI have higher levels of career planfulness, exploration, and decision making, and are more likely to perceive growth opportunities within their careers than students with low PGI (Ashton & Robitschek, 2013).

PGI also seems to play a role in how well students do academically. The research in this area is minimal, but results are promising. In fact, PGI may be related to college GPA at a higher rate than the SAT. According to The College Board (Kobrin, Patterson, Shaw, Mattern, & Barbuti, 2008), when all components of the SAT are used (i.e., regular test scores), they account for 12.25% of the variability in first-year GPA. Among a group of predominantly first- and second-year students, PGI (specifically, the Readiness for Change, Using Resources, and Intentional Behavior dimensions) accounted for 22% of the variability in GPA (Robitschek & Anderson, 2011). Perhaps it is not surprising that the Using Resources and Intentional Behavior dimensions seem to be critically important parts of PGI in predicting college GPA. In this context, Using Resources could encompass such things as studying with friends, making use of tutoring and instructor office hours, or using online study aids often provided with textbooks. These are pragmatic resources that can have important influences in a college student's level of success. The Intentional Behavior component may be needed to keep the use of resources identified as an intentional personal growth mechanism. Interestingly, within the context of all dimensions of PGI, students with relatively higher levels of Readiness for Change have *lower* GPAs. We interpret this to mean that students with *only* a readiness to change their GPA, but without the requisite use of resources or engagement in intentional change behaviors, may have much less success raising their GPAs than their peers with higher levels of all PGI components. This may be similar to New Year's resolutions in which people can identify things they want to change about themselves (i.e., high Readiness for Change) but do not have a sufficiently detailed plan for how to make the change (i.e., high Planfulness), have not enlisted the help of others to make the change (i.e., Using Resources), and do not follow through with making the change (i.e., Intentional Behavior).

Finally, college students with high PGI have better interpersonal relationships than their low PGI colleagues. More specifically, it is hypothesized that positive family functioning helps young people develop PGI by teaching them the value of personal growth as well as the requisite skills for this growth (Whittaker & Robitschek, 2001). Perhaps not surprisingly then, students with high PGI report facilitative conditions within their families of origin, including better relationships with family members, experiencing more commitment, support, freedom to express their feelings, encouragement to participate in a wide range of activities outside the family, and less conflict with family members than reported by students with low PGI (Robitschek & Kashubeck, 1999; Whittaker & Robitschek, 2001). High PGI students also are more likely to have current relationships characterized by trust, satisfaction and intimacy, concern for others' well-being, and the ability to compromise in relationships (Robitschek & Kashubeck, 1999; Robitschek & Keyes, 2009), which is the operational definition of Ryff's (1989) *positive relations with others*. One possible explanation for these positive relationships with others is through PGI's impact on other dimensions of well-being. We know that PGI likely is a protective factor against depressive symptoms (Robitschek & Anderson, 2011; Robitschek & Kashubeck, 1999) and seems to promote well-being (Robitschek & Keyes, 2009). When people are happy, satisfied with their lives, and in good mental health, they have more internal resources to invest in productive and satisfying interpersonal relationships. Another possibility is found in the tenet that people with high PGI seek out opportunities for growth and capitalize on opportunities found in the environment (Robitschek, 1998). In this case, people with high PGI should view interpersonal relationships as opportunities for growth. This growth-oriented attitude leads to openness to self-exploration (Ashton & Robitschek, 2013) and specifically in the context of relationships, willingness to explore how to be a better partner, friend, and family member.

Well-Being and Distress

Research indicates that PGI likely plays several important roles in the development of mentally healthy college students. First, PGI seems to have a direct effect on maximizing students' mental health. Keyes (2002) describes mental health as having three dimensions of well-being: psychological (having a sense of purpose and self-acceptance), emotional (perceptions of quality of life and positive affect), and social (thriving in interpersonal relationships within a community). In college students, PGI strongly predicts all three of these components of mental health, accounting for one fifth to one half of the variability in each type of well-being (Hardin, Weigold, Robitschek, & Nixon, 2007; Robitschek & Keyes, 2009). The relationship seems quite clear; when students have higher PGI they also have higher levels of overall mental health. This is important because social, emotional, and psychological well-being are importantly different dimensions of mental health (Keyes, 2003). Factors that impact any one of these dimensions may increase overall well-being. But factors impacting all of the dimensions, as PGI can, have the potential to function as efficient, parsimonious mechanisms to improve overall mental health (Robitschek & Keyes, 2009).

A second important role for PGI in the development of healthy college students is as a protective factor against psychological distress (Robitschek & Keyes, 2009). This role has been investigated in two ways, examining direct effects of PGI on distress and by studying the extent to which PGI can explain the relationships between various constructs and distress. PGI consistently has been found to be directly related to low levels of distress, such as depression and anxiety in college students (e.g., Robitschek & Kashubeck, 1999; Weigold & Robitschek, 2011). In addition, PGI explains the associations of both internal and external factors with psychological distress. In terms of external factors, when college students reported positive functioning in their families of origin they also typically reported high levels of PGI; in turn, they experienced low levels of depression, anxiety, and overall psychological distress (Robitschek & Kashubeck, 1999). An internal factor considered in this literature is self-discrepancies, that is, when the type of person a student thinks he or she should be or wants to be differs from the type of person the student perceives herself or himself to be (Higgins, 1987). Research has found that when college students have lower levels of detrimental self-discrepancies (either because they have fewer or smaller self-discrepancies) they tend to have higher PGI, which in turn, predicts lower levels of social avoidance and distress (Hardin et al., 2007).

There are several possible explanations for these findings. Perhaps college students with high PGI are more likely to be resilient and recover more quickly from distress (Hardin et al., 2007). Another possibility is that students with high PGI easily recognize when they experience distress and quickly try to remedy it by changing their own behavior or the situation before the distress increases or becomes long-lasting (Robitschek & Kashubeck, 1999). Additional research is needed to untangle this complicated mechanism, but sufficient evidence does exist to indicate that PGI is an important factor in helping to increase well-being and decrease psychological distress in college students.

Application and Practice

Although theory and research have focused on learning what PGI might predict or lead to (e.g., improved well-being and lower distress) and what might predict or lead to high levels of PGI (e.g., effective family functioning), PGI theory and research have begun to crossover successfully to applications and practice. For example, current knowledge about PGI can be used to create ways to increase students' PGI. Increasing students' PGI is pragmatic because higher levels of PGI should lead to higher levels of student well-being and success in school. Knowledge of a student's current level of PGI also may be helpful. The research cited in this chapter demonstrates PGI's use as a predictor for a variety of important outcome variables, including emotional well-being, career development, and academic success. Identifying students with low PGI can serve as a preliminary screening to identify students who may have difficulty in one or more areas of student development currently or in the future. From a strengths perspective, we also might screen for high levels of PGI to identify internal resources that can be utilized during the college experience. More specific applications are described in the next several sections.

University Counseling Centers

Perhaps the most obvious place that PGI can be applied is university counseling centers (UCCs). Research shows that people with high PGI are more likely to seek out psychosocial support than their low PGI colleagues (Klockner & Hicks, 2008), suggesting that students who come for services at UCCs likely will have higher levels of PGI than students with similar levels of distress who are not seeking services. This is useful information because it suggests that extra effort is needed to reach distressed students with low PGI who might be reluctant to access available student services. Among clients who do seek counseling, those with higher levels of PGI tend to have more personal commitment to the counseling process (i.e., expectations of taking responsibility for the change process) than clients with lower PGI, and this relation is particularly strong for women (Robitschek & Hershberger, 2005).

Weigold and colleagues (Weigold, Joyce, Spieth, Russell, & Kimbrell, 2010) outlined several ways that PGI can be used during the counseling process. Counselors can assess PGI at the beginning of therapy to aid in client conceptualization and treatment planning. For example, clients with relatively low levels of PGI may need to learn the process and steps of intentional personal growth and change before they will be ready to make major changes in themselves. Conversely, clients with high PGI may be more able to work on important changes from the beginning of counseling because of previous knowledge and experience with the self-change process. PGI also can be assessed on an ongoing basis to track changes in a client's knowledge of and engagement in the intentional growth process. Given the ability of PGI to predict a wide range of well-being, functioning, and distress dimensions, perhaps PGI could be tracked as a simple proxy for broadly defined mental health. In contrast, PGI could be used in conjunction with other measures, either of strengths or struggles, to obtain a more complete picture of a student's current functioning and ability to handle the challenges of college.

PGI also can be used as a core topic in therapy (Weigold et al., 2010). When PGI is introduced to clients at the beginning of therapy it can quickly orient a client to active involvement in the counseling process, goal-setting specifically for personal growth, and a planful, focused approach to personal change. The four components of PGI (Readiness for change, Planfulness, Using resources, and Intentional behavior) also can be specific foci in therapy. For example, clients who have particularly low levels of Using Resources may benefit from explicit skills training on how to use resources outside of themselves (e.g., social support, self-help books, and more advanced students) to assist in their efforts to improve. Clients who have relatively high levels of Planfulness compared with their other components of PGI may not yet be aware of the utility of their Planfulness and may benefit from help recognizing and building on this strength. Helping clients to recognize their strengths is an important part of using positive psychology in counseling.

Thus far, we have focused on using PGI with individual clients. However, PGI is also relevant in UCC programming targeting groups of students. Thoen and Robitschek (2013) created a brief workshop-based intervention, Intentional Growth Training (IGT), that can be used within UCCs to increase students' PGI. The intervention has both an educational component and an activity component. The educational component is an interactive presentation about PGI, which includes defining PGI, discussing how to utilize PGI in daily life, explaining how PGI can be increased through repeated intentional attempts at self-change with positive outcomes, and teaching the process of self-change. This educational component also promotes insight into current life circumstances and emotional states. This is done through guiding workshop participants through an interactive reflective process about a past attempt at self-change. Participants explore issues of stress and risk taking related to their personal growth experiences through a description that change usually involves stepping outside of one's comfort zone. This portion of the intervention takes approximately 20–30 min.

The activity component is presented immediately following the educational component when knowledge about PGI is fresh. Participants self-select a personal growth activity they have wanted to do for some time but have yet to try. The activity needs to be something that will put them outside of their comfort zone but that can be completed within one week. Although the activity might seem to be quite minimal from an outsider's perspective (e.g., participants take a risk and simply try something new rather than actually changing a characteristic or behavior), we have found that the benefits of the activity occur, nonetheless (Thoen & Robitschek, 2013). Steps in this activity component of the intervention include setting specific goals, identifying steps needed to accomplish these goals, and developing action plans for the future activity. The workshop ends when participants have a plan of action. One week later participants return and process the activity, either orally or through expressive writing. Research has shown that college students participating in this intervention experienced a significant increase in both PGI and psychological well-being over this 1-week time period (Martinez & Robitschek, 2010). Students who did not receive the interventions did not experience these benefits (Robitschek et al., 2012). The complete manual for Intentional Growth Training (Thoen & Robitschek, 2012) is available for free use in clinical, educational, and research purposes. The manual can be downloaded at https://pgilab.wordpress.com/intentional-growth-training-igt/.

By teaching about the components of PGI and guiding students through specific intentional efforts to improve themselves, college students can use their acquired skills for future intentional personal growth, with greater psychological well-being as a byproduct. Students will acquire the skills of evaluating when they are ready to change, the process of planning for a change, finding and using the resources needed for change, and then implementing the change process. This workshop can be used in outreach programming or group therapy in the UCC. Although developed for use with groups, the content of the workshop also can be adapted for use with individual clients and can easily be adapted for multiple UCC needs.

Career Services

PGI has several important applications to career services that are offered on campus. The PGIS-II can be used as a quick indicator of students' readiness for the vocational tasks expected in college. The measure could be included with more traditional career assessments when helping students with career decision making and planning to assist with tailoring career interventions to the specific needs of each client (Ashton & Edwards, 2010). For example, when students have low levels of PGI, career counselors might direct clients to explicitly growth-oriented career experiences, such as explicit self-exploration or development of career adaptability as a means of addressing both vocational concerns and the intentional personal growth process. In contrast, when students have high levels of PGI, career counselors can focus less on the process of intentional personal growth and more on the content of career development (Ashton & Edwards, 2010).

Another important use for PGI is to help students prepare for the rapidly changing world of work, which requires students to be adaptable (Savickas, 1997). When students leave college, they need to be prepared to grow their skills as their jobs change with new technology. They also need to be prepared to retool if their existing skill set becomes obsolete or if their segment of the labor market takes a hard hit in an economic down turn and they are unable to get a job in their current field. When the concept of intentional personal growth is incorporated into career counseling it can provide college students with an explicit framework from which to respond to these types of career transitions, helping them become more adaptable in these increasingly uncertain economic times.

Academic Advising

Given the strong predictive relationship of PGI with academic success (Robitschek & Anderson, 2011), it seems prudent for college academic advisors to consider how they might incorporate and promote PGI in their setting. One possibility is to talk explicitly with students about the personal growth that is required to truly succeed in college, explaining the relationship between intentional personal growth and academic success. A second possibility is to offer PGI workshops through an academic advising office. In this setting, advisors could help students generate personal growth goals that target academic growth. A more specific possibility is to focus efforts on helping students access resources in the college community. College and university communities typically do quite well at providing information *about* resources. Using a PGI approach to resources is different; it involves teaching students *how to access* the resources. This includes such things as addressing the roadblocks to accessing campus resources (e.g., student shyness or lack of assertiveness) and teaching students how to talk with faculty who they experience as intimidating. These activities also will help students who are struggling with grades to increase academic functioning (e.g., by teaching them to make better use of academic resources).

Intercollegiate Athletics

The unique challenges and stressors experienced by student athletes make PGI particularly relevant to intercollegiate athletics. Many university and college athletic departments have a mental health professional who is a liaison to the sports teams. This person (or persons) takes into account the specific considerations that must be made for student-athletes regarding their mental health, such as the need to perform at an elite level despite major and minor psychological stressors that easily could impede performance. Just as an academic advisor may discuss with a student the importance of seeking resources when needed and identifying changes that need to be made, so too can an athletic liaison discuss these considerations with student-athletes. In addition, the concept of intentional personal growth may have special significance for developing as student-athletes, who are expected to continue their athletic development during the college years. Typically this requires personal commitment to the self-improvement process, the ability to identify what needs to change in one's skill set, the ability to access and use resources such as trainers and coaches, and the ability to implement the self-improvement strategy. If coaches, trainers, and even athletics directors added PGI as a process dimension to the specific content of each sport, it is possible that training college athletes would be more effective and student athletes would learn a process of personal growth that they could take with them even after their athletic careers end.

PGI in the Classroom

Consider how teaching might differ from the status quo if the activities were approached from a perspective of intentional personal growth. We tend to conceptualize the classroom as a location for intellectual endeavors, for learning.

Two definitions of learning are: "knowledge or skill acquired by instruction or study" and "modification of a behavioral tendency by experience (as exposure to conditioning)" (http://www.merriam-webster.com/dictionary/learning). These definitions suggest that some force outside of the student, whether this force is an *experience* or the instructor, creates an environment in which skills or knowledge are increased. Although the student can have an active role in this process, the active role is not requisite to the process. In contrast, the term *grow* is defined as "to spring up and develop to maturity," "to assume some relation through or as if through a natural process," and "to increase in size by assimilation of material into the living organism . . ." (http://www.merriam-webster.com/dictionary/grow). These definitions suggest that some force *within* the students is responsible for change. Thus, if students are *growing* in the classroom, they are doing so because of a natural tendency within themselves and due to their own actions. Certainly faculty can structure experiences to facilitate this growth. But the major impetus for the growth comes from within the student.

Several implications of the PGI approach in the classroom are evident. First, students are responsible for their own growth in the classroom, and instructors are responsible for supporting and facilitating this growth. This is important information for students to have, and should be provided directly through syllabi, descriptions of assignments, expectations of in-class participation, and instructor facilitation of this participation, to name a few. Second, teaching strategies can be designed to increase students' PGI. For example, when the process of intentional personal growth is made explicit early in the semester, instructors can begin with an assignment that requires most students to grow and is likely to have a high rate of success for all students. For example, in Introductory Psychology classes an assignment could be to identify a topic of interest anywhere in the field of psychology; use the college library's online catalog to locate and access a recent journal article addressing that topic; read the article; and write a report about the article, summarizing what the student understands about the article and identifying the parts of the article that the student does not understand. After students complete the assignment, instructors can debrief the *process* of growth/ learning in this assignment to help students understand and solidify the process so that they can apply it again in future assignments and growth activities. In this example, students will have learned the PGI concepts of Using Resources, Intentional Behavior, and how to identify areas for future learning and growth (i.e., Readiness for Change). Thus, the activity parallels key components of the PGI activity described in the University Counseling Center section.

PGI can also be used to work one-on-one with students. Instructors can include consideration of PGI in their conceptualization of a wide range of potential problems and experiences students might have. For example, a student who has earned a failing grade in the class by mid-term may be either low in PGI or not using PGI in this class. When an instructor takes a PGI approach to this situation, conversation with the student would include discussion of the *growth process* the student is using in the class, with an assessment by the instructor of how to improve this process. For example, keeping in mind the four components of PGI, instructors could assess the degree to which the student is viewing class content as an opportunity to learn and grow, making a useful plan for learning the material, knowledgeable about available resources to help with the learning process, and is putting the learning plan into action and actually making use of the available resources. Perhaps the student needs better Planfulness, or maybe more Intentional Behavior. For students not doing well in class who are not using instructor office hours or available tutoring, the instructor might consider how to increase the Using Resources dimension of PGI for these particular students or for the class as a whole if that is warranted. Finally, PGI can also be used to conceptualize success in class. When students are doing well, instructors can invite these students to attend instructor office hours to discuss the students' personal growth process. This type of discussion can help students make their growth processes more explicit, thereby increasing the intentionality of the process, and in turn, increasing overall well-being (Robitschek, 1999) and the likelihood that the process will be used again.

Multicultural Considerations

Throughout this chapter, we have presented an emphasis on *self-directed personal improvement*. Given this emphasis, it is reasonable to wonder if PGI is unique to cultures and groups that emphasize independent functioning, such as European Americans and men more so than women. Fortunately, this is not the case. Instead, research suggests that PGI is similarly relevant across many different cultures within the United States and throughout the world (e.g., Joshanloo & Ghaedi, 2009; Solcova & Kebza, 2005). For example, in a sample of several thousand college students, including Latina/os, African Americans, and European Americans, average scores (and distributions of scores) on the PGIS were virtually identical (Robitschek, 2002). However, culture does play a role in that an individual's culture impacts perceptions of the ways in which it is important to grow and develop as a person by affecting values and beliefs (Robitschek, 2003).

There are several important implications of the role of culture in the expression of PGI on college campuses. Perhaps most importantly, students will have different culturally based definitions of what it means to be a *good student*. For example, some students from immigrant families might value getting good grades above all else, with their families perceiving good grades as a direct predictor of future work success. Other students from cultures of privilege might value studying something they love, having grown up with the assumption that they will be able to support themselves in any field they choose. Still other students from working-class backgrounds might value successfully balancing school, work, and family roles, perhaps because of a need to support themselves through college, while contributing emotionally and financially to their families. It is important to consider how personal growth goals may vary for students in each of these groups. Students in the first group might focus on developing study skills, writing skills, or becoming more comfortable seeking assistance from tutors. Students in the second group might set goals to learn more about their interests and how those interests might be related to the world of work. Finally, students in the last group might set personal growth goals of crystallizing their values and priorities to help them make specific plans for a more balanced approach to their multiple life-roles. Students in all of these groups could be focused on being a *good student*, but they would be approaching this shared goal from quite different perspectives; therefore, they have very different specific goals that are grounded in their cultural values.

College staff and faculty working with students to increase their PGI need to incorporate culture into their activities by following several guidelines:

a. be aware of our own cultural values and how they might affect our definitions of personal growth, particularly during the college years;
b. be careful to avoid imposing our own culturally-based operationalizations of areas for personal growth;
c. incorporate the topic of culture and cultural values into every discussion with students about intentional personal growth—this can be accomplished by simply and directly asking students how they want to grow and how their values play important roles in these growth goals; and
d. be respectful of students' personal and cultural definitions of appropriate domains for intentional personal growth.

Case Study

When Gabriela went through new student orientation at a large public university, she received IGT. Through IGT, Gabriela learned about the four components of PGI (Readiness for Change, Planfulness, Using Resources, and Intentional Behavior) and the benefits of having a high level of PGI; she also planned and carried out an intentional growth activity. During this training, she realized that she had an average level of PGI. Gabriela was particularly good at Readiness for Change (recognizing what she could improve about herself and when it was a good time to make those changes) and Planfulness (creating a strategy for how to make changes). She also learned that she was less adept at Using Resources (asking for help from others or using material resources) and Intentional Behavior (actually carrying out the plans she made for self-improvement). Through the discussion in IGT, Gabriela realized that as part of her Mexican heritage she did not consider the things family members did for one another as asking for help or Using Resources. Instead, Gabriela perceived this as "just what we do." In addition, Gabriela would not want to impose on anyone outside her family by asking them for help with any problems she was having. Altogether, Gabriela learned that she was better at thinking about personal growth than she was at actually carrying out her plans for growth.

As the fall semester started, Gabriela readily made friends. But just as she learned in IGT, Gabriela did not want to impose on her friends or anyone else at the university by asking them for any type of assistance. So despite her close network of friends and many available resources, Gabriela was not Using Resources to any large extent. This was not a problem until she began to struggle with the material in her Cultural Anthropology class. She talked with family members about her struggles, but because Gabriela was a first generation college student, her family could provide support but little specific assistance with this problem. Gabriela needed help from resources more familiar with what she was experiencing. She had a cousin, Rocio, who had graduated from college several years earlier, and Gabriela's family encouraged her to talk with this cousin about the problem. On a weekend trip home, Rocio asked Gabriela how school was going. When Gabriela shared her struggles, Rocio told her about the importance of using university resources, such as meeting with faculty and TAs, and joining study groups to be successful in college. She stressed that it was OK to ask for help from these sources and gave Gabriela some tips on how to approach her instructors with questions. Rocio even helped Gabriela write and send an email to her Anthropology instructor, Dr. Jermaine Williams, asking to set up a meeting to discuss the course material. This is an example of Rocio teaching Gabriela how to Use Resources.

Shortly after Gabriela returned to school, Dr. Williams responded by email and they set up a meeting. Because the student had been struggling for some time, Dr. Williams, who knew about PGI, asked why she didn't come in sooner. He realized there might multiple factors influencing this, including cultural issues, PGI, and personal style. Gabriela stated that it is hard for her to ask for help, that she was taught to do things on her own and not burden others with her problems. Dr. Williams recognized these reasons as both cultural and a low level of Using Resources. He quickly assessed several things during the conversation with Gabriela: (1) if she had received any messages from family members that it was OK to ask for help in a school setting; (2) if she had taken IGT during orientation; and (3) her skills in the other dimensions of PGI. Through this conversation Dr. Williams found out that her cousin had encouraged Gabriela to contact him. He also learned that Gabriela had relatively high levels of Readiness for Change and Planfulness. So he focused on Using Resources in their discussion.

Dr. Williams focused on Using Resources in two ways. First, he provided Gabriela with the resources she needed to be more successful in his class, things like study skills and answering her specific questions about course material. Second, he discussed the process of Using Resources (in the context of PGI) specific to his class. Dr. Williams explicitly acknowledged that Gabriela was, in fact Using Resources by coming to talk with him. They discussed the cultural and personal barriers that had made it difficult for Gabriela to ask for help from Dr. Williams. He reinforced the benefits of using available resources in this way and discussed Using Resources as part of the personal growth process for Gabriela during her first year in college. Finally, Dr. Williams not only encouraged Gabriela to come back when she again had questions about course material, but also helped her set a small behavioral goal for how to use additional resources at school. This encouraged her to take what she had learned about the process of personal growth and apply it in another context.

Because both Gabriela and Dr. Williams were well-versed in the language and concepts of PGI, this process of promoting PGI did not take long. Dr. Williams primarily was reminding Gabriela of what she already had learned and was simply teaching her to apply the concept of Using Resources in a new context. This brief intervention provided Gabriela with two attempts to practice Using Resources, one of which already included a positive outcome. Dr. Williams' actions could have important effects on Gabriela's grades and well-being, particularly in combination with similar experiences elsewhere in Gabriela's college experience.

Conclusion

We began this chapter with several students, all of whom were experiencing the rude awakening that college was much more difficult than high school. Some of these students faced this challenge with low PGI and experienced the challenge as a threat to who they were and what they were capable of doing. These low PGI students might have foreclosed on career options that required them to overcome the academic challenges of college. Other students met the challenge of increased demands in college with high PGI and experienced the challenge as an opportunity to grow and improve themselves. These high PGI students made important changes in themselves to overcome the challenge, continued to grow in similar ways throughout college, and thrived in the face of this challenge. Armed with knowledge about PGI, college and university staff and faculty can intervene in multiple aspects of campus life and in the classroom to address and increase the PGI of every student, so that all college students have the opportunity to thrive in the face of the inherent challenges college will provide.

Personal Growth Initiative Scale—II
© Christine Robitschek, Ph.D., 2008

For each statement, please mark how much you agree or disagree with that statement. Use the following scale:

0 = Disagree Strongly
1 = Disagree Somewhat
2 = Disagree a Little
3 = Agree a Little
4 = Agree Somewhat
5 = Agree Strongly

	0	1	2	3	4	5
1. I set realistic goals for what I want to change about myself.	0	1	2	3	4	5
2. I can tell when I am ready to make specific changes in myself.	0	1	2	3	4	5
3. I know how to make a realistic plan in order to change myself.	0	1	2	3	4	5
4. I take every opportunity to grow as it comes up.	0	1	2	3	4	5
5. When I try to change myself, I make a realistic plan for my personal growth.	0	1	2	3	4	5
6. I ask for help when I try to change myself.	0	1	2	3	4	5
7. I actively work to improve myself.	0	1	2	3	4	5
8. I figure out what I need to change about myself.	0	1	2	3	4	5
9. I am constantly trying to grow as a person.	0	1	2	3	4	5
10. I know how to set realistic goals to make changes in myself.	0	1	2	3	4	5
11. I know when I need to make a specific change in myself.	0	1	2	3	4	5
12. I use resources when I try to grow.	0	1	2	3	4	5
13. I know steps I can take to make intentional changes in myself.	0	1	2	3	4	5
14. I actively seek out help when I try to change myself.	0	1	2	3	4	5
15. I look for opportunities to grow as a person.	0	1	2	3	4	5
16. I know when it's time to change specific things about myself.	0	1	2	3	4	5

References

Ashton, M. W., & Edwards, A. E. (2010, August). Personal growth initiative and vocational functioning. In C. Robitschek (Chair), *Personal growth initiative in mental health, vocational functioning, and intervention.* Symposium conducted at the meeting of the American Psychological Association, San Diego, CA.

Ashton, M. W., & Robitschek, C. (2013, July). *Career adaptability and personal growth initiative: A moderated mediation model.* Poster presented at the annual meeting of the American Psychological Association, Honolulu, HI.

Ashton, M. W., Robitschek, C., Geiger, A. N., & Murray, D. D. (2010, August). *Reliability and validity of the Personal Growth Initiative Scale—II.* Poster presented at the annual meeting of the American Psychological Association, San Diego, CA.

Bartley, D. F., & Robitschek, C. (2000). Career exploration: A multivariate analysis of predictors. *Journal of Vocational Behavior, 56*(1), 63–81.

Chemers, M. M., Hu, L., & Garcia, B. F. (2001). Academic self-efficacy and first-year college student performance and adjustment. *Journal of Educational Psychology, 93*(1), 55–64.

Hardin, E. E., Weigold, I. K., Robitschek, C., & Nixon, A. E. (2007). Self-discrepancy and distress: The role of personal growth initiative. *Journal of Counseling Psychology, 54*(1), 86–92.

Higgins, E. T. (1987). Self-discrepancy: A theory relating self and affect. *Psychological Review, 94*(3), 319–340.

Joshanloo, M., & Ghaedi, G. (2009). Psychometric characteristics of "Personal Growth Initiative" scale in university students. *Journal of Behavioral Sciences (Iran), 3*, 121–125.

Keyes, C. L. M. (2002). The mental health continuum: From languishing to flourishing in life. *Journal of Health and Social Behavior, 43*(2), 207–222.

Keyes, C. L. M. (2003). Complete mental health: An agenda for the 21st century. In C. L. M. Keyes & J. Haidt (Eds.), *Flourishing: Positive psychology and the life well-lived* (pp. 293–312). Washington DC: American Psychological Association.

Klockner, K. D., & Hicks, R. E. (2008). My next client: Understanding the Big Five and positive personality dispositions of those seeking psychosocial support interventions. *International Coaching Psychology Review, 3*(2), 148–163.

Kobrin, J. L., Patterson, B. F., Shaw, E. J., Mattern, K. D., & Barbuti, S. M. (2008). *Validity of the SAT for predicting first-year college grade point average* (Technical Report No. 2008-5). Retrieved from College Board website: http://professionals.collegeboard.com/profdownload/Validity_of_the_SAT_for_Predicting_First_Year_College_Grade_Point_Average.pdf

Martinez, M. A., & Robitschek, C. (2010, August). *Increasing Personal Growth Initiative through Education and Growth Activity.* Poster presented at the annual meeting of the American Psychological Association, San Diego, CA.

Prochaska, J. O., & DiClemente, C. C. (1982). Transtheoretical therapy: Toward a more integrative model of change. *Psychotherapy: Theory, research and practice, 19*, 276–288.

Prochaska, J. O., & DiClemente, C. C. (1986). The transtheoretical approach. In J. C. Norcross (Ed.), *Handbook of eclectic psychotherapy* (pp. 163–200). New York: Brunner/Mazel.

Robitschek, C. (1998). Personal growth initiative: The construct and its measure. *Measurement and Evaluation in Counseling and Development, 30*(4), 183–198.

Robitschek, C. (1999). Further validation of the Personal Growth Initiative Scale. *Measurement and Evaluation in Counseling and Development, 31*(4), 197–210.

Robitschek, C. (2002). Normative data for the PGIS across culturally diverse college samples. Unpublished raw data.

Robitschek, C. (2003). Validity of Personal Growth Initiative Scale scores with a Mexican American college student population. *Journal of Counseling Psychology, 50*(4), 496–502.

Robitschek, C., & Anderson, L. A. (2011, August). *Personal growth initiative: Predicting depression, well-being, and functioning in college students.* Poster presented at the annual convention of the American Psychological Association, Washington DC.

Robitschek, C., Ashton, M. W., Spering, C. C., Geiger, N., Byers, D., Shotts, G. C., & Thoen, M. (2012). Development and psychometric properties of the Personal Growth Initiative Scale—II. *Journal of Counseling Psychology, 59*(2), 274–287.

Robitschek, C., & Cook, S. W. (1999). The influence of personal growth initiative and coping styles on career exploration and vocational identity. *Journal of Vocational Behavior, 54*(1), 127–141.

Robitschek, C., & Hershberger, A. R. (2005). Predicting expectations about counseling: Psychological factors and gender implications. *Journal of Counseling and Development, 83*(4), 457–469.

Robitschek, C., & Kashubeck, S. (1999). A structural model of parental alcoholism, family functioning, and psychological health: The mediating effects of hardiness and personal growth orientation. *Journal of Counseling Psychology, 46*(2), 159–172.

Robitschek, C., & Keyes, C. L. M. (2009). Keyes' model of mental health with personal growth initiative as a parsimonious predictor. *Journal of Counseling Psychology, 56*(2), 321–329.

Ryff, C. D. (1989). Happiness is everything, or is it? Explorations on the meaning of psychological well-being. *Journal of Personality and Social Psychology, 57*(6), 1069–1081.

Savickas, M. L. (1997). Career adaptability: An integrative construct for life-span, life-space theory. *Career Development Quarterly, 45*(3), 247–257.

Savickas, M. L. (2000). Renovating the psychology of careers for the 21st century. In A. Colins & R. A. Young (Eds.), *The future of career* (pp. 53–68). New York: Cambridge University Press.

Solcova, I., & Kebza, V. (2005). Predictors of well-being in a representative sample of Czech population. *Ceskoslovenska Psychologie, 49*, 1–8.

Super, D. E. (1957). *The psychology of careers.* New York: Harper & Row.

Super, D. E., & Knasel, E G. (1981). Career development in adulthood: Some theoretical problems and a possible solution. *British Journal of Guidance and Counselling, 9*(2), 194–201.

Thoen, M. A., & Robitschek, C. (2012). *Intentional Growth Training.* Unpublished manual. Retrieved from http://www.myweb.ttu.edu/crobitsc/IGT.html

Thoen, M. A., & Robitschek, C. (2013). Intentional growth training: An intervention to increase personal growth initiative. *Applied Psychology: Health and Well-being, 5*(2), 149–170.

Weigold, I. K., Joyce, N. R., Spieth, R. E., Russell, E. J., & Kimbrell, M. T. (2010, August). Personal growth initiative and mental health. In C. Robitschek (Chair), *Personal growth initiative in mental health, vocational, functioning, and interventions.* Invited symposium presented at the annual meeting of the American Psychological Association, San Diego, CA.

Weigold, I. K., & Robitschek, C. (2011). Agentic personality characteristics and coping: Their relation to trait anxiety in college students. *American Journal of Orthopsychiatry, 81*(2), 255–264.

Whittaker, A. E., & Robitschek, C. (2001). Multidimensional family functioning: Predicting personal growth initiative. *Journal of Counseling Psychology, 48*(4), 420–427.

10

Social Development and Relationship Enhancement

SARAH L. HASTINGS AND TRACY J. COHN

Memorable times are those shared with others. Indeed, for most people, happiness and a sense of meaning in life are not only enhanced by social connections, but are defined by them (Baumeister, Vohs, Aaker, & Garbinsky, 2013; Krause, 2007). People with ample social support enjoy important far-reaching benefits including better health, lower rates of mental health concerns, and increased longevity (Berkman & Syme, 1979; House, Landis, & Umberson, 1988). Any examination of the many facets of positive psychology (e.g., strengths, well-being, gratitude, happiness) would be incomplete without attending to the interpersonal context of these phenomena.

The importance and value of friendships during college are particularly salient given that these years of development are essential in shaping personal identity for the late adolescent or emerging adult. For traditional-aged college students, the transition to university life is frequently a time during which the individual moves away both psychologically and physically from one's family (Rice, 1992). Indeed, findings suggest that emerging adults are likely to be more comfortable with their friends and have more reliance on their peer networks than on their parents (Youniss & Smollar, 1985). This closeness parallels the developmental task of separation and individuation (Lopez, Campbell, & Watkins, 1988) found in many Western cultures. College students with strong social support networks tend to have higher academic achievement lower dropout rates, and higher academic engagement (Gerdes & Mallinckrodt, 1994; Mallinckrodt, 1988). College years become an opportunity to enhance personal understanding of differences as well as to enrich the complexity of friendships.

Students enter the university setting possessing a wide range of skills necessary to build and sustain relationships. They have typically learned their relationship skills vicariously from their families, and have developed social patterns which enabled them to meet their needs in that setting. Rarely, however, have students received instruction or feedback regarding how to develop effective personal bonds beyond their immediate circle of family and social contacts. The college years provide a new arena in which to learn how to work and live effectively with people who are different from oneself, and the skills developed on campus lay the foundation for close relationships across the lifespan.

In this chapter, we explore findings from the positive psychology literature dealing with human relationships particularly as they apply to college students. Much of the material we will discuss addresses both friendships and romantic involvements, but our goal is to think more broadly than romantic ties. As Friedrich Nietzsche remarked, "It is not a lack of love, but a lack of friendship that makes unhappy marriages." Certainly, the skills that nourish friendships also nurture meaningful romantic relationships, and it is our hope that readers can extract the findings from the friendship literature and apply these to enhance their romantic relationships where appropriate. The following sections explore why having friends is one of the strongest predictors of overall satisfaction with life and general levels of happiness (Reis & Gable, 2003). As college students refine their adult identity and prepare to step into vocational roles, social interactions potentially provide a practice arena where students can learn about peer relationships and develop life-long skills in nurturing them. This chapter is designed for anyone who works with college students in a supportive or advisory role. Effective helpers, whether they are residence life staff, career development professionals, or student affairs administrators know that establishing trusting relationships with students creates a welcoming space for guidance or mentoring to occur. Students are more likely to be open to suggestions, feedback, and instruction when they feel respected and valued as people. The bonds of warm caring relationships help pave the way for the business of mentoring to occur. Warm caring relationships also help students function better in the university environment overall.

Benefits of Close Relationships

Relationships play a central role in human development across the lifespan. From an evolutionary perspective, relationships provided many advantages to early humans. Membership in a tribe or family group increased one's likelihood of survival by providing protection and procuring food. The emergence of division of labor allowed the responsibilities associated with survival to be shared and distributed among group members, ensuring a more efficient use of resources. Today, in many universities, honor societies or organizations associated with academic majors serve a similar function by providing their members access to information about internships or professional networking opportunities. Psychological researcher John Bowlby argued that close relationships not only enhanced the survival of early humans, but continue today to direct the path of healthy human development. He termed the establishment of emotional bonds between people *attachment* and went on to develop a detailed explanation for how bonds between children and their caregivers increase one's chances of survival and provide a template for adult relationships into adulthood (Bowlby, 1988).

Beyond the evolutionary benefits, human relationships are believed to help buffer an individual from the stresses of life, and can influence behavior, shaping and molding it according to the norms of an established group. Having friends influences how likely people are to achieve their goals. Close friends increase motivation to pursue goals, and individuals are more likely to meet those goals if they believe that their friends will appreciate their efforts (Shah, 2003). Having friends can also make people healthier. Socializing with a friend who eats healthily makes it more likely that a person will also eat healthily (Rath, 2006). People with a medical condition who have friends live longer than those who share the same medical condition but do not have friends. In one study examining a group of individuals with heart disease who had four or more friends compared to a similar group who had fewer than four friends, individuals in the group with fewer friends were more likely to die (Brummett et al., 2001).

Perhaps not surprisingly, engaging in an unpleasant or mundane activity, such as studying for a final exam, is made more enjoyable with the presence of a friend (Kahneman, Krueger, Schkade, Schwarz, & Stone, 2004). Although studies have not shown that students study longer when doing so with a friend, the overall level of displeasure has been found to be lower. Given the importance that college students place on their friendships for social and emotional support, it is not surprising that the literature reflects the necessary and essential function of friendships on mental and physical health. Of particular relevance to individuals in higher education, college students who report having at least one close friend or best friend in college are more likely to persist in their academic track (Goguen, Hiester, & Nordstrom, 2010). Findings from Goguen, Hiester, and Nordstom suggest that a friendship cultivated in the first year of college that is based on trust, similar interests, and lower-conflict is associated with higher GPA and greater likelihood of attending a second year.

Selecting Friends

How do students choose friends from among their many acquaintances? The relationships established by college students are generally seen as similar and proximal (Ebbsen, Kjos, & Konecni, 1976). That is, college-age students pick friends who are close to them physically (e.g., down the hallway of the same residence hall) or similar to them in age, race, or ethnic group (Way & Chen, 2000). In high school, this pattern of selecting friends who are close and culturally similar is largely based on ethnic segregations of school and neighborhoods (Mouw & Entwisle, 2006). During college years, it becomes increasingly likely that students will be exposed to individuals with backgrounds different from their own and become friends with those from various cultures. However, exposure alone does not guarantee that students will expand their social networks to include people who are different from themselves, as according to Syed and Juan (2012), homophily (i.e., the tendency of people from similar cultures to group together) tends to happen among college-aged students if efforts are not focused on building networks between groups of diverse people. Therefore, if universities are committed to the idea of friendships, administrators, faculty and members of residence life may benefit from creating opportunities that require collaboration rather than competition. For example, at the University of Kansas, students compete to be included in the "Rock Chalk Review" musical and in turn, those selected groups work together to raise money for a common charitable organization.

In order to establish close relationships, it pays to behave in ways that signal to others one is likely to serve as a valued friend. What kinds of behaviors help create bonds between people? Given that friendship is associated with so many important outcomes, how can one increase the likelihood of finding and keeping friends? The following sections describe factors associated with establishing and maintaining relationship bonds.

Empathy and Communication Skills

Much of what experts in human behavior have come to believe about establishing supportive relationships has emerged from the literature in counseling and psychology. Carl Rogers (1951), arguably one of the most influential figures in the field, advocated that good listening skills, grounded in an attitude of authenticity, provide the foundation for supportive relationships. He viewed listening, not as a passive process, but as an engaged, active stance assumed by the listener as that individual strives to see the world as the other person sees it. Active listeners attend to the total meaning communicated, tuning into emotions both expressed and implied. They focus in not only to the words spoken, but also to nonverbal cues, voice inflection, and eye movements to help clarify the underlying meaning expressed. Rogers further emphasized that respectful listening includes communicating back to the speaker that the listener understands the content and the emotion that was communicated. In other words, it is not enough to say, "I know exactly what you mean," or "I understand how you feel." Rather, Rogers advocated showing one's understanding through action—the action of reflecting back both the content and emotion that were communicated. Responding to a distressed student by saying, "You're really hurt by what your roommate said, and you're wondering whether the two of you can work through this problem," is likely to help a student feel heard and valued. This expressed empathy was included as one of the central conditions that Rogers conceptualized as necessary for personal development to occur, along with congruence and unconditional positive regard.

Listening in this way is not an easy task. The skills involved in active listening require time and commitment. It is difficult to tune out distractions in order to truly listen to another person. There is little question that the contemporary environment provides many competing sources for our attention. Our love of technology and the push to do more in less time has made multitasking skills critical in most settings. However, what threatens to become lost is the focused attention that helps build and nurture intimacy. Professional helpers turn off their cell phones, close their office doors, and set systems in place to assure that the time with their client will not be interrupted. Although we are not proposing to equate friendship to counseling, we are suggesting there are aspects of the counseling relationship and of the stance taken by a professional helper that can inform how we approach meaningful relationships. Namely, deep listening takes energy, requires commitment, and calls us to prioritize the relationship by setting boundaries in place to protect it from outside intrusions.

Most people find that active listening skills are acquired over time with repeated practice. That practice includes *un*learning other styles of communication that are mistakenly construed as helpful, including advice giving, minimizing problems, comparing the other person's situation to one's own, or changing the subject to cheer up the other individual. Helping professionals are trained to be cautious in giving advice, knowing that telling people what to do often minimizes the complexity of their situations and can impede autonomous decision making. This granting of autonomy is especially important with college students, who may, for the first time, be in a position of making important decisions on their own without parental influence. Peer helpers in universities are often taught to restrain themselves from giving advice regarding complex personal decisions. Rather, students can be better assisted when peer and professional helpers alike demonstrate empathic understanding, educate about available resources, and help students access those resources in an efficient manner. There are a number of resources university peer and professional helpers can use to enhance their listening and responding skills. More than Listening: A Casebook for Using Counseling Skills in Student Affairs Work (Harper, 2010) is designed for those who want to make a difference in students' lives, but who may not have professional training in counseling and helping skills. Likewise, Applied Helping Skills: Transforming Lives (Brew & Kottler, 2008) provides an introduction to basic responding skills. Many universities student affairs divisions invite professional counseling center staff to provide training in listening skills to resident advisors or other peer helpers during orientation. Many colleges offer courses in helping skills for peer facilitators or other students in helping roles. All of these resources can provide professionals and peer helpers alike, with skills that will enable them to be more empathic communicators.

The value of empathy extends beyond immediate contacts and close relationships. Feeling empathy for members of stigmatized groups (e.g., minorities, people diagnosed with mental illnesses, or human immunodeficiency virus) and for social causes (e.g., animal rights, the environment) has important implications for promoting tolerance and fostering social action. Capitalizing on empathy can improve attitudes toward a broad range of people and groups. It can reduce prejudice and discrimination against ethnic or sexual minorities and improve attitudes toward protecting the environment (Batson, 1991). Actively trying to understand what a person is thinking and feeling will increase empathic feelings, which lead to valuing the person's welfare, which in turn, leads to generalizing to the stigmatized group as a whole. Thus, the benefits of empathy have the potential to impact understanding and appreciation of entire groups of people and to counter attitudes which lead to discrimination and marginalization (Batson, 1991). Understanding the power of empathy can help organizers of diversity training events or multicultural planning staff to deepen the impact of their programming by engaging students' perspective taking abilities in a positive way.

How do we know whether listening skills and empathy really matter? Do people truly value being heard and understood? Most of us, reflecting on our own experiences with skilled and unskilled listeners, would argue listening does matter, and research findings bear this out as well. Researchers have found, for example, that people seek out social environments where they believe others understand them. According to self-verification theory, people enjoy interacting with those who confirm their self-views (Swann, Rentfrow, & Guinn, 2002). In romantic relationships, people tend to remain with partners longer if the two individuals share similar emotional reactions to life events (Anderson, Keltner, & John, 2003; Oishi & Sullivan, 2006) or similar goals (Sanderson & Evans, 2001). People experience greater positive affect when they feel that their partner understands them (Oishi, Koo, & Akimoto, 2008) and shares their joy for positive life events (Gable, Reis, Impett, & Asher, 2004). Perceiving close others to be responsive and understanding of a stressful experience mitigates the stressful experience's negative impact on one's health and subjective well-being (Sarason, Sarason, & Gurung, 1997). Thus, people orient toward social environments where they perceive others understand their subjective thoughts and relate to their feelings. They seek out those who communicate warmth, acceptance, understanding, and validation. Thus, empathy *does* matter, and student affairs personnel, advisors, and other support professionals who display empathy and who create opportunities for students to experience empathic feelings for one another, can impact the campus community on a larger scale. A challenge for professionals who plan student events or who organize student activities is to find ways to help students step beyond the comfort they feel in their immediate groups, and to experience empathy for and work together with others who may be different from themselves. Universities have embraced this challenge by creating opportunities for marginalized groups to tell their stories. At Radford University, for example, several student groups organized a concert with Music 4 Mental Health, featuring a musician and former Virginia Tech running back who integrated positive messages about mental health with his musical performance in an outdoor space accessible to a large audience.

Mutuality and Autonomy Support

Another way of conceptualizing supportive relationships is through the lens of mutuality. Acceptance of another person comes easily when a friend holds opinions and beliefs that dovetail neatly with one's own. However, few relationships are so tidy, and people will inevitably find themselves at odds regarding some aspect of their friendship. How can people balance attending to their own needs and honoring the needs of their companion when differences arise? Is it possible to still be connected with another person while supporting that individual's identify as a separate being? Set forth in the relational/cultural theory articulated by researchers from the Stone Center at Wellesley College (Jordan, Kaplan, Miller, Stiver, & Surrey, 1991) mutuality describes the process in which both people in a relationship display empathic consideration for each other, acknowledge and honor the uniqueness of the other, and are willing to both affect and be affected by the other. Mutuality is a bidirectional interpersonal process in which both parties are willing to share and explore their inner experiences with one another while refraining from trying to change or manipulate the other person (Jordan, 1991). The process has been studied along with autonomy support, which is when one person acknowledges another's perspective, helps provide choices, and encourages self-initiation, while being responsive to the other. An academic advisor may want a good student to continue in her chosen major, because the advisor recognizes the student is a good writer, has helped the advisor in his research, and has potential to go to graduate school. However, the advisor, in learning the student is considering changing majors, would display autonomy support if he bracketed his own needs and agenda in order to help the student come to a decision that is best for her though it may be different from what is the advisor's best interests.

Although autonomy support has generally been examined between two individuals with varying levels of power within a relationship (e.g., between an authority figure and a subordinate), researchers have begun examining whether the same benefits occur in peer relationships where there is a greater expectation of mutuality. Might both people in a relationship benefit from giving and receiving autonomy support? Studies have found that, in fact, they do. Receiving autonomy support from a close friend prompts the recipient to perceive greater relationship quality and greater well-being. However, the giver of autonomy support also benefits, the way a friend who gives a gift to another experiences the pleasure of giving something of meaning and value. As an example, a student, Jenny, has invited her roommate, Savannah, to attend a sorority pre-rush event designed to recruit new members. Savannah is debating whether or not to go. Savannah feels a sense of loyalty to her roommate, but she worries joining a sorority would interfere with her other activities. Although Jenny would like to have her roommate and friend be a part of her sorority, she recognizes that Savannah is a person with different priorities and interests, so Jenny talks with Savannah about the advantages and potential disadvantages of joining the sorority, but she refrains from pressuring her to participate. Jenny respects Savannah's position, states she knows Savannah will make the best decision for herself, and honors whatever Savannah ultimately chooses. Close friends who equally support each other's independence provide a clear example of autonomy support. The benefits extend both to perceptions regarding the quality of the relationship and to perceptions regarding higher levels of general psychological well-being for the individuals involved (Deci, La Guardia, Moller, Scheiner, & Ryan, 2006). Interestingly, perceived autonomy support from the friend also predicted a greater willingness to express both positive and negative feelings within the relationship. The results applied both to women and to men, suggesting that autonomy is as important for women as it is to men and that connectedness has relevance for men as well as for women.

Communication and Capitalization

Most people have experienced the support and reassurance gained by leaning on a trusted friend during times of need. However, people also seek one another for social support when things go well in addition to when things are not going well. Langston (1994) described this process as capitalization, meaning that the act of telling others about a positive event capitalizes or provides benefits *beyond* those experienced as a result of the event itself. Furthermore, the benefits of sharing positive events affect both the person who tells the event and the one to whom the event is disclosed (Gable et al., 2004; Gable, Gonzaga, & Strachman, 2006). Capitalization is very common in daily interactions. In surveys, people indicated they told at least one other person about the most positive thing that had happened to them that day between 70% and 80% of the time (Gable et al., 2004). Furthermore, when people shared positive events, they reported experiencing positive feelings, enhanced well-being, a sense of greater self-esteem, and less loneliness beyond the effects of the positive events themselves. In other words, the *sharing* of positive happenings seems to benefit the person who has experienced the event. Indeed, the more people with whom individuals indicate they shared positive events, the more benefits they experienced (Gable et al., 2004).

With whom do people choose to share positive life events? Most choose close friends or family members. In fact, capitalization seems to provide an opportunity for friends and others in close relationships to cultivate intimacy. How friends and others respond to hearing positive news can have a powerful effect on the relationship. These responses can be classified on two dimensions. The active-passive dimension assesses whether the partner's response to good news is actively engaging or whether it is inactive and minimally engaging. The constructive-destructive dimension measures whether the partner's response affirms the good news or detracts from it. These two dimensions, if arranged perpendicularly, result in four quadrants, and serve as a grid on which to classify a partner's reaction to good news. Active-constructive responses, those that are present in most satisfying relationships, communicate enthusiasm about the positive event and signal the other partner the receiver of the good news is actively engaged. Passive-constructive responses convey a positive response to the event, but the response is minimal given that the partner does little to elicit more information or communicate excitement. Active-destructive responding describes reactions that deliver negative feedback to the good news. Perhaps the responder presents a less desirable interpretation of the event or highlights its negative implications. Finally, passive-destructive responses fail to acknowledge the event. Perhaps the partner changes the subject or focuses on his or her own experiences in relation to it.

An example may help in illustrating the four responses. Karen tells her roommate, Lynn, she was accepted into an academic honor society. If Lynn responds with an active-constructive response, she would say something like, "Fantastic! I knew you could do it. Give me the details!" A passive-constructive response would be, "That's nice." Lynn's response would be active-destructive if she said, "Time to give up any hopes of a social life. You'll be spending every weekend studying to keep your grades up so you can stay in there." Finally, if Lynn were to deliver a passive-destructive response, she may say nothing or reply, "Guess what happened to me today?"

Studies have linked relationship quality to the pattern of responses people typically receive from their relationship partners. In dating couples, greater relationship satisfaction, trust, and intimacy were reported in relationships where active-constructive responses predominated in the interactions (Gable & Gosnell, 2011). The pattern applied for both men and women. The other three response classifications were associated with less desirable evaluations of the relationships studied (Gable et al., 2004). In experimental studies where individuals were asked to relay a positive event to an experimenter who responded in one of the four ways, participants reported feeling closer to those who delivered active-constructive responses. When people respond with active-constructive comments, they communicate their understanding of the importance of the event to the relationship partner in particular.

Furthermore, the communication conveys validation and an attitude of affection and care. Research on capitalization demonstrates that friends and roommates' responses to positive news can play an important role in shaping the quality of the relationship. Having relationship partners who are skilled in responding to good news of events has important benefits both to the individual and to the relationship.

Conflict Resolution

Conflict is an inevitable byproduct of human relationships. As social beings, humans orient toward groups, yet group members have competing needs and agendas. Conflict is certain to erupt at one time or another. In close friendships, strong bonds and a shared history can provide a safety net helping to support the relationship while conflict is addressed. Partners' attitudes about conflict can influence the way differences are conceptualized. Do the partners believe conflict is the "beginning of the end," for example, or do they view conflict as natural and manageable? There are benefits to conflict. Conflict challenges people to think more carefully, to be more flexible, to work toward greater understanding, and to be creative in identifying new pathways to problem-solving (Scannell, 2010). However, unresolved conflict can lead to the unraveling of a relationship or a group; therefore, finding ways to successfully navigate through troubling conflict is critical to emerging on the other side. Often people tend to avoid conflict. They have seen the scorched landscape left behind quarreling family members or grieved their own severed relationships resulting from unresolved differences. Student development professionals and college students in leadership roles may find themselves in positions where they are called to mediate student conflicts. A number of resources about conflict resolution reason that talking about conflict before it occurs can lay the groundwork for successful problem-solving. Furthermore, helping people identify and classify their knee-jerk reactions to conflict and enabling them to experience conflict in controlled or even playful ways can help people gain confidence in their ability to successfully resolve problems (Scannell, 2010). A common exercise led by resident advisors, for example, asks freshman roommates to articulate preferences regarding sleep and study schedules, guests in the room, and habits related to organization skills so that the students can know what to expect from one another and will have already broached potentially difficult topics in advance of problems. Likewise, having roommates complete a self-assessment about one's personality and habits and then sharing results with the new roommate can give students a common language to use when differences emerge. Although the skills of conflict mediation are beyond the scope of this chapter, we encourage readers to consider two resources that may be helpful including The Essential Guide to Workplace Mediation & Conflict Resolution: Rebuilding Working Relationships (Doherty & Guyler, 2008) and The Big Book of Conflict Resolution Games (Scannell, 2010).

The Different Roles of Friends

The intimacy and connectedness that individuals feel when they are a part of a romantic/intimate relationship is similar to the feelings individuals have with their best-friend. Research suggests that best-friend relationships are similar to romantic/love relationships in many ways, including the level of acceptance, trust, respect, degree of disclosure, and mutual understanding (Yarber, Sayad, & Strong, 2012). Levels of relationship satisfaction are generally similar for both groups and solid friendships are the foundation of strong love relationships (Yarber, Sayad, & Strong). Although one may be a friend to one's intimate/romantic partner, it is likely that one will also need additional friends outside of the primary intimate/romantic relationship.

If having friends is important to optimal functioning, does having fifty friends make one five times happier than if one has only ten friends? Research findings have generally indicated that three to four friends are the essential number to increase overall levels of happiness and physical health (Brummet et al., 2001; Rath, 2006). However, what about the complexity, quality, depth, and breadth of those three to four friendships? Do all friends play the same role? Data from two sources suggest that there may be a variety of roles that friends play in a person's life. A model proposed by Rath (2006), using data collected by The Gallup Organization (Carr, 2006), delineates types or styles of friends. The findings from Rath and Carr's research suggests that there are eight types of friends:

Builders are motivators and encouragers. They are the motivational speakers of an individual's life, encouraging people to move toward their goals.

Champions are personal public relations firms for his/her friends. Champions talk about their friend's talents and skills to others. The stand up for their friends when they are down and encourage their friends to live up to their personal potential.

Collaborators are the mirrors to friends. They have similar beliefs, likes, and dislikes as their friends. They have a similar approach to the world that brings comfort.

Companions are Plato's notion of the platonic other half. The intimacy and connectedness is deep and rich. Individuals who are companion friends are friendship soul mates.

Connectors are the social engineers of the friendship world. They link individuals together and create networks of collaboration.

Energizers are the socializers and "party" friends. Their abundance of energy and playfulness makes these individuals important in increasing overall levels of positive moods.

Mind Openers are those who push their friends into new and unusual experiences. Mind openers encourage individuals to take risks and work against the status quo.

Navigators are the travel guides of the world. They help individuals identify and understand their goals. They help individuals understand the pathways to reach those goals.

A model proposed by Spencer and Pahl (2006) also proposes eight different types of friendships based on qualitative analysis of sixty interviews. Types of friends are organized by complexity of friendship and level of engagement. Findings are similar to Rath (2006) and include:

a) *associates* are those who enjoy similar tasks, activities, hobbies and sports;
b) *useful contacts* share information and guidance related to vocational decisions;
c) *favor friends* exchange resources in a "function manner" but do not necessarily offer emotional resources;
d) *fun friends* socialize but do not engage in emotional exchanges or intimacy;
e) *helpmates* are a blend of favor friends and fun friends in that they are social friends and help out each other in a utilitarian way;
f) *comforters* provide emotional support and intimacy as well as socializing and fun;
g) *confidants* are those individuals who may not be proximal but are individuals one confides important or personal information and;
h) *soul mates* are those who display all of the elements of the other types.

Although we may have many people we consider friends, teammates, roommates, or coworker, what makes an essential or "vital" friend? Rath (2006) suggested the definition of "vital friends" as those individuals who significantly improve one's life ". . . a person at work or in your personal life whom you can't afford to live without" (p. 76). These vital friends are those that help people get through challenging times, motivate us, and help increase our overall satisfaction with life.

Understanding Relationship Strengths

Righetti, Rusbult, and Finkenauer (2010) proposed that close friends who have good relationship fit may have a sort of synergistic effect, shaping people into ideal selves. Coined the Michelangelo effect or Michelangelo phenomenon, it is thought that once an individual is paired with the correct friend(s), these friends serve to guide the individual toward an optimal level of functioning, "chipping away" at the stone of the psyche so that the ideal form can emerge that is buried within (Righetti, Rusbult, & Finkenauer, 2010). In order for the stone to be chipped away, however, one must have the right fit with one's friends. One way to understand fit is by determining the strengths of the current relationships an individual has in his/her life. Both informal and informal means can be used to assess the relationship strengths.

Less formal measures for determining strengths and satisfaction with relationships include assessing perceptions of the relationship by querying about the general level of satisfaction. Asking oneself, "How satisfied am I with my friendships," has been found to be a good predictor of general satisfaction with relationships (Oswald, Clark, & Kelly, 2004). If general satisfaction is low, determining whether additional friendships may foster greater satisfaction will help an individual recognize strengths and types of friendships to seek out in future friends. In a way, it becomes akin to selecting a special dessert to pair with a main course to script a satisfying meal. In addition, other formal assessments may then be helpful to clarify where growth may be beneficial.

Rath (2006), along with The Gallup Organization has developed an online assessment called the Vital Friends Assessment that individuals can complete to determine which of the eight friendship styles best represent their friends (https://www.vitalfriends.com). Friends are then categorized in the top three styles of friendship. Once the assessment is complete, each friend is ranked on the top three friendship styles that he or she represents based on intensity. Following the ranking, Rath suggests that having different friends to meet different needs increases overall satisfaction with life and if one area or friendship style is not filled, people can actively cultivate or seek out individuals to help meet those needs.

Another formal assessment of both individual and group strengths is the Clifton StrengthsFinder personality inventory [CSF] (Asplund, Lopez, Hodges, & Harter, 2009). Chara and Eppright (2012) reported that the CSF is the most popular personality inventory in the world, with over 6 million people having completed the assessment and 600 universities using the assessment as part of student development. The 177 items, once completed, generate a list of the top five themes for the person who completed the assessment. Based on those five themes, called Signature Themes, individuals can then explore who supports or discourages individual strengths and subsequently make decisions about who may be needed as a friend in order to increase overall relationship satisfaction and optimal functioning. With this knowledge about personal strengths, individuals can search and cultivate friendships that maximize individual strengths and increase overall relationship satisfaction. At a university setting, administrators and school officials might help students find opportunities to connect with others who might help meet his or her friendship needs. For example, universities might create opportunities for students who are interested in volunteering to join a club or organization, cultivating "help mate" friendships.

Increasing Satisfaction with Unsatisfying Friendships

Satisfying relationships are essential to both mental and physical health (Baumeister & Leary, 1995), yet what makes a friendship satisfying is not clear. The investment model of friendship (Thibault & Kelley, 1959), proposes that satisfaction is a product of perceived relationship benefits rewards/positive aspects of the relationship, minus the perceived costs or negative aspects of the relationship, and the degree to which the rewards and costs meet or exceed an individual's expectation. Pierce, Saronson, and Saronson (1991) argue that people develop two types of expectations surrounding friendships and relationships in general: general perceptions of friendship support (e.g., if I need to borrow $10 I have someone I can ask) and specific support for specific relationships (e.g., if Kim will allow me to borrow $10 from her). These perceptions and expectations grow out of the relationship history (e.g., how many times *has* Kim loaned me money). Thus, individuals may feel satisfied or dissatisfied with their friendships in general (e.g., "I generally feel good about my friendships"), or they may feel specifically satisfied or dissatisfied with one relationship in particular (e.g., "My relationship with Kat is close but I wish my relationship with Brian was closer"). Both forms of satisfaction and dissatisfaction are important, as satisfaction is associated with psychological happiness and dissatisfaction is associated with psychological frustration and distress (Calmes & Roberts, 2008).

Part of responding to and managing the frustration of friendship dissatisfaction is understanding from where the dissatisfaction emerges. As was noted earlier, satisfaction is an equation of investment that measures inputs and outputs (Thibault & Kelley, 1959). In other words, how many rewards does an individual get for the cost of being in the relationship? It is a natural response to experience frustration, anger, and sadness when relationships are out of balance and the costs or negatives are more than the positives or rewards. Individuals may benefit by examining whether their perceptions of costs and rewards are realistic. Perhaps an individual who wants to spend most of her time on campus and participate in numerous student groups may not hold expectations that are realistic for her current friends. Individuals may also benefit from evaluating whether their friends can offer them the rewards and benefits that they want from friendships. For example, if an individual *does* believe that each and every event on campus should be spent in the company of one's friends and the person perceives that this is a reasonable expectation yet the person's friends disagree, the individual may benefit from actively seeking out additional friends to amend this perception, such as a finding a "Fun friend" (Spencer & Pahl, 2006) to engage in social activities and relying on his/her "Comforters" to obtain emotional support. Two key components of managing frustration with relationship mismatch are apparent. First, individuals need to understand that all things need not come from one person (Rath, 2006). In fact, it may be healthier to anticipate that many things can come from many people. Second, individuals need to honor and recognize the strengths of their current friendship while also cultivating new friendships that will round out their friendship team. For example, an individual through formal or informal assessment may determine that the individual has several "Comforters" but has few "Fun friends." Recognizing the areas for expansion in friendships honors what current friends provide while at the same time identifying areas that need to be nurtured in order to manage the frustration of the absence of a "Fun Friend." Again, the message from Rath (2006) and The Gallup Organization is that individuals need to make a concerted and focused effort of finding and cultivating friendships that respond to relationship expectations and needs. Universities provide the ideal setting for both learning about individual strengths, assessing the strengths of current friendships, and providing opportunities for cultivating new friendships.

Integrating Friendships into University Planning

In addition to the emphasis that universities place on educational opportunities afforded to students, attention must also be placed on developing social opportunities. The following suggestions are made for universities to enhance relationships for students:

1. Universities may want to consider service-learning opportunities including internships and externships that bring students together in meaningful ways to contribute while also socializing. For example, the Virginia Polytechnic Institute and State University since 2002 has hosted the "Big Event" where 6,852 student volunteers engage in service activities in the community. However, because of the possibility of in-group and out-group formation, universities may want to consider establishing a culture that promotes these events as opportunities to not only do good in the community but also to do good toward others in developing relationships and fostering fellowship. Findings generally support the importance of student interaction and engagement on campus for student development and retention and discourage

competition when resources are limited (Astin, 1984; Brief, Umphress, Dietz, Burrows, Butz, & Scholten, 1985; Pascarella, 1985).

2. Physical environments matter in making friends and relationships. In one study, people were three times more likely to develop close networks of friends in the work environment when there were designated spaces for socializing (Rath, 2006). Universities and administrative units that are focused on building fellowship need to focus on removing barriers to friendship. For example, designing buildings that create administrative and staff "wings" and placing faculty and employees in cubicles or offices with closed doors, inhibit opportunities for informal but important contact. Libraries, frequently seen as the heart of the university, may need to be reorganized around a central gathering area that is clearly designed for socializing. Increasingly, libraries are creating cafes and coffee shops that promote active engagement with the environment. Universities may want to integrate what innovative start up companies have known for years—build work environments tailored for socializing. For example, when Google headquarters was built in Zurich, the designers recognized the need for spaces that were flexible but also facilitated conversation and fellowship (Vinnitskaya, 2009). The design of the building is organized around multiple living-spaces with sofas and furniture that are easily rearranged for small or large social gatherings. One need not worry about decreased academic productivity of students engaging in too much socializing. Findings on workplace behavior and productivity overwhelming support that having friends and socializing at work increase overall levels of satisfaction (Markiewicz, Devine, & Kausilas, 2000) and increase productivity (Bandiera, Barankay, & Rasul, 2010).

3. Having conversations about friendship can increase the overall likelihood of developing relationships. Findings from the Gallup Organization (Rath, 2006) suggest that when managers in the business field talk with their employees about friendships on a regular basis, overall rates of friendships increased. The same may be true about faculty, staff, and administrators at universities. Although data are not available, it may be that highlighting the importance of peer relationships may increase the likelihood of individuals forming these relationships. University officials and faculty may want to select a common book related to friendships (such as Vital Friends) that the entire campus community might read and discuss within different classes and disciplines. Administrators and members of residence life may want to bring in guest speakers or facilitate conversations related to the importance of friendships and teambuilding.

4. Universities may benefit from designating an individual to coordinate opportunities to interact with individuals from diverse cultures. Although birds of a feather may flock together, giving opportunities to interact with

individuals from different cultures may increase the likelihood of creating friendship networks and prompt greater cultural acceptance (Pettigrew, Tropp, Wagner, & Christ, 2011). One example, proposed by the editor of this book, is the conversation partner program common at many universities, where native English speakers volunteer to meet with international students simply to talk, giving the international students a way to practice their language skills. Almost invariably, greater understanding develops through this process.

5. Competition between groups increases cohesion among potential friends who are in a group together. Opportunities for individuals who are randomly assigned to groups and challenged to complete a task against another group may increase group cohesion and led to friendships (Kennedy & Stephan, 1977).

6. Ambassador programs for new and transfer students may help facilitate introductions. This may mean paring senior students with junior students in housing arrangements, creating formal peer-mentoring programs in learning resources centers, or opportunities in the classroom for senior students to introduce junior students to new friends or resources. University ambassadors can serve to introduce new students to the university community and also facilitate introductions to new friends.

In addition to suggesting practical interventions to increase the likelihood of fostering social networks on university campuses, the following vignette is provided as a means of illustrating the multiple levels at which universities can support students and enhance student skills in relationship, academic, or vocational levels.

Case Study

Matt, a senior at a public university of 12,000 students, serves as a resident advisor for a wing of male and female students. Matt works hard to engage his residents in hall events and to get to know his residents on more than just a superficial basis. He makes a point of remembering birthdays and having at least a brief conversation with every resident once a week. When his building launched a used clothing drive for a community shelter, Matt organized a contest between the various wings, prompting a sense of camaraderie among those teams working together to collect the most bags of clothing. Matt looks for creative ways to unite his residents to work together on both service projects and to participate in community gatherings.

Toward the end of the first semester, some of Matt's residents alerted him to concerns about Derek, a 19-year-old sophomore on his wing. The residents remark that Derek has been moody and has begun isolating himself with his door closed and turning down invitations to join others for meals and social events. Their concern culminated when Derek recently got into a yelling match with his roommate, and based upon reports from students in adjacent rooms, there appeared to be a physical altercation, although neither roommate would acknowledge this. Earlier that day, Matt had received an e-mail from Derek requesting a private room.

Matt meets with Derek and listens carefully to his concerns, trying hard to acknowledge Derek's frustration with his roommate without choosing sides. He ultimately refers Derek to the hall director, Sabrina, a member of the professional housing staff. Sabrina listens attentively to Derek. In addition to clarifying the problems he has encountered in his roommate situation, she asks questions about his family, his interests, and his goals for the future. She learns Derek is a first-generation college student who managed, largely on his own, to apply for college and complete applications for student loans while a high school senior. Last year, Derek was involved in intramural sports along with two of his best friends, but, ultimately, the friends both left college, leaving Derek to room with someone he did not know well. Finances are tight. Derek depends on a scholarship that he may lose if he does not get better grades, and he works parttime on campus. Sabrina discovers that Derek is struggling to maintain his 2.9 GPA. He is a business major and would like to go on and earn an MBA, but he is uncertain about what will be required of him in graduate school and how the application process works. He is considering withdrawing from the university at the end of the current semester because of his accounting grades. Sabrina observes that Derek has encountered some disappointments in his first year and a half of college, but she notes that he has demonstrated considerable resourcefulness in facing challenges. She points out he is working hard to support himself, and that he has clear goals for his future. She acknowledges he is good at tackling details like the paperwork necessary for college admission and financial aid on his own. She expresses empathy for the fact that his best friends left the university, and that he has had to make the most of rooming with someone he did not know well. Sabrina asks whether Derek would be willing to include his roommate in a joint meeting to see whether their differences can be resolved. Furthermore, she asks Derek whether he would be willing to talk to the staff of the Student Success Office to help address his academic struggles. She also notes the hall is recruiting for students to play on spring intramural sports teams and hopes that Derek, having been involved last year, will participate again. Sabrina calls the Student Success Office and learns someone is available to meet with Derek within a half hour. Sabrina finishes her conversation with Derek and walks him over to their office and introduces him to the staff. The next day, Sabrina follows up with Derek to see how his appointment with the Student Success Office went. She learns he liked the staff member he talked with and plans to go back for tutoring help in accounting. Derek agrees to serve as a co-captain for the hall's intermural team in the spring and to help with recruiting efforts in the coming weeks.

Upon examining this case scenario, it is apparent that helping relationships can provide both a safety net and direction in helping a student who is struggling in several life areas. Because of the early investment on the part of his resident director to get to know residents well, Derek felt comfortable making that first contact and asking for assistance. Upon being referred to Sabrina, the Residence Hall Director, Derek found a compassionate listener who quickly sized up Derek's strengths and was able to both communicate empathy for his situation and engage in effective problem-solving and referral. Sabrina saw that Derek lacked social support, and she tried to involve him in an aspect of college life (intramurals) that had been meaningful to him last year. She recognized that he needed academic support to improve his grades and assisted with the referral by walking him over and introducing him to the Student Success Center staff. The next day, she followed up with Derek, and continued to monitor his progress and offer support for the next several months. Derek's resident advisor, Matt, also followed up with Derek. He learned that Derek and his roommate had agreed to meet with Sabrina and that they have set some ground rules in place to try and address their differences. Matt agrees to help with intramural recruiting and, for those who do not want to participate on the intramural team, to help organize a group to attend games and cheer on their hall.

Conclusion

Decades of research examining helping relationships have revealed that an essential ingredient in prompting growth and change is the quality of the relationship the helper brings to the table (Lambert & Barley, 2001). Student development professionals and student leaders on campus can have a profound impact on helping students find their footing and progress to more satisfying levels of development if they focus on improving their ability to relate to students and tailor their relationship skills to individual needs. They can also serve as role models as students attempt to expand their own repertoire of relationship skills beyond those developed during childhood and adolescence. Students who learn to respond empathically, provide autonomy support to others, deal proactively with conflict, and select friends who meet a variety of their interpersonal needs will be well-equipped for establishing nurturing relationships over the course of their lives.

References

Anderson, C., Keltner, D., John, O. P. (2003). Emotional convergence between people over time, *Journal of Personality and Social Psychology, 84*, 1054–1068.

Asplund, J., Lopez, S. J., Hodges, T., & Harter, J. (2009) The Clifton StrengthsFinder 2.0 technical report: development and validation. Princeton, NJ: The Gallup Organization. Retrieved from http://strengths.gallup.com/private/Resources/CSFTechnicalReport031005.pdf

Astin, A. W. (1984). Student involvement: A developmental theory for higher education. *Journal of College Student Personnel, 25*, 297–308.

Bandiera, O., Barankay, I., & Rasul, I. (2010). Social incentives in the workplace. *Review of Economics Studies, 77*, 417–458.

Batson, C. D. (1991). *The altruism question: Toward a social-psychological answer.* Hillsdale, NJ: Erlbaum Associates.

Baumeister, R. F., Vohs, K. D., Aaker, J. L., & Garbinsky, E. N. (2013). Some key differences between a happy life and a meaningful life. *Journal of Positive Psychology, 8*(6), 505–516. doi :10.1080/17439760.2013.830764.

Baumeister, R., & Leary, M. (1995). The need to belong: Desire for interpersonal attachments as a fundamental human motivation. *Psychological Bulletin, 117*, 497–529.

Berkman, L. F., Syme, S. L. (1979). Social networks, host-resistance, and mortality—9-year followup-study of alameda county residents. *American Journal of Epidemiology, 109*(2), 186–204.

Bowlby, J. (1988). *A secure base: Parent-child attachments and healthy human development.* New York: Basic Books.

Brew, L., & Kottler, J. A. (2008). Applied helping skills: Transforming lives, Thousand Oaks: Sage Publications.

Brummett, B. H., Barefoot, J. C., Siegler, I. C., Clapp-Channing, N. E., Lytle, B. L., Bosworth, H. B., et al. (2001). Characteristics of socially isolated patients with coronary artery disease who are at elevated risk for mortality. *Psychosomatic Medicine, 63*, 267–272.

Calmes, C. A., & Roberts, J. E. (2008). Rumination in interpersonal relationships: Does co-rumination explain gender differences in emotional distress and relationship satisfaction among college students? *Cognitive Therapy and Research, 32*, 577–590.

Carr, J. A. (2006). *A test-retest evaluation of the Vital Friends Assessment.* Omaha, NE: The Gallup Organization.

Chara, P. J., Jr., & Eppright, W. J. (2012). The item-number distortion effect in rank order testing: An example using the Clifton Strengths Finder Inventory. *Psychological Reports, 111*(1), 219–227. doi:10.2466/01.03.07.PR0.111.4.219-227

Deci, E. L., La Guardia, J. G., Moller, A. C., Scheiner, M. J., & Ryan, R. M. (2006). On the benefits of giving as well as receiving autonomy support: Mutuality in close friendships. *Personality and Social Psychology Bulletin, 32*, 313–327.

Doherty, N., & Guyler, M. (2008). *The essential guide to workplace mediation & conflict resolution: Rebuilding working relationships.* Kogan Page: Philadelphia.

Ebbsen, E. B., Kjos, G. L., & Konecni, V. J. (1976). Spatial ecology: Its effects on the choice of friends and enemies. *Journal of Experimental Social Psychology, 12*, 505–518.

Gable, S. L., & Gosnell, C. L. (2011). The positive side of close relationships. In Sheldon, K. M., Kashdan, T. B., & Steger, M. F. (Eds.). *Designing positive psychology: Taking stock and moving forward* (pp. 265–279). New York: Oxford University Press.

Gable, S. L., Reis, H. T., Impett, E. A., Asher, E. R. (2004). What do you do when things go right? The intrapersonal and interpersonal benefits of sharing positive events. *Journal of Personality and Social Psychology, 87*(2), 228–245.

Gable, S. L., Gonzaga, G. C., Strauchman, A. (2006). Will you be there for me when things go right? Supportive responses to positive event disclosures. *Journal of Personality and Social Psychology, 91*, 904–917.

Gerdes, H., & Mallinckrodt, B. (1994). Emotional, social, and academic adjustment of college students: A longitudinal study of retention. *Journal of Counseling and Development, 72,* 281–288.

Goguen, L. M. S., Hiester, M. A., & Nordstrom, A. H. (2010). Associations among peer relationships, academic achievement, and persistence in college. *Journal of College Student Retention: Research, Theory and Practice, 12*(3), 319–337. doi:10.2190/CS.12.3.d

Harper, R. (2010) More than listening: A casebook for using counseling skills in student affairs work. Washington, DC: National Association of Student Personnel Administrators.

House, J. S., Landis, K. R., & Umberson, D. (1988). Social relationships and health. *Science, 241*(4865), 540–545.

Jordan, J. W. (1991). The meaning of mutuality. In J. V. Jordan, A. G. Kaplan, J. B. Miller, I. P. Stiver, & J. L. Surrey (Eds.), *Women's growth in connection: Writings from the Stone Center* (pp. 81–96). New York: Guilford.

Jordan, J. W., Kaplan, A. G., Miller, J. B., Stiver, I. P., & Surrey, J. L. (Eds.). (1991). *Women's growth in connection: Writings from the Stone Center.* New York: Guilford.

Kahneman, D., Krueger, A. B., Schwarz, N., & Stone, A. A. (2004). A survey method for characterizing daily life experience: The day reconstruction method. *Science, 306,* 1776–1780.

Kennedy, J., & Stephan, W. G. (1977). The effects of cooperation and competition on ingroup-outgroup bias. *Journal of Applied Social Psychology, 7*(2), 115–130. doi:10.1111/j.15591816.1977.tb01333.x

Krause, N. (2007). Longitudinal study of social support and meaning in life. *Psychology and Aging, 22,* 456–69.

Lambert, M. J., & Barley, D. E. (2001). Research summary on the therapeutic relationship and psychotherapy outcome. *Psychotherapy: Theory, research, practice, training, 38*(4), 357–361. doi:10.1037/0033-3204.38.4.357

Langston, C. A. (1994). Capitalizing on and coping with daily-life events: Expressive responses to positive events. *Journal of Personality and Social Psychology, 67,* 1112–1125.

Lopez, F. G., Campbell, V. L., & Watkins, C. E., Jr. (1988). Family structure, psychological separation, and college adjustment: An investigation of sex differences. *Journal of Counseling Psychology, 33,* 52–56.

Mallinckrodt, B. (1988). Student retention, social support, and dropout intention: Comparison of Black and White students. *Journal of College Student Personnel, 29,* 60–64.

Markiewicz, D., Devine, I., & Kausilas, D. (2000). Friendships of women and men at work: Job satisfaction and resource implications. *Journal of Managerial Psychology, 15,* 161–184.

Mouw, T., & Entwisle, B. (2006). Residential segregation and interracial friendship in schools. *American Journal of Sociology, 112*(2), 394–441.

Oishi, S., & Sullivan, H. W. (2006). The Predictive value of daily vs. retrospective well-being judgments in relationship stability. *Journal of Experimental Social Psychology, 42,* 460–470.

Oishi, S., Koo, M., & Akimoto, S. (2008). Culture, interpersonal perceptions, and happiness in social interactions. *Personality and Social Psychology Bulletin, 34,* 307–320.

Oswald, D. L., Clark, E. M., & Kelly, C. M. (2004). Friendship maintenance: An analysis of individual and dyad behaviors. *Journal of Social and Clinical Psychology, 23*(3), 413–441. doi:10.1521/jscp.23.3.413.35460

Pascarella, E. T. (1985). College environmental influences on learning and cognitive development: A critical review and analysis. In J. Smart (Ed.). *Higher education: Handbook of theory and research.* New York: Agathon.

Pettigrew, T. F., Tropp, L. R., Wagner, U., & Christ, O. (2011). Recent advances in intergroup contact theory. *International Journal of Intercultural Relations, 35*(3), 271–280. doi:10.1016/j.ijintrel.2011.03.001

Pierce, G. R., Sarason, I. G., & Sarason, B. R. (1991). General and relationship-based perceptions of social support: Are two constructs better than one? *Journal of Personality and Social Psychology, 61*, 1028–1039.

Rath, T. (2006). *Vital friends: the people you can't afford to live without.* New York: Gallup Press.

Reis, H. T., & Gable, S. L. (2003). Toward a positive psychology of relationships. In C. L. M. Keyes & J. Haidt (Eds.), *Flourishing: Positive psychology and the life well-lived* (pp. 129–159). Washington DC: American Psychological Association.

Rice, K. G. (1992). Separation-individuation and adjustment to college: A longitudinal study. *Journal of Counseling Psychology, 39*, 203–213.

Righetti, F., Rusbult, C., & Finkenauer, C. (2010). Regulatory focus and the michelangelo phenomenon: How close partners promote one another's ideal selves. *Journal of Experimental Social Psychology, 46*(6), 972–985. doi:10.1016/j.jesp.2010.06.001

Rogers, Carl (1951). *Client-centered therapy: Its current practice, implications and theory.* London: Constable.

Sanderson, C. A., & Evans, S. M. (2001). Seeing one's partner through intimacy-colored glasses: An examination of the processes underlying the intimacy goals-relationship satisfaction link. *Personality and Social Psychology Bulletin, 27*, 461–471.

Sarason, B. R., Sarason, I. G., & Gurung, R. A. R. (1997). Close personal relationships in health outcomes: A key to the role of social support. In S. Duck (Ed.), *Handbook of personal relationships: Theory, research, and interventions* (2nd ed, pp. 547–573). United Kingdom: Wiley & Sons.

Scannell, M. (2010). *Big book of conflict resolution games: Quick, effective activities to improve communicaiton, trust, and collaboration.* New York: McGraw-Hill.

Shah, J. (2003). The motivational looking glass: How significant others implicitly affect goal appraisals. *Journal of Personality and Social Psychology, 54*, 424–439.

Spencer, L., & Pahl, R. (2006). *Rethinking friendship: Hidden solidarities today.* Princeton, NJ: Princeton University Press.

Syed, M., & Juan, M. J. D. (2012). Birds of an ethnic feather? Ethnic identity homophily among college-age friends. *Journal of Adolescence, 35*(6), 1505–1514. doi:10.1016/j.adolescence.2011.10.012

Swann, W. B., Jr., Rentfrow, P. J., & Guinn, J. (2002). Self-verification: The search for coherence. In M. Leary and J. Tagney (Eds), *Handbook of self and identity* (pp. 367–383). Guilford: New York.

Thibault, J., & Kelley, H. (1959). *The social psychology of groups.* New York: Wiley.

Vinnitskaya, I. (2009, November). Google emea engineering hub. Retrieved from http://www.archdaily.com/41400/google-emea-engineering-hub-camezind-evolution/

Way N., & Chen, L., (2000) Close and general friendships among African American, Latino, and Asian American adolescents. *Journal of Adolescent Research, 15*, 247–301.

Yarber, W. L., Sayad, B. W., & Strong, B. (2012). *Human sexuality: Diversity in contemporary America*, 8th Ed. New York: McGraw-Hill.

Youniss, J., & Smollar, J. (1985). *Adolescent relations with mothers, fathers, and friends.* Chicago, IL: University of Chicago Press.

11

The Role of Positive Psychology in Fostering Spiritual Development and a Sense of Calling in College

BRUCE W. SMITH, BELINDA VICUNA, AND GLORY EMMANUEL

What is the role of positive psychology in relation to spirituality in college? Although little has been written about positive psychology in relation to spiritual development or a sense of calling, there is a great deal of overlap between the goals of positive psychology and those who are on a spiritual path and seeking to discover or answer a sense of calling. This chapter will explore ways positive psychology may help college students foster spiritual development and their own unique sense of calling. First, we will propose working definitions of spirituality, spiritual development, and a sense of calling. Second, we will discuss how college may be an important context for spiritual development and discovering a sense of calling. Third, we will identify the aspects of positive psychology that may be most important for fostering spiritual development and a sense of calling. Finally, we will propose a set of specific guidelines and suggestions for using positive psychology to improve spiritual development in a college setting and for making it possible for students to discover and fulfill a sense of calling.

What Is Spirituality and Spiritual Development?

One of the greatest challenges in understanding the role of college in spirituality and spiritual development is that there has not been broad agreement on a concise or inclusive definition of spirituality (Zinnbauer et al., 1997). On the one hand, spirituality has been used in a very limited and narrow way to mean only that which is related to organized religion or belief in a deity or supreme being. On the other hand, the word spirituality has also been used in a great variety of ways to include whatever may be considered to be good or positive including all aspects of human relationships, nature, art, music, and literature (Zinnbauer at al., 1997).

Psychologists have defined spirituality in ways that find a middle ground between tying it to organized religion and being so broad and ambiguous that it loses all of its meaning (Dyson, Cobb, & Forman, 1997; Selway & Ashman, 1998). Pargament and Mahoney (2002) have summarized some of the most important definitions of spirituality as what is the best of being human, a quest for existential meaning, and a search for that which is transcendent or sacred. In positive psychology, spirituality has been identified as a human character strength that may also be closely related to purpose, faith, and religiousness. Peterson and Seligman (2004) have stated that spirituality "is the most human of the character strengths as well as the most sublime. We define spirituality the strength of spirituality and religiousness as having coherent beliefs about the higher purpose and meaning of the universe and one's place within it" (p. 533).

We would also like to propose a middle ground definition of spirituality as living according to that which brings the greatest or highest authentic meaning and purpose to one's life. When using the word "meaning," we are referring to a coherent world view about what is most important in life and by "purpose" we mean a highly motivating direction or goal to which one is passionate and committed (Antonovsky, 1979; Emmons, 1999; Reker, Peacock, & Wong, 1987; Steger, 2009). In saying "greatest or highest," we mean that which the person thinks is most important to both them and to society. Finally, by "authentic," we mean what it is meaningful and purposeful to that particular individual rather than something that is externally imposed. If we use this definition for spirituality, then spiritual development would involve moving towards living according to what might bring the greatest authentic meaning and purpose.

By using this definition, we are drawing on the thought of broad thinkers in the areas of psychology, philosophy, and religion such a Paul Tillich and Viktor Frankl. Tillich defined religious faith as that which one is primarily concerned with or an individual's "ultimate concern" (Tillich, 1957). The way he used the word "faith" was similar to the way that we use the word "spirituality" today, in the sense that it went beyond organized religion to embrace the full range of human experience. The advantage of thinking about spirituality as an ultimate concern or our phrase, "that which brings the greatest or highest authentic meaning and purpose," is that it is inclusive, because everyone has a potential ultimate concern whether or not it is tied to organized religion.

Viktor Frankl wrote "Man's Search for Meaning" (1946), one of the most widely read books of the 20th century, and developed a form of psychotherapy that aims to increase a person's sense of meaning and purpose in life. In "Man's Search for Meaning," he wrote about how the experience of love for him was the ultimate or highest meaning in his life and that it was this meaning that enabled him to survive being in concentration camps during World War II. As with

Tillich, Frankl's conception of meaning is universal in the sense that it is something that everyone can find and experience. The idea of an ultimate or highest meaning is very similar to Tillich's idea of ultimate concern. Both ideas can incorporate the concept of a supreme being as espoused by most of the world's religions or the idea of a higher power as set forth in 12-step programs such as Alcoholics Anonymous (Alcoholics Anonymous, 2001). Yet, they also do not exclude people who are atheists or agnostics or otherwise outside the realm of organized religion.

Finally, although a variety of meanings have been associated with both the word "spirituality" and the word "religion," we would like to highlight a key distinction between them that points to the broad way that we are defining spirituality. Although the word "religion" has been used to refer to the search for that which brings higher meaning and purpose (Pargament, 1997), during the past 20 years the word religion has been more often associated with organized religion that involves a specific set of beliefs and practices (Zinnbauer et al., 1997). Although organized religion may be one way for people to discover and live according to their highest meaning and purpose, we use the word spirituality in a way that may include many other pathways up the same proverbial mountain. Thus, although colleges and universities may not be in the business of promoting organized religion, they can do much to foster spirituality through enabling students to discover and begin to more fully live the kind of life that brings the greatest authentic meaning and purpose.

What Is a Sense of Calling?

Spiritual development shares similar themes with the concept of calling. Although spiritual development can be conceptualized as moving towards living according to what brings the greatest authentic meaning and purpose, the concept of a calling involves a specific path or the unique way that a particular individual comes to understand and embark on this journey. If everyone has something that potentially brings great meaning and purpose to their lives, then a sense of calling might involve the unique path that enables one to more fully and completely realize and live out this meaning and purpose.

Traditionally, the concept of a calling has entailed religious and spiritual connotations, such as a transcendent summon from God or from the sacred to use personal talents in the service of others. However, there has also been considerable attention to the concept of a calling from a secular perspective (Steger, Pickering, Shin, & Dik, 2010). In general, the concept of calling has been characterized as *how* one's career or other life role can be infused with meaning and purpose (Dik & Duffy, 2009). In their attempt to develop an empirically testable definition, Dik and Duffy (2009) provide key elements of a calling: (1) a transcendent summons for a particular life role (e.g., career), (2) deriving a sense of purpose and meaning, and (3) primarily motivated by others-oriented values and goals.

Put simply, a sense of calling can be conceptualized as a meaningful, prosocial endeavor prompted by both an internal and an external source (Duffy, Allan, & Bott, 2012). A calling serves both the self and society (Conklin, 2012). At the initial stages of developing a sense of calling in particular, and also at a more mature level in which one is living out one's calling, being embedded in a supportive community is crucial. True to the nature of having a sense of calling, the prosocial orientation speaks to the invaluable role of one's community to foster and enable a person to live out his or her calling. Having a sense of calling means being rooted in a community, not only having the yearning to contribute to the greater good of one's community but also gaining support and strength from one's home community.

Vocation is another concept that has a similar meaning to calling. It is described as the intersection between gifts, talents, and the world's needs (Thompson & Feldman, 2010). In the words of Frederick Buechner (1973), vocation is "the place where your deepest gladness and the world's deepest hunger meet" (p. 95). There is a considerable overlap between the two descriptions, but essentially both conceptualizations meet one another in acknowledging talent, passion, greater good, orientation toward others, and the meaning derived from living out one's calling. Another rendition of vocation offers a more simplistic definition, as an internal motivation to pursue a meaningful, prosocial life role (Dik & Duffy, 2009).

Because living out one's calling or vocation inherently has implications for living a meaningful and purposeful life, it is not surprising that it would have a great deal to do with overall happiness and well-being—central foci of positive psychology (Lyubormirsky, 2007; Seligman, 2011). Being involved in work that embodies one's calling has been shown to be related to higher work satisfaction and better health (Wrzesniewski, McCauley, Rozin, & Schwartz, 1997). Research on the impact of fulfilling and living out one's calling in an occupation or career consistently shows major benefits including greater life satisfaction (Davidson & Caddell, 1994), greater meaning in life, intrinsic work motivation, career decision self-efficacy (Dik, Sargent, & Steger, 2008), greater occupational commitment (Serow, Eaker, & Ciechalski, 1992), greater career-decidedness (Dik & Sedlacek, 2008), and more adaptive coping strategies (Treadgold, 1999).

Why Might College Be an Important Context for Fostering Spiritual Development and Calling?

If spiritual development is about moving towards a higher meaning and purpose, and a calling is one's unique path toward it, then college might provide a critical context for this search. During the college years, many students begin a journey of "meaning-making" (Nash & Murray, 2010). Students are confronted with courses, topics, and others' world views/values that make them think about the larger world. They are confronted with discussions about politics, international relations, historical controversies and conflicts, world problems such as poverty and trade, and other issues that may challenge them to think about their role in the world. This can lead to asking existential questions of meaning and purpose and possibly to formulating unique and authentic answers to questions about the meaning of their lives. Students are also often presented with questions about what major they want to select and what career they want to pursue. These questions and responses to them can be a critical part of the development of a sense of calling.

As Nash and Murray (2010) describe, the existential questions of meaning are a "fascinating admixture of the abstract and the practice, the universal and the particular. They represent well the tensions that exist for so many college students who seek to find the delicate balance that exists in the difficult space between idealism and realism, between macro- and micro-meaning" (p. xvi). Students often go through the process of trying to address these issues and develop responses that shape their values, worldview, and the direction of the rest of their lives. Colleges may fail to address these issues altogether or they may provide a supportive community where students can discover the values and life directions that are most meaningful to them. They can leave students to flounder alone or they may provide mentors and experiences that can help students sort through their potential vocations and discover a unique calling.

In the distant past, there were many colleges that attempted to help emerging adults develop spiritually. In early American history, the primary role of the first colleges was to provide a seminary-like curriculum established by religious groups to foster the education of future clergy, who often had a religious sense of calling (Rudolph, 1991). However, over the past 200 years, there has been a dramatic shift in the academic curriculum. Spirituality and spiritual development have become rare topics in higher education and student affairs literature (Astin, Astin, & Lindholm, 2011; Love & Talbot, 1999). Many consider the current inability of colleges to openly address issues related to spirituality and calling to be a loss for students. Recently, many psychologists, researchers, and mental health professionals have argued that the investigation of meaning and purpose is an integral part of students' overall development that is too often ignored by universities and colleges (Temkin & Evans, 1998).

Astin et al. (2011) believe that spiritual education is critical for students' academic careers because it enables them to make meaning of their education and their lives. In college, they can cultivate a sense of purpose and experience dilemmas that form and refine their values and beliefs and make choices about what they want to do. They also may consider and reconsider their world view and the role that it plays in their lives. Astin et al. (2011) state that, "spirituality involves aspects of our students' experience that are not easy to define, such as intuition, inspiration, creativity, and their sense of connectedness to others and the world" (p. 40). They describe the imbalance universities have shown in focusing on "outer" aspects of students' development through course completion, honors and awards, and degree attainment but neglecting "inner" development that targets values, beliefs, emotional maturity, moral development, spirituality, and self-understanding. The focus on developing a meaningful philosophy of life has been overshadowed by the desire to help students obtain financial satisfaction (Astin, Oseguera, Sax, & Korn, 2002).

Although colleges have tended in the past to focus on "objective" and "value-free" knowledge and have stayed away from spirituality (Palmer, 1993), academia is slowly allowing meaning and purpose to be discussed and studied more and to play a more significant role in the social sciences (Tierney & Rhoads, 1993). College faculty and staff have come to realize how important it is for their students to have a sense of meaning and direction for their lives. This can help to build a foundation of personal values and goals that can be maintained when students are later challenged by a variety of individual and societal problems (Nash & Murray, 2010). For example, college professors have begun to attend to the role of spirituality in leadership development activities because it provides a foundation for communicating core values, creating a diverse community, promoting holistic learning, and providing a framework for moral behavior (Nash & Scott, 2009).

Astin (2004) calls for spirituality to be a central component in college education. He conducted a pilot study of 3,700 students enrolled at 46 colleges and universities and a full-scale study of 90,000 students enrolled at 150 institutions and found that spirituality directly impacts students' sense of community. He wrote that "more than anything else, giving spirituality a central place in our institutions will serve to strengthen our sense of connectedness with each other, our students, and our institutions. This enrichment of a sense of community will not only go a long way toward overcoming the sense of fragmentation and alienation that so many of us now feel, but will also help our students to lead more meaningful lives as engaged citizens, loving partners and parents, and caring neighbors" (Astin, 2004, p. 34). This sense of community might provide the context where students can identify the best expressions of their own unique gifts and talents which can become the foundation for a sense of calling.

The college community may play a critical role for enabling students to explore questions related to a higher meaning and purpose and their place in the world. Another large scale study investigated increases and decreases in spirituality in a sample of precollege individuals, and found that social context played an important role in spiritual development (Regnerus, Smith, & Smith, 2004). In addition, being in an environment where spirituality is valued has been found to increase personal control and decrease feelings of depression (Powell, Shahabi, & Thoresen, 2003). Traditionally, religious institutions have provided the context for exploring spirituality in relation to organized religion. However, it is certainly not necessary to confine the exploration of meaning, purpose, and a sense of calling to religious institutions. Secular college and universities have the added advantage of people with a greater diversity of values and beliefs and can foster the open exploration of a variety of spiritual perspectives and life callings.

How Can Positive Psychology Foster Spiritual Development and a Sense of Calling?

So far, we have defined spiritual development as moving towards a sense of higher meaning and purpose and calling as a person's unique and authentic path towards greater meaning and purpose. In addition, we have tried to show how college may provide a critical window of opportunity to enable students to discover this path and begin to answer this call. What does positive psychology offer that may uniquely contribute to the discovery of this path? Moreover, how can positive psychology enable people to actually begin to live a life of higher meaning and purpose? Before we present specific suggestions for how this can be accomplished in a college setting, we want to present some examples of what positive psychology may have to offer all people who are on a spiritual journey. Although the positive psychology movement does not specifically advocate organized religion, it has much to say about spirituality as a life of authentic meaning and purpose.

The first and most important thing to point out is that the purpose and goals of positive psychology are entirely consistent with enabling people to discover and live a life that has authentic meaning and purpose. Christopher Peterson has defined positive psychology as "the science of what make's life most worth living" (2013, p. 3). This life worth living, or "the good life" as Seligman often refers to it, may essentially be nothing other than what we have defined as the essence of spirituality (Seligman, 2011): an authentic life of the greatest and highest meaning and purpose. Martin Seligman has been developing what he is calling the PERMA theory of the good life, which includes positive emotions, engagement or flow, relationships, meaning, and accomplishment (Seligman, 2011). Rather than focusing on reducing psychopathology and returning people to some imaginary zero point of average of normal functioning, positive psychology has focused on thriving and flourishing and enabling human beings to reach their own level of optimal functioning (Peterson, 2013; Seligman, 2011; Seligman & Csikszentmihalyi, 2000).

Second, although positive psychology can be thought of as a specific set of findings by a specific group of researchers who have been labeled positive psychologists, it can also be considered a particular approach to discovering: (1) What is at the heart of the good life? and (2) How to enable human beings to reach it? For thousands of years, philosophy and religion have focused on coming up with answers to both of these kinds of questions. This has resulted in rich and nuanced answers to the questions of what is the good life and what kinds of practices may enable us to experience it. Positive psychology has brought the discipline and rigor of the scientific method to each of these critical questions. It has provided a way for people to begin to address what have been sometimes dismissed as values questions that have been off-limits in more reductionistic approaches to science. Most importantly, positive psychology has provided a way to use the best empirical research methods to test and consensually identify and validate ideas about what is the good life and how to achieve it.

Third, positive psychology has begun to actually provide answers to the question of what kind of life is worth living, or, in other words, what does the life of the greatest meaning and purpose actually look like and entail? This is undoubtedly a challenging question to approach from a scientific perspective because it involves questions of value and value judgments. An approach that has been taken by Martin Seligman has been to try to identify the core elements of human well-being (Seligman, 2011). As noted above, he has proposed and presented initial evidence for his PERMA theory of well-being that includes five primary elements including a sense of meaning that is at the heart of our definition of spirituality (Seligman, 2011). Whether or not the PERMA theory is correct about the five most important elements of well-being, we think this is an example of how a scientific approach can be applied to try to understand what is most important to particular individuals and to humanity as a whole. Positive psychology can continue to use quantitative as well as qualitative methods to discover what makes life most meaningful and worth living.

Fourth, and most relevant for our goal of spiritual development and a sense of calling, positive psychology is also bringing science to bear on the question of how to enable people to live a life that is meaningful and worthwhile. We think that positive psychology has specifically contributed to this by focusing on human character strengths and virtues, developing ways to exercise these strengths, and developing other practices that may increase a person's sense of meaning and purpose. The development of a classification of human character strengths and virtues has provided a way to understand all of the human qualities that may foster the life worth living (Peterson & Seligman, 2004). The six categories of virtues include wisdom, courage, humanity, justice, temperance, and transcendence which all can be seen as ways to enable people to live a life of meaning and purpose. Indeed, they have been called "values in action" (VIA)—and can be seen as qualities that may lead to the good life—if not fully embody it (Peterson & Seligman, 2004).

The VIA classification system may be particularly relevant and useful for a sense of calling. Positive psychologists have developed the VIA survey that can be used to enable people to identify their top character strengths in the VIA classification system (Peterson & Seligman, 2004; Peterson & Park, 2009). The ideas of both calling and vocation involve knowing one's self and identifying what one is best at, and this kind of self-knowledge may be critical for identifying one's calling in life. Positive psychologists have also developed practical suggestions regarding ways to best use and express each of the character strengths (Rashid & Anjum, 2005). This may provide a straightforward way for many people to begin to discover, experiment with, and exercise what may be a life's calling. There is empirical support for the notions that both identifying and using one's top character strengths may be beneficial in relation to improving well-being (Gander, Proyer, Ruch, & Wyss, 2013; Seligman, Steen, Park, & Peterson, 2005), and there may be ways to begin to authentically live out one's unique values in a way that both improves well-being and leads to a life of meaning and purpose.

Finally, positive psychology has also focused on developing specific exercises and practices that may foster spiritual development. Even though organized religion has not been a primary focus in positive psychology, many positive psychology researchers have studied human qualities and strengths that have long been a focus of organized religion but which have often been ignored in psychology. Robert Emmons has developed a line of research examining gratitude and some of the interventions that may enhance it (Emmons & McCullough, 2003; Emmons, 2008). He and others have shown that gratitude can be increased and that gratitude may increase various elements of well-being. Everett Worthington, Michael McCullough, and Robert Enright have done seminal work in studying forgiveness and interventions that may promote it (Enright, 2001; McCullough, 2001; Worthington, 2006). As with gratitude, they and others have shown how forgiveness may be increased and that it too may have positive effects on other aspects of well-being. Sonja Lyubomirsky and Barbara Fredrickson have focused on the development of exercises and interventions that may increase kindness and love and have shown beneficial effects on both mental and physical health and well-being (Lyubomirsky, 2007; Fredrickson, 2013). All of these exercises may serve as ways to enhance spirituality as that which is most meaningful and gives a person a sense of purpose in life. For example, Lyubomirsky has developed and tested exercises that involve the practice of random acts of kindness.

How Can Positive Psychology Foster Spiritual Development and Calling in College?

Positive psychology principles and practices have much to offer in enabling people to discover and live out the kind of life that may bring them the most meaning and purpose. We will now present a set of specific guidelines and suggestions for using positive psychology to accomplish this with students in college and university settings. In order to have the greatest impact and to be relevant to the largest number of students, we will give suggestions for a variety of contexts including the classroom, academic advising, residence halls, administration, departments, and athletics and extracurricular activities. Also important for our approach, we want to provide opportunities for faculty and staff to take advantage of positive psychology to further their own spiritual development and sense of calling, as well as that of the students with whom they work.

Before we get started, we want to state the key principles and components of positive psychology that we think are important across all of these settings. First, a positive psychology approach should foster discussions about what a life of meaning and purpose consists of—or what is the good life that is worth living (Peterson, 2013; Seligman, 2011). Second, a positive psychology approach should foster an appreciation of individual differences and help each student identify what a life of meaning and purpose might be and look like for them as unique individuals. This can be done by discussions and writing and by using formal questionnaires such as the VIA survey (King, 2001; Peterson & Seligman, 2004). Third, a positive psychology approach should help students actually answer their own unique call and make progress in their own spiritual journey—as defined as moving toward a life of the greatest authentic meaning and purpose. This can be done by providing them with a variety of exercises and resources to try out and use to enable them to see what fits and works for them best—such as those suggested for each of the VIA strengths and those developed more specifically for things like gratitude, forgiveness, love, and kindness (Emmons, 2008; Enright, 2001; Fredrickson, 2013; Lyubormirsky, 2007).

Positive Psychology Courses

In our own state university setting, we have designed three kinds of positive psychology courses that may be particularly useful in helping students develop spiritually and discover and pursue a sense of calling. We have taught each several times and found them to be well-received and highly rated by students. The first is a basic positive psychology course called "Positive Psychology" where the students learn what positive psychology has discovered about (1) well-being and the good life (Seligman, 2011), (2) the human strengths and positive qualities that enable a person to live it (Peterson & Seligman, 2004), and (3) what each individual student can do to move towards the kind of life that is most important to him or her (Rashid & Anjum, 2005). Over a period of eight years, this has become a large class (200 students) that is taught every semester where students initially identify what kind of life and goals would be most meaningful to them (e.g., what is their calling?), identify their strengths using the VIA survey (e.g., how can I reach my calling?), and apply these strengths for achieving their own idea of a life worth living.

The second course that we have developed is an advanced undergraduate seminar called "Positive Psychology Lab" (20–25 students) for those who want to further explore their own sense of calling and how to use their strengths to achieve the kind of life that they think is most worth living. This course involves students giving a brief presentation on what their unique strengths are, how they have been expressed in their lives, and how they can apply them to reach their most important goals (e.g., to answer their own unique calling). After each presentation, students are given written feedback by all of the other students as to what they as observers see as the presenter's strengths and how they might use them to reach their goals. This enables everyone in the class to become experts in recognizing and supporting the call to a life of meaning and purpose for themselves and for other people. The students in this course also give group presentations on how to help others identify and use different collections of strengths to reach their goals. These group presentations have served as a model and as training for these more advanced students to work with at risk students who are struggling to identify and follow their own sense of calling.

The third course that we have developed is a seminar called "First in Family to College" for first year first generation students (20–25 students) who may be at risk for dropping out of college. Many of these students are from lower income families or are ethnic minority students. There are several ways that positive psychology is used in this course to help motivate students to stay in college. The instructor meets with each student to do a "motivational interview" (Miller & Rollnick, 2012) to help them identify what is most important for them to accomplish at school and help them use that to increase and maintain their motivation for being in college. The students use the VIA survey to identify their own strengths, talk about them in class, and receive feedback on how to reach their most important academic and life goals. Finally, the students are mentored by students in the advanced undergraduate seminar course that was discussed above. Thus, the students who have a more developed sense of how to apply positive psychology in discovering and living a meaningful life mentor students who may be struggling to discover a meaningful and sustaining calling for their own lives.

Focusing on Meaning and Purpose in Other Courses

There are several ways that the key positive psychology principles and components that we have identified could be applied in other classes. We would encourage instructors for courses related to psychology, the social sciences, philosophy and religion, and the humanities to find ways to relate their classes to the questions that students may have about what is important to them and what they want to do with their lives. For example, a philosophy course could include various approaches to understanding a life of meaning and purpose, which could lead to discussions on how that may vary for individual students. A literature or cinema course could involve introducing students to the VIA classification of character strengths and then having them write about or discuss how different characters they are studying live them out (Niemiec & Wedding, 2008, 2014). Students in other social sciences and humanities courses could be encouraged to think about, write about, and discuss what these disciplines may have to say about achieving the good life and how students can use information and ideas they learn in the class to discover and live it for themselves.

In addition, colleges could incorporate questionnaires, writing exercises, and discussions in first year survey or last year capstone courses that may mark major times of transition for college students. For example, students in freshman English or writing courses could be given assignments to write about what kind of life they are seeking or would be most important to them. Introductory psychology courses could include taking the VIA survey and getting students to think about how their strengths may translate into specific majors or career directions. Similarly, senior honors courses and programs could include taking the VIA survey and discussing or writing about the results to enable students to identify their own unique strengths, gifts, and talents and how they may use them after they graduate. For example, King (2001) has developed and tested an excellent writing exercise that involves writing about a best possible future self that can be used to help students envision living out a sense of their own calling.

Academic Advising and Residence Halls

Beyond the classroom, there are several other programs and settings for students where positive psychology may be applied to enhance spiritual development and a sense of calling (Gehrke, 2008). Positive psychology may be easily integrated into academic advising where there is a strong emphasis on identifying majors and making career choices. Advisors can be trained to talk with students about issues related to meaning and purpose and about how they may discover and follow a pathway to what is most meaningful to them (Thompson & Feldman, 2010). Of course, a variety of psychological instruments are already used to help students identify their interests and career preferences. The VIA survey could be an excellent addition to these and could supplement the strength-based assessment that colleges are increasingly supporting (Park & Peterson, 2008). The VIA and other strength-based assessments can serve as a starting point for helping students think about how they can apply their own unique strengths with regard to choosing a major or a career (Peterson & Seligman, 2004; Rath, 2007).

Positive psychology may also be particularly applicable to helping students in dormitory and residence hall settings. Living in a college residence facility can be a formative experience for students in terms of building community and learning to live with people with diverse personalities and backgrounds. It can also be a time of major stress that sometimes brings out the worst in people that can become a major distraction from success in school. Life in a residence hall may provide one of the best opportunities for students to learn to use and apply positive psychology in helping to get to know other people and themselves. We suggest that an important part of resident advisor training could be to have them take the VIA survey and train them to administer it to their residents and discuss how they can use it to help others best use their strengths. In addition, life in a residence hall can be a crucible for discussions about the meaning of life. We think that helping students see each other in light of their strengths could go far in helping them discover a life of meaning and purpose.

Administration and Departments

If the college administration and individual departments do not value spiritual development and a sense of calling, it is difficult to imagine that they would do much to support their development in students. One key to creating an environment where students can find their own unique way to a life of meaning and purpose may be to support faculty and staff in doing the same (Dik & Steger, 2008). As an example from our own university, there was a woman who worked in student affairs who took our basic positive psychology course. She was later promoted to serve as a dean of student affairs where she played an important role in helping the university develop other positive psychology classes and in providing funds to do research on them. Her enthusiasm spread to others in the university administration who have continued to value and support the role of positive psychology in the lives of students, faculty, and staff.

There are four ways we propose for increasing awareness and support of the role of positive psychology in spiritual development and calling in college administration and across departments. The first is to encourage faculty and staff to take the positive psychology courses or simply to suggest sitting in on days that may be particularly relevant for them. The second is to conduct one time workshops or seminars for faculty and staff where they take the VIA survey and then are asked to discuss the results in the context of what is most important to them and their own sense of calling (McGovern & Miller, 2008). The third is to encourage individual departments, offices, or workgroups to take the VIA survey as a way of learning how to better work together and appreciate each other strengths. The fourth is to show a movie that emphasizes positive psychology themes to the whole college community to raise awareness about positive psychology and begin a discussion on what is a meaningful life and how to help students, faculty, and staff achieve it (Niemiec & Wedding, 2008, 2014).

Athletics and Other Extracurricular Activities

Although sports and hobbies do not always translate directly into one's primary vocation or source of income, they can be the places or even laboratories where students discover and develop some of their most important strengths and talents.

Thus, extracurricular activities in college may provide some of the best opportunities for enabling students to discover and respond to their own unique and authentic sense of calling. There are a couple of ways that colleges may begin to do a better job of this in the context of sports and other extracurricular activities. First, we suggest that coaches and leaders of campus organizations themselves have the opportunity to be a part of discussions about the meaning of their own sport or activity and whether and how they may have a sense of calling for it. We also think it could be beneficial for them to take the VIA survey to help them identify their own unique strengths and begin to think about how they are related to activities they are leading. Second, we suggest that they have the students in their sports teams/groups/organizations or extracurricular activities take and discuss the VIA. The coaches and leaders can help the students understand how their strengths may be related to each of the activities and to other ways of expressing who they are and what they want to do.

Case Example

We present the story of a student who took advantage of the positive psychology course sequence at our large state university to discover a higher, authentic sense of meaning and purpose. Although some of the details of the story have been changed to protect her identity, the most important points regarding finding a sense of meaning and purpose have been retained. This student is representative of what we have seen in many other students who have had both the introductory Positive Psychology course and the more advanced Positive Psychology Laboratory course described above.

Ashley was a 23-year-old Latina woman who was the first in her family to attend college. Although she was a psychology major, she had already been in school for four years and still did not have a good idea of what she wanted to do with her life. In addition, she often focused on her weakness in math and felt handicapped by the emotional abuse she suffered as a child. When she took the Positive Psychology course, for the first time in her life, she began to think about what she wanted in life and realized that she had some strengths. She completed an assignment designed to help identify her goals, the most important of which was being of help to others who had been abused as children. The VIA survey helped Ashley to see that her greatest strengths involved love and kindness and the appreciation of beauty and excellence. For a class exercise to use her strengths, she volunteered for a crisis hotline and discovered that she really enjoyed talking with other people under distress. In addition, she used her appreciation of beauty by taking a continuing education art class that involved telling her life story through drawing and painting. She found that free-style drawing helped her express and work through some of her past abuse. At the end of the semester, for the first time in her life, she had hope and greater confidence that she could be successful in spite of her childhood and that she really had something to offer.

Ashley enjoyed the Positive Psychology class so much that she also took the Positive Psychology Laboratory class the following the semester. Whereas the Positive Psychology class enabled her to begin to what she wanted in life, she was still not very clear about how to achieve it and had few friends who understood or supported her. In the Positive Psychology Laboratory class, she had what she later called a life-changing experience when she gave a presentation to the class about her strengths and goals. She had always been terrified of public speaking, but she was amazed to find that the class not only paid attention but gave her a great deal of feedback about her strengths and how she could reach her goals. There was another female student in the class who told her about a master's program in counseling and how she may even be able to establish a practice where she could specialize in art therapy. Ashley was delighted to hear that it may be possible for her to find a career combining her core strengths of love and kindness and the appreciation of beauty in helping others overcome challenges similar to what she had faced. She wrote her final paper on her plan to become a counselor and use art in her work to help people who had experienced abuse as children. She remained friends with the student who suggested the masters in counseling program and the two women attended the program together.

Although Ashley's story may sound almost too good to be true, we have seen something very similar happen with many of the students who have taken the Positive Psychology and Positive Psychology Laboratory classes. The most important aspects of positive psychology that seem to have made a difference for these students are that they are (1) given ways to identify what kind of life would be most meaningful to them, (2) enabled to identify their strengths and find ways to use them for a life of meaning and purpose, and (3) supported by other students who recognize and affirm their strengths and what they are seeking. For Ashley and other students like her, positive psychology can help turn college into a place that enables them to discover and begin to live out an authentic sense of meaning and purpose.

Conclusion

College is a critical time for developing spiritually and discovering a sense of calling. It is a time when students begin to envision what their life can be like, consider which career is best suited for them, and decide how they can most fully live out what they want to do and who they want to be (Braun, 2005). As the science of what makes life worth living (Peterson, 2013), positive psychology is ideally placed to enable college students to find a life of meaning and purpose. Through this chapter, we have tried to identify and illustrate the ways that positive psychology can foster spiritual development and calling in college students. By entering college life through courses, advising, residence halls, extracurricular activities, administration, and individual departments, it can provide students with multiple opportunities for exploring what kind of majors and career paths may be most meaningful to them. Through making exercises like the VIA survey (Peterson & Seligman, 2004) available to the whole college community, positive psychology can increase the awareness of the unique strengths and callings of all students, faculty, and staff. In making use of new discoveries about how to develop and use strengths such as love, kindness, gratitude, and forgiveness, it will continue to add to the ways that college can help students live out their callings. Positive psychology has only just begun to fulfill its tremendous potential for making college a place where people can discover and realize their own authentic sense of meaning and purpose.

References

Alcoholics Anonymous. (2001). *Alcoholics Anonymous,* 4th ed. New York: A.A. World Services.

Antonovsky, A. (1979). *Health, stress, and coping.* San Francisco: Jossey-Bass.

Astin, A. (2004). Why spirituality deserves a central place in liberal education. *Liberal Education, 90*(2), 34–41.

Astin, A. W., Astin, H. S., & Lindholm, J. A. (2011). Assessing students' spiritual and religious qualities. *Journal of College Student Development, 52*(1), 39–61.

Astin, A. W., Oseguera, L., Sax, L. J., & Korn, W. S. (2002). *The American freshman: Thirty-five year trends, 1966–2001.* Los Angeles: Higher Education Research Institute, UCLA.

Braun, P. (2005). Employees are looking for students who reflect on life's bigger questions. *Campus Career Counselor, 3*(1), 6.

Buechner, F. (1973). *Wishful thinking: A theological ABC.* New York: Harper & Row.

Conklin, T. A. (2012). Work worth doing: A phenomenological study of the experience of discovering and following one's calling. *Journal of Management Inquiry, 21*(3), 298–317.

Davidson, J. C., & Caddell, D. P. (1994). Religion and the meaning of work. *Journal for the Scientific Study of Religion, 33*(2), 135–147.

Dik, B. J., & Duffy, R. D. (2009). Calling and vocation at work: Definitions and prospects for research and practice. *The Counseling Psychologist, 37*(3), 424–450.

Dik, B. J., Sargent, A. M., & Steger, M. F. (2008). Career development strivings assessing goals and motivation in career decision-making and planning. *Journal of Career Development, 35*(1), 23–41.

Dik, B., & Steger, M. (2008). Randomized trial of a calling-infused career workshop incorporating counselor self-disclosure. *Journal of Vocational Behavior, 73*(2), 203–211.

Duffy, R. D., Allan, B. A., & Bott, E. M. (2012). Calling and life satisfaction among undergraduate students: Investigating mediators and moderators. *Journal of Happiness Studies, 13*(3), 469–479.

Dyson, J., Cobb, M., & Forman, D. (1997). The meaning of spirituality: A literature review. *Journal of Advanced Nursing, 26*(6), 1183–1188.

Emmons, R. A. (1999). *The psychology of ultimate concerns: Motivation and spirituality in personality.* New York: The Guilford Press.

Emmons, R. A. (2008). *Thanks!: How practicing gratitude can make you happier.* New York: Mariner.

Emmons, R. A., & McCullough, M. E. (2003). Counting blessings versus burdens: An experimental investigation of gratitude and subjective well-being in daily life. *Journal of Personality and Social Psychology, 84*(2), 377–389.

Enright, R. D. (2001). *Forgiveness as a choice: A step-by-step process for resolving anger and restoring hope.* Washington, DC: American Psychological Association.

Frankl, V. E. (1946). *Man's Search for Meaning.* New York: Bantam Books.

Fredrickson, B. L. (2013). *Love 2.0.: How our supreme emotion affects everything we feel, think, do, and become.* New York: Hudson Street Press.

Gander, F., Proyer, R. T., Ruch, W., & Wyss, T. (2013). Strength-based positive interventions: Further evidence for their potential in enhancing well-being. *Journal of Happiness Studies, 14*(4), 1241–1259.

Gehrke, S.J. (2008). Leadership through meaning-making: An empirical exploration of spirituality and leadership in college students. *Journal of College Student Development, 49*(4), 351–359.

King, L. A. (2001). The health benefits of writing about life goals. *Personality and Social Psychology Bulletin, 27*(7), 798–807.

Lyubormirsky, S. (2007). *The how of happiness: A new approach to getting the life you want.* New York: Penguin Books.

Love, P., & Talbot, D. (1999). Defining spiritual development: A missing consideration for student affairs. *NASPA Journal 37*(1), 361–375.

Lyubomirsky, S. (2007). *The how of happiness: A new approach to getting the life you want.* New York: Penguin Books.

McCullough, M. E. (2001). Forgiveness: Who does it and how do they do it? *Current Directions in Psychological Science, 10*(6), 194–197.

McGovern, T. V., & Miller, S. L. (2008). Integrating teacher behaviors with character strengths and virtues for faculty development. *Teaching of Psychology, 35*(4), 278–285.

Miller, W.R., & Rollnick, S. (2012). *Motivational interviewing: Helping people change*, 3rd ed. New York: The Guilford Press.

Nash, R. J., & Murray, M. C. (2010). *Helping college students find purpose: The campus guide to meaning-making.* New York: Jossey-Bass.

Nash, R. J., & Scott, L. (2009). Spirituality, religious pluralism, and higher education leadership development. In A. Kezar (Ed.), *Rethinking leadership in a complex, multicultural, and global environment: New concepts and models for higher education* (pp. 131–150). Sterling, VA: Stylus.

Niemiec, R. M., & Wedding, D. (2008). *Positive psychology at the movies: Using films to build virtues and character strengths.* Toronto, CA: Hogrefe.

Niemiec, R. M., & Wedding, D. (2014). *Positive psychology at the movies 2: Using films to build and well-being.* Toronto, CA: Hogrefe.

Palmer, P. J. (1983). *To know as we are known: A spirituality of education.* San Francisco: Harper & Row.

Pargament, K. I. (1997). *The psychology of religion and coping: Theory, research, and practice.* New York: The Guilford Press.

Pargament, K., & Mahoney, A. (2002). Spirituality: Discovering and conserving the sacred. In C. R. Snyder & S. J. Lopez (Eds.), *Handbook of positive psychology* (pp. 646–659). New York, NY: Oxford University Press.

Park, N., & Peterson, C. (2008). Positive psychology and character strengths: Application to strengths-based school counseling. *Professional School Counseling, 12*(2), 85–92.

Peterson, C. (2013). *Pursuing the good life: 100 reflections on positive psychology.* New York: Oxford University Press.

Peterson, C., & Park, N. (2009). Classifying and measuring strengths of character. In C. R. Snyder & S. J. Lopez (Eds.), *Oxford handbook of positive psychology* (pp. 25–34). New York, NY: Oxford University Press.

Peterson, C., & Seligman, M. E. P. (2004). *Character strengths and virtues: A handbook and classification.* New York: Oxford University Press.

Powell, L. H., Shahabi, L., & Thoresen, C. E. (2003). Religion and spirituality: Linkages to physical health. *American Psychologist, 58*(1), 36–52.

Rashid, T., & Anjum, A. (2005). 340 ways to use VIA character strengths. Retrieved from http://www.viastrengths.org/Applications/Exercises/tabid/132/Default.aspx

Rath, T. (2007). *StrengthFinder 2.0.* New York: Gallup Press.

Regnerus, M. D., Smith, C., & Smith, B. (2004). Social context in the development of adolescent religiosity. *Applied Developmental Science, 8*(1), 27–38.

Reker, G. T., Peacock, E. J., & Wong, P. T. P. (1987). Meaning and purpose in life and well-being: A life-span perspective. *Journal of Gerontology, 42*(1), 44–49.

Rudolph, F. (1991). *The American college and university: A history.* University of Georgia Press.

Seligman, M. E. P. (2011). *Flourish: A visionary new understanding of happiness and well-being.* New York: Free Press.

Seligman, M. E. P., & Csikszentmihalyi, M. (2000). Positive psychology: An introduction. *American Psychologist, 55*(1), 5–14.

Seligman, M. E. P., Steen, T. A., Park, N., & Peterson, C. (2005). Positive psychology progress: Empirical validation of interventions. *American Psychologist, 60*(5), 410–421.

Selway, D., & Ashman, A. F. (1998). Disability, religion and health: A literature review in search of the spiritual dimension of disability. *Disability and Society, 13*(3), 429–439.

Serow, R. C., Eaker, D., & Ciechalski, J. (1992). Calling, service, and legitimacy: Professional orientations and career commitment among prospective teachers. *Journal of Research and Development in Education, 25*(3), 136–141.

Steger, M. F. (2009). Meaning in life. In C. R. Snyder & S. J. Lopez (Eds.), *Oxford handbook of positive psychology* (2nd ed., pp. 679–687). New York, NY: Oxford University Press.

Steger, M. F., Pickering, N. K., Shin, J. Y., & Dik, B. J. (2010). Calling in Work Secular or Sacred? *Journal of Career Assessment, 18*(1), 82–96.

Temkin, L., & Evans, N. J. (1998). Religion on campus: Suggestions for cooperation between student affairs and campus-based religious organization. *NASPA Journal, 36*(1), 61–89.

Thompson, E., & Feldman, D. (2010). Let your life speak: Assessing effectiveness of a program to explore meaning, purpose, and calling with college students. *Journal of Employment Counseling, 47*(1), 12–18.

Tierney, W. G., & Rhoads, R. A. (1993). Postmodernism and critical theory in higher education: Implications for research and practice. In J. C. Smart (ed.), *Higher education: Handbook for theory and research* (Vol. 9, pp. 308–343). New York: Agathon.

Tillich, P. (1957). *Dynamics of faith.* New York: Harper and Row.

Treadgold, R. (1999). Transcendent vocations: Their relationship to stress, depression, and clarity of self-concept. *Journal of Humanistic Psychology, 39*(1), 81–105.

Worthington, E. L., Jr. (2006). *Forgiveness and reconciliation: Theory and application.* New York: Brunner/Routledge

Wrzesniewski, A., McCauley, C., Rozin, P., & Schwartz, B. (1997). Jobs, careers, and callings: People's relations to their work. *Journal of Research in Personality, 31*(1), 21–33.

Zinnbauer, B. J., Pargament, K. I., Cole, B., Rye, M. S., Butter, E. M., Belavich, T. G., Hipp, K. M., Scott, A. B., & Kadar, J. L. (1997). Religion and spirituality: Unfuzzying the fuzzy. *Journal for the Scientific Study of Religion, 36*(4), 549–564.

12

The Intersection of Positive Psychology and Leadership Development

SHARRA DURHAM HYNES

We live in a time when there is a critical need for effective leaders—those who can and will take up the challenge to create positive change within our society. We are living in a new world that is bombarded by conflict, profound transformation, loss, disaster, unmet needs, ineffective responses, and a lack of solutions. Within our own borders of the United States, we see issues of poverty, hunger, human trafficking, political division, natural disasters, and so much more. For just one example, after Hurricane Sandy struck the eastern shore in October 2012, touted as the worst natural disaster on the East Coast, lawmakers, communities, and churches struggled to find a way of meeting the vast losses of so many communities and individuals. One can easily think of other examples in which, even in one of the most technologically advanced nations in the world, leaders still struggle to address prolific and severe problems. On a smaller but still impactful scale, other complex and difficult situations are sometimes combined with ineffective leadership on our college campuses today.

Although statements that identify a lack of progress or success may be discouraging, there is growing interest in new and existing models of leadership development that more appropriately address the challenges of the society in which we now live (Durham Hynes, 2009). Indeed, these critical needs present an opportunity for a new and different kind of leadership (Boyatzis & McKee, 2005). Societies worldwide need leadership that will result in positive change for communities and civilizations. Higher education institutions provide one of the best avenues through which individuals can learn critical leadership information and gain valuable and applicable leadership experiences. It is often said that the children of today will be the leaders of tomorrow, thus making training and development in leadership of paramount importance. Although leadership experience does occur before college, higher education settings offer many opportunities to more fully develop and solidify the leaders of tomorrow.

Simultaneous to the emergence of the need for effective leadership and positive change within society was the birth of the positive psychology movement. In 1998, Martin Seligman, who was president of the American Psychological Association (APA) at the time, promoted the science of positive psychology (Fowler, Seligman, & Koocher, 1999) and encouraged psychologists to consider a broader way of thinking with regard to psychology. Since then, he and many others have suggested that psychologists and researchers not be merely concerned with how to treat pathology and/or study traditional psychological concepts but also focus on how to move individuals, organizations, and communities to a place of flourishing (Seligman & Csikszentmihalyi, 2000; Seligman, 2011).

Furthermore, the field of positive psychology is seeking to strengthen the base of knowledge around human resilience, strength, growth, and development as well as ways in which people experience feelings of joy, expressions of altruism, and examples of healthy family and institutions (Myers, 2000; Gable & Haidt, 2005). "Unlike the popular 'feel good' positive approaches of the past, such as Norman Vincent Peale's famous message of the 'power of positive thinking', or the recent best-sellers by [Stephen] Covey and Spencer Johnson, positive psychology follows its heritage of insisting on sound theory and research before moving on to application and practice" (Luthans, 2002, p. 697). Based on the science, in the past decade, there has been an expanding array of positive psychology applications. Individuals who study leadership, particularly postindustrial forms of leadership, often resonate with the aforementioned goals of positive psychology.

With the fields of leadership development and positive psychology both experiencing fast-paced growth in the time between 1990 and today, there is great optimism for a cumulative, positive impact on our world. As described by Frank Shushok and Vera Kidd in Chapter 2 of this volume, today's college students are members of the Millennial generation, born after 1981. They have emerged as a powerful force and will shape the economic and social demands of the next decade. They are focused on teamwork, doing good works on behalf of others, and they desire tangible outcomes to their work (Howe & Strauss, 2000). Being able to leverage the gifts and talents of these students is critical to stimulating and implementing change initiatives in organizations and in societies across the world.

This chapter will outline and explore the points of intersection between positive psychology and leadership, including a section on civic engagement. College student personnel who teach, research, promote, and facilitate leadership development will be able to draw on the connection between positive psychology and leadership theories and practices to enhance the learning experience for students. Six models of leadership will be referenced in this chapter: Leadership Identity Development, Mindful Leadership, Relational Leadership, Resonant Leadership, Social Change Leadership, and Transformational Leadership. Although many varying theories of leadership are available, these postindustrial models of leadership seem to have synergy with the principles and goals of positive psychology. These models also stand out as being more relevant and appropriate for the college student population. In particular, the Social Change model and the Leadership Identity Development model were created with college students as the primary audience and the group through which the research for these models was conducted.

The following four basic principles of positive psychology will be highlighted and examined, and their respective connections with models of leadership will be discussed:

- Shifting the focus from negative to positive
- Developing a language of strengths
- Utilizing strategies that foster hope
- Building emotional intelligence

These four principles were selected because they share a common thread of agency. Within each principle, the individual chooses a course of action or a focus and then acts on his/her choice, insight, or awareness. Suggestions for leadership practitioners in higher education will be offered with an emphasis on practical ideas for helping students to apply their strengths and talents (a key principle of positive psychology) in order to become agents of positive change within their respective communities.

Shifting the Focus from Negative to Positive

As was previously mentioned, Martin Seligman brought to bear his professional interest in optimism on the field of psychology when he served as the leader of the APA in 1998. He encouraged research into methods, strategies, and mindsets that would help shift both individual and collective interest from a negatively focused paradigm to a positive one. Given this shift, advances in psychological research and practice have now returned to the original mission: understanding the whole person.

At least two leadership theories appear to synchronize with shifting the focus from negative to positive. These theories are Transformational Leadership and the Social Change Model of Leadership Development. Transformational Leadership, which was created and developed by Burns (1978), is focused on the mutual benefits gained for both leaders and followers in the process of leadership development, such as gains in motivation and morality. In other forms of leadership, the amount and extent of the leader's power differentiates the leader and follower; however, in Transformational Leadership, the differences in power between the leader and follower are counterweights that provide mutual support to each other (Burns, 1978). Therefore, the inherent power difference between leader and follower is not a negative aspect of leadership in the Transformational Leadership theory. The difference in power is an understood and appreciated balance, and both the leader and the follower benefit. Transformational leaders generally find ways of developing common goals and purposes with their followers. They engender trust, respect, and a positive relationship with their followers. It should be assumed that human resilience (the ability to move through adversity), strength, and development would be natural byproducts of the achievement of the common purpose that is desired as an outcome of Transformational Leadership.

Transformational Leadership differs from many of the previously researched and developed forms of leadership that tended to focus more exclusively on the attributes or behaviors of the positional leader, not the impact that he/she could have on those who follow. Industrial forms of leadership such as the "great man theory" tended to focus more on power and authority and not on the process of leadership (Rost, 1991). Therefore, the leadership of the individual was often dependent on his/her morals and values. If a positional leader used negative values, he/she could have a dramatic impact, but it would not always be for the good of the whole or for the good of those who were following. For example, dictators of past societies such as Hitler and Stalin had positional power and used this power to achieve their own desired outcomes, often at the expense of others. Yes they were leaders, but they certainly were not transformational nor did they desire positive outcomes for everyone involved in the leadership process. Transformational Leadership principles confirm that a shift from perceiving power and authority as negative to seeing that it can be positive is in agreement with the aforementioned principle of positive psychology—shifts from negative to positive.

The Social Change Model of Leadership is designed for college students and advocates for leadership development, grounded in social responsibility and change for the common good. This definition shows the overlap with the principle of shifting the focus to the positive and away from the negative. The model comprises seven values: consciousness of self, congruence, commitment, collaboration, common purpose, controversy with civility, and citizenship. There is also an overall value of change that synthesizes the other seven values (Higher Education Research Institute, 1996). A quick review of these values signals an emphasis on the more positive outcomes of the leadership process. For example, it can be assumed that developing an understanding of how to practice controversy with civility will frame differences between individuals and groups in the most productive and positive light. Although differences are unavoidable, emphasis is placed on how to address these differences with respect, care, and concern for the viewpoint of the other person.

The Social Change Model has two primary goals. The first is to enhance student learning and development. Specifically, this goal seeks to increase students' greater self-knowledge and understanding of their talents, values, and personal interests. The second goal is to create positive social change at the community or institutional level. This positive change is intended to help organizations function more effectively and to treat individuals with more civility (Higher Education Research Institute, 1996).

Another way in which the social change model aligns with the principle of shifting the focus from negative to positive is the stated goal of creating change agents; i.e., those who will be mobilized to understand themselves and commit to making positive change within groups, organizations, and the broader world. Roberts (2007), one of the original creators of the Social Change Model, encourages students to start at a place where they can be effective, nurture big dreams, continue to build new resources, and become lifelong learners who learn not only from their own experiences but also from the experiences of others. If students are able to apply this suggestion, they will realize that leadership for positive social change requires constant attention and diligence. A focus on the desired positive end (shifting away from the negative) will hopefully keep students motivated and encouraged through the very hard work that is required to achieve their goal(s).

Developing a Language of Strengths

Many in leadership understand that before you can effectively lead and manage others, you must know and understand yourself (Goleman, Boyatzis, & McKee, 2002). To this end, it is helpful for students to understand their unique abilities and positive qualities and develop a language for discussing these strengths with others. This focus on strengths corresponds with the focus of positive psychology where there is an emphasis on what is right and good rather than on what needs to be remedied or fixed. Those who teach and develop leadership in students can help in the process of developing a language of strengths by providing opportunities for reflection, use of instruments, and targeted mentoring that draws on natural talents. There are several approaches available for helping students to develop a language of strengths. From simple personal reflection exercises that encourage students to identify things in which they excel to the use of instruments such as the Gallup StrengthsFinder (Rath, 2007), students can identify their strengths and develop a language and greater understanding of themselves around these strengths. If resources are available to have students take a normed instrument, such as the StrengthsFinder, it can be helpful in creating shared vocabulary around personal strengths. It can also be helpful in giving students written resources to better explain the nuances of their particular set of talents and offer opportunities to reflect on the intersection of talents. An accessible and appropriate resource for this purpose is the book *StrengthsQuest* (Clifton, Anderson, & Schreiner, 2006), which includes a single use access code to the StrengthsFinder instrument. *StrengthsQuest* and *StrengthsFinder 2.0* (Rath, 2007) have descriptions of all 34 of the themes of talent as well as sections on how students can utilize their strengths for academics and careers. Based on the experience of many professionals in higher education, this instrument is highly beneficial in helping students to identify talents, even those talents that have previously gone unrecognized or have been underdeveloped.

In 2008, Gallup Press published *Strengths Based Leadership* (Rath & Conchie, 2008), which is a book about how strengths can be effectively applied in leadership situations. This book also contains research about what followers are looking for in a leader. Interestingly, according to the authors, followers want someone who can demonstrate compassion, hope, stability, and trust. These four areas of leadership correspond suitably with the principles of positive psychology, specifically the emphasis on hope. Although this text is not focused on the college student population, it may be another useful resource for those professionals who desire to build the leadership capacity of students. The text includes a unique access code that allows a student to take a leadership version of Gallup's StrengthsFinder instrument. The leadership version provides the individual with strategies for leading with strengths and also aligns strengths with four domains of leadership: executing, influencing, relationship building, and strategic thinking. Gallup promotes the philosophy that leaders do not need strengths in all four of the leadership domains. However, teams will function best when there is a broad representation of strengths across the four domains in the team as a whole. Someone can be an exceptional leader even if their strengths fall primarily into one domain. What may set the leader apart from others is his/her understanding of what it means to have strengths grouped within a single area rather than dispersed across the four domains. This level of self-awareness correlates with a deep understanding of the ways in which the leaders' behaviors can impact both individuals within the group and the group as a whole. For example, if a leader's strengths are primarily grouped in the executing domain, he/she should be more aggressive in seeking out leaders from the group who can help with relationship building and strategic thinking.

Recognizing that many institutions do not have resources to purchase texts or access codes for each student, they can use other personal reflection exercises or free online tools to define a student's talents and create a plan for turning that talent into a well-developed strength. For example, students can register for free to take the VIA Institute on Character's inventory of personal strengths at www.viacharacter.org. One reflection exercise that may be beneficial is to have students journal or blog about moments of great success or accomplishment and the activities or behaviors that are characteristic of these particular moments. They can also reflect on things that come easily to them, areas of performance or learning that simply are natural fits with their particular talents or gifts. For example, some people are natural communicators and have a very easy time putting thoughts into words, either written or verbal. If one has this type of talent, they may not recognize it as being unique because they may assume that everyone has this same ability. Taking intentional time to reflect on "what comes easily" may allow them to identify this as something that is special and unique about their particular ability. They might also think about the subjects in school where they have excelled with minimal effort.

Two leadership development models that appear to have synergy with this principle of developing a language of strengths are the Leadership Identity Development Model (LID) and the Social Change Model (previously described in more detail). The LID Model was developed by a team of researchers from the University of Maryland (Komives, Longerbeam, Owen, Mainella, & Osteen, 2006; Komives, Owen, Longerbeam, Mainella, & Osteen, 2005). These researchers used a grounded theory approach and based their findings on qualitative data gathering from interviews with college students. The findings of this research resulted in a six-stage model that moves leadership identity from being leader centered to viewing leadership as a collaborative, relational process where one does not have to hold a position of leadership to effectively serve as a leader and participate in the process of leadership development. The LID model utilizes six distinct stages of leadership, and students progress through one stage before entering another. That being said, the linear nature of the stages is perhaps too simplistic of a visual representation of the model because individuals can regress or revisit aspects of a stage even after they have progressed beyond that stage. The six stages include: (1) Awareness, (2) Exploration/Engagement, (3) Leader Identified, (4) Leadership Differentiated, (5) Generativity, and (6) Internalization/Synthesis.

Most college students find themselves in stage two or three where they are exploring the concept of leadership or have identified themselves or others as positional leaders. They are still leader-centric at these stages and do not see leadership happening throughout the organization or group at this point in their development. Between each of the stages is a transition where the individual realizes and understands the next stage, but he/she is not fully operating in the new stage. A key transition occurs between stages three and four, and it can be assisted through experiences and the guidance of mentors or coaches. This transition moves students into a more refined understanding of leadership development, specifically with developmental gains in seeing leadership as a process and acknowledging that leadership is not dependent on position or role. Few individuals ever reach stage six of the model, in college or otherwise. The overlap with principles of positive psychology is not as obvious with the LID Model as with the Social Change Model. With close examination, however, one can see that identifying strengths in their own life and within fellow team members would help students move toward stage four where they are learning about group and team skills and the importance of each person's contributions to the greater whole. Similarly, emotional intelligence, as will be discussed later in this chapter, can help students to maximize their relationships with peers and adults at each stage of their leadership journey. The LID model also corresponds suitably with the dimension of fostering hope as it moves students toward generativity where they recognize that leadership is a developmental process. Students in stage five and six give hopeful examples to peers who are moving through lower levels of the LID model, specifically stages one, two, and three.

Finally, if coaches, mentors, and peers use a strengths lens for their work with students, they may help the students to make faster and more comprehensive gains in their Leadership Identity Development. For example, a student may have a talent for creating order and structure even in chaotic situations. This talent can be particularly helpful in getting things done and accomplishing goals within a group. When a coach or mentor can recognize these strengths and draw them out of a student, while also pointing to the important roles that other team members play in the process of achieving the group's goals, they may be adding to the developmental gains for the student.

Perhaps what is common to both the LID model as well as the Social Change Model of Leadership is the importance of knowing and understanding oneself. Being aware of one's strengths and natural abilities is a critical aspect of knowing and understanding one's self. When individuals know that they have a keen ability to provide a vision for the future, they can use this strength to move themselves and the group forward more expeditiously. The Social Change Model includes the important value of Consciousness of Self. Not only does the student become more aware of himself or herself, they also become aware of how they interact with group members, their communities, and the world in which they live. The depth of understanding around these relationships can reinforce self-knowledge because others help to confirm and affirm what is already understood at the individual level.

Utilizing Strategies that Foster Hope

The third principle of positive psychology is how strategies can be developed and implemented to foster hope in students. Fostering hope means building (1) capacity within students to overcome adversity and (2) know-how to attack challenges and problems in productive and effective ways. It is helping students to incorporate both agency thinking and pathways thinking into their problem solving, which Snyder (1994) defined as the essence of hope. Fostering this kind of hope moves students beyond pure aspiration and helps them to have vision for a different outcome as well as mental strategies for achieving that outcome. For example, a student who is thrust into a leadership role because his peer has left school will need encouragement from others that he is capable of performing in this new role, even if he did not initially intend to lead or serve. He will need to be affirmed in his strengths, to be challenged to cast a vision for the organization, and to live the values of the organization through his day-to-day leadership. In addition, a student who finds herself struggling in a class may need help brainstorming different study strategies or learning techniques.

The leadership theory that best aligns with this principle of positive psychology is the Relational Leadership model (Komives, Lucas, & McMahon, 1998). This model is driven by vision and process, not position and authority. "This approach to leadership is *inclusive* of people and diverse points of view, *empowers* those involved, is *purposeful* and builds commitment toward common purposes, is *ethical*, and recognizes that all four of those elements are accomplished by being *process-oriented*" (Komives et al., 1998, p. 68). Ultimately, the model supports the healthy, ethical, and effective development of a group of people or a community. Naturally, the relational model seems to focus more on the benefits for the whole rather than simply for the good of the individuals who are practicing leadership. As Bolman and Deal (1995) state, "Effective leadership is a relationship rooted in community. Successful leaders embody their group's most precious values and beliefs. Their ability to lead emerges from the strength and sustenance of those around them" (p. 56).

Although the components of relational leadership may not automatically foster hope in an individual, the experience of making a meaningful contribution within an organization is an inherently hope-building experience. For example, if I know that my personal contributions or my team's contributions are improving the experience for the whole community or organization, I will be more energized to continue to serve and/or lead. I will also be willing to work harder to overcome adversity that may come in the process of making a contribution. Student leadership positions often bring with them adversity and challenge because of the very nature of the leadership position. Student leaders are not exclusively practicing leadership, they are also balancing the role of student—perhaps the role of athlete or student worker—and still have to maintain other roles such as son or daughter and friend. All of these competing priorities often create adverse situations or dynamics, and the student needs to be reminded that she can overcome these challenges as she draws on her unique abilities and the support of others who are part of her relationship circle. She can develop a hopeful perspective knowing that her skills and abilities, along with the resources that are available to her, will help her overcome the situation.

Building Emotional Intelligence

The final principle of positive psychology is the importance of building emotional intelligence. Much of our historical emphasis in business, industry, and education has been on intelligence levels; that is, the amount of brainpower that someone has to apply to given situations. Goleman et al. (2002) and many others posit that a different kind of intelligence, emotional intelligence, is equally important to success in any aspect of our lives. Emotional intelligence refers to the way in which leaders handle relationships and interactions with others, being attuned not only to the words and actions of others but also to the emotions that are accompanying these words and actions (Goleman et al., 2002).

This principle of positive psychology has gained momentum as more organizations experience adversity and setbacks. The leadership realizes that survival of the organization depends not only on the bottom line but also on the organization's human resources and their ability to be resilient through times of challenge and struggle. Studies have demonstrated a link between organizational climate and business performance, quantifying the difference that "feel" makes within an organization (Goleman et al., 2002). The leader's behavior is one of the key facets of creating a positive feeling for both employees and customers.

Linking closely to the principle of emotional intelligence are two final leadership models: Mindful Leadership and Resonant Leadership. Mindful leadership, an outgrowth of mindfulness (Kabat-Zinn, 1994), focuses on self-awareness and self-compassion. Practices such as meditation and reflection allow a leader to tap into his/her emotional state and become aware of what emotions are present and how they are impacting behavior and relationships. Mindful leadership encourages authenticity; that is, the leader is vulnerable and allows his/her followers to see emotions being processed and balanced in healthy ways. William George, a leader in the Mindful Leadership arena, has promoted this emerging model of leadership as a way for leaders to learn self-awareness and self-regulation (Silverthorne, 2010). Leaders who become attuned to their own emotions and are self-compassionate can emerge as healthy models for others within their unit. These leaders can also mitigate stresses and emotional strain because they practice compassion with themselves and therefore are more likely to practice compassion to others. Moreover, practicing mindful leadership cultivates focus, clarity, and an ability to be present in each moment (Marturano, 2014).

Resonant leadership (Boyatzis & McKee, 2005) is the other leadership model that aligns with the principle of building emotional intelligence. Resonant leaders are those who are attuned to self and others. This approach helps leaders address some of the inherent stresses of leading and helps leaders to remain "close" to members of the organization even with power differences that exist. Resonant leaders have developed skills in showing compassion, providing hope, and being mindful. These three skill areas are critical to being an emotionally intelligent leader and managing the many complexities that come with leadership—both positional and influential leadership. For a student leader on a campus, resonant leadership may be a good approach because (1) peers often respond very well to each other and (2) the leader sees that the peer can relate to their individual circumstance. For example, if a student leader in a service organization sees one of the members struggling with financial stress, he/she can demonstrate compassion and hope by listening to the other student, pointing them toward campus resources, being sensitive to the financial need with regard to involvement in organization activities, etc. Mindfulness might be less easy to demonstrate, but being attentive to the wide-reaching implications of financial stress on body, mind, and spirit can show that the leader is attuned. The leader might show the student that they are being mindful by following up and showing empathy.

Building on emotional intelligence, positive psychology researchers also address the value of positive emotions (e.g., joy, gratitude, hope, inspiration). Positive emotions significantly contribute to well-being and success for leaders and followers by expanding creative thinking, openness to ideas, and resources for coping with complex issues (Fredrickson, 2013; Higgs, 2010). Leaders using a mindful or resonant leadership approach can work to develop positive emotions and well-being in themselves and others.

Positive Psychology and Civic Engagement

The way an individual grapples with and resolves the salient social issues of the period when he or she comes of age becomes an integral part of personality thereafter (Stewart & Healy, 1989). Although it is certainly beneficial to diagnose problems within our society and identify all of the varied needs that individuals and groups of people have, it is more beneficial to develop strategies for actually addressing these problems in purposeful and effective ways. Civic engagement can serve as a vehicle for connecting a student's desire to serve and make a difference with real needs in the community. Civic engagement is defined as "working to make a difference in the civic life of our communities and developing the combination of knowledge, skills, values and motivation to make that difference. It means promoting the quality of life in a community, through both political and non-political processes" (Ehrlich, 2000, p. vi). We certainly should not be proponents of service for service sake; rather, we should help students to find ways to make a significant and lasting difference with their service experiences. The four principles of positive psychology that were explored previously in this chapter can also be utilized to align positive psychology, leadership, and civic engagement (See Figure 12.1.)

All of the leadership theories mentioned above can be used to create what Richard Couto calls "citizen leaders" (Wren, 1995). These leaders are not necessarily seeking out leadership positions and sometimes shy away from being placed in the "leadership role." They engender respect from others and often are supported by many others within their communities. This support leads them to be bolstered and energized for the cause that they are working toward. They are inherently problem solvers, and therefore others enjoy working with them

	Positive Psychology Principles			
	Focus on positive rather than negative	Developing a language of strengths	Utilizing strategies that foster hope	Building emotional intelligence
Civic Engagement/ Civic Leadership Application	Engage students in identifying ways in which they can serve to address and improve needs/issues within their communities	Help students to locate service opportunities where they can use their unique strengths	Encourage students to be a hopeful presence within their communities, to cast a vision for a better future, and to become involved in order to make that vision a reality	Encourage students to connect relationally with those whom they are serving and to be authentic in their relationships

Figure 12.1   Positive Psychology and Civic Engagement.

because they are more apt to identify and implement solutions. "In stimulating citizen leadership we must take our eyes off the leader as authority figure, solver of problems, maker of meaning, and creator of vision. Instead we must look toward developing interactive systems in which every citizen will lead" (Secor & Tyasto, 2005, p. 130). Higher education institutions are in a unique place to develop and encourage citizen leadership. By affording students the opportunity to volunteer, i.e., to become involved in their home community as well as their college or university community, students can begin to identify their own leadership skills and abilities as well as encouraging the leadership growth of every citizen within the community. Extended service-learning experiences are one way in which students can create positive change within their communities. A study by Eyler & Giles (1999) demonstrates that students who are involved in service-learning develop higher levels of tolerance, and they are able to apply their college learning to the community needs that surround them. These are two skills that will allow citizen leaders to make a positive difference in their community for the duration of their lives, not just while they are in college.

Suggestions for Application

Although college student personnel staff are often best at identifying ways to apply information to their particular campus environments, the suggestions listed below will perhaps spark creativity and brainstorming in the application of focusing on the positive, developing a language of strengths, providing hope, and building emotional intelligence within student leaders.

- In either curricular or cocurricular contexts, one should explore a variety of leadership theories with students and identify those that align best with principles of positive psychology. Once these theories are identified, students can be asked to conduct research on a person of influence within their own lives whom they see embodying at least one principle of positive psychology and one of the relevant leadership theories. For example, a student may have a mentor or coach who has been instrumental in noting talents within the lives of others. This person fits the role of mentor/leader within the Leadership Identity Development model and has perhaps been instrumental in moving the student through the critical transition between stages three (Leader Identified) and four (Leadership Differentiated) of the model.

- Encourage students to participate in international service experiences and keep a journal or photo blog of their learning and observations. It has been demonstrated through empirical research that international service experiences enhance moral reasoning, cultural intelligence, and leader adaptability (Wilson, 2008). Students should be asked to specifically reflect on the leader adaptability area and discern whether transformational leadership was occurring through the service experiences.

- Offer opportunities for students to identify their natural talents and create a plan for adding skills, knowledge, and experiences to those talents in order to solidify them for future use. Ask students to keep a journal (either written, video, audio, or photographic) of ways in which their strengths are developing over time.

- Encourage student leaders to identify the strengths in their teammates or group members and to find ways of supporting others' use of their strengths in creative ways to benefit the aims of the group as a whole. Identifying individual strengths within a group allows students to appreciate the value that they and their diverse peers bring to the group.

- When inevitable challenges arise that a student leader must confront, they have an opportunity to respond in a variety of ways. Leadership advisors can helps students identify possible responses based on different theories of leadership and reflect on how the issue or challenges can be viewed and responded to as a chance for positive growth, change, and/or learning to occur rather than a stressful problem area.

- Engender the positive emotion of hope by having leaders dialogue or write about past and current success, emphasizing the role they played in achieving a particular goal. Emphasize the interpersonal interactions that occurred to facilitate this positive outcome.

- Consider hosting a workshop or day-long retreat for student leaders that would include activities such as becoming more mindful as well as some common team-building exercises. In doing so, be sure to include the important piece of processing the experience in terms of the positive psychology principles at work. The workshop could also serve as a model for a workshop that leaders may want to have for their student groups.

- Provide opportunities for student leaders to increase their emotional intelligence and positive emotions, through strategies such as exploring the impact of their civic engagement experiences, journaling, mindfulness, or expressing gratitude.

Multicultural Implications

In both leadership and civic engagement experiences, an appreciation for difference is a critical component for success, particularly in a world that is becoming increasingly interconnected and globalized. Although a focus on difference may present a challenge because of the natural friction and stresses that can occur between those who are different, ultimately teaching students to value difference is setting them up for success for the duration of their life. It is imperative for student affairs personnel involved with leadership as well as across campus to not only have a diversity lens but to promote and teach issues related to diversity to students (Pope, Mueller, & Reynolds, 2009; Pope, Reynolds, & Mueller, 2004). Three steps can be taken to help students begin to see the positive value of multiculturalism and diversity: increasing awareness and knowledge, serving others, and developing a social justice perspective. Through these tangible steps, students see the value of differences and how an appreciation for diversity can advance leadership and create positive change within our broader society.

First, students should be exposed to as much difference (cultural, ethnic, socioeconomic, religious, age, gender, etc.) as possible. As a student's exposure to difference increases, they are more likely to develop an awareness of what it is like to experience life differently. Awareness involves knowledge of one's own culture and beliefs as well as those of others. Awareness will identify how cognizant a student is of her values, culture, and assumptions and will ultimately impact the way that a student leads.

Studying culture and leadership can help increase the awareness and knowledge of staff and students. Significant work has been done on culture and leadership by House, Hanges, Javidan, Dorfman, and Gupta (2004), and they have published an 800-page set of findings titled *Culture, Leadership, and Organizations: The GLOBE Study of 62 Societies*. This work indicates a clear relationship between culture and leadership and includes a set of nine cultural dimensions. These cultural dimensions can be utilized to help students see typical leadership values that are associated with each of the nine cultural dimensions. The dimensions are intended to be a description or general framework of cultural behaviors, not a rigid prescription. For those who are interested in more fully understanding the impact of culture on leadership, this comprehensive research would be a top resource.

For example, Middle Eastern countries tended to cluster into a group that indicated that the population in these countries showed high scores in collectivism and conversely scored low in areas such as gender egalitarianism and uncertainty avoidance. Women did not often hold the same status as men. This single finding influences leadership because both women and men of all cultures must understand the impact of gender on the ways in which they lead and perceive the leadership of others.

Another example of a country cluster is the Anglo cluster, which included Canada, the United States, Australia, Ireland, England, South Africa (White sample), and New Zealand. These countries showed low scores in collectivism, which is the converse of the aforementioned Middle Eastern cluster. Although the collectivism was low, performance orientation was high. This result is consistent with our understanding of "Western" individualism. Certainly, a divergence from collectivism means that individual leadership aspirations might be more prevalent in this culture and there may be relatively less emphasis on communities and families.

Ultimately, to be effective as a leader, one must understand the cultural implications on both leader and follower behavior. If one is to lead a group of multicultural individuals, there has to be awareness, sensitivity, understanding, and a willingness to modify leadership style and approach to best meet the needs of the cultural understanding of team members. Developing experiences and content knowledge of other cultural groups helps students have an awareness of others and can help them develop new respect for people who come from different backgrounds and perspectives. Ignoring culture and its implications on behaviors and perceptions is one of the quickest ways to undermine even the best leadership efforts and strategies and shows a lack of emotional intelligence.

Second, students should be encouraged to serve others. Encourage service experiences where students can come to realize and understand that altering social conditions is not an event but rather a process that demands ongoing attention and care (Rhoads, 1997). Service can be accomplished through service-learning, volunteerism, civic engagement activities or through internships/field experiences. When students become engaged in acts of service to others, they are more likely to make a commitment to social justice (Monard-Weissman, 2003). Service opportunities can help students to increase awareness of stereotypes and assumption and aid students in understanding larger societal and systemic issues (Einfeld & Collins, 2008; Jones & Hill, 2001). Students are able to address injustices with their acts of service and change the situation of others. There is a positive correlation of volunteerism with civic responsibility, specifically outcomes of helping others, promoting racial understanding and serving the community (Astin & Sax, 1998).

Finally, students can be encouraged to adopt a lifestyle of social justice where they move beyond acts of charity and begin to address root causes of systemic societal issues either through their vocational choice, their community engagement, or through leadership (formal or informal) (Eyler & Giles, 1999). Students must learn the importance of increasing one's awareness of inequalities in our world and also become equipped with skills, experiences, and empowerment to address these inequalities through sustained service and strategies for positive change (Adams, 2007). Social justice moves beyond one-time acts of service or even longer periods of service. It is a way of thinking, a paradigm, and a way of seeing the world. When students adopt a commitment to social justice, they are demonstrating advancement in the LID model to higher levels of leadership, to generativity, and to synthesis of values with actions.

Several of the positive psychology principles and leadership models mentioned previously support a commitment to multiculturalism and a value for diversity. For example, the positive psychology principle of developing a language of strengths may help to put a positive perspective on differences. Framing differences as strengths rather than points of conflict can be immeasurably beneficial. Two students who are working on a project together and find completely different worldviews may at first believe their work will be arduous and conflict ridden. However, if they can identify strengths within each other, even simply acknowledging that their different worldview will bring a fresh perspective on the situation, it will help them in accomplishing the goal. This kind of respect for difference is also present within the Social Change Model of Leadership, specifically within the value of controversy with civility.

In citizen leadership roles, individuals are committed to addressing societal issues through service. "Participation in service is found to show increases in students' tolerance, commitments to equal opportunity, and cultural diversity and reductions in stereotyping, prejudice and blaming others" (Flanagan, 2004, p. 727). These ideological changes should produce a shift away from the negative and toward the positive. They also should foster hope within students as they become committed to social justice and positive change within our world.

Case Study

Erica, a 20-year-old Hispanic female, is a Junior majoring in advertising. She attends a large university and is involved in her sorority, which arranges a large-scale service event within the community. The Annual Heritage Days event has a very positive reputation based on years of past success achieved by other student leaders. Erica's sorority has approximately 30 members and relies heavily on volunteers. Although Erica is not the president of the sorority, she holds a position of leadership within the group that focuses on finances and fundraising. The event is approximately 2 months away, and her group is working very hard to finish the final organizational tasks as well as preparing for the actual day of the event. Upon reviewing the sorority's budget and finances, she realizes there were insufficient funds allotted for the upcoming event to cover the necessary expenses (e.g., advertising, supplies, etc.).

Erica's situation can demonstrate how principles of positive psychology applied to leadership are necessary to effectively address the situation. First, Erica is aware that she is not the sole leader of this organization and that leadership is happening throughout the organization to accomplish the goals of the service event. Erica uses her emotional intelligence by taking time to reflect on the situation instead of acting hastily. She met with her sorority's advisor to discuss her approach. She convenes a committee of other leaders and members who are working on the event. Drawing on Mindful and Resonant Leadership as well as shifting the focus from negative to positive, Erica explains the situation to the group, reminding them of the meaningful implications of this service event on the community, the positive reputation of their sorority, and her confidence that, although problematic, they can find a workable solution. Erica then facilitates a brainstorming session of potential solutions including shifting funds around from other areas, raising additional funds before the event, and developing creative ways of accomplishing tasks with less money. Erica reminds the group of the retreat they had earlier in the semester where they all discussed their strengths, and she suggests that they talk about who could be assigned to various tasks based on their strengths. The committee presents the issue to the larger group, and after careful thought, they are able to present the issue in a way that rallies the group to work together rather than causing conflict or blaming. This process instills hope in the members that there are options that they have and that they do have the resources—other than money—to still have a successful event.

Conclusion

The American public perceives a crisis of leadership in our nation. Major public and private institutions appear increasingly incapable of dealing constructively with an ever-expanding list of social and economic problems, and individuals are becoming more cynical about government. We need a new generation of leaders who can bring about positive change in local, national, and international affairs (Zimmerman-Oster & Burkhardt, 1999). As described in this chapter, an approach to leadership theory and practice that emphasizes principles of positive psychology may effectively and more thoroughly address the crisis points within our nation and our world.

Our future leaders are developing their skills and potential in college today, and leadership should be a planned result of a higher education. Developing leadership among college students may be the best way for us to build civic capacity for our nation (Zimmerman-Oster & Burkhardt, 1999). Many institutions of higher education may have good intentions to build the leadership capacity of their students but may still be relying on traditional approaches that do not incorporate the valuable principles of positive psychology.

This chapter begins to elucidate the connections between established leadership theories and select principles of positive psychology. Moving forward, those leadership approaches that draw on positive psychology will likely be more effective because they can truly bring out the best in leaders and followers. Indeed, some leadership models are already reflecting this perspective more directly. For example, in their model of Authentic Leadership, Luthans and Avolio (2003; Luthans, Youssef, & Avolio, 2007) emphasize four positive psychological capacities: confidence, hope, optimism, and resiliency, and they assert that these core attributes of authentic leaders can be developed. Staff in higher education who work with student leaders can use the contents of this chapter as a starting point for identifying new approaches and strategies for developing leaders that can foster a well-founded, realistic hope for the future.

References

Adams, M. (2007). Pedagogical frameworks for social justice education. In M. Adams, L. A. Bell, & P. Griffin (Eds.), *Teaching for diversity and social justice* (pp. 15–33). New York: Routledge.

Astin, A. W., & Sax, L. J. (1998). How undergraduates are affected by service participation. *Journal of College Student Development, 39,* 251–263.

Bolman, L. G., & Deal, T. E. (1995). *Leading with soul: An uncommon journey of spirit.* San Francisco: Jossey-Bass.

Boyatzis, R. E., & McKee, A. (2005). *Resonant leadership: Renewing yourself and connecting with others through mindfulness, hope, and compassion.* Boston: Harvard Business School Press.

Burns, J. M. (1978). *Leadership.* New York: Harper & Row.

Clifton, D. O., Anderson, E. C., & Schreiner, L. A. (2006). *Strengths Quest: Discover and develop your strengths in academics, career, and beyond* (2nd ed.). New York: Gallup Press.

Durham Hynes, S. L. (2009). *Perceptions of the capacity for change as a component of leadership development as reported by select populations of college students: Implications for college student leadership development.* (Order No. 3370691, Texas A&M University). ProQuest Dissertations and Theses.

Ehrlich, T. (2000). *Civic responsibility and higher education.* Phoenix: Oryx Press.

Einfeld, A., & Collins, D. (2008). The relationships between service-learning, social justice, multicultural competence, and civic engagement. *Journal of College Student Development, 49,* 95–109.

Eyler, J., & Giles, D. E. (1999). *Where's the learning in service-learning?* San Francisco: Jossey-Bass.

Flanagan, C. A. (2004) Volunteerism, leadership, political socialization, and civic engagement. In R. Lerner & L. Steinberg (Eds.), *Handbook of adolescent psychology* (pp. 721–745). Hoboken, N.J: John Wiley & Sons, Inc.

Fowler, R. D., Seligman, M. P., & Koocher, G. P. (1999). The APA 1998 annual report. *American Psychologist, 54*, 537–568. doi:10.1037/0003-066X.54.8.537

Fredrickson, B. L. (2013). Positive emotions broaden and build. In P. Devine & A. Plant (Eds.), *Advances in experimental social psychology* (Vol. 47, pp. 1–54). San Diego, CA: Academic Press.

Gable, S. L., & Haidt, J. (2005). What (and why) is positive psychology? *Review of General Psychology, 9*, 103–110. doi:10.1037/1089-2680.9.2.103

Goleman, D., Boyatzis, R., & McKee, A. (2002). *Primal Leadership.* Boston, MA: Harvard Business School Press.

Higgs, M. (2010). Change and its leadership: The role of positive emotions. In P. A. Linley, S. Harrington, & N. Garcea (Eds.), *Oxford handbook of positive psychology and work* (pp. 67–80). New York: Oxford University Press.

Higher Education Research Institute. (1996). *A social change model of leadership development* (Version III). Los Angeles: University of California Los Angeles, Higher Education Research Institute.

Howe, N., & Strauss, W. (2000). *Millennials rising: The next great generation.* New York: Random House.

House, R. J., Hanges, P. J., Javidan, M., Dorfman, P. W., & Gupta, V. (2004). *Culture, leadership, and organizations: The GLOBE study of 62 societies.* Thousand Oaks, CA: Sage.

Jones, S. R., & Hill, K. (2001). Crossing high street: Understanding diversity through community service-learning. *Journal of College Student Development, 42*, 204–216.

Kabat-Zinn, J. (1994). *Wherever you go, there you are: Mindfulness meditation in everyday life.* New York: Hyperion.

Komives, S. R., Lucas, N., & McMahon, T. R. (1998). *Exploring leadership: For college students who want to make a difference.* San Francisco: Jossey-Bass.

Komives, S. R., Longerbeam, S. D., Owen, J. E., Mainella, F. C., & Osteen, J. (2006). A Leadership Identity Development model: Applications from a grounded theory. *Journal of College Student Development, 47*, 401–418.

Komives, S. R., Owen, J. E., Longerbeam, S. D., Mainella, F. C., & Osteen, L. (2005). Developing a leadership identity: A grounded theory. *Journal of College Student Development, 46*, 593–611.

Luthans, F. (2002). The need for and meaning of positive organizational behavior. *Journal of Organizational Behavior, 23*, 695–706.

Luthans, F., & Avolio, B. J. (2003). Authentic leadership development. In K. S. Cameron, J. E. Dutton, & R. E. Quinn (Eds.), *Positive organizational scholarship,* (pp. 241–261). San Francisco, CA: Berrett-Koehler.

Luthans, F., Youssef, C. M., & Avolio, B. J. (2007). *Psychological capital: Developing the human competitive edge.* Oxford, England: Oxford University Press.

Marturano, J. (2014). *Finding the space to lead: A practical guide to mindful leadership.* New York: Bloomsbury Press.

Monard-Weissman, K. (2003). Fostering a sense of social justice through international service-learning. *Academic Exchange Quarterly, 72*(2), 164–169.

Myers, D. G. (2000). The funds, friends, and faith of happy people. *American Psychologist, 55*, 56–67.

Pope, R. L., Mueller, J. A., & Reynolds, A. (2009). Looking back and moving forward: Future directions for diversity research in student affairs. *Journal of College Student Development, 50*, 640–658.

Pope, R. L., Reynolds, A. L., & Mueller, J. A. (2004). *Multicultural competence in student affairs.* San Francisco: Jossey-Bass.

Rath, T. (2007). *StrengthsFinder 2.0.* New York: Gallup Press.

Rath, T., & Conchie, B. (2008). *Strengths based leadership: Great leaders, teams, and why people follow.* New York: Gallup Press.

Rhoads, R. A. (1997). *Community service and higher learning: Explorations of the caring self.* Albany, NY: State University of New York Press.

Roberts, D. R. (2007). *Deeper learning in leadership: Helping college students find the potential within.* San Francisco, CA: Jossey-Bass.

Rost, J. (1991). *Leadership for the twenty-first century.* Westport, CT: Praeger.

Secor, J., & Tyasto, M. (2005). Leadership for social change: Cross-cultural development of citizen leaders. In N. S. Huber, & Walker, M. C. (Eds.), *Emergent Models of Global Leadership, Building Leadership Bridges.* Silver Spring, MD: International Leadership Association.

Seligman, M. E. P. (2011). *Flourish: A visionary new understanding of happiness and well-being.* New York: Free Press.

Seligman, M. E. P., & Csikszentmihalyi, M. (2000). Positive psychology: An introduction. *American Psychologist, 55,* 5–14.

Silverthorne, S. (2010, September). Mindful leadership: When East meets West. *Harvard Business School Working Knowledge.* Retrieved from http://hbswk.hbs.edu/item/6482.html

Snyder, C. R. (1994). *The psychology of hope: You can get there from here.* New York: Free Press.

Stewart, A. J., & Healy, J. M. (1989). Linking individual development and social changes. *American Psychologist, 44,* 30–42.

Wilson, C. E. (2008). *The impact of international service experiences on adult development in moral reasoning and cultural intelligence.* Unpublished dissertation manuscript. North Carolina Agricultural and Technical State University.

Wilson, C. E. (2008). Faith-based motivation and leader development: International service experiences as catalyst for moral development and cultural intelligence. *Culture & Religion, 9*(3), 287–300. doi:10.1080/14755610802535637

Wren, J. T. (1995). *The leader's companion.* New York: The Free Press.

Zimmerman-Oster, K., & Burkhardt, J. C. (1999). *Leadership in the making: Impact and insights from leadership development programs in U.S. colleges and universities.* Battle Creek, MI: Kellogg Foundation Monograph.

13

Positive Psychology in College Sport and Exercise

LISA M. MILLER

Positive psychology synergistically created a new approach to the vital importance of developing the body as well as the mind in college. Physical development and athletic performance provide foundations of holistic health and well-being. The acquisition of knowledge, skills, and motivation in this synergy of positive psychology and the body is a significant contributors to positive self-perceptions and performance enhancement (Korn, Gonene, Shaked, & Golan, 2013). For many college students and college student athletes, with the pressures of demanding curriculum, part-time employment, and other responsibilities, sport and exercise improvements often become a low priority. This chapter will highlight the many benefits of innovative positive psychology techniques to enhance college sport and exercise experiences in various dimensions for the overall improvement of student well-being. Innovative research and practice on topics such as creating peak performance, managing the flow of focus, and initiating positive visualization will be explained. The content will focus on positive psychology for sport and exercise enhancement, ways to implement a positive psychology-based approach to sport and exercise performance, and recommendations for future positive psychology usage for college sport and exercise leaders. In addition, a case study will be included to more closely connect current literature to the realities of actual inclusion of positive psychology techniques in college sport and exercise. This chapter may be of particular interest for college students, recreation and wellness center staff, college coaches, athletic directors, athletic department staff, intramural sports coaches and advisors, student activity coordinators, and faculty in Sport Psychology, Sport and Exercise Science, and Recreation in order to innovatively assist both college students and student athletes.

Positive psychology as applied to college sport and exercise is devoted to reinforcing the positive aspects of fitness, health, nutrition, and athletics. With physical development, the body and mind respond together with much potential for well-being and authentic happiness through the increase of positive emotions, social engagement, and meaningful health advancement (Seligman, 2004). Some of the specific positive benefits from sport and exercise include increased energy, better weight control, higher perseverance, elevated mood enhancement, increased self-esteem, revitalized creativity, improved hopefulness, and greater optimism (Anderson & Brice, 2011; Duckworth, Peterson, Mathews, & Kelly, 2007; Ross & Thomas, 2010). Although connections have been established between positive psychology and physical development (Crescioni, et al., 2011), the theory and research are still at a relatively new stage of development. More research is needed to explore the use of new positive psychology initiatives on college campuses for sport and exercise enhancements.

College students may feel alone and alienated without peer groups for interaction as they transition from their high school support group to their new academic life (Boyle, Mattern, Lassiter, & Ritzler, 2011). Physical activities often involve a sense of relatedness and connectedness to others (Seligman, 2011). Although different students will have different levels of need, sport and exercise participation provides a source of coping through relationship building. Physical activity may also help students with the emotional challenges that occur as part of college life and development. The use of positive psychology in sport and exercise could be directed toward building teamwork and self-esteem. This could facilitate improved social-emotional interactions and adjustment to college life. Given the high demands of many college courses, physical activity also functions as a positive stress reliever (Welle & Graf, 2011).

College life poses many challenges to maintaining physical development (Topp et al., 2011). For example, many students need to work a part-time job. They likely also have challenging and rigorous academic requirements within their majors and minors, as well as personal and social issues that accompany the transition to college. Some students experience family or home life stress as well, even when living away from home (Misra & McKean, 2000; Pedersen, 2012). Other research indicates that college students often experience a new routine of health risk behaviors including binge drinking, physical inactivity, lack of sleep, and low consumption of fruits and vegetables (Kwan, Faulkner, Arbour-Nicitopoulos, & Cairney, 2013). Pressures may exist for drug use and engaging in risky sexual behaviors. The responsibilities and pressures that college students face can accumulate to high levels of stress where proactive wellness routines become less possible, and the appropriate amounts of exercise, healthy nutrition, social connections, and sleep become less likely to occur.

Even student athletes may experience challenges related to physical development. Student athletes report not receiving the type of help needed due to a misperception that they are all self-motivated, confident in themselves, and self-disciplined (Cole, 2006). The athletic environment often encourages self-reliance and a focus on a win-at-all-costs mentality without consideration of the knowledge, skills, and motivation needed for habits establishing a mentality for long term well-being. The academic portion of college skill building has received increased attention for student athletes (Brown, 2007), however the psychological side of college skill building lacks as much concern in the athletic culture. Time management challenges occur with the demands of classes, practice, competitions, and study time. This creates yet another barrier to student athletes gaining the benefits of sport and exercise habit formation. Positive psychology techniques in physical development and athletic performance are methods geared toward "maximizing human potential" through positive skill building (Delligatti, 2004, p. 161). These positive psychology methods are well-suited for meeting the unique challenges of college students and student athletes. Seligman (2011) proposed a theoretical perspective for positive psychology dimensions by defining five pillars of well-being: positive emotion, engagement, relationships, meaning, and achievement (PERMA). The five pillars will be addressed as applied to sport and exercise in college. In addition, the various categories of positive psychology techniques including cognitive, interpersonal, strengths based, and emotions based (Snyder & Lopez, 2002) will be discussed. Students and student athletes will hopefully benefit from the research findings from positive psychology. The goals of sport and exercise related to creating the conditions for optimal performance, coping with stress and anxiety, being present in the moment, and visualizing positive outcomes with hope and optimism.

Positive Psychology Techniques and Approaches

One role of positive psychology can be to understand the factors necessary for the creation of a positive environment for proactive and holistic development. This type of culture provides support for students in developing positive coping skills that could help prevent burnout or underperformance. Students often tend to not ask for assistance until they have exhausted all their own personal resources and consequently feel overwhelmed. By then, the help arrives too late or will take extensive time and resource management to reverse the negative patterns that became entrenched. One key tactic of the positive psychology model is to maintain focus on strengths and wellness. Students may benefit from more deliberate education about positive psychology approaches for achieving holistic wellness within the college culture. Such approaches provide proactive promotion of positive psychology coping skills by encouraging strengths-based efforts rather than a focus on correcting weaknesses (Gilpin, 2008).

However, participation in athletics cannot always be assumed to provide the same positive outcomes as exercise. For example, athletics may be a stress producer for highly competitive athletes that may lead to burnout and other negative consequences (Gould & Whitley, 2009). Therefore, sports teams could benefit from positive psychology approaches to deal with the negative side effects of high competition, whereas exercise itself in moderation may function as a stress reliever. Examples of positive psychology techniques to cope with highly competitive situations may include meditation, visualization, resiliency training, strength-based initiatives, mindfulness, or relationship building. Two recent advancements include appreciative inquiry and altruistic leadership. Appreciative inquiry is a technique that focuses attention on appreciating strengths rather than criticizing deficits or problems within a team or organization (Thachenkery, Avital, & Cooperrider, 2010). The goal of appreciative inquiry is to improve performance through asset utilization that builds upon one's experience and current potential rather than high pressure scare tactics. Altruistic leadership (Miller & Carpenter, 2009) is based on the ultimate goal of improving the well-being of others. In sport and exercise, this would be indicated by the leader making decisions based on what is best for his or her followers. These positive psychology approaches offer ways to encourage excellent performance without adding additional pressure through a developmental approach with emphasis on improving strengths and wellness.

The drive for excellence in athletics can have both positive and negative effects. On the positive side, student athletes learn skills to achieve excellence and optimal performance. They learn to set several types of goals and learn to have hope that they will achieve those goals (Curry, Snyder, Cook, Ruby, & Rehm, 1997). On the negative side, athletics may take priority over academics. The pressure for high performance may create a loss of holistic wellness, a loss of balanced social interaction, less amount of time to pursue career development, problems with eating disorders, and possible involvement with performance enhancing substances (Kisaalita & Robinson, 2014). Learning to apply practical positive psychology approaches provides a pathway for coping with pressures in more effective ways.

Practical Applications of Positive Psychology

Positive psychology aimed to combine the conceptual framework with practical applications to promote a proactive approach to personal development and assessment, including sports and exercise. This positive psychology approach has shifted the focus from individuals' areas of weakness to examining strengths and realms of effectiveness (Clonan, Chafouleas, McDougal, & Riley-Tillman, 2004). The overarching aim of positive psychology is to treat and celebrate the whole person, and physical sport and exercise are crucial areas for proactive application. For example, Gilpin (2008) cited practical applications for encouraging a mindset of gratitude by teaching students to use positive, self-affirming language on a regular basis; listing goals for obtaining a more satisfying life with hopefulness; and openly naming negative thought patterns so that they can be more easily replaced by positive thoughts. Gilpin's applications apply to sport and exercise as well. With physical activities, students may learn to use self-affirming language about their bodies, listing athletic or exercise goals, and replacing negative self-comments with positive reinforcement. These positive strategies may also help support excellence in performance.

Positive physical development is not only for students. The health and well-being of faculty and staff are also important to the campus culture as a whole. A positive, proactive approach means all constituents in the campus culture take notice of their personal attitudes and outlooks toward health, fitness, and well-being, as well as recognizing how their attitudes positively or negatively impact the culture (Peterson & Park, 2011). Peterson and Park from the University of Michigan created a "theme semester" where the whole campus focused on positive psychology as related to what makes life worth living (George, 2010). Practical strategies to communicate the theme included positive psychology oriented course topics, essay writing, film making, lecture series, movies, campus events, and off-campus activities. The goal was to promote overall wellness and meaningfulness of life. This is a new approach intended to produce a large scale application of positive psychology in education to maximize the benefits in institutional settings.

One pathway includes the healthfulness of the environment itself as a practical place for positive sport and exerice development. With a healthfulness approach, various departments and agencies intentionally influence one another to achieve a healthy atmosphere for performance excellence in academics and in athletics. This could foster positive energy within the classroom setting, creating a synergistic condition between the mind and the body (Strout, 2005). Practical positive psychology approaches for physical development could include yoga classes, meditation groups, campus recreation and athletic department advisory groups on positive approaches to sport and exercise, acknowledging research agendas that promote positive techniques, grant programs for projects on positive physical development or athletic performance, or experiments that include positive sport and exercise on campus (Thurston, 2011). This may also include proposing an innovative course in positive sport and exercise psychology. The campus culture of students, faculty, and staff engaging in physical development together could stimulate improved rapport and connectedness across campus, and students may receive other positive developmental outcomes from informal interaction with faculty and staff (Wilson & Ryan, 2013). This positive engagement could lead to higher gains on academic performance. Students may develop positive ways of being respectful and confident in their communications through increased social opportunities and social self-efficacy (Annesi & Tennant, 2013). Most often, the two main types of skill sets featured in the campus setting are academic-based and social-based. A focus on positive sport and exercise could provide a realm for reinforcement and additional individual attention for students. It is important to communicate that even among highly competitive athletes, students must keep in mind that professional athletics as a career is rare, and their well-rounded development is vitally important.

Another pathway of connecting students, faculty and staff through physical development could occur through campus challenges or wellness organizations. Students, faculty, and staff at San Jose State University compete in a 6-week wellness challenge. Teams comprise any combination of students, faculty, and staff. Likewise, students at Portland State are able to engage in a 9-week wellness challenge where the staff and faculty compete against the students. The Ohio State University organized the inaugural 2013 Building Healthy Academic Communities Conference, which included special wellness activities, self-led massage, mindfulness meditations, and zumba exercise. University programs such as these support the inclusiveness of all individuals on campus engaging together to develop and maintain a healthy lifestyle.

With athletic performance, not only student athletes could gain from practical applications in positive psychology. Fans of the athletic program could also gain in terms of spirit clubs with positive emotions, positive relationship building, feelings of shared achievement, ongoing hopefulness, and meaningfulness that are brought to the entire campus community through athletic excellence. One line of research in sport management relates to BIRGing, also known as basking in reflective glory with one's athletic team (Cialdini, Borden, Thorne, Walker, Freeman, & Sloan, 1976). The feeling of "we" won, even though the actual performance was won by the players and coaches, may boost campus constituents' self-esteem and social identity (Lee, 1985).

The aim of nurturing positive psychology character traits in sports and exercise is to create an environment to build on success in various areas of a students' lives. From success comes a healthier mindset from which students can draw to better face the challenges of everyday living (Martens & Witt, 2004). Having positive skills produces self-satisfaction and confidence. As a confident and resilient mindset develops, the person begins to view experiences in a more positive manner. These experiences may in turn create motivation for personal improvement and goal setting for the future. The realm of physical development and athletic performance provides opportunities for having confidence in one's personal abilities and skills leading to a mindset of hopefulness and perseverance through adversity (Delligatti, 2004). In addition, sport and exercise may boost optimism (Jenson, Olympia, Farley, & Clark, 2004). Positive psychology researchers have connected optimism to more productive and self-satisfying achievement, which is formed in large part on the basis of past accomplishments and the hope of future success.

A role also exists for campus constituents to provide praise and reinforcement in the category of physical development and athletic performance. Recreation and fitness center leaders may consider a system of providing praise and reward to frequent users. One such system is used at Marquette University where students, faculty and staff involved in the wellness program earn rewards from various departments at the school and are entered into a grand prize drawing. More emphasis could also be placed upon consistency in giving feedback in a positive manner. For example, the University of Minnesota offers students ongoing opportunities to earn points for their Wellness Bank. Accumulated points are rewarded by perks such as a reduction in medical program premiums or wellness rewards with cash value. In addition, some form of reward systems could be put in place with group contingencies for peer collaborative effort, such as the program that occurs now for teams that compete in wellness activities at the University of Michigan, where students are encouraged to invite their spouses or significant others to participate in the program with them. Orlick (1978) encouraged recreation and sport leaders to consider the design of games that influence responses to be individualistic, competitive, or cooperative. The added positive peer collaborative interaction could be an additional motivator for students in physical and athletic development. Cooperative designs typically have a superordinate goal that the group aims toward achieving together. A strengths-based approach could also be added to take advantage of each person's character strengths to achieve the superordinate goal. Results indicate that cooperative designs have increased sharing and greater altruistic concern for others (Orlick, McNally, & O'Hara, 1978).

Another possibility for a practical application of positive psychology in physical development and athletic performance would be to have the student athletes on an athletic team reflect on how utilizing a certain positive character strength would benefit them and their team culture. Each student athlete would complete a strengths-based survey to determine his or her strengths. Several surveys would be applicable to the sport setting, such as the VIA (www.viacharacter.org) or StrengthsFinder surveys (www.strengthsfinder.com). A sport psychology practitioner, who may be a sport psychology consultant or a campus counselor, could administer and discuss the survey with the student athletes. One goal would be to encourage group discussion and appreciation of each team member's contributions. Questions that could be posed may include: what strength does each player bring to the team, and how could the team best utilize these strengths? This would encourage student athletes to spot the strengths of teammates and contemplate how these positive strengths could be utilized. For example, a student athlete with the strength of vitality could be encouraged to use this energy, zest, enthusiasm, and vigor to motivate the team during difficult times. Focus would shift to the positives of team functioning rather than criticisms or negatives. Each campus athletic leader may consider and possibly conduct a needs assessment of the athletic department or the specific athletic team before applying this positive psychology strategy. The setting and culture of the campus may also impact the optimal application of positive psychology strategies. For example, a smaller university may provide a more flexible way for the athletic director or coach to try new approaches, whereas a larger university culture may have more levels and procedures that delay and perhaps require more standardization. A useful research starting point would be to begin with the special needs of particular teams or organizations on campus. This could be influenced by who is willing to participate and promote the application of positive psychology. Coaches, for example, may have varying levels of openness to psychological strategies. One way to increase receptivity of coaches to positive psychology applications would be to involve more integration into their current practice schedules rather than requesting additional time when coaches already feel a strain on their schedules (Martínková & Parry, 2011).

An additional practical application would be to implement research to collect the results of the implementation of positive psychology techniques for fostering physical or athletic development. This may include interviews or surveys for the participants. Results of the research could be presented in speaking events on campus. Such speaking events could include feedback regarding the benefits and challenges of implementing positive psychology for sport and exercise on campus. However, suggestions may also be offered for spreading positive psychology practices around campus to academic units, student activities, career services, or campus ministry. One best practice would be for campus sport and exercise leaders to begin observing and documenting well in advance of the implementation of positive psychology applications. Leaders could write about the planning, progress, and tips for success of various positive psychology strategies. Forethought may be noted as to what impact the leaders want to have on the students or the student athletes as a legacy of the positive psychology approach.

One trend in current research practices that aligns with positive psychology science translation into real world exercise and sport experience is called translational research (Woolf, 2008). The translational research approach has the goal of more closely connecting scientific thinking with application based implementation with meaningful outcomes. Researchers accomplish this by applying theoretical knowledge to situations in the field requiring problem solving. Outcomes in the research for exercise and sport campus programs could be medical, behavioral, social, or psychological. With translational research, multidisciplinary collaboration on campuses becomes more acceptable and valued. Exercise and sport settings on campuses typically experience this type of multidisciplinary collaboration on a daily basis as various campus constituents come together to serve the athletic program or become involved in fitness initiatives. Translational research would be one option for adding a research component to positive psychology in physical development and athletic performance on campus.

The type of research to use for assessing practical applications would be important to consider. As with translational and action research where the researcher is actively involved, bias of the practitioner may occur depending on the practitioner's position, history, and interaction with physically active students or student athletes. There could be positives and negatives to utilizing a person unfamiliar to the students. Perhaps this alternative creates a collaborative effort between a campus representative and an outside constituent who is unknown to the students. This consideration of "who" conducts the application is a key influence on the positive psychology results on campus. Another possible component to add to the endeavor of research on positive psychology techniques would be to interview fitness leaders, coaches, or the athletic director about the actual application. This further helps measure the validity of the impact (White, 1975; Beaman & Wheldall, 2000) and could then be utilized in the future to continue to add best practices for insight on implementation around campus.

Other positive psychology techniques could be followed through research with case study approaches where a single subject or single organization examines the technique. One example of a case study approach would to encourage optimal performance in the athletic department through a workshop on flow or how to "get into the zone" (Csikszentmihalyi, 1990). While the research is being conducted, student athletes may learn to utilize techniques such as the flow state through optimal arousal levels, balance of challenge and skill, maintaining focus, plans for preparation and competition, optimal control of situational conditions, effortless attitude, sense of control, loss of self-consciousness, complete absorption in the activity, confidence, positive mental attitude, and feeling good toward the performance. Another area for research consideration could involve an innovative approach to positive psychology in physical development and athletic performance through evaluating the positive development of student athletes in the athletic program using a longitudinal approach over time (Douglas, Harwood, and Minniti, 2010). The goal of this education program for student athletes would be to achieve optimal psychological, social, and emotional development through their challenging years in competitive athletics. The key areas of measurement would be self-analysis skills, behavioral skills, social skills, attitude approach characteristics, and emotional competence. Outside of athletics, a case study of exercise adherence utilizing positive psychology techniques for college students would add additional research findings.

Campus fitness directors may deliver training on motivational quality in addition to motivation quantity where we are not only addressing how much motivation exists but also what type of motivation occurs. This training would involve the distinction between intrinsic mastery motivation versus ego-centered, competition-based motivation. Ego-centered competition often includes too much focus on winning and achieving an overall outcome goal. Quality intrinsic motivation involves gaining competence in exercise techniques, consciously choosing preferred ways of exercising, and building supportive relationships related to exercise goals (Duda, 2011). Each participant could be encouraged to keep a 14-day diary of needs being met and feelings of well-being after the training. The positive psychology techniques aim toward meeting important needs or desires of the participants, such as positive emotions and meaningful interactions. Routines and psychological skill practice would be emphasized during the training in addition to enjoyment, altruism, relationship appreciation, and meaningfulness in the experience of exercise and sport.

Positive practices could be adopted on a campus-wide basis and include the physical activity of intramurals, recreation, fitness, and athletics. The goals of positive development will depend on assessment of community needs, student diversity, and surrounding factors such as campus culture or demographics (Clonan et al., 2004). Several programs could come together to provide a health and wellness college committee focused on integrating positive approaches into campus life, including physical activities and athletic performance. The best results may come from campus committees dedicated to creating overarching positive campus-wide goals that allow for innovation in ways that positive prosocial skills could be infused across physical and academic setting (Clonan et al., 2004).

Multicultural Positive Psychology for Sport and Exercise

Physical development and athletic performance depends on several cultural factors. These factors may include gender, race, religion, sexual orientation, age, disability, and socioeconomic status. Multicultural sensitivity is needed in considering approaches to exercise and athletics (Watson, 2006). The nuance of cultures and experiences is an important factor to consider when planning implementation of positive psychology techniques for sport and exercise. Some campus locations may be at a level of optimizing experiences for students, whereas other locations may be in the process of just meeting students' basic needs. A racial and gender report card has been developed to closely examine special circumstances for different colleges for these multicultural groups (Lapchick, 2011). This report card is relevant as an indication of who needs extra help for holistic achievement and success beyond the playing field. Cultures will vary a considerable amount nationally and internationally due to factors such as frameworks of power and change (Doherty, Fink, Inglis, & Pastore, 2010). At the level of unique student athletes, awareness of multicultural experiences of stereotypes, exploitation, and discrimination of typical cultural groupings in the United States could be helpful, such as the different experiences of female student athletes, African American students, Muslim students, and lesbian, gay, bisexual, or transgender groups (Zimbalist, 1999). Research also suggests that sport and recreation leaders should consider multicultural differences related to physical and intellectual disabilities (Hutzler & Barak, 2013) to customize techniques and meet individual differences. Positive approaches are needed for diversity to be respected and valued in physical and athletic centered environments on campus. To provide a specific example in relation to positive psychology, one approach would be to utilize the VIA Character Strengths survey to discuss similarities and differences on teams.

For relationship building, athletes could learn to interpret interactions with team-mates and coaches as positive rather than negative. For example, a coach helps an athlete interpret criticism as a way to learn rather than as an attack on the athlete's expertise. A consultant for the athletic department could also use the intervention of gratitude letters that athletes would write to diverse others who helped their athletic career.

Perceptions of positive psychology practices may vary by gender, religion, age, race, sexual orientation, type of physical development, and location of the campus being suburban, rural, or urban. For example, female athletes may view positive psychology in alignment with physical or athletic developmental goals, and male athletes may perceive the intent and purpose of positive psychology interventions in different ways (Ailsa, Ken, David, & Scott, 2004). The multicultural viewpoints could provide demographic and sociocultural information for future implementation in the physical or athletic domain of campus in order to understand barriers or perspectives that need to be addressed. For example, racial climate on campus may help the positive psychology practitioner gain a better sense for the exercise, recreation, or athletic environment for trust and safety of the students. In addition, particular positive psychology techniques may provide benefits in different ways for physical development or athletic performance. Therefore, the positive psychology practitioner may consider implementing a variety of techniques and determine effectiveness of each approach with multicultural factors being considered in the physical or athletic culture. Despite the type of culture, the practitioner could consider the issue of rapport building with the students or student athletes. Will the participants feel able to take risks, to openly participate, and to value the work being presented for physical development or athletic performance? This will help to establish a positive motivational climate for learning. Cultural considerations may impact various ways of reaching students and student athletes. These techniques may involve reward systems, charting progression, or partnership initiatives by the students or teams.

Ways to effectively deal with barriers must be noted and considered during implementation (Van Niekerk, 2010). One barrier may be the nuances of positive psychology programming in the physical or athletic campus environment. More specifically, student athletes may not have been exposed to much emphasis or awareness of the psychological side of sport. Many schools and coaches do not teach students about flourishing skills. Another barrier may be just gathering support from campus leaders. The current issues of multiculturalism may create an initial bias against anything related to psychology where current and previous student relationships impact the success of the program. Lastly, respectful relationships may not be the norm for particular physical or athletic groups on campus. These barriers could be assessed prior to implementation, but some barriers will not be revealed until implementation started. For example, coaches of athletic teams may utilize negative consequences too often. Coaches and athletes find themselves feeling detached and negative toward the team. Leaders in sport and student recreation may not know how to create a positive environment. Athletes may try to meet expectations set by the sport leaders but experience a negative climate when the goals focus too much on winning in an ego orientation rather than a task mastery or altruistic orientation. These and other barriers to effectively implementing positive psychology techniques may be difficult to understand and surpass. However, research must continue to address the best and most effective ways of teaching and promoting the positive transformations that are needed in the physical and athletic college setting that are appropriate to each and every diverse individual.

Case Study

The case study chosen for this chapter involved one sport psychologist from Boston University. This section examines the specific case of Dr. Amy Baltzell's work as a certified sport psychology consultant through the Association of Applied Sport Psychology. Her position is with Boston University as the Sport Psychologist and Director of the Sport Psychology Track in the Counseling Program. She recently wrote a book entitled "Living in the Sweet Spot" (Baltzell, 2011) about preparing for performance in sport and life using positive psychology for daily fulfillment and high performance. Her book contains many examples of top athletes dealing with the pressure to perform at their best. Baltzell herself was an Olympian and America's Cup sailor.

In an interview (A. Baltzell, personal communication, October 5, 2012), Dr. Baltzell provided a detailed and specific example of the practical application of positive psychology research and theory. During her work with college athletes, teams, and coaches, she addressed many topics that focus on flourishing rather than addressing problems. Baltzell said, "I have found that it is not enough to just focus on helping athletes jump higher or run faster. To truly help them optimize performance, to the competitor's maximum potential, it is essential to keep the commitment to helping them thrive on my radar in all of my consulting work." For both individuals and groups, she focuses on helping athletes and coaches become aware of strengths for positive focus and self-determination. She supports using positive psychology as the most effective way to integrate these strengths into performance and training.

In her daily work, she emphasizes the value of several positive psychology topics. The first she described was positive emotions. She helps athletes notice and strengthen their positive emotions associated with sport through mindfulness of positive moments. The topic of flow has also strongly influenced her work. Baltzell stated, "Based on Csiksentmihayli's initial research using experiential sampling, he found that it was possible to experience flow in ordinary daily experiences.

In both my workshops and individual consulting, I aspired to help athletes and coaches be more engaged in their daily training in a way that would cultivate full focus on tasks that are authentically compelling." She describes how this can require either adjusting the task at hand or adjusting how one appraises the experience, such as a student athlete re-framing an extra hour of running not as a chore but rather as purposeful with positive feelings of pace and rhythm.

Another topic that Baltzell discusses is the positive imagery she uses in her consulting work with student athletes. She frequently has athletes imagine the moment in competition that would represent achieving an outcome goal that is highly valued by the athlete. Her example included the last one hundred meters of a 1500 meter race. The athlete is encouraged to imagine crossing the finish line. Baltzell stated, "I would have such an athlete practice imagining the thoughts and points of mental focus that would facilitate optimal racing and, in the imagery, emphasize the moment of crossing the finish line. I encourage special attention to the positive emotions that the runner would have in this moment. Consistent with one pathway recommended by Albert Bandura to strengthen self-efficacy, filling one's mind with future success contributes to enhancing self-efficacy for the particular event." Therefore, student athletes are taught to bring the anticipated positive emotions to mind that accompany the anticipated success.

One of the topics that she most values is the concept of cultivating mindfulness with student athletes. She supports mindfulness by commenting that "Awareness and in-the-moment acceptance of all that has already transpired may be essential for optimal athletic performance. When the athlete is able to accept all negative and positive experiences that have occurred, in addition to all negative to positive emotions and thoughts that occur, they are more able to focus on the task at hand that will allow optimal performance." Many athletes and coaches struggle with shifting from thinking about negative events to being in the moment. If athletes and coaches cannot shift from negative thoughts that interrupt high performance thoughts, performance is likely to decline. She approaches the reframing by helping athletes and coaches tolerate the negatives if thought stoppage or shifting does not work. They must allow themselves to move forward in a positive way by accepting the challenges and letting the distress go without judgment of being positive or negative.

The topics of optimism and hope also integrate into Baltzell's practice. She works with student athletes to create optimism that their optimal potential will be accomplished. With hopefulness, she teaches the athletes to hope for maximization. This maximization is accomplished through pathways of hope for attaining goals through resources and finding various capabilities to overcome challenges. For example, a coach or athletic trainer helps an athlete hope for the best possible recovery from injury.

On the intervention side of using positive emotions, Baltzell refers back to Seligman's (2011) work on flourishing. She explained that, "Helping athletes and coaches both notice and nurture positive emotion is an untapped well of opportunity. I have adopted Seligman's idea of the three-good things exercise and have both athletes and coaches, individually and in group/team settings, bring to mind three-good things that happened in practice and in competition." Baltzell also adds focusing on the athletes' strengths to this appreciation of positive thinking by having the athletes distinguish how their strengths helped bring about the three good things that happened in their sport.

In terms of engagement, much of her work focuses on helping athletes and coaches create the possibility of flow in their daily experience. She explains, "Quality of daily experience is under-valued in sport psychology practice. I fully believe that when the performer has better quality of psycho-emotional experience while training and competing, the better the performer will do when it counts." For example, part of this intervention is to help athletes reclaim and recall their love of the game. This can help to cultivate the possibility of full engagement. A coach or counselor may also help an athlete reconnect psychologically and emotionally to the pure fun of sports.

She also helps student athletes recognize the benefits they gain from their relationships. Often overlooked by athletes, the athlete to coach relationship is a rich source of learning and resources. Baltzell intentionally helps student athletes to recognize the benefits they might gain from these relationships. She discussed, "I've worked with hundreds of athletes at this point who have had a hard time with how they are coached. They take the yelling, criticism personally." Her intervention technique involves teaching the athletes to take the good information, depersonalize the feedback, and become aware of the positive intention of most coaches. This skill of positively interpreting an interaction instead of assuming the worst helps build positive relationships with coaches and teammates.

The topics of meaningfulness, goal setting, and achievement linked together as Baltzell describes her work with student athletes. "Having athletes get very clear on what is in it for them is essential. As we know for Deci and Ryan's self-determination theory, it is important to personally value intrinsically motivated goals." Without a doubt, achievement plays a major role in work with athletics, but meaningful connections must also be established.

The sport psychology services at Boston University seemlessly integrate sport psychology and positive psychology without many challenges from coaches or athletes. "I think any workshop or program needs to feel like it is created to match the audience. I don't see a conflict. I used to. Approximately 5 years ago I thought I would have to leave the field of sport psychology. I felt like I cared too much about the athlete as a human being, I cared more about their flourishing as a human being." Baltzell then decided to bring positive psychology into her sport psychology work. "Since that time I have continued to be delightfully surprised, and often inspired, about how the ideas in positive psychology just made my teaching and consulting work that much better."

In summary, positive psychology integrates smoothly into athletic endeavors on campus. Baltzell recommends more research to support the use of positive psychology in sport psychology. Empirical work must continue to develop. She supports expanding positive psychology beyond the athletic realm and into other areas of campus, "I brought in an expert mindfulness meditation teacher to teach a three class series on mindfulness and meditation to my graduate sport psychology students. I have given talks that included mostly positive psychology ideas to all of the Boston University freshman athletes and, separately, to the Boston University coaching staff for all sports. I have conducted research on the impact of mindfulness meditation with athletes. I have worked with entire collegiate coaching staffs which included a series of talks that were positive psychology inspired, with one series entitled, 'Positive Coach: Positive Results.' I have given talks to kindergarten teachers, to middle and high-school teachers. I have given talks to youth sport coaches who are coaching in cities across the country with under-served urban youth." For Batzell's work, positive psychology is infused throughout her interventions and speaking engagements for both athletic and nonathletic audiences.

Conclusion

This chapter illustrated the potential benefit of using positive psychology to understand the physical and athletic developmental needs of college students and student athletes. Many approaches included here could be integrated into a variety of situations for self-improvement. This illustrated the power of positive sport and exercise leaders who endeavor to make experiences more engaging for college students. Even with all of the innovative positive psychology techniques, the basics of positive reinforcement are still important to implement. In summary, this is an vital area for theory development, awareness raising, quality distinctions, and behavioral change.

Positive psychology for sport and exercise could be designed uniquely and specifically to meet the developmental needs of the students. The environment may nurture optimization and flourishing with structured interventions (Seligman, 2011). Positive interventions have the potential to build a sense of community for physical development and athletic performance. Positivity is often reciprocated and resonated, and physical activity and sport provides a fitting environment for additional exploration. The positive techniques could provide positive adult attention and positive role modeling from campus leaders in exercise, sport, or fitness. Students would be actively involved in their own and their team's flourishing. By actively including students in the design, democracy, and upkeep of the positive physical and athletic climate, the students would be more invested in positive learning. Students would also better understand how to reach out to others in physical activities and sport through positive psychology techniques. They could be involved in developing positive psychology outcomes into their customized sport psychology profile, such as adding a measurement of hardiness for assessing the three dimensions of commitment, control, and challenge (Sheard & Golby, 2010) or adding measurement of character, passion, or sportsmanship (Peterson & Seligman, 2004; Vallerand, Briere, Blanchard, Provencher, 1997).

Ultimately, recognizing and determining that one's physical development and athletic performance can be controlled, at least to some degree, is a powerful factor in the ability to view exercise and sport positively. Feelings of helplessness and hopelessness often follow when a person views circumstances as being out of one's own control (Meeker, Stankovich, & Kays, 2000). Competence, freedom, and engagement in sport and exercise are important. Consequently, self-determinism, fostered by the use of positive psychology practices, places the control into the hands of the individual empowering him or her to make changes in views and actions. Students and faculty may also value utilizing positive psychology practices beyond exercise development and sport performance.

Lastly, strategies exist for ongoing innovative implementation of positive psychology for sport and exercise campus practitioners. One recommendation for college campus exercise and sport specialists today is for better training in the use of positive psychology techniques and interventions. A key component to reinforce here is the importance of practicing positive psychology like practicing a physical skill. Practice. Practice. Practice. Mental skills need practice through visualization, imagery, and metacognitive self talk. An option may be to develop an in-house planning committee that is able to collectively target the most important and effective areas for positive psychology influence. Increased collaboration of coaches, counselors, student-life leaders, and recreation directors could promote additional empowerment of positive psychology techniques in physically active student, staff, and faculty groups. Most exercise and sport programs are likely implementing some form of positive psychology already, but an additional step would be to encourage deliberate practice of positive psychology skills. More innovative strategies may be needed as impetus to deeper study and consistent monitoring for effective application of positive psychology practice. A final recommendation would be for college campuses to provide the appropriate professional development for implementing training to maintain positive psychology practices for optimal exercise and sport experiences. In addition, longitudinal studies may be conducted that better detail best practices for teaching the various techniques of positivity for student flourishing and institutional effectiveness with physical development and athletic performance.

References

Ailsa G., A., Ken P., H., David, L., & Scott B. (2004). New Zealand athletes' attitudes towards seeking sport psychology consultation. *New Zealand Journal Of Psychology, 33*(3), 129–136.

Anderson, R., & Brice, S. (2011). The mood enhancing benefits of exercise: Memory biases augment the effects. *Psychology of Sport and Exercise, 12* (2), 79–84.

Annesi, J. J., & Tennant, G. A. (2013). Mediation of social cognitive theory variables in the relationship of exercise and improved eating in sedentary adults with severe obesity. *Psychology, Health & Medicine, 18*(6), 714–724.

Beaman, R., & Wheldall, K. (2000). Teachers' use of approval and disapproval in the classroom. *Educational Psychology, 20,* 431–447.

Baltzell, A. (2011). *Living in the sweet sport: Preparing for performance in sport and life.* Morgantown, WV: Fitness Information Technology.

Brown, G. (2007). Knight panel urges educational intervention for recruits. *NCAA News, 44*(3), p.8.

Boyle, J., Mattern, C., Lassiter, J., Ritzler, J. (2011). Peer 2 Peer: Efficacy of a course-based peer education intervention to increase physical activity among college students. *Journal of American College Health, 59*(6), 519–620.

Cialdini, R. B., Borden, R. J., Thorne, A., Walker, M. R., Freeman, S., & Sloan, L. R. (1976). Basking in reflected glory: Three (football) field studies. *Journal of Personality and Social Psychology, 34,* 366–375.

Clonan, S., Chafouleas, S., McDougal, J., & Riley-Tillman, T. C. (2004). Positive psychology goes to school: Are we there yet? *Psychology in the Schools, 41*(1), 101–110.

Cole, K. (2006). *An examination of school counselors' knowledge and perceptions of recruited student-athletes* (Doctoral dissertation). Retrieved from University of Iowa, Proquest Digital Dissertations Database (AAT 77649442).

Crescioni, A., Ehrlinger, J., Alquist, J. L., Conlon, K. E., Baumeister, R. F., Schatschneider, C., & Dutton, G. R. (2011). High trait self-control predicts positive health behaviors and success in weight loss. *Journal Of Health Psychology, 16*(5), 750–759.

Csikszentmihalyi, M. (1990). Flow: The psychology of optimal experience. New York, NY: Harper & Row.

Curry, L., Snyder, C., Cook, D., Ruby, B., & Rehm, M. (1997). Role of hope in academic and sport achievement. *Journal of Personality & Social Psychology, 73*(6), 1257–1267.

Delligatti, N. (2004). A preventative model of school consultation: Incorporating perspectives from positive psychology. *Psychology in the Schools, 41*(1), 155–162.

Doherty, A., Fink, J. Inglis, S., & Pastore, D. (2010). Understanding a culture of diversity through frameworks of power and change. *Sport Management Review, 13*(4), 368–382.

Douglas, J., Harwood, C., & Minniti, A. (2010). The psychological assets of positive youth development: A developmental framework for sports. *The Association of Applied Sport Psychology Conference Abstracts,* Providence, RI.

Duckworth, A. L., Peterson, C., Matthews, M. D., & Kelly, D. R. (2007). Grit: Perseverance and passion for long-term goals. *Journal of Personality and Social Psychology, 92*(6), 1087–1101.

Duda, J. (2011). Promoting positive psychology in sport, dance, and exercise settings: The role of motivational processes. *World Congress on Positive Psychology Abstracts,* Philadelphia, PA.

George, M. (2010, September). *LSA theme semester asks questions about life.* Retrieved from http://ur.umich.edu/1011/Sep07_10/1458-lsa-theme-semester

Gilpin, J. (2008). Teaching happiness: The role of positive psychology in the classroom. *Salve's Dissertations and Theses, 24,* 1–23.

Gould, D., & Whitley, M. (2009). Sources and consequences of athletic burnout among college athletes. *Journal of Intercollegiate Sport, 2*(1), 16–31.

Hutzler, Y., Oz, M., & Barak, S. (2013). Goal perspectives and sport participation motivation of Special Olympians and typically developing athletes. *Research In Developmental Disabilities, 34*(7), 2149–2160.

Jenson, W. R., Olympia, D., Farley, M., & Clark, E. (2004). Positive psychology and externalizing students in a sea of negativity. *Psychology in the Schools, 41*(1), 67–79.

Kwan, M. W., Faulkner, G. J., Arbour-Nicitopoulos, K. P., & Cairney, J. (2013). Prevalence of health-risk behaviours among Canadian post-secondary students: descriptive results from the National College Health Assessment. *BMC Public Health, 13*(1), 1–6.

Kisaalita, N. R., & Robinson, M. E. (2014). Attitudes and motivations of competitive cyclists regarding use of banned and legal performance enhancers. *Journal of Sports Science & Medicine, 13*(1), 44–50.

Korn, L., Gonen, E., Shaked, Y., & Golan, M. (2013). Health perceptions, self and body image, physical activity and nutrition among undergraduate students in Israel. *Plos ONE, 8*(3), 1–7.

Lapchick, R. (2011). *Racial and gender report card.* Retrieved from http://www.bus.ucf.edu/sportbusiness/?page=1445

Lee, M. (1985). Self-esteem and social identity in basketball fans: A closer look at basking-in-related-glory, *Journal of Sport Behavior, 8,* 210–223.

Martens, B. K., & Witt, J. C. (2004). Competence, persistence, and success: The positive psychology of behavioral skill instruction. *Psychology in the Schools, 41*(1), 19–30.

Martínková, I., & Parry, J. (2011). Two ways of conceiving time in sports. *Acta Universitatis Palackianae Olomucensis. Gymnica, 41*(1), 23–31.

Meeker, D., Stankovich, C., & Kays, T. (2000). *Positive transitions for student-athletes.* Scottsdale, AZ: Holcomb Hathaway.

Misra, R., & McKean, M. (2000). College students' academic stress and its relation to their anxiety, time management, and leisure satisfaction. *American Journal of Health Studies, 16,* 1.

Miller, L., & Carpenter, C. (2009). Altruistic leadership strategies in coaching: A case study of Jim Tressel at The Ohio State University. *Strategies: A Journal for Physical and Sport Educators, 22*(4), 9–12.

Orlick, T. (1978). *The cooperative sports and games book.* New York, NY: Pantheon.

Orlick, T. McNally, J., O'Hara, T. (1978). Cooperative games: Systematic feedback and cooperative analysis. In F. Smoll & R. Smith (Eds.), *Psychological perspectives in youth sports* (pp. 203–228). New York, NY: Hemispheres.

Pedersen, D. E. (2012). Stress carry-over and college student health outcomes. *College Student Journal, 46*(3), 620–627.

Peterson, C., & Park, N. (2011). Positive education: Different approaches. *World Congress on Positive Psychology Abstracts,* Philadelphia, PA.

Peterson, C., & Seligman, M. (2004). *Character strengths and virtues: A handbook and classification.* Oxford: American Psychological Association.

Ross, A., & Thomas, S. (2010). The health benefits of yoga and exercise: A review of comparison studies. *Journal of Alternative and Complementary Medicine, 16*(1), 3–12.

Seligman, M. (2004). *Authentic happiness: Using the new positive psychology to realize your potential for lasting fulfillment.* New York, NY: Free Press.

Seligman, M. E. P. (2011). *Flourish: A visionary new understanding of happiness and well-being.* New York, NY; Free Press.

Sheard, M., & Golby, J. (2010). Personality hardiness differentiates elite level sport performers. *International Journal of Sport & Exercise Psychology, 8*(2), 160–170.

Snyder, C. R., & Lopez, S. J. (2002). *Handbook of positive psychology.* New York, NY: Oxford University Press.

Strout, M. (2005). Positive behavioral support at the classroom level: Considerations and strategies. *Beyond Behavior, Winter,* 3–8.

Thachenkery, T., Avital, M., Cooperrider, D. L. (2010). Advances in appreciative inquiry. In Thachenkery, Cooperrider, A. (Ed.), *Introduction to positive design and appreciative construction* (Vol. 3, pp. 25). London: Emerald Publishing.

Thurston, M. (2011). A model for university academic programs in positive psychology and consciousness studies. *World Congress on Positive Psychology Abstract,* Philadelphia, PA.

Topp, R., Edward, J., Ridnar, S., Jacks, D., Newton, K., Keiffner, P., Woodall, D., & Conte, K. (2011). Fit into college: A program to improve physical activity and dietary intake lifestyles among college students. *Recreation Sports Journal,* 35(1), 69–79.

Vallerand, R., Briere, N., Blanchard, C., & Provencher, P. (1997). Development and validation of the multidimensional sportsmanship orientation scale. *Journal of Sport and Exercise Psychology, 19,* 197–206.

Van Niekerk, R. L. (2010). Understanding the barriers to and reasons for phsycial exercise among university students. *African Journal for Physical, Health Education, Recreation, & Dance, Supplement,* 172–182.

Watson, J. (2006). Student-athletes and counseling: Factors influencing the decision to seek counseling services. *College Student Journal,* 40(1), 35–43.

Welle, P., & Graf, H. (2011). Effective lifestyle habits and coping strategies for stress tolerance among college students. *American Journal of Health Education,* 42(2), 96–106.

White, M. A. (1975). Natural rates of teacher approval and disapproval in the classroom. *Journal Of Applied BehaviorAnalysis, 8,* 367–372.

Wilson, J. H., & Ryan, R. G. (2013). Professor-Student Rapport Scale: Six Items Predict Student Outcomes. *Teaching Of Psychology,* 40(2), 130–133.

Woolf, S. (2008). The meaning of translational research and why it Matters. *Journal of American Medical Association, 299,* 211–213.

Zimbalist, A. (1999). *Unpaid professionals.* New Jersey: Princeton University Press.

14

Life Coaching for Students

LAWRENCE I. MARKS

Students enter college with dreams of developing personal and professional success, and they look to the college faculty and staff to educate them in how to achieve these goals. There are many different ways that success can be defined for a particular individual, and many different avenues that educators use to develop student success. In discussing positive psychology on the college campus, Shushok and Hulme (2006) stated, "The promotion of success begins with the study of success" (p. 6). The science of positive psychology examines factors that lead to success, and life coaching provides an excellent means of using positive psychology to develop student success.

Life coaching as an area of practice and research has enjoyed tremendous growth over the past 15–20 years. With roots in consultation services for business executives and managers, the term "executive coaching" became increasingly used throughout the 1980s and 1990s (Kilburg, 1996). Recognizing that addressing the whole person and all aspects of the person's life, not just their time at work, was the most effective approach toward change and improved performance, coaches expanded the practice of executive coaching to "life coaching," although coaches that focus exclusively on the work setting remain valued. In addition, the growth of Humanistic psychology beginning in the 1950s, including the influential work of Carl Rogers and Abraham Maslow, and the focus on personal development in the following decades set the stage for the emergence of life coaching. Notably, Maslow coined the term "positive psychology" in his 1954 book in which he explains the hierarchy of needs model and describes self-actualization. Through these developments, in the 1990s life coaching became more popular for individuals outside of the corporate world who wished to have a coach as a guide toward personal development and goal achievement (Williams & Davis, 2007).

In terms of scholarly publications, Grant's (2011) annotated bibliography showed a dramatic increase in articles on executive and life coaching between the 1930s and 2010, with the majority occurring since 2000, and a current review of the PsycINFO database reveals that publications on coaching have continued to expand exponentially. The largest professional association for coaches, the International Coach Federation (ICF), was founded in 1995, and it currently has over 22,000 members. There are many organizations, including some universities, which offer training in executive and life coaching. The ICF manages accreditation of training programs as well as offers different levels of credentialing for coaches.

This aim of this chapter is to provide an introduction to life coaching, describe the connections between positive psychology, coaching, and student development, and discuss how coaching can take place on campus. Research and strategies related to working with students on achieving goals, increasing well-being, and focusing on strengths are included to demonstrate the value of coaching on campus, and to offer an overview of some practical applications involved in the coaching process. A section on cultural considerations serves as a reminder that being tuned in to and responsive to the cultural background of the students in coaching is essential for the students and coaches to have the most enriching and effective experience and outcome. Finally, a case study is presented to illustrate some of the chapter's concepts.

Depending on their roles and responsibilities, almost any faculty, staff, and/or student affairs professional might be able to take on the role of a coach. Although many of the positive psychology coaching strategies discussed here can be practiced by college personnel, professionals wanting to develop their coaching skills further are encouraged to seek out additional training. Training ensures competent coaching and teaches how to manage different coaching situations, additional interventions, as well as addresses the ethics related to coaching practice.

Life Coaching and Positive Psychology

Just what is life coaching? Life coaching involves a collaborative professional relationship between a coach and the individual being coached, with the focus on facilitating the individual's pursuit of personal and professional growth, specific goals, improving performance, and/or enhancing well-being. The coach may take the role of encourager, supporter, listener, motivator, guide, and challenger. The individuals being coached tend to not have any major mental health-related dysfunctions. Instead, coachees typically are getting along in life fairly well, with normal life struggles, and likely have certain life areas in particular that they wish to either change or develop. Having a life coach allows individuals to pursue their goals with greater clarity, helps them stay on course, and provides the support to stretch further in achieving their goals. A growing body of research has demonstrated that life coaching leads to improved outcomes including increased well-being and goal attainment (Grant, Cavanagh, Parker, & Passmore, 2010). Furthermore, life coaching is well suited for college students desiring to make positive changes.

Often the term "coach" is associated with the world of sports, and although life coaching and athletic coaching are distinct professions, a comparison can be made in the benefits of having a coach. Consider an athlete who participates in systematic training with an athletic coach versus an athlete who attempts to win competitions independent of any assistance. Yes, there may be some exceptions, but virtually all successful athletes, including those who seem to be naturally gifted, work with a coach to refine their skills, build endurance, remain focused during competitions, and hold them accountable for keeping to practice and health maintenance schedules. People outside of athletics also achieve impressive personal or professional success on their own through talent, time, effort, and persistence. Therefore, coaching is not a replacement for the effort put in by the individual. Instead, a coach can enhance the process of goal achievement or personal and professional growth by developing a collaborative relationship and using various coaching techniques. This is especially important with an increasing amount of distractions in life that may move people, including professional athletes, away from pursuing their goals and living a healthy life. Today, individuals seek out coaching to work on a variety of issues such as work-life balance, completing dissertations, starting a business, increasing productivity, time management, career transition, improving team performance, developing leadership skills, and improving diet/nutrition.

Having read the previous chapters in this book and following the brief introduction to life coaching thus far, you may already see the natural fit between life coaching and positive psychology. Linley, Joseph, Maltby, Harrington, and Wood (2009) identified four aspects of both fields that create this synergy. First, positive psychology and life coaching both focus on enhancing performance and well-being. Second, by giving attention to factors that contribute to success and achievement, both diverge in the same manner from traditional psychological views that tend to focus more on psychological dysfunctions. Third, positive psychology's identification of and attention to personal strengths provides a tool that makes coaching toward goal achievement more effective. And fourth, positive psychology offers research-based support for various coaching interventions. Although life coaches may approach their work with a variety of orientations and methods, positive psychology provides an additional set of research-based theories and interventions that are particularly well suited for the coaching field. For example, increasing positive emotions and focusing on strengths are two major emphases within positive psychology, both described later, that create a solid foundation for life coaching (Biswas-Diener & Dean, 2007). An important note to make here is that life coaching, from a positive psychology perspective (or from any approach for that matter), must occur within a cultural context, an issue that will be discussed later in this chapter.

Coaching on Campus

In a series of articles, Schreiner (2010a, 2010b, 2010c) described "student thriving," a concept which is rooted in positive psychology. Thriving for college students consists of multiple factors including being engaged in learning, a determination to succeed academically, having an optimistic outlook, meaningful relationships with others, and an openness to and embracing of others from diverse backgrounds. The different aspects of thriving significantly contribute to student success including achieving higher grades, intention to graduate, effective coping, and greater life satisfaction (Schreiner, 2010a, 2010b, 2010c). Most colleges and universities include in their stated mission or goals not only to develop the academic knowledge and skills of students, but also to develop well-rounded students who are self-aware, engaged in learning, able to problem-solve in various situations, and who can contribute productively in society and build relationships in a diverse community. In other words, facilitating students' thriving directly supports higher education institutions' goals of providing opportunities for academic and non-academic student growth. In their review of highly effective educational institutions and practices, Kuh, Kinzie, Schuh, Whitt, and Associates (2005) recommend investing in programs and activities that foster student engagement for enhancing student success. As you would expect and have probably witnessed, because of their differences in background, individual experiences, and dispositions, students vary on how much they are engaged, let alone thriving, while in college. And, you may also have known students who, with some encouragement, support, and a gentle or not so gentle nudging, have made a shift in their perspective and performance from an average student to an exceptional one. Life coaching can provide an effective means for creating and sustaining just such a positive development.

Although the growth of life coaching in businesses, organizations, and the public at large has been rapid, life coaching on college campuses has been fairly limited. The shortage of coaching on campus may be due to lack of awareness or information about coaching and/or not having staff trained to provide coaching. Fortunately, because of its popularity and effectiveness, many colleges and universities are now starting to offer coaching services. Of the higher education institutions which do have such programs, many, though not all, are often focused primarily on academic success, and these services are sometimes labeled academic coaching or success coaching. Wellness coaching, which focuses on improving areas such as health, exercise, and nutrition, is another area that some schools are implementing. Robinson & Gahagan (2010) described a coaching program for academic success at the University of South Carolina, and they reported that their program led to improved academic performance in terms of

GPA for the participants. Schreiner (2010b) suggested that academic advisors, with their one-on-one relationship with students, are in a unique position to foster hope, thriving, and academic determination in students. Beyond advisors, faculty or staff members in a variety of departments potentially may also take on the role of a coach for a student. In addition, in some cases, appropriately trained students could be in the role of a peer coach. There also are private coaches and agencies that offer coaching to students directly or who are hired by universities to provide coaching for students.

Life coaching has some overlap with other traditional helping type relationships found on campus including counseling/therapy and mentoring, and it is important to distinguish the features of coaching that make it unique from these other professional roles that staff or faculty may have with students. Counseling professionals (e.g., psychologists, mental health counselors, social workers) typically focus on a range of issues from coping with normal, developmental life struggles to alleviating mental health problems and symptoms, whereas coaches would not necessarily work with students who are experiencing psychological issues that are impairing their functioning. In some cases, a student may be in counseling and also participate in a coaching relationship at the same time, and, in these situations, it is best if the two professionals can consult regarding their approaches and the areas/issues of attention when working with a student. Mental health clinicians may use some interventions also used by coaches (see examples later in the chapter), but the focus or desired outcomes as a result of these interventions will likely be different. Life coaching, especially from a positive psychology perspective, can be viewed as picking up where counseling ends to enhance and further students' growth and flourishing (Linley & Joseph, 2004). The diagram in Figure 14.1 illustrates this relationship between counseling/therapy and coaching along a continuum of time orientation and area of emphasis.

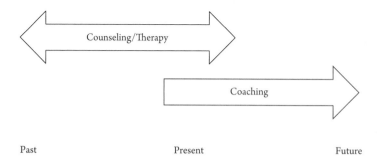

Figure 14.1 Relationship between counseling/therapy and coaching along a continuum of time orientation and area of emphasis

Mentoring in a college environment shares with life coaching (and counseling) the importance of a supportive relationship and often a focus on setting and achieving goals. However, mentoring differs from coaching in that the attention is typically singularly focused on career related issues, the mentor is usually in the same field as the mentee with more experience or expertise in that area, and role modeling the process of achievement is an important aspect of the relationship. With coaching, the emphasis is broader in scope, the coach and student do not have to be in the same academic or career discipline, and while role modeling may be present, the coach facilitates the student finding her own individualized path to success (Jacobi, 1991).

Life Coaching in Practice

The relationship between the life coach and student is fundamental to facilitating positive change and development. Research findings on what makes a successful learning experience for college students almost invariably include positive interactions with a faculty or staff member (Kuh, et al., 2005; Lundberg & Schreiner, 2004; Schreiner, Noel, Anderson, & Cantwell, 2011). Indeed, most student affairs professionals know the value of positive relationships with students, and they are well versed in expressing genuine interest and support. They do this through using the reliable skills of empathy, understanding, and good listening. Similar to a mentor or mental health counselor, the relationship between a life coach and student involves more than routine or cursory interactions. Although campus professionals may engage in certain coaching activities with students, being a coach for a student requires professionals to step out of their ordinary roles to engage more fully in the coaching process. For example, a career counselor may recommend career exploration activities and ask a student to report back, but this is only a limited aspect of coaching and the coaching relationship. With coaching, an ongoing commitment to students' success is important, helping them to identity and reach their goals through posing challenging questions and holding them accountable, but within the context of a supportive, encouraging relationship. Life coaching is a collaborative or coactive relationship in which the students feel an openness to grow and make changes that they may not have done before, not because of the expert advice given by the coach, but because of the trust felt as a part of their working alliance. Thus, instead of only telling students what to do, a coach working in a collaborative manner facilitates increasing students' awareness of themselves and their strengths and empowers them to take action steps that will move them closer to their goals (Stober & Grant, 2006; Whitworth, Kimsey-House, Kimsey-House, & Sandahl, 2007). In this manner, life coaches on campus are essentially teaching lifelong skills of the process of effectively identifying, setting, and attaining goals.

Coaching students on campus can take place individually or in groups, and each modality has advantages. In individual meetings, students may experience a closer connection to their coach and receive more focused attention. In group meetings, a small group of five or six students come together to receive coaching. The group modality has several benefits for students including receiving support from peers, a feeling of accountability to the group, and an increase in the ideas, strategies, and resources that may be generated for a particular topic or goal. Coaches also may choose to check in with their students between meetings through phone calls, email, texting, or a coaching-related website. In this manner, the coach may share resources or have students report on their progress. Maintaining regularly scheduled meetings, which may occur individually, in groups, or even through a form of electronic communication (e.g., video calls) contributes to a dependable and collaborative relationship and helps keep the student focused on meeting their goals. Students may benefit from having a life coach for just one semester or throughout their college career.

The content of the meetings between the coach and student will initially be about describing the positive psychology coaching process, screening for other problems and making referrals if necessary, establishing a collaborative relationship, assessment of the situation as well as the strengths and resources of the student, and identifying goals. The coach and student can cocreate an ongoing meeting agenda. The coach may offer information on goal setting and motivation, or suggest positive psychology-related exercises, but most of the meeting will likely be addressing the students' goals. Given the academic setting, students may often choose raising their grades, improving study habits, or deciding on a career as their goal. However, other goals that might be helpful for students to address through life coaching might include improving physical wellness (such as starting and maintaining an exercise/fitness routine or improving nutrition), becoming involved or increasing engagement in campus or community activities, or managing finances. From a holistic perspective, addressing any appropriate goals will facilitate student success. That is, when students strive for and achieve goals that they set for themselves, they not only learn from the process but develop a feeling of accomplishment. These two factors in turn can lead to increased motivation to work toward other goals. The next section will describe how coaches can help students in the process of identifying and achieving their goals.

Developing the Old College Try: Facilitating Students' Striving Toward Goals

"Give it the old college try" is a sentiment in the United States culture that encourages adults to recall the energy, determination, perseverance, and skills that led them to strive for and achieve goals during their college days. However, this process of working toward goals is often one that college students must navigate on their own. Students who work with a coach can master this life-long skill because setting and achieving goals is a fundamental piece of life coaching.

Coaches might begin the process of coaching students by presenting a basic model of setting and achieving goals. The first step is to identify the desired goal. Next, the coach and student can develop a plan and actions to take. Between coaching sessions, the expectation is that the student will carry out the plan. Evaluation of the plan and progress toward the goal occurs throughout the process and can lead to modifying the plan and/or possibly adjusting the goal. This cycle is repeated until the goal is accomplished. Grant, Curtayne, and Burton (2009) described using Whitmore's (1992) GROW model (Goal, Reality, Options, Way forward) in each coaching session. Their model involves setting goals for the coaching session, examining the current situation and what is working or not working, discussing what can be done next, and developing a specific plan. Considerations for the various steps in setting and achieving goals are discussed below.

Many student affairs professionals may be familiar with the useful SMART acronym when discussing goals. SMART stands for specific, measureable, attainable, realistic, and timely or time bound. Reviewing the SMART approach to goal setting can be a beneficial starting place when helping students learn the best way to set goals. Discussing the idea that short-term goals are steps that should always lead toward long-term goals also provides a valuable context for how to work on student goals. That is, when developing goals, one should start by identifying longer term goals, and then break those goals down into small steps which can become the shorter term goals. In this way, students can see the connection between how what they are working on today will lead toward their ultimate ambitions. When addressing goals, have students write down, not just talk about, their long-term and short-term goals, which will clarify their thoughts and priorities (King, 2008). The process of writing down goals also seems to make them feel more real and important versus just keeping the goals in mind.

When identifying goals or steps toward goals, the coach should brainstorm options and solutions to challenges or obstacles with the student. Trusting in the creativity and resourcefulness of students helps them to build trust in themselves in the future. When a student feels the coach's support of their autonomy, it leads to higher achievement and positive outcomes (Reeve, 2002). For example, when working on setting deadlines for goals, avoid the tendency to impose your own timeline. Instead, as the student's coach, discuss both realistic expectations for goal completion and the need to challenge oneself.

A coach working from a positive psychology perspective will want to discuss with the student the self-concordance of their goals, that is, if and how their goals fit with their personal values, interests, and passions (Grant, 2006; Sheldon, 2001). It is essential to help students identify goals that are important to them and explore the values that are driving attainment of a particular goal. With college students, there may be other influences, such as parents, peers, or former teachers, who have had an impact on their choices and aspirations.

Another distinction of goals to highlight is the difference between intrinsic and extrinsic goals. Intrinsic goals involve connecting with others, serving others, or personal growth, whereas extrinsic goals involve achieving visible rewards such as wealth, attractiveness, or popularity. Research has demonstrated that pursuing and attaining goals that are more self-concordant and intrinsic is related to greater overall well-being for the individual (Kasser & Ryan, 2001; Sheldon, 2001; Sheldon & Schmuck, 2001). Moreover, Sheldon and Lyubomirsky (2006) found that when students made intentional activity changes such as exercising, studying more, embracing a new perspective, or eating healthier, they reported greater and longer-lasting positive emotions and well-being compared to students who made or experienced changes in circumstances such as taking a new class, moving, getting a new cell phone, or being awarded a scholarship.

It is not uncommon for students struggling to achieve goals to express concerns about motivation. The coach can help to motivate students by agreeing on specific steps and having the students report back on their progress. Indeed, accountability to the coach is a key aspect of the coaching process. The coach could also discuss with the student ways of increasing motivation through such positive psychological strategies as visualizing a successful outcome, developing and using a social support network, and being optimistic. Coaches might also have the student write down all the personal benefits of reaching their goal and identify the reasons a goal is important or meaningful as a way of increasing intrinsic motivation. With this strategy, do not let the student stop at a few benefits, but work with them to think more deeply if necessary; this process will help the students uncover their own values and choices.

If obstacles continue to arise for the student, the coach can help the student reevaluate the goals and discuss how the goal or steps to reaching the goal may need to be modified to be more attainable. Examining the initial assessment of the students' strengths and resources can provide useful information about the realism of their goals (Biswas-Diener & Dean, 2007). Coaches might also consider the students' readiness for making changes, following Prochaska, Norcross, and DiClemente's (2013) stages of change model. Students may need to be engaged in awareness raising conversations about areas for potential improvements before setting goals and action steps (Grant, 2006). Learning and experiencing the process of setting personal goals, steps to achievement, sustaining motivation, and overcoming obstacles is a process that not only will lead to students' success in college but instill skills and perspectives that they can draw on in the future, when they want to "give it the old college try."

When students understand the goal-setting process and are successful in making progress toward or achieving their goals, a feeling of hope is engendered

(Schreiner, Hulme, Hetzel, & Lopez, 2009). Snyder (2002) described two elements in his theory of hope: thoughts about how one will go about achieving a goal (pathways thinking) and thoughts about one's ability to reach a goal (agency thinking). Hope is positively correlated with numerous markers of success or well-being including self-esteem, academic performance, athletic performance, and mental health. Coaching students through the goal-setting process, including brainstorming ideas, developing specific steps, and visualizing success can increase both components of hope (Kauffman, 2006). When a student experiences achieving a goal, hope is increased, and the student may feel more confident to take on a different or even more challenging goal. The positive emotion of hope thus serves to facilitate desired outcomes and reinforces future efforts. The process is similar to Fredrickson's concept of the upward spiral, that positive emotions lead to increased well-being (Fredrickson, 2009; Fredrickson & Joiner, 2002). The role of well-being in coaching is explored further in the next section.

How Coaching toward Happiness and Well-Being Can Lead to Success

One of the hallmarks of life coaching from a positive psychology perspective is that increasing individuals' happiness and well-being can directly and indirectly lead to successful outcomes for the individual. Many students may be in a mindset that if they are just able to "find a girlfriend/boyfriend" or "get a job" then they will be happy, but research in positive psychology suggests the process works the other way around. That is, happiness and greater well-being is what causes individuals to be successful and achieve desired goals (Achor, 2010; Biswas-Diener & Dean, 2007; Boehm & Lyubomirsky, 2008; Lyubomirsky, King, & Diener 2005). Happiness, although somewhat of a subjective and ubiquitous term, is often operationalized by life satisfaction or subjective well-being, and it has been found to be positively associated with improved physical immunity, increased financial income, high-quality social relationships, work satisfaction and productivity, and increased resiliency (Diener & Biswas-Diener, 2008; Pavot & Diner, 2004). Individuals' overall well-being has been conceptualized as comprising different components. For example, Ryff's (1989, 2014) model describes six factors: autonomy, environmental mastery, personal growth, positive relations with others, purpose in life, and self-acceptance. In his 2011 book, Seligman posits that well-being has five elements: positive emotions, engagement, meaning, accomplishment, and positive relationships.

Students may not state a goal of increasing their happiness or well-being, although that can and does occur, but they may talk about components that for them would lead to happiness such as improving social support, increasing their GPA, gaining confidence in a certain area, or exercising more. Either way, it is a worthwhile endeavor to explore how they view their own happiness and well-being, what these concepts mean to them, the multiple factors that contribute to happiness and well-being, and the relationship between these concepts and setting and achieving goals. Happiness and well-being can be enhanced by educating about realistic expectations and impactful factors (Pavot & Diener, 2004). According to Gilbert (2006), people often misjudge what actually contributes to their own happiness. This may be particularly true with college students, as they transition developmentally from the intense joys and struggles of adolescence to increasingly mature adults.

Research findings by Barbara Fredrickson have contributed extensively to the understanding of how positive emotions contribute to happiness and well-being and, in turn, optimal performance, particularly within Western culture. Fredrickson's (1998, 2001, 2009) broaden-and-build theory holds that with increased experiences of positive emotions, such as joy, gratitude, hope, inspiration, interest, and serenity, thinking is broadened, and people become more open-minded, creative in their thinking, and able to see more solutions to problems. In addition, with increased positive emotions, individuals build resiliency (physical, social, psychological, and emotional), learn more, and develop new skills. In contrast, with increased negative emotions, thinking tends to be limited and resiliency tends to be depleted. Robust research has demonstrated that experiencing a greater amount of positive emotions to negative emotions leads to flourishing in life (Fredrickson, 2013a, 2013b).

Although students are typically open to self-improvement, the improvement that they often focus on is centered on what they see as their weaknesses or alleviating distress rather than enhancing strengths or positive emotions. This outlook usually stems from years of parents, athletic coaches, and educators emphasizing where a student is falling short, albeit with the aim of having the student mend or advance in these areas of needed attention. Life coaching with students from a positive psychology approach offers an opportunity to reconceptualize the process of growth and self-improvement. This is not to say that coaches should ignore or avoid problem areas. A life coach should acknowledge where the student is struggling; and, equipped with the knowledge of how enhancing well-being leads to success, coaches can offer a new framework for student growth and development. Furthermore, this positive approach and focus on well-being and goal achievement is often one that is well received. The next section describes examples of select positive psychology coaching interventions.

Positive Psychology Coaching Interventions

There are numerous positive psychology coaching interventions that can enhance happiness and well-being by increasing positive emotions (which facilitates goal achievement), and a few popular and empirically supported strategies will be described here. Fredrickson's broaden-and-build theory (described above) under-lies the power of these strategies. One technique involves having students reflect on their day or week, and write down three things that went well and what role they had in the situation. Participants who engaged in this exercise daily for 1 week scored higher on measures of happiness and lower on measures of depres-sion at a 1-, 3-, and 6-month follow up. This finding was especially true for those individuals who continued to practice the exercise after the first week (Seligman, Steen, Park, & Peterson, 2005). Having students do this exercise in a group set-ting, such as a coaching workshop, offers several benefits including a boost to their mood or energy level as they describe their events or listen to others' good happenings, feeling they are getting to know the other group members and maybe feeling drawn to hear more, perhaps a sense of feeling more connected to each other, and a likely shift in their perspective to a more positive mind set. Not too bad for a simple group activity.

A similar intervention can be done through expressing gratitude, which can be accomplished through having students write down a list of things that they are grate-ful for either recently or in the past. Studies show that experiencing and express-ing gratitude leads to improved well-being, greater resiliency, improved physical health, helpfulness to others, increases in other positive emotions, and progress toward goals (Bono, Emmons, & McCullough, 2004; Emmons & McCullough, 2003; Emmons & Mishra, 2011). Interestingly, engaging in this reflection once per week actually appears to be more beneficial than multiple times per week, to keep the practice meaningful (Lyubomirsky, Sheldon, & Schkade, 2005). Related powerful strategies for developing gratitude include keeping a gratitude journal over time in which students can write about people, things, and events that occur in their day to day lives for which they are thankful and writing a letter (which can later be delivered) expressing appreciation to a person in the past who the students recall as someone who was particularly helpful to them.

"Practice random acts of kindness" is a trendy directive to hopefully bolster goodwill and benevolence for others. Although the "random" aspect implies some-thing unexpected or unplanned for which the surprise can add to the positive experience, coaches can also recommend that students practice intentional acts of kindness. Finding ways to be helpful and/or kind to others almost always yields positive feelings on the part of the doer and receiver. Helping others through engag-ing in volunteer work and service learning is associated with increased well-being, although the process through which this occurs is still in need of further research (Piliavin, 2003; Schwartz, 2007). Lyubomirsky, Sheldon, and Schkade (2005) reported that being intentional about doing several kind deeds one day per week increased well-being in students more than in students who did occasional kind acts throughout the week or in a control group. Altruism is a common human trait, although its expression among individuals can vary depending on familial and cul-tural influences, especially when faced with societal challenges. When students are provided with suggestions or opportunities, their prosocial behavior may increase (Barber, 2004). In addition, practicing loving-kindness meditation, in which the person quietly and mindfully contemplates warm feelings first toward oneself and then to others, was found to increase positive emotions which led to increases in self-acceptance, social support, and life satisfaction, and decreases in physical symptoms (Fredrickson, Cohn, Coffey, Pek, & Finkel, 2008).

When positive experiences occur in life, savoring allows one to expand and continue the positive emotions connected to the experience, and thereby the wellness benefits of these emotions. Students can be encouraged to savor positive experiences through several strategies. First, being fully present when experiencing something enjoyable or rewarding and mindfully taking in the experience through all of one's senses can heighten the positive impact. Sharing the experience or accomplishment with supportive others either in person or via social media offers an extension of the experience through retelling what occurred. Displaying mementos or pictures of the experience in one's room or office can serve as a reminder of the experience, such as a spring break vacation. Keeping connected with other people, places, or organizations involved in the experience also promotes savoring the experience. For a thorough review of the concept of savoring and a description of other ways of savoring, see Bryant and Veroff (2007).

Presenting a variety of strategies for building positive emotions allows students to choose what they believe will work best for them, although in most cases students should be encouraged to at least attempt a number of different strategies. Sheldon and Lyubomirsky (2004) suggested that the better the fit between the intervention and the person's interests, strengths, and culture, the more successful that activity will be in increasing positive emotions. Moreover, they also suggested considering labeling the activity for the content of what it is (e.g., increasing gratitude) versus as a happiness raising exercise, to avoid a potential defeating effect of overfocusing on the happiness goal. Explaining these exercises as interventions to increase overall wellness that will help lead to goal achievement may be preferable. Whether students are reflecting on what went well in their week, expressing gratitude, or doing a kind act, it is important for the student to take time to fully connect to the positive emotion rather than carrying out the activity as only a cognitive exercise (Fredrickson, 2009). Again, it is the felt experience of the positive emotion that can facilitate success. Furthermore, recognizing that one was intentional about creating the positive emotion can contribute to greater self-efficacy.

Focusing on Strengths

Similar to emphasizing positive emotions, identifying and using strengths is a major contribution of positive psychology that is also useful in life coaching.

When I have asked students to list their strengths or positive qualities, they often quickly write five to seven areas, pause for a few moments as they reflect more deeply, and perhaps come up with a few more to add to the list, and then get stuck. Surely, they have more than a handful of strengths, but they often find it difficult to think of them. This may be because thinking of their strengths is not something they typically do, they may not consider a particular strength as a strength, they may have a cultural norm to be humble, or they may feel uncomfortable with self-identifying strengths. Mood also can influence the number of strengths listed, with feelings of depression tending to cause more trouble with this activity. Using an established strengths assessment such as the VIA survey (Peterson & Seligman, 2004) or the StrengthsFinder (Rath, 2007), two of the most widely used strengths assessments, can provide students with additional ideas and language when describing their strengths. Besides asking directly about strengths, a coach can ask other exploratory questions such as "What are you doing when you are at your best?" "Tell me about something you are looking forward to," "Describe one of your greatest past accomplishments," or "What have others said to you about what they like about you or what you do well?". To spot strengths from students' responses, listen closely and look for changes in tone and energy level (Biswas-Diener, 2010; Linley & Burns, 2010). Having students identify their strengths has a number of benefits and applications including facilitating increased self-awareness, understanding of how they can contribute in a diverse group, seeing strengths in others, selecting extracurricular activities (e.g., participation in campus or community organizations), and making a career choice (Shushok & Hulme, 2006).

Identifying strengths can be constructive by itself, but additional value comes in applying one's strengths. Govindji and Linley (2007) reported that knowledge of strengths and use of strengths are positively correlated. Both variables were also correlated with different measures of well-being, but not surprisingly strengths use seemed to have a stronger impact than knowledge of one's strengths. Students who learn to apply their strengths in different areas of their lives, especially when it comes to the pursuit of their coaching goals, are more likely to be successful in achieving their goals by directly using their best tools and the consequent increase in positive emotions (Fredrickson, 2009). Applying strengths to areas of interests and goals can contribute to a state of flow, in which students are fully engaged in and absorbed in an activity, and thereby exercises their strengths muscles so to speak. Coaches also can discuss with students how they can use their strengths, perhaps in new ways, by providing service to individuals, groups, or communities (Kauffman, 2006). Based on their qualitative research, Bowers and Lopez (2010) suggested that capitalizing on strengths is influenced by social support which brings positive emotions, experiencing success which engenders hope, and feeling reinforced to use strengths because of the beneficial outcomes. All of these factors can be attended to in the life coaching process by exploring how students use their strengths, the factors that influence strengths use, and the outcomes experienced when applying strengths.

Beyond identifying and using strengths is the dynamic concept of strengths development (Biswas-Diener, Kashdan, & Minhas, 2011). Through practicing using one's strengths, strengths can be further developed. Even when it comes to strengths, there typically can be room for growth or refinement. Coaches should also discuss with students when and where they can optimally use their strengths. There may be some occasions when students may not want to use strengths. For example, a student who has outstanding skills in organization and who can be detail oriented can benefit from applying these strengths when it comes to a number of different activities including working on class assignments or arranging events for an extracurricular club. However, there can be a point in the process when action steps need to be implemented and the detailed planning needs to play less of a role. Thus, the context or situation in which strengths are applied is important.

Strengths may be manifested in different ways depending on students' interests, values, and culture. For example, individuals strong in leadership could pursue being a rabbi or a CEO, depending on their interests and backgrounds. Furthermore, examining and developing a profile of strengths may be more useful than thinking about one strength at a time, as strengths may interact with each other in unique ways. Talking with students about these different aspects of strengths development can facilitate their self-awareness and thriving (Biswas-Diener et al., 2011).

A final comment about strengths applies to staff and faculty members themselves. Taking time to consider students' strengths while working with them can help the staff member change or at least balance any potential negative judgments or biases that may occur. For example, if a student elicits feelings of frustration, considering her or his strengths allows that staff or faculty member to see the whole person and see more possibilities for the student. Being mindful of students' strengths is useful not just in coaching, but in other contexts as well such as teaching, advising, and counseling. Moreover, a staff member who knows her or his own strengths can use those in providing coaching services.

Cultural Considerations in Life Coaching with Students

For organization and flow, this section on cultural considerations is near the end of the chapter, however, it is regarded as a primary consideration. The concepts of and within life coaching, as within positive psychology in general, are not inherently positive but their meanings are culturally embedded (Pedrotti, Edwards,

& Lopez, 2009). Individuals across different countries report various levels of subjective well-being and positive affect, and along with these differences, the strategies to increase wellbeing need to fit for the individual given her/his culture (Diener & Tov, 2009; Pedrotti, et al., 2009). Similarly, what it means to be happy, live well, or function at an optimal level can differ within and between cultural groups. Examples of these differences might include personal development, accomplishments or performance, social harmony, balance, material possessions, personal enlightenment, or serenity (Diener & Biswas-Diener, 2008; Leong & Wong, 2003; Snyder, Lopez, & Pedrotti, 2011). Thus, when coaching students, it is essential to assess what happiness, success, and achievement means to them as individuals, and to recognize that these individual meanings will vary by cultural background and other demographic variables.

As previously discussed, how strengths are identified and used by students also is influenced by their background and culture (Pedrotti, et al., 2009). To help students appreciate the strengths in themselves and others, in a coaching group activity, the facilitator can ask students to write down their strengths, and then go around the room having each individual share one strength, but not repeat a strength that has been previously said. This experiential activity demonstrates that students in any group or team will bring different strengths. The exercise can also highlight how a diverse group of students can find value in working together when using their strengths, and how embracing these strengths can lead to success for the individual and group. The participants will be able to see that if they were working on a group project, they could tap the strengths of each individual in the group in deciding who is going to work on what aspects of the project and how they all might best work together, resulting in increased engagement and a successful outcome for their project. Having one's strengths identified by others may not be commonplace, and the encouragement to do so by a university staff member can have positive outcomes including demonstrating interest and support for the student and providing a valuable learning experience. This might be especially impactful when the coach and student are from different cultural backgrounds. Moreover, talking about strengths can provide a nonthreatening way to begin diversity related discussions (Shushok & Hulme, 2006).

Coaches should be careful not to be ethnocentric in considering the strengths of any individual. Underrepresented groups who may have experienced bias or prejudice from living in a society where they may not have as much power or privilege can be encouraged to examine what strengths they have developed as a result of managing through these experiences (Constantine & Sue, 2006). Chang and Banks (2007) found that the ethnic/racial minority groups of college students in their research (African Americans, Asian Americans, and Latinos) had as much if not more hope than Euro-Americans, despite, or as the researchers suggest, possibly because of anticipating obstacles toward meeting goals. Although potentially generated in different ways, hope is a positive expectancy that has benefits toward goal achievement across cultural groups. To uncover students' strengths, consider asking the questions cited above in the section on focusing on strengths.

Life coaching is about enhancing, growing, or improving aspects of one's self. The inherent driving force toward growth is a universal phenomenon. In addition, pursuing goals that are more self-concordant and intrinsic in nature has been found to predict well-being across different cultures (Kasser & Ryan, 2001; Sheldon, Elliot, Ryan, Chirkov, Kim, Wu, Demir, & Sun, 2004). However, as noted above, the specific direction and outcome of students' efforts and goals are determined by the individual, based on her or his values, interests, and culture. To this end, it is important for a coach to assess a student's cultural identity and be mindful of culture throughout the coaching process.

Case Study

David is a 20-year-old, multiracial (White/Hispanic) male, majoring in digital media. He saw a flyer on campus about a Life Coaching for Students workshop being held at his university counseling center and was interested in participating. At the initial meeting with the staff member leading the workshop, David expressed that he was doing fairly well in classes, but believed he could be more organized and manage his time better. He enjoyed his classes, had a good network of friends, and had a pleasant disposition, but often fell behind on his school work. In the first session of the workshop, David completed an exercise in which he rated the importance of and his satisfaction in different areas of his life. One area that he felt needed particular improvement was managing his finances, and this seemed to stem from his organization issues. His bank account had dipped below zero on several occasions and he had been assessed several banking fees. He understood the need to keep a balance in his account and to attend to it; however, this was one of the areas that got put off as he tried to catch up and keep up with the responsibilities and activities of college life.

The workshop that David participated in was 6 sessions, and it met weekly for one and a half hours. There were five students in the workshop including David. The four other students in the workshop had identified different goals. Natalia set goals around being in better physical shape by improving exercise and nutrition, Jayden aimed to complete his undergraduate honors thesis, Jessica wanted to figure out her future career plans, and Anita focused on wanting to develop and improve her friendships, finding it hard to balance time for school and friends. Each week in the workshop the leader began by incorporating a positive psychology coaching exercise such as sharing what went well during the week, and/or talking about topics such as goal setting and motivation. David found the activities of identifying his strengths and the interventions to increase his positive emotions to be refreshing, and he liked that the other students in the workshop also seemed engaged in the activities and process. The majority of the time in each session was spent focusing on each student's goals, initially creating a vision for their longer-term goals, and then each week writing down on 3 × 5 cards the short-term goals or action steps that they would commit to that week that would lead to achieving their ultimate goals. David kept his cards each week, and he later found it helpful to review his progress.

Through the group discussion, a first step identified for David was to talk with his bank about the assessed fees and determine what services or special accounts may be available to him. He had been avoiding talking with the bank, but, with the encouragement of the coach and the other students, he set a goal for the week to talk with his bank. Choosing a specific date and time helped him keep that commitment. He was excited to report back the next week that, much to his surprise, the banker he met with was very helpful and friendly and waived all but one of his fees. Building on this motivation, David set another goal to develop a budget for himself, something he had not done before. A couple workshop members shared ideas and helpful websites on how to get started, and David appreciated their support. The coach asked David to list the benefits of making and sticking to a budget and asked him to identify the reasons this was important to him. With that set, David turned his attention to increasing his income. The coach, David, and other group members brainstormed ideas for David including finding a parttime job (and resources to do so), offering tutoring in a class in which he was excelling but he knew others were struggling, organizing a fundraiser for his extracurricular club and his efforts would go toward his dues, becoming a mystery shopper, and other creative ideas. When David wrote about his best possible future self (King, 2001), a positive psychology intervention that was done in the workshop, he described being financially secure and confident, among other positive aspects of his life, and this reinforced his commitment to his goals. David commented that it felt good to envision himself in the future in this positive way.

David made significant progress toward his goals and toward his feeling that he was thriving as a student. David's accomplishments each week led to him feeling increased hope and optimism. His success also bolstered his motivation in other areas of his life. Having the accountability of the weekly workshop helped David stay on track with his budgeting and other action steps. He felt inspired by seeing others in the workshop make progress on their goals. At the end of the 6-week workshop, the members decided to make a Facebook group to continue their efforts. Although not addressed during the workshop, David said he planned to start getting organized and managing his time better in other areas of life, such as academics, and he felt confident in his ability to meet this next goal.

Conclusion

Nutrition is widely known to be one of the most critical factors for an individual's physical health. Those who eat unhealthy meals, overindulge in eating, skip meals, or otherwise do not give attention to their food consumption suffer health consequences including low energy, weight gain, and hypertension. In contrast, maintaining a relatively balanced, healthy diet allows the body to maintain homeostasis and function normally. People can also take their nutrition another step by being committed to following guidelines of eating plenty of fruits and vegetables, understanding ingredients, eating in moderation, and limiting unhealthy foods. This attention to nutrition, combined with an appropriate amount of exercise, will generally lead to excellent physical health and aid the body to function at an optimal level.

Life coaching, particularly from a positive psychology perspective, is like the nutrition of mental health. There are many personal issues and distractions in life that can lead to stress, depression, and falling short of achieving goals. However, with social support and other effective ways of coping, individuals can manage through the inevitable life challenges and live relatively happy and productive lives. People can also take their well-being another step by seeking out a life coach and incorporating the positive psychology strategies described in this chapter and book. This further attention can lead to successful accomplishment of goals, optimal performance, and living a thriving and flourishing life.

Overall wellness/well-being and success in college is likely a reciprocal relationship, although aspects of wellness including positive emotions have been shown to unilaterally facilitate beneficial outcomes, as described previously. College and university staff who take on the role of a life coach can help students understand this relationship and encourage the implementation of relevant strategies that lead to success. Within academic settings, coaches can educate students on the scientific and practical research findings related to positive psychology, happiness and well-being, goal setting, and achievement.

Several institutions have incorporated academic coaching that has contributed to the retention and success of students. The focus discussed in this chapter is on life coaching, of which academics are an important piece for students. That is, life coaching for students may focus on academic performance, but it may instead or in addition address other aspects and goals of students' lives. From a holistic wellness perspective, when gains are made in one area, they can have a positive impact and facilitate gains in other areas of life. The learning outcomes for students actively participating in a coaching relationship include understanding and being able to apply the process and steps of achieving goals. Student success breeds further hope, resiliency, and success. Life coaching with students allows colleges and universities to develop students' skills and approaches for enhanced performance in academics and other realms that not only contribute to productive and engaged students, but to the development of healthy, thriving alumni after the students graduate and take this knowledge with them. With colleges and universities always on the lookout for valuable initiatives to enhance student success, life coaching for students is a promising endeavor.

References

Achor, S. (2010). *The happiness advantage: The seven principles of positive psychology that fuel success and performance at work.* New York: Crown Business.

Barber, N. (2004). *Kindness in a cruel world: The evolution of altruism.* Amherst, NY: Prometheus Books.

Biswas-Diener, R. (2010). *Practicing positive psychology coaching: Assessment, activities, and strategies for success.* Hoboken, NJ: John Wiley & Sons, Inc.

Biswas-Diener, R., & Dean, B. (2007). *Positive psychology coaching: Putting the science of happiness to work for your clients.* Hoboken, NJ: John Wiley & Sons, Inc.

Biswas-Diener, R., Kashdan, T. B., & Minhas, G. (2011). A dynamic approach to psychological strength development and intervention. *Journal of Positive Psychology, 6,* 106–118. doi:10.10 80/17439760.2010.545429

Boehm, J. K., & Lyubomirsky, S. (2008). Does happiness promote career success? *Journal of Career Assessment, 16,* 101–116. doi:10.1177/1069072707308140

Bono, G., Emmons, R. A., & McCullough, M. E. (2004). Gratitude in practice and the practice of gratitude. In P. Linley, S. Joseph (Eds.), *Positive psychology in practice* (pp. 464–481). Hoboken, NJ: John Wiley & Sons Inc.

Bowers, K. M., & Lopez, S. J. (2010). Capitalizing on personal strengths in college. *Journal of College & Character, 11*(1), 1–11. doi:10.2202/1940-1639.1011

Bryant, F. B., & Veroff, J. (2007). *Savoring: A new model of positive experience.* Mahwah, NJ: Lawrence Erlbaum Associates.

Chang, E., C., & Banks, K. S. (2007). The color and texture of hope: Some preliminary findings and implications for hope theory and counseling among diverse racial/ethnic groups. *Cultural Diversity and Ethnic Minority Psychology, 13,* 94–103. doi:10.1037/1099-9809.13.2.94

Constantine, M. G., & Sue, D. W. (2006). Factors contributing to optimal human functioning in people of color in the United States. *The Counseling Psychologist, 34,* 228–244. doi:10.1177/0011000005281318

Diener, E., & Biswas-Diener, R. (2008). *Happiness: Unlocking the mysteries of psychological wealth.* Malden, MA: Blackwell Publishing.

Diener, E., & Tov, W. (2009). Well-being on planet earth. *Psychological Topics, 18,* 213–219.

Emmons, R. A., & McCullough, M. E. (2003). Counting blessings versus burdens: An experimental investigation of gratitude and subjective well-being in daily life. *Journal of Personality and Social Psychology, 84,* 377–389. doi:10.1037/0022-3514.84.2.377

Emmons, R. A., & Mishra, A. (2011). Why gratitude enhances well-being: What we know, what we need to know. In K. M. Sheldon, T. B. Kashdan, M. F. Steger (Eds.), *Designing positive psychology: Taking stock and moving forward* (pp. 248–262). New York: Oxford University Press. doi:10.1093/acprof:oso/9780195373585.003.0016

Fredrickson, B. L. (1998). What good are positive emotions? *Review of General Psychology, 2,* 300–319. doi:10.1037/1089-2680.2.3.300

Fredrickson, B. L. (2001). The role of positive emotions in positive psychology: The broaden-and-build theory of positive emotions. *American Psychologist, 56,* 218–226. doi:10.1037//0003-066X.56.3.218

Fredrickson, B. L. (2009). *Positivity*. New York: Crown Publishers.

Fredrickson, B. L. (2013a). Positive emotions broaden and build. In P. Devine & A. Plant (Eds.), *Advances in experimental social psychology* (Vol. 47, pp. 1–54). San Diego, CA: Academic Press.

Fredrickson, B. L. (2013b). Updated thinking on positivity ratios. *American Psychologist, 68*, 814–822. doi:10.1037/a0033584

Fredrickson, B. L., Cohn, M. A., Coffey, K. A., Pek, J., & Finkel, S. M. (2008). Open hearts build lives: Positive emotions, induced through loving-kindness meditation, build consequential personal resources. *Journal of Personality and Social Psychology, 95*, 1045–1062. doi:10.1037/a0013262

Fredrickson, B. L., & Joiner, T. (2002). Positive emotions trigger upward spirals toward emotional well-being. *Psychological Science, 13*, 172–175.

Gilbert, D. (2006). *Stumbling on happiness*. New York: A.A. Knopf.

Govindji, R., & Linley, P. A. (2007). Strengths use, self-concordance, and well-being: Implications for strengths coaching and coaching psychologists. *International Coaching Psychology Review, 2*, 143–153.

Grant, A. M. (2006). An integrative goal-focused approach to executive coaching. In D. R. Stober, & A. M. Grant (Eds.), *Evidence based coaching handbook: Putting best practices to work for your clients* (pp. 153–192). Hoboken, NJ: John Wiley & Sons, Inc.

Grant, A. M. (2011). *Workplace, executive and life coaching: An annotated bibliography from the behavioural science and business literature*. Coaching Psychology Unit, University of Sydney, Australia.

Grant, A. M., Cavanagh, M. J., Parker, H. M., & Passmore, J. (2010). The state of play in coaching today: A comprehensive review of the field. In G. P. Hodgkinson, & J. K. Ford (Eds.), *International Review of Industrial and Organizational Psychology* (Vol. 25, pp. 126–167). Hoboken, NJ: John Wiley & Sons, Ltd.

Grant, A. M., Curtayne, L., & Burton, G. (2009). Executive coaching enhances goal attainment, resilience and workplace well-being: A randomised controlled study. *Journal of Positive Psychology, 4*, 396–407. doi:10.1080/17439760902992456

Jacobi, M. (1991). Mentoring and undergraduate academic success: A literature review. *Review of Educational Research, 61*, 505–532. doi:10.3102/00346543061004505

Kasser, T., & Ryan, R. M. (2001). Be careful what you wish for: Optimal functioning and the relative attainment of intrinsic and extrinsic goals. In P. Schmuck & K. M. Sheldon (Eds.), *Life goals and well-being: Towards a positive psychology of human striving* (pp. 116–131). Kirkland, WA: Hogrefe & Huber Publishers.

Kauffman, C. (2006). Positive psychology: The science at the heart of coaching. In D. R. Stober, & A. M. Grant (Eds.), *Evidence based coaching handbook: Putting best practices to work for your clients* (pp. 219–253). Hoboken, NJ: John Wiley & Sons, Inc.

Kilburg, R. R. (1996). Toward a conceptual understanding and definition of executive coaching. *Consulting Psychology Journal: Practice and Research, 48*, 134–144. doi:10.1037/1061-4087.48.2.134

King, L. A. (2008). Personal goals and life dreams: Positive psychology and motivation in daily life. In J. Y. Shah and W. L. Gardner (Eds.), *Handbook of motivation science* (pp. 569–578). New York: Guilford Press.

King, L. A. (2001). The health benefits of writing about life goals. *Personality and Social Psychology Bulletin, 27*, 798–807. doi:10.1177/0146167201277003

Kuh, G. D., Kinzie, J., Schuh, J. H., Whitt, E. J., & Associates (2005). *Student success in college: Creating conditions that matter*. San Francisco: Jossey-Bass.

Leong, F. T. L., & Wong, P. T. P. (2003). Optimal human functioning from cross-cultural perspectives: Cultural competence as an organizing framework. In W. B. Walsh (Ed.), *Counseling psychology and optimal human functioning* (pp. 123–150). Mahwah, NJ: Lawrence Erlbaum Associates.

Linley, P. A., & Burns, G. W. (2010). Strengthsspotting: Finding and developing client resources in the management of intense anger. In G. W. Burns (Ed.), *Happiness, healing, enhancement: Your casebook collection for applying positive psychology in therapy* (pp. 3–14). Hoboken, NJ: John Wiley & Sons.

Linley, P. A., & Joseph, S. (2004). Applied positive psychology: A new perspective for professional practice. In P. A. Linley & S. Joseph (Eds.), *Positive psychology in practice* (pp. 3–12). Hoboken, NJ: John Wiley & Sons, Inc.

Linley, P. A, Joseph, S., Maltby, J., Harrington, S., & Wood, A. M. (2009). Positive psychology applications. In S. J. Lopez & C. R. Snyder (Eds.), *Oxford handbook of positive psychology* (pp. 35–47). New York: Oxford University Press, Inc.

Lundberg, C. A., & Schreiner, L. A. (2004). Quality and frequency of faculty-student interaction as predictors of learning: An analysis by student race/ethnicity. *Journal of College Student Development, 45,* 549–565. doi:10.1353/csd.2004.0061

Lyubomirsky, S., King, L., & Diener, E. (2005). The benefits of frequent positive affect: Does happiness lead to success? *Psychological Bulletin, 6,* 803–855. doi:10.1037/0033-2909.131.6.803

Lyubomirsky, S., Sheldon, K. M., & Schkade, D. (2005). Pursuing happiness: The architecture of sustainable change. *Review of General Psychology, 9,* 111–131. doi:10.1037/1089-2680.9.2.111

Maslow, A. H. (1954). *Motivation and personality.* New York: Harper & Row.

Pavot, W., & Diener, E. (2004). Findings on subjective well-being: Applications to public policy, clinical interventions, and education. In P. A. Linley & S. Joseph (Eds.), *Positive psychology in practice* (pp. 679–692). Hoboken, NJ: John Wiley & Sons, Inc.

Piliavin, J. A. (2003). Doing well by doing good: Benefits for the benefactor. In C. L. M. Keyes & J. Haidt (Eds.), *Flourishing: Positive psychology and the life well-lived* (pp. 227–247). Washington, DC: American Psychological Association.

Pedrotti, J. T., Edwards, L. M., & Lopez, S. J. (2009). Positive psychology within a cultural context. In S. J. Lopez & C. R. Snyder (Eds.), *Oxford handbook of positive psychology* (pp. 49–57). New York: Oxford University Press.

Peterson, C., & Seligman, M. E. P. (2004). *Character strengths and virtues: A handbook and classification.* Washington, DC: American Psychological Association.

Prochaska, J. O., Norcross, J. C., & DiClemente, C. C. (2013). Applying the stages of change. In G. P. Koocher, J. C. Norcross, & B. A. Greene (Eds.), *Psychologists' desk reference* (3rd ed.) (pp. 176–181). New York: Oxford University Press.

Rath, T. (2007). *StrengthsFinder 2.0.* New York: Gallup Press.

Reeve, J. (2002). Self-determination theory applied to education settings. In E. L. Deci & R. M. Ryan (Eds.), *Handbook of self-determination research* (pp. 183–203). Rochester, NY: University of Rochester Press.

Robinson, C., & Gahagan, J. (2010). In practice: Coaching students to academic success and engagement on campus. *About Campus, 15*(4), 26–29. doi:10.1002/abc.20032

Ryff, C. D. (1989). Happiness is everything, or is it? Explorations on the meaning of psychological well-being. *Journal of Personality and Social Psychology, 57,* 1069–1081. doi:10.1037/0022-3514.57.6.1069

Ryff, C. D. (2014). Psychological well-being revisited: Advances in the science and practice of eudaimonia. *Psychotherapy and Psychosomatics, 83,* 10–28. doi:10.1159/000353263

Schreiner, L. A. (2010a, May/June). The "thriving quotient." *About Campus, 15*(2), 2–10. doi:10.1002/abc.20016

Schreiner, L. A. (2010b, July/August). Thriving in the classroom. *About Campus, 15*(3), 2–10. doi:10.1002/abc.20022

Schreiner, L. A. (2010c, September/October). Thriving in community. *About Campus, 15*(4), 2–11. doi:10.1002/abc.20029

Schreiner, L. A., Hulme, E., Hetzel, R., & Lopez, S. J. (2009). positive psychology on campus. In S. J. Lopez & C. R. Snyder (Eds.), *Oxford handbook of positive psychology* (pp. 569–578). New York: Oxford University Press, Inc.

Schreiner, L. A., Noel, P., Anderson, E., & Cantwell, L. (2011). The impact of faculty and staff on high-risk college student persistence. *Journal of College Student Development, 52*, 321–338. doi:10.1353/csd.2011.0044

Schwartz, C. (2007). Altruism and subjective well-being: Conceptual model and empirical support. In S. G. Post (Ed.), *Altruism and health: Perspectives from empirical research* (pp. 33–42). New York: Oxford University Press.

Seligman, M. E. P. (2011). *Flourish: A visionary new understanding of happiness and well-being.* New York: Free Press.

Seligman, M. E. P., Steen, T. A., Park, N., & Peterson, C. (2005). Positive psychology progress: Empirical validation of interventions. *American Psychologist, 60*, 410–421. doi:10.1037/0003-066X.60.5.410

Sheldon, K. M. (2001). The self-concordance model of healthy goal striving: When personal goals correctly represent the person. In P. Schmuck & K. M. Sheldon (Eds.), *Life goals and well-being: Towards a positive psychology of human striving* (pp. 19–36). Kirkland, WA: Hogrefe & Huber Publishers.

Sheldon, K., Elliot, A., Ryan, R., Chirkov, V., Kim, Y., Wu, C., Demir, M., & Sun, Z. (2004). Self-concordance and subjective well-being in four cultures. *Journal of Cross-Cultural Psychology, 35*, 209–223. doi:10.1177/0022022103262245

Sheldon, K. M., & Schmuck, P. (2001). Suggestions for healthy goal striving. In P. Schmuck & K. M. Sheldon (Eds.), *Life goals and well-being: Towards a positive psychology of human striving* (pp. 216–230). Kirkland, WA: Hogrefe & Huber Publishers.

Sheldon, K. M., & Lyubomirsky, S. (2004). Achieving sustainable new happiness: Prospects, practices, and prescriptions. In P. A. Linley & S. Joseph (Eds.), *Positive psychology in practice* (pp. 127–145). Hoboken, NJ: John Wiley & Sons, Inc.

Sheldon, K. M., & Lyubomirsky, S. (2006). Achieving sustainable gains in happiness: Change your actions, not your circumstances. *Journal of Happiness Studies, 7*, 55–86. doi:10.1007/s10902-005-0868-8

Shushok, F., & Hulme, E. (2006, September/October). What's right with you: Helping students find and use their personal strengths. *About Campus, 11*(4), 2–8. doi:10.1002/abc.173

Snyder, C. R. (2002). Hope theory: Rainbows in the mind. *Psychological Inquiry, 13*, 249–275. doi:10.1207/S15327965PLI1304_01

Snyder, C. R., Lopez, S. J., & Pedrotti, J. T. (2011). *Positive psychology: The scientific and practical explorations of human strengths* (2nd ed.). Los Angeles: Sage Publications.

Stober, D. R., & Grant, A. M. (2006). Toward a contextual approach to coaching models. In D. R. Stober & A. M. Grant (Eds.), *Evidence based coaching handbook: Putting best practices to work for your clients* (pp. 355–365). Hoboken, NJ: John Wiley & Sons, Inc.

Whitmore, J. (1992). *Coaching for performance.* London: Nicholas Brealey.

Whitworth, L., Kimsey-House, K., Kimsey-House, H., & Sandahl, P. (2007). *Co-active coaching: New skills for coaching people toward success in work and life.* Boston: Davies-Black.

Williams, P., & Davis, D. C. (2007). *Therapist as life coach: An introduction for counselors and other helping professionals* (Revised and Expanded). New York: W. W. Norton & Company.

15

Creating a Positive Campus Culture

TIM HODGES AND JESSICA KENNEDY

Mainstream and social media outlets love antacid-popping headlines from college campuses about campus violence, grade inflation, cheating, and ill-advised choices by members of a campus community. Fortunately, those same media channels are getting better about celebrating positive news, student accomplishments, and meaningful breakthroughs also coming from education.

This chapter seeks to provide answers to the question posed by Don Clifton, the American Psychological Association's Father of Strengths Psychology: "What would happen if we studied what is right with people?" (Lopez, Hodges, & Harter, 2005, p. 3).

The past several years have included many advances in the field of Positive Psychology (see Lopez & Snyder, 2011 for a review). Included in the many areas of study have been several constructs with implications for improving the health of our campus communities. Many institutions of higher education focus efforts on studying what is right with people and developing ways to build more positive cultures on their campuses.

The research is emerging, expansive, and encouraging because it builds upon approaches around strengths, hope, engagement, and well-being within campus communities. These four constructs will receive primary attention in this chapter in part because they meet three key criteria for inclusion:

1. Each has demonstrated reliable measurement properties.
2. Each has meaningful relationships with outcomes that lead to success for students.
3. Each is malleable and can be enhanced through deliberate action.

Although each of the topics covered here (strengths, hope, engagement, and well-being) meet these criteria on their own merit, they have also been studied in relationship to one another and have been found complimentary in pursuit of improving student success (Lopez, 2012).

Strengths

Following Clifton's directive to focus on people's positive attributes, a team of Gallup researchers undertook a major research project focused on studying the characteristics of successful people. The population studied included individuals from a wide range of occupations, including full-time students. The criterion used to identify successful individuals was specific to the role and included measures such as sales volume, customer service ratings, attendance, turnover, satisfaction, and a variety of other outcome measures (see Asplund, Lopez, Hodges, & Harter, 2009 for a more in-depth description of the research). Scientists conducted in-depth interviews, focus groups, and surveys in an effort to understand attributes leading to success. Over time, and across a wide variety of roles and types of groups, the researchers began to see distinct patterns in people's responses. Regardless of the task at hand or the situation in which they found themselves, successful people tended to find a unique ways of doing things. These "naturally recurring patterns of thought, feeling, or behavior that can be productively applied" later were termed "talents" (Hodges & Clifton, 2004, p. 257). These talents represent the inherent potential inside each person. Talent can be combined with knowledge and skills to form strengths, defined as the abilities to produce "consistent, near-perfect performance in a given activity" (Clifton & Anderson, 2002, p. 8). In 2001, Gallup launched StrengthsFinder (later renamed "Clifton StrengthsFinder" after Don Clifton's death in 2003), an online talent assessment utilized by millions of people (Asplund, Lopez, Hodges, & Harter, 2009).

Although Gallup's discoveries in strengths science included a broad study of success across many roles, much of the original theory building and field testing was completed by educators and students. Many of the early "strengths champions" were in higher education. These research leaders convened several gatherings and dedicated their research efforts to the study of strengths assessment and development. They presented findings at major academic conferences including the American Psychological Association and the Academy of Management. By putting what they learned into action on campus, these scholars' efforts aided in the development of the "StrengthsQuest" curriculum (Clifton & Anderson, 2002; Clifton, Anderson, & Schreiner, 2006) to assist students in developing strengths in general academic life, study techniques, relationships, class selection, and extracurricular activities.

After a thorough literature review, Lopez & Louis (2009) introduced a five-stage process of strengths development. The first stage involves assessing the student and educator's strengths, along with consideration of achievements and other factors leading to positive outcomes. The assessment utilized in many of the studies was the Clifton StrengthsFinder, often introduced as a component of the StrengthsQuest program for students. Second, individualizing the student interaction with strengths allows the development process to become real and personal to the individual student, taking into account their unique goals, needs, and interests. Third, cultivating relationships was found to be key to the development process. Sharing results and having conversations with meaningful peers, advisors, and mentors provides a context for encouragement and feedback and builds relevance for strengths language and practice through integration into the daily experience. Fourth, involving the thoughtful application of strengths both in and outside the classroom context is critical to strengths development. This often involves (1) classroom experiences in strengths-based teaming or (2) written assignments designed for further process one's unique strengths. Outside the classroom, common contexts for strengths application include new student orientation, residence life programming, student government, and activities associated with the campus career center. Finally, the ongoing process of strengths development requires intentional effort. Strengths are not to be seen as an outcome in and of themselves but rather as a lens through which one can more positively approach his or her life. Intentionally and frequently revisiting the strengths feedback over time can help build this more positive approach.

Hundreds of college and university campuses have made the investment to provide a context for strengths discovery and development (see Lewis, 2009, 2012 for a review), and a variety of approaches have been applied to introduce strengths to students. Although many factors lead to the success of any developmental intervention, the most successful seem to have certain themes in common and in terms of successful strengths development program. Lopez (2012) provides several tips:

- Program goals must be clearly specified. Simply "doing strengths" without a goal in mind will not likely yield as successful outcomes.
- Successful strengths development tends to follow best practices outlined in the literature and have intentional follow-through.
- Quality research often includes participant pre- and post-testing, as well as control groups, to better understand the change able to be attributed to the specific strengths program.

Although the context for strengths development varies widely, common settings for strengths development include new student orientation seminars, sophomore experience programs, residence life, leadership classes, student organizations, and programs offered through career centers.

Case Study: Strengths Development at a Large
Midwestern Public University

Among the many success stories of strengths development on campus, one large Midwestern public institution stands out for its inclusive approach, focused effort, and research rigor. Although its 3-year effort primarily focused on nearly 20,000 first-year and transfer students, the institution has also involved more than 5,000 faculty and staff and thousands of parents, alumni, and other members of the extended campus community. A cross-disciplinary office orchestrated consistent efforts while preserving the local culture necessary to integrate strengths into the daily activity on campus.

The institution had big goals from the beginning. Organizers believed a common language across campus would help facilitate integrated strengths thinking and action. More importantly, leaders did not just set out to "do strengths" as an outcome of its own, rather strengths development was purposively integrated with campus objectives including increased appreciation of others, self-awareness, confidence, goal pursuit, overall retention, graduation, and student satisfaction.

Campus research leaders were involved from the start, reviewing an extensive list of campus surveys, data sources, and success markers to understand the overall student experience. Nearly all students completed the Clifton StrengthsFinder during orientation or in their first few days on campus. In addition, the institution conducted frequent surveys to obtain information about student activity and performance. These surveys were collected at the beginning and end of the first semester and at the end of the spring semester of students' freshman and sophomore years. Qualitative data were collected throughout the study, adding a richness and explanatory power to the story.

The initiative seems to be working. Preliminary evidence suggests several areas in which strengths development is progressing towards the intended goals. Student retention and GPA is higher among students participating in the strengths development programs. Participants report feeling a higher sense of belonging and believe that they are making more progress towards the institution's learning and development outcomes. Students report that higher levels of self-awareness aided their career planning efforts. There also seems to be an additive effect of strengths development: students with more frequent interactions with strengths programming also had improved levels of student engagement.

The institution was intent on addressing the needs of all student populations and was pleased to find that recipients of Pell grants who took the Clifton StrengthsFinder had higher first- and second-year retention rates. Moreover, students who reported having strengths discussions had higher academic self-efficacy, hope, and engagement than their peers who did not report having strengths discussions. Students of color also seemed to benefit from the programming, with higher participation rates and self-reported levels of leadership development, community service, and overall satisfaction than White students in their cohort. It appears that the institution's focus on strengths development is helping students and the overall campus progress towards important goals.

Hope

Hope is not to be brushed aside or looked down upon as a frivolous concept. Science shows that hope is a significant determinant of individual success across a range of roles covering both college and career (Lopez, 2013).

Do you believe the future will be better than the present, and that you play an active role in making that belief a reality? If so, psychologists would likely refer to you as a hopeful person (Lopez, 2013). Hope has been studied for decades, with its recent resurgence beginning in the early 1990s by C. R. "Rick" Snyder (Snyder, et al., 1991) and continuing through the work of Shane Lopez (Lopez, 2013). The Lopez and Snyder framework of hope involves both agency and pathways thinking. Agency, based on Bandura's (2001) work, involves the belief that one can play an active and important role in his or her own situation. Pathways thinking acknowledges that we will all be faced with challenges and setbacks, and that we should draw on a variety of resources and think of many possible ways to persist in overcoming these situations (Snyder, 1994). A broad body of research looks at the effects of hope across many contexts, most notably in the workplace and in education.

The word "hope" has been used widely in popular culture, the media, and even politics, and in some ways it has been watered down or used to mean many different things. However, in the educational arena, there is significant rigor around the definition of hope. Although not significantly related to income (Gallup, 2009a) or native intelligence (Snyder, McDermott, Cook, & Rapoff, 2002), researchers have discovered a link between hope and educational goals of attendance, credits earned, and academic achievement (Gallup, 2009b). For instance, "hopeful" students have higher college grade point averages than their less hopeful peers (Gallagher and Lopez, 2008; Snyder, Shorey et al., 2002). Furthermore, hope's predictive power remained significant even when controlling for high school grade point average or scores on college entrance exams such as the ACT or SAT (Gallagher and Lopez, 2008; Snyder, Shorey et al., 2002).

Hope is often observable, because hopeful students carry themselves with a different level of energy and enthusiasm, as well as demonstrate critical thinking skills. They regularly think about and talk about the future, making their current experiences more relevant and powerful in the context of their contributions to future success. Hopeful students are not Pollyannas; however, they bring a healthy sense of realism about the difficulties and obstacles life throws at them. Rather than being surprised and discouraged about these obstacles, hopeful students know these contests are a part of life, planning accordingly and reframing them as challenges to be overcome in pursuit of a goal. Using this approach, they are likely to come up with multiple pathways to a successful outcome, and, as a result, hopeful students often experience less damaging amounts of stress, frustration, loss of confidence, and lowered self-esteem than their stuck or discouraged peers (Snyder, 1994).

Thankfully, hope is malleable and can be increased through relatively simple strategies. Institutions of higher education are often filled with departments offering resources to support students in their time of need—academic advising, writing centers, and student organizations with numerous opportunities to access relevant content, relationships, and experiences. The key for campus leaders is to clearly communicate what resources are available to students and to do so in ways that break through the message clutter all around students today.

- Campuses can nurture hope in students by better organizing and promoting the many available resources available to students who are stuck or discouraged, to provide or remove financial or social barriers to getting assistance.
- Too many students have their first meaningful interaction with the career center near the end of their time on campus. Many career centers are redefining their mission and practice in an effort to better support students throughout their college experience by helping students understand what a good job can look like and by exposing them to the many possible future pathways beyond graduation.
- Campuses need to embrace social media and other electronic forms of communication to provide multiple channels for students to receive this critical information and provide interventions.
- Higher education often loses students in times of transition, including the transition from high school to college, from first to second semester of the freshman year, and from freshman to sophomore year (Foote, Hinkle, Kranzow, Pistilli, Rease Miles, & Simmons, 2013). This attrition could be reduced through the work of hopeful students at the next phase of the collegiate experience who can serve as a sort of "cultural broker," helping students in transition see a realistic and relevant model of what is possible in the future.

Case Study: Hope at a Public 2-Year College

Advances in hope research have caught the attention of institutional research and student affairs professionals. Among the many institutions focused on the measurement and development of student hope is a large public Community College serving students in the Western United States. Their story involves two main components: (1) measuring student hope and studying it in relation to student outcomes and (2) investing in faculty better prepared to build hope in students.

The institution's strategic vision is vested in the relationship between hope and student success and championed by top leadership. Adding items from the hope scale (Snyder et al., 1991) to the Accuplacer assessment (a test to determine readiness for college-level work in reading, mathematics, and writing) allowed the institution access to the baseline hope levels of thousands of prospective students. Armed with this baseline hope measurement, a cohort of more than 600 first-time college students enrolled in the institution. Student success measures were collected at several momentum points, including the following: first semester course success and completion, persistence rates, and completion of 12 and 24 units of academic credit.

The initial results from this case study, consistent with previous research, indicated that high-hope students had meaningful observed differences (effect size differences of .20 or higher) than their low- or average-hope peers on many of the student success measures: higher first-semester success rates, persistence, and completion of both 12 and 24 units than their peers, suggesting that those students with sufficient ideas and energy for the future were able to better succeed in the college environment.

The institution also appreciated the developmental nature of hope and focused on fostering a more hopeful environment for all students. Believing it takes high-hope leaders to improve the institution's ability to foster student success, substantial efforts were made in faculty development. Instructors came together to address teaching strategies with a goal of ensuring that their student interactions were building the agentic nature of hope—helping the students know that they are an owner and an active participant in creating their desired future. Instead of simply accepting excuses, faculty attempted to respond with encourage language about what could be done differently or better next time. When giving homework assignments, instructors were more likely to use a "when-where" strategy (Gollwitzer, 1999), helping students visualize when they would complete the assignment and where they would be when doing it, helping break down barriers, and minimizing excuse-making and procrastination. Although the long-term effects of developing hope in students is still being studied, early feedback from students and faculty seems supportive of the refined and hopeful approach to student success.

Engagement

Think about the best educator you have ever known. What words or phrases would you use to describe him or her?

Rarely do we hear descriptors about the credentials of the professor, where they earned their doctorate, whether they are tenured or not, or how many top-tier articles they have authored, or how many millions of dollars in research grants they have won. Researchers have, in fact, found answers to the "best educator" question often revolve around certain themes: descriptors about how the instructor set their students up for success; how they made the classroom environment feel like a one-on-one conversation (even if it was a large lecture hall or online forum with hundreds of participants); and how the instructor helped the student prepare for a future that went beyond the content presented in the class. In short, the instructor created an environment where the students were both involved and enthusiastic about school—known as "engagement" (Gordon, 2006).

Engagement is good for the employee and good for the employer. In the workplace, engagement is defined as an individual's involvement and satisfaction with as well as their enthusiasm for work (Harter, Schmidt, & Hayes, 2002). Although related to satisfaction, engagement goes further in describing one's emotional relationship with their occupation (whether their occupation is as a full-time student or employee). Extensive research across many types of industries around the world has shown a strong linkage between engagement and productivity (which can mean pay in many environments), retention, quality, and a host of other positive outcomes (Harter, Schmidt, & Hayes, 2002). When employees are involved with and enthusiastic about their work, they are more productive in the short term and more likely to stay with their employer for the long term. Employers who create a great place for their employees to work enjoy meaningful benefits over those who simply define their relationship with employees as transactional. These positive outcomes lower stress and increase aspects of well-being for employees.

The same appears to be true in educational institutions. When employees have a great place to work, there are benefits to the students. Research in K-12 education has shown a linkage between teacher engagement and student engagement, which in turn is predictive of student achievement on standardized tests (Gallup, 2009a). Great principals are more likely to build a great place to work in many ways, including:

- selecting talented teachers,
- creating a culture of recognition, and
- ensuring teachers see the importance of building strong relationships with each other and with the students they serve (Gordon, 2006).

From the student perspective, their engagement involves the emotional relationship they have with their school. Engaged students feel safe, have close relationships with other students, have instructors who help them see how their coursework is relevant, and receive regular and meaningful recognition for doing good schoolwork. They also have frequent opportunities to use their strengths

to do what they do best. When students strongly agreed that their institution is committed to building the strengths of each student, they were more than seven times as likely to be engaged as their peers who strongly disagreed with the same statement (Lopez & Calderon, 2011).

Engaging students is an ongoing process, and educators need to search out new and effective techniques to build engagement over time, which requires hard work and diligent practice. Unfortunately, in a study of more than a half million students in grades 5–12, Gallup found student engagement drops with each school year. Although 76% of elementary students are engaged, the same is true of just 61% of middle school and 44% of high school students (Busteed, 2013). Ongoing research is underway explore whether the same trends hold true in higher education as well.

Building student engagement can be achieved through a variety of practices. Students who know their strengths and have regular opportunities to put them into practice are more likely to be engaged. Instructors and campus leaders who have the right talent for the job, and who are personally engaged in their work, seem more likely to lead classrooms where students are more involved and enthusiastic.

Case Study: Engagement at a Midwestern Community College

A Midwestern Community College has been focused on building a great place to work and learn. They were concerned with the downward trend in student engagement throughout middle and high school and wanted to ensure that their students would not suffer the same trend. The institution committed to building the engagement of employees at the college through selection and development, acknowledging that employees need more than knowledge and skills to do the job, but also the inherent talent that leads to success in the role. Furthermore, the institution is committed to helping engage students through strengths-based relationships.

When faculty and staff are active and enthusiastic participants in their work, students benefit from a more energetic and engaging environment. Having the right staff in the right roles to fit their talent is critical. The institution began a process of behavior-based interviewing to better ensure that each hiring decision would strengthen the institution. These job interviews are designed from a process of identifying the top performers in a given role and then discerning how those top performers are predisposed for success. The interview questions are scored in a way that top applicants answer at a high level of agreement with successful job incumbents (Schmidt & Rader, 1999). Furthermore, new employees were introduced to their strengths in a professional development context as part of their orientation program. Individual strengths-based conversations involved the new employee and their direct supervisor, facilitated by trained human resources professionals, to better facilitate the likelihood that employees were able to do what they do best, a key element of workplace engagement. All campus employees were invited to participate in an employee engagement survey. Department leaders carefully reviewed the results, shared them with their teams, and led conversations focused on building a more engaged workplace into the future. These conversations revealed roadblocks to employee success, often related to communication, recognition, relationships, or unclear performance expectations. When these issues were uncovered, teams often realized that they could be resolved with relatively simple actions.

At the same time that the staff engagement efforts were underway, the college intentionally fostered an engaging learning environment for students. Many new students at the college had been previously disenfranchised with higher education having previously gone through negative experiences in the traditional campus environment. At this college, many students appreciated the efforts by the institution to identify and celebrate the unique talents of each student through specific written and verbal feedback on their potential for success. The campus invested in a student success center, designed to get new students off to a great start and support all students as they encountered challenges in their college experiences, typically related to overcoming financial, psychological, academic, or relational barriers. More than 10,000 students have participated in strengths assessments and counseling sessions with certified strengths coaches to better understand and apply their strengths to their coursework, relationships, career planning, and a variety of other situations. This firsthand experience with knowing their institution is committed to getting to know them as individuals, and set them up to do more of what they do best every day, has created many opportunities for students to experience improved engagement.

Well-Being

Take a trip to your favorite bookstore, either physical or online, and you'll find thousands of titles on the topic of wellness and well-being. Most of these books promote the latest fad diet or exercise program designed to perfect your favorite muscle group and allow you to fit into a certain size of clothing by the holidays. A few aisles (or mouse clicks) away, you will find another entire section devoted to personal finance, with divergent yet sure-fire ways to get rich by buying or selling precious metals or real estate, offering advice on how to get into or out of debt, and touting a variety of ways to invest your money for short- or long-term gain. In an entirely different section of the bookstore, you will find titles offering career advice to new graduates seeking employment for the first time, or those who desire to be self-employed, or those trying to successfully bring their careers to a close and transition into retirement.

Although many of these ideas are compelling and some are even well-researched, almost all focus on only one aspect of well-being, as if true well-being happened in a vacuum. What the science shows is that good—and great—overall well-being is inter-connected. After a comprehensive global study of more than 150 countries, Tom Rath and Jim Harter came to the conclusion that our well-being results from several life domains—purpose (career), social, financial, physical, and community—and are not independent, they are highly related and interdependent (Rath & Harter, 2010).

Purpose well-being addresses how one occupies their time and whether they like what they do each day. Colleges and universities can no longer view purpose well-being as something that students experience after graduation and job placement. All members of the campus community—faculty, staff, administrators, and students—have experiences that influence their purpose well-being on a daily basis. There is satisfaction that comes from knowing the pursuit of activities, knowledge, and growth are investments in your long-term well-being. Successful cultivation of purpose well-being has a short game (something to look forward to on a daily basis) and a long game (deep purpose in life and a plan to achieve goals over time).

Research on engagement in the workplace provides ample evidence for the need for and value in building high career well-being. Employees who are engaged in their jobs are more productive, less likely to steal from their employer, less likely to call in sick, more likely to show up for work and build a long-term career with the organization, and much more (Harter, Schmidt, Killham, & Agrawal, 2009). Great career well-being builds great culture in that people like being at work, want to be working, and enjoy the people with whom they get to work.

Social well-being addresses the existence of strong relationships and the experience of strong positive emotions, including love. One's social well-being involves a broad network of friends and colleagues and is especially influenced by the closest of relationships (Rath & Harter, 2010). Interestingly, the research also supports the use of technology and social media for building and nurturing our social relationships (Rath & Harter, 2010). Social well-being can happen in a 21st century construct.

Our personal level of well-being seems to be closely related to the well-being of those with whom we live. Those living with someone with thriving (strong, consistent, and progressing) overall well-being are twice as likely to be thriving themselves (Agrawal & Harter, 2010). This finding suggests that we should both appreciate the value of our roommate and also accept the responsibility that comes with knowing our decisions and behaviors have a meaningful impact on those around us.

Financial well-being is not just about how much money one brings in; it is about the actual relationship with money. Recent research suggests that financial security has nearly three times the impact of income alone on employees' overall well-being (Rath & Harter, 2011). Those with strong financial well-being effectively manage their economic life in the short term, which reduces their level of stress. Furthermore, they experience increased security that comes with having a long-term plan for their finances. For students, this may mean that they participate in their employer's 401(k) plan, contributing $20 per pay check or automatically deducting a few dollars a month for an IRA. Furthermore, some students may opt for community colleges or state universities to minimize the amount of student loan debt they will carry into their future.

Physical well-being is characterized by good health and enough energy to get things done on a daily basis. Although bookstores are filled with specific plans and recommendations about how to increase one's physical well-being, it seems that the most successful strategies involve a combination of a healthy diet, adequate rest, and regular exercise. Rath (2013) provides a thorough review of the well-being research and straightforward strategies to improve one's well-being.

Campus leaders are acutely aware of the rising costs of healthcare for employees and students. Double-digit percentage increases in health insurance impact the finances of both the institution and the individual enrolling in the plan. Although some grudgingly accept that that the financial realities of our healthcare system are inevitable, others predict that as much as three fourths of American healthcare costs are related to preventable decisions including smoking, poor diet, and inadequate exercise (Rath & Harter, 2011). At an individual level, it seems that more informed and healthy daily choices can have a major impact on our physical well-being.

Community well-being involves the sense of engagement and involvement you have with the area where you live. Those who experience thriving levels of community well-being feel safe and secure in their physical environment, and they are also emotionally connected to their communities. They take pride in their neighborhoods and are more likely to promote the positive aspects of their communities. Furthermore, they are more likely to get involved in projects to make things even better. Those with the highest levels of community well-being can readily think of recent times when they were recognized for positive contributions to their local community (Rath & Harter, 2010). Involvement in community service has benefits that seem to include both the receiving organization as well as the volunteer themselves. Research has found that the benefactor may actually benefit through reduced stress and other negative emotions (Piliavin, 2003).

One final thought on the power of well-being in creating a positive campus culture: well-being can be contagious—good or bad. A Harvard study found that if one of your social connections is happy, your chances of being happy increase 15%. Moreover, if an indirect connection is happy and they make one of your connections happier by 15%, the odds that you are happier will increase by 10%; simply by knowing someone who knows someone who is happy can make you happy. Now, this all goes in the opposite direction as well: an increased chance of starting bad habits like smoking also "catches" in a community. (Rath & Harter, 2010, p. 34).

Case Study: Building Well-Being on Campus

In late 2010, a group of researchers from higher education institutions across the country gathered to start a new discussion about the well-being of people who learn and work at colleges and universities. They came from both public and private institutions and from different regions of the country, all setting out to build campus communities committed to creating a culture where every student and every employee was thriving. Bringing their varied and deep expertise as physicians, therapists, counselors, administrators, institutional researchers, and student affairs professionals, the group shared ideas, designed research, and took steps toward increasing well-being on their respective campuses.

Although each institution stayed true to its unique mission, student population, and strategic goals, the group agreed on a common and inclusive conceptualization of well-being across domains of career/purpose, social, financial, physical, and community. They explored the resources currently available on campus, and they convened meetings of leaders across campus to share best practices and encourage collaboration. They assessed a variety of populations of faculty, staff, and students and shared feedback to individuals and groups. Further activity included research designed to study well-being in relation to campus goals and success measures. Results were shared at a variety of local, regional, and national conferences.

In summarizing their experiences, the group discussed the following discoveries and questions to guide future inquiry in each of the five areas of well-being:

- Purpose: Although career preparation is a benefit and goal of higher education, it is important for students to also acknowledge that their current experience—how they occupy their time and whether they like what they do each day while still in college—is also important and deserving attention.
- Social: The benefits of strong social relationships are well documented. However, future research should explore the implications of technology-mediated social interaction.
- Financial: Recent reports indicate that the amount of outstanding student loan debt has passed $1 trillion, passing credit cards in total outstanding loan volume. Although investing in higher education has documented benefits, at what point do the costs outweigh the benefits?

- Physical: The traditional rhythms of campus life often involve all-night study sessions and frequent pizza parties. How can we change conversations on campus so we celebrate the "freshman fit" rather than the "freshman fifteen," or where we brag about a good night of sleep before a test rather than an all-nighter?
- Community: Do students identify with their campus community as their home, or do they see themselves as reluctant to get involved as they are "just passing through"?

Conclusion

These cornerstones in building a positive campus culture should not feel overwhelming. Most campuses and organizations have some of these components and structures in place. You might find it is time for a revived mission or clarification purpose or renewed strategic direction. For your campus, it might be a matter of aligning organizations and resources in new ways that better meet the needs of your students. Moreover, it might take bold leadership on the part of the stakeholders to (1) truly examine their campus and programs and (2) assess what areas opportunities and strengths can be built on to improve the overall positive culture on campus.

References

Agrawal, S., & Harter, J. K. (2010). *How much does the wellbeing of others in the same household influence our own wellbeing?* Omaha, NE: Gallup.

Asplund, J., Lopez, S. J., Hodges, T., & Harter, J. (2009). *The Clifton StrengthsFinder 2.0 technical report: Development and validation*. Princeton, NJ: Gallup.

Bandura, A. (2001). Social cognitive theory: An agentic perspective. *Annual Review of Psychology, 52*, 1–26.

Busteed, B. (2013, January 7). The school cliff: Student engagement drops with each school year. The Gallup Blog. Retrieved from http://thegallupblog.gallup.com/2013/01/the-school-cliff-student-engagement.html

Clifton, D. O., & Anderson, C. E. (2002). *StrengthsQuest*. Washington, D.C.: Gallup.

Clifton, D. O., Anderson, C. E., & Schreiner, L. A. (2006). *StrengthsQuest* (2nd ed.) New York, NY: Gallup Press.

Foote, S. M., Hinkle, S. M., Kranzow, J., Pistilli, M. D., Rease Miles, L., & Simmons, J. G. (2013). *College students in transition: An annotated bibliography*. Columbia, SC: NRC Publications.

Gallagher, M. W., & Lopez, S. J. (2008). Hope, self-efficacy, and academic success in college students. Poster presented at the annual convention of the American Psychological Association, Boston.

Gallup (2009a). Hope, engagement, and well-being as predictors of attendance, credits earned, and GPA in high school freshmen. Unpublished raw data, Omaha, NE.

Gallup (2009b). Relationships between hope, income, and teacher-student ratio in March 2009 Gallup Student Poll. Unpublished raw data, Omaha, NE.

Gollwitzer, P. M. (1999). Implementation intentions: Strong effects of simple plans. *American Psychologist, 54,* 493–503.

Gordon, G. (2006). *Building engaged schools: Getting the most out of America's classrooms.* New York: Gallup Press.

Harter, J. K., Schmidt, F. L., & Hayes, T. L. (2002). Business-unit-level relationship between employee satisfaction, employee engagement, and business outcomes: A meta-analysis. *Journal of Applied Psychology, 87,* 268–279.

Harter, J. K., Schmidt, F. L., Killham, E. A., & Agrawal, S. (2009). *Gallup Q12® meta-analysis: The relationship between engagement at work and organizational outcomes.* Omaha, NE: Gallup.

Hodges, T. D., & Clifton, D. O. (2004). Strengths-based development in practice. In P. A. Linley & S. Joseph (Eds.), *International handbook of positive psychology in practice: From research to application* (pp. 256–268). New York, NY: Wiley.

Lewis, M. C. (2009). *A summary and critique of existing strengths-based educational research utilizing the Clifton StrengthsFinder.* Omaha, NE: The Gallup Organization.

Lewis, M. C. (2012). *The Clifton StrengthsFinder and student strengths development: A review of research.* Omaha, NE: Gallup.

Lopez, S. J. (2012). *Strengths rules.* Omaha, NE: Gallup.

Lopez. S. J. (2013). *Making hope happen: Create the future you want for yourself and others.* New York: Atria Books.

Lopez, S. J., & Calderon, V. J. (2011). Gallup Student Poll: Measuring and promoting what is right with students. In S. I. Donaldson, M. Csikszentmihalyi, & J. Nakamura (Eds.), *Applied positive psychology: Improving everyday life, health, schools, work, and society* (pp. 117–133). New York: Routledge.

Lopez, S. J., Hodges, T. D., & Harter, J. K. (2005). *The Clifton StrengthsFinder technical report: Development and validation.* Princeton, NJ: Gallup.

Lopez, S. J., & Louis, M. C. (2009). The principles of strengths-based education. *Journal of College and Character, 10*(4), 1–8.

Lopez, S. J., & Snyder, C. R. (2011). *The Oxford handbook of positive psychology* (2nd ed.). New York: Oxford University Press.

Piliavin, J. A. (2003). Doing well by doing good: Benefits for the benefactor. In C. L. M. Keyes & J. Haidt (Eds.), *Flourishing: Positive psychology and the life well-lived* (pp. 227–247). Washington, DC: American Psychological Association.

Rath, T. (2013). *Eat move sleep: How small choices lead to big changes.* Arlington, VA: Missionday.

Rath, T., & Harter, J. (2010). *Wellbeing: The five essential elements.* New York: Gallup Press.

Rath, T., & Harter, J. (2011). *The economics of wellbeing.* Omaha, NE: Gallup.

Schmidt, F. L., & Rader, M. (1999). Exploring the boundary conditions for interview validity. *Personnel Psychology, 52,* 445–465.

Snyder, C. R. (1994). *The psychology of hope: You can get there from here.* New York: Free Press.

Snyder, C. R., Harris, C., Anderson, J. R., Holleran, S. A., Irving, L. M., Sigmon, S. T., et al. (1991). The will and the ways: Development and validation of an individual-differences measure of hope. *Journal of Personality and Social Psychology, 60,* 570–585.

Snyder, C. R., McDermott, D., Cook, W., & Rapoff, M. (2002). *Hope for the journey* (Rev. ed.). Clinton Corners, NY: Percheron Press.

Snyder, C. R., Shorey, H. S., Cheavens, J., Pulvers, K. M., Adams, V. H., III, & Wiklund, C. (2002). Hope and academic success in college. *Journal of Educational Psychology, 94,* 820–826.

INDEX

Please note: page numbers in italics indicate tables or illustrations

academic ability, ethnic stereotypes
    regarding, 84–86
academic advising
    and fostering spiritual development, 272–273
    and personal growth and development,
        229–230
    supporting autonomy in, 245
academic coaching, 118–119
Academic Determination factor, in Thriving
    Quotient, 8, 9
academic success
    and academic coaching, 337–338
    and academic self-efficacy, 103–104
    and curiosity, 107–108, 110–111, 122
    encouraging and enhancing, 99–100
    encouraging and enhancing (case example),
        121–124
    and engaged learning, 108–109
    factors contributing to, 100–101
    and family of origin, 224–225
    and implicit self-theory, 101–103
    learning communities, 119
    learning styles, 117–118
    and mentoring, 157
    and microaggressions, 119–121
    multicultural considerations, 119–121
    and perceived academic control, 104–105,
        114–117
    role of sports and exercise, 303
    and sense of hope, 105–107, 123, 155
    and shaping students' self-theories, 111–113
academic support services, reinforcing value
    of, 113
academic thriving, 9–10
active-constructive response, in the classroom,
    153–154

admissions selectivity, detriments of, 5
Adult Dispositional Hope Scale, 106
advising, student
    culturally competent practice, 92–95
    and positive psychology, 13–15
    reinforcing value of, 113
    strengths-based advising, 118–119
African American students
    and pathways to engaged learning, 10
    spirituality and intrapersonal
        thriving, 10–11
Aging Well (Vaillant), 32
Ahuvia, A., positive psychology and
    multiculturalism, 87
alcohol use, among Millennial
    generation, 39–40
Allport, G., deficit model and racial
    stereotyping, 85–86
altruism, expressing, 330–331
altruistic leadership, and athletics, 302
A Mind That Found Itself (Beer), 58
Anderson, E. C.
    Clifton Strengths Finder and Self-Reflection
        Survey, 146–147
    developing a language of strengths,
        283–284
    identifying and nurturing teacher
        strengths, 135
    remediation *vs.* strengths-based approach,
        148, *149*
Applied Helping Skills: Transforming Lives (Brew &
    Kottler), 243
appreciative advising, 118–119
appreciative inquiry
    and athletics, 302
    and supervision and training, 207–208

appreciative inquiry, and career counseling, 177–180
    design stage of, 179
    destiny stage of, 179–180
    discovery stage of, 177–178
    dream stage of, 178–179
Aristotle, *Nicomachean Ethics*, 49
Arum, R., and market-driven education, 3
Asian American students, optimism and pessimism among, 89–90
Asian students
    and pathways to engaged learning, 10
    spirituality and intrapersonal thriving, 10–11
Aspirations for Student Learning, 52
assessment and evaluation practices
    applying motivational interviewing concepts, 202–203
    providing effective feedback, 201–202
    and students' active role in learning, 114, 124
Astin, A. W.
    spiritual development among college students, 265–266
    spirituality and higher education, 49
    theory of talent development, 7
Astin, H. S., spirituality and higher education, 49
athletics
    and altruistic leadership, 302
    and building relationships, 304
    and personal growth and development, 230
    and spiritual growth and development, 273–274
    See also sports and exercise
attributional retraining, and perceived academic control, 105, 114–117
Attributional Style Questionnaire, 75
authentic happiness and well-being theory, 66, 68
Authentic Leadership Model, 296
autonomy
    and academic advising, 245
    in life coaching, 326
    and psychological well-being, 67
    significance of in relationships, 245–246
Avolio, B. J., authentic leadership, 16, 296
Aware-Explore-Apply model, of strengths development, 200–201

Baby Boom generation, and environmental concerns, 32
Bain, K.
    encouraging student curiosity, 111
    positive expectations of students, 120

Bandura, A.
    hope and campus culture, 347
    self-efficacy, 184, 196, 208
Banks, K. H., cross-cultural research, 87, 90, 334
Barkley, E. F., shaping students' self-theories, 112
Baumeister, R. F., strengths-based supervision, 197–198
Beers, C. W., *A Mind That Found Itself*, 58
behavioral *vs.* psychological engagement, 6
Belvet, B., culturally relevant strengths, 91–92
benevolence, practice of, 330
Bickman, L., feedback in learning process, 201
Big Book of Conflict Resolution Games, The (Scannell), 249
Binet, A., early theories of student success, 7, 133–134
Birnbaum, R., "crises" in higher education, 29
Bolman, L. G., relational leadership, 287
Borders, L. D., effective supervision, 194–195
Bowers, K. M.
    capitalizing on strengths, 332
    creating opportunities for success, 173
Bowlby, John, benefits of close relationships, 240–241
Branigan, C.
    the broaden hypothesis, 62
    the undoing hypothesis, 63–64
Brashears, M., Millennials and social isolation, 39
Braskamp, L., benefits of *StrengthsQuest* program, 146
Brew, L., active listening skills, 243
broaden and build theory of positive emotions, 60–66
    applying in the classroom, 152–153
    the broaden hypothesis, 61–62
    the build hypothesis, 62–63
    the flourish hypothesis, 65–66
    and identifying student strengths, 173
    and life success, 329, 330
    the resilience hypothesis, 64–65
    and supervision and training, 194–195
    the undoing hypothesis, 63–64
Bryant, F. B., savoring positive experiences, 331
Buechner, Frederick, vocational calling, 264
Burns, J. M., Transformational Leadership theory, 281–282
Burton, G., life coaching and goal-setting, 326

campus culture, creating a positive
    case studies, 346–347, 348–349, 351–352, 355–356
    and engagement in campus life, 349–351

and a sense of hope, 347–349
and a sense of well-being, 352–355
strengths-based approach, 344–347
Cantwell, L., strengths-based practice,
147–148
capitalization, and enhancing relationships,
246–248
career counseling, positive model of
career flow, 171–172
case example, 185–186
counselor perspective, 186–187
eliciting client wisdom, 176–181
lifelong decision making, 182–184
multicultural concerns, 184–185
narrative and constructivist counseling,
180–181
and personal growth and development, 229
planned happenstance perspective,
174–176
premises for, 167–168
reframing expectations, 168–169
and strengths-based approach, 172–174
vs. life coaching, 324
work as a calling, 169–171, 263–264
career planning, reinforcing value of, 113
Carr, J. A., friendship roles
case studies
career counseling, 185–186
engagement in campus life, 351–352
fostering spiritual development, 274–275
leadership development, 294–295
life coaching for students, 335–336
personal growth and development, 233–235
positive psychology and academic success,
121–124
positive psychology in the classroom,
159–161
a sense of hope, 348–349
social development and relationships,
255–257
sports and exercise, 310–313
strengths development, 346–347
supervision and training, 212–213
Chang, E. C.
cross-cultural research, 90, 334
optimism and pessimism among college
students, 89–90
pessimism and cultural difference, 205
positive psychology and multiculturalism, 87
change
readiness for, 221–222, 224
Stages of Change model, 327
change, societal
Millennial reaction to, 34–35
and technology, 35–37
Chara, P. J., Jr., personality inventories, 251

character strengths, and finding one's
calling, 269
Charness, N., moving beyond competence to
excellence, 210
Chickering, A., early theories of student
success, 7, 134
civic engagement
and leadership, 289–290, *290*
and multicultural understanding, 293
classroom behavior, among
Millennials, 46–48
"clearness committees," Quaker tradition of,
170–171
Clifton, Donald
developing a language of strengths,
283–284
origins of strengths psychology, 343
strengths-based supervision, 198
strengths theory, 59, 60
Clifton Strengths Finder
and career counseling, 172
case study of, 159–160
completion by students, 146
definitions of 34 talent themes
measured, 73–75
and friendships, 251
history and uses of, 70
identifying and nurturing student
strengths, 143
identifying teaching talent, 136
origins of, 344
strengths-based supervision, 199
coaching, and positive psychology approaches,
306, 309–310
Cochran, L., career counseling models, 169
co-curricular activities
opportunities for positive psychology,
15–16
and self-knowledge, 51–54
and time away from technology, 36–37
Cohn, Tracy J., 239–260
collaboration, opportunities for in college, 242
collectivism
and constructs of happiness, 87–88
and culture, 293
Colvin, G., deliberate practice, 211
Common Fire (Keen, Keen, Parks, & Daloz), 32
communication
and capitalization in relationships, 246–248
importance of in friendships, 242–245
and teaching success, 138
community, sense of
community well-being, 354
and institutional effectiveness, 18–19
and interpersonal thriving, 11–12
and organizational effectiveness, 17

competence, moving beyond to excellence, 209–212
Complete State model of mental health, 68–69
Compton, W. C., strengths-based supervision, 198–199
conceptual equivalence, 83
Conchie, B., *Strengths Based Leadership,* 284
confidence, and motivational interviewing techniques, 203
conflict resolution, in social relationships, 248–249
Constantine, M G., multicultural competence in counseling, 205
constructivist counseling, 180–181
consumer mentality in higher education, 2–4
content mastery, and positive psychology in the classroom, 13
coping skills
    as culturally relevant strength, 91, 205
    helping students develop, 15
counseling centers
    culturally competent practice, 92–95
    and student personal growth and development, 227–229
    and using positive psychology, 15
counseling services
    reinforcing value of, 113
    vs. life coaching, 323, 323
courage, and strengthening teaching success, 144
coursework in positive psychology, 270–272
Couto, Richard, civic engagement and leadership, 289–290
Crabb, S., strengths-based practice in the workplace, 142
Csikszentmihalyi, M., thriving communities, 17
cultural competence
    cross-cultural practice, 84
    cross-cultural research, 82, 83–84, 85–86, 89–90, 93–94
    culturally relevant strengths, 91–92
    cultural pluralism, emergence of, 86
    and strengths-based practice, 92–95
culture, definition of, 82
Culture, Leadership, and Organizations (House et al.), 292
curiosity
    and academic success, 107–108
    encouraging development of, 110–111, 122
Curtayne, L., life coaching and goal-setting, 326

Daloz, L. A. P., *Common Fire,* 32
Deal, T. E., relational leadership, 287
Dean, D.
    classroom behavior among Millennials, 47

economic downturns and Millennials, 44–45
Generation on a Tightrope: A Portrait of Today's College Student, 33
Millennials as "digital natives," 36
self-expression among Millennials, 39–40
sheltered upbringing of Millennials, 41, 42
societal change and Millennials, 35
traits of Millennials, 28–29
Deci, E. L., authentic motivation, 12–13
decision-making, processes of, 182–184
Deficit and Inferiority models
    and racial and ethnic stereotyping, 85–86
    vs. strengths-based approach, 148, *149,* 150
Deficit Remediation model
    and studying student success, 31
    vs. strengths-based model, 148
    vs. strengths development, 6–7, *149,* 150
deliberate practice, and fostering excellence, 210–211
depression, among college students, 225–226
developmental perspective, on supervision, 192–193
Dewey, J., early theories of student success, 7, 134
DiClementes, C. C., stages of change model, 327
Diener, E., theory of subjective well-being, 5
dining options, for Millennial students, 52–53
discipline, and teaching success, 139
discrimination and oppression
    and academic success, 119–121
    dealing with external manifestations, 95
Diverse Citizenship factor, in Thriving Quotient, 11
diverse student populations
    growth of, 3
    interpersonal thriving, 11–12
    in Millennial generation, 37–38
    and pathways to engaged learning, 10
    spirituality and intrapersonal thriving, 10–11
    and strengths development model, 7–8
diversity
    human diversity models, 86
    in training and supervision, 204–207
Doherty, N., conflict resolution, 249
Dorfman, P. W., culture and leadership, 292
drug and alcohol use, among Millennial generation, 40
Dum, M., feedback and supervision, 202
Dweck, C. S.
    challenges in supervision and training, 197
    implicit self-theory, 101, 102–103
    learning orientations, 210
    shaping students' self-theories, 112

economic downturns, and optimism of
Millennials, 43–44, 55
economy, knowledge, 3
Eden, D., "Pygmalion effect" in management,
195–196
Edison, Thomas, 174
Edwards, L. M., strengths and goal-setting
behavior, 199–200
Elliott, E. S., implicit self-theory, 102
Emmanuel, Glory, 261–278
Emmons, Robert, importance of gratitude, 269
emotions
building positive emotions, 330–331
emotional intelligence and leadership,
287–289
emotional well-being *vs.* happiness, 65
role of positive emotions in providing
feedback, 204
empathy
importance of in friendships, 242–245
and motivational interviewing, 203
positive empathy in the classroom, 154–155
and teaching success, 139
Engaged Learning factor, in Thriving
Quotient, 8, 9
engagement
an engaged life, 66
behavioral *vs.* psychological engagement, 6
and campus culture, 349–351
and career counseling, 174–176
and decision making, 183–184
engaged learning and academic success,
108–109, 123–124
Enright, Robert, promoting forgiveness, 269
entity theory, 101–102
environmental concerns, generational
patterns, 31–32
environmental mastery
and academic thriving, 9
and psychological well-being, 67
Eppright, W. J., personality inventories, 251
Ericcson, K. A., moving beyond competence to
excellence, 210
*Essential Guide to Workplace Mediation & Conflict
Resolution, The* (Doherty & Guyler), 249
Estévez, E. F., *StrengthsQuest* self-assessment, 147
ethnic and racial minorities, cultivating safe
learning environments, 95, 120
ethnicity
and access to higher education, 1–2
and career counseling services, 184–185
and coping skills, 91, 205
and Millennial generation, 38
and pathways to engaged learning, 10
stereotypes *vs.* multiculturalism, 84–86
and strengths development model, 7–8

evaluation and assessment practices
applying motivational interviewing concepts,
202–203
providing effective feedback, 201–202
and students' active role in learning,
114, 124
excellence, fostering in the workplace,
209–212
executive coaching, history of, 319
expectations and pressures, faced by Millennial
generation, 49–50
extracurricular activities, and spiritual
development, 273–274
Eyler, J., service learning and leadership
development, 290

failure
failure prevention *vs.* success promotion, 14
responses to, 102–103
familism, as culturally relevant strength, 91
feedback
applying motivational interviewing concepts,
202–203
providing effective feedback, 201–202
role of positive emotions in, 204
financial well-being, description of, 354
Fineburg, A. C., teaching positive
psychology, 13
Finkenauer, C., synergistic effect of friendship,
250–251
Fischer, N., culturally relevant
strengths, 91–92
fixed mindset
and intellectual development, 101–103
and learning, 210
and strengths-based approaches, 116
Flores, L. Y., multicultural considerations in
career counseling, 184
flourish hypothesis
applying in the classroom, 153
of broaden and build theory, 65–66
flourishing people
and construct of thriving, 8
definition and description of, 4–5
five pillars of, 66, 301
flow experiences
and career counseling, 173
and sports and exercise, 307
Fordyce Emotions Questionnaire, 75
forgiveness, among Hmong Americans, 88–89
Frankl, Viktor, spiritual development,
262–263
Fredrickson, B. L.
attaining happiness, 269
the broaden hypothesis, 61, 62

Fredrickson, B. L. (*cont.*)
  positive emotions and happiness, 329, 330
  the undoing hypothesis, 63–64
  upward spiral of positive emotion, 328
friendships
  benefits of close friendships, 240–241, 257
  case study, 255–257
  communication and capitalization in,
    246–248
  conflict resolution in, 248–249
  developing among students, 39, 41, 253–255
  empathy and communication in, 242–245
  importance of during college, 239
  increasing satisfaction with, 252–253
  mutuality and autonomy support, 245–246
  selecting friends, 241–242
  skills for building, 239–240
  and spirituality, 49
  types of friendships, 249–250
  understanding relationship strengths,
    250–252
Frijda, N. H., the broaden hypothesis, 61

Gable, S. L., active-constructive response,
    153–154
Gahagan, J., coaching for academic success,
    322–323
Gallup Strengths Finder, 283
Gardner, H., and consumer mentality in higher
    education, 2–3
Gellat, H. B.
  planned happenstance theory, 175
  "positive uncertainty," 168
General Happiness Scale, 75
Generation on a Tightrope (Levine & Dean), 33
Generation X, and environmental concerns, 32
George, William, Mindful Leadership
    model, 288
Gilbert, D., attaining happiness, 329
Giles, D. E., service learning and leadership
    development, 290
Gilpin, J., mindset of gratitude, 302–303
Gladwell, Malcolm, *Outliers: The Story of
    Success,* 204
global knowledge economy, and higher
    education, 3
goal-setting behavior
  and career flow, 172
  intrinsic *vs.* extrinsic goals, 327
  and life coaching, 325–328
  pathways thinking and agency
    thinking, 328
  and sense of hope, 107, 123, 157, 158, 327
  SMART goals, 194, 326
  and sports and exercise, 304

strengths-based approach to, 199–200
Goguen, M. L. S., benefits of college
    friendships, 241
Goleman, D., emotional intelligence and
    leadership, 288
Gonzalez, R. C., multicultural competence in
    counseling, 206
Govindji, R., knowing and using strengths, 332
graduation rates
  and admissions selectivity, 5
  continued low rates, 1
Grant, A. M.
  bibliography on life coaching, 319–320
  life coaching and goal-setting, 326
gratitude, benefits of expressing, 330
group work in classrooms, 153, 158
growth, fostering in supervision and
    training, 194
growth mindset
  and intellectual development, 101–102,
    122–123, 124
  and learning, 210
  and training, 207
Gupta, V., culture and leadership, 292
Guyler, M., conflict resolution, 249

Haidt, Jonathan, decision-making
    processes, 182
Hanges, P. J., culture and leadership, 292
happiness
  authentic happiness and well-being
    theory, 66, 68
  in collectivist *vs.* individualist
    societies, 87–88
  life coaching toward, 328–329
  vs. emotional well-being, 65
Harper, R., counseling in student affairs
    work, 243
Harrington, S.
  group work in classroom, 153
  positive psychology and life coaching, 321
Harter, J., sense of well-being, 353
Harzer, C., strengths-based practice in the
    workplace, 142
Hastings, Sarah L., 239–260
Haynes, T. L., attributional retraining, 115
Hays, P., culturally competent practice, 93
helplessness, as response to failure, 102–103
Heppner, M. J., multicultural considerations in
    career counseling, 184
Heppner, P. P., decision-making processes, 182
Hess, A. K., developmental model for
    supervision, 193
Hetzel, R., positive psychology in higher
    education, 4

Hiester, M. A., benefits of college friendships, 241
higher education
  as context for spiritual development, 264–267
  generational patterns in, 29–30
  and leadership development, 279–280
  life coaching in, 322–324
  U. S. history of, 2–4
  use of positive psychology, 4–5
Hill, P. C., forgiveness, 88
Hmong Americans, manifestations of forgiveness among, 88–89
Hodges, Tim, 343–357
Hoffman, E., strengths-based supervision, 198–199
Holloway, E., importance of supervisory process, 191
Hook, J. N., culturally relevant strengths, 91–92
hope, sense of
  and academic achievement, 105–107, 123
  applying in the classroom, 155–159
  and career flow, 171
  and goal-setting behavior, 327–328
  leadership and fostering a sense of hope, 286–287
  and positive campus culture, 347–349
  and student advising relationships, 14–15
  in supervision and training, 194
House, R. J., culture and leadership, 292
Howe, N.
  expectations of Millennial generation, 50
  generational change in society, 31
  Millennials Rising: The Next Great Generation, 33, 39
  optimism of Millennial generation, 43
Hulme, E.
  appreciating strengths in others, 185
  emphasizing positive student traits, 30–31
  identifying student strengths, 173
  positive psychology in higher education, 4
  studying success, 319
human diversity models, 86
Hurlock, E. B., early theories of student success, 133–134

implicit self-theory
  and academic success, 101–103
  and academic support services, 113
  shaping students' self-theories, 111–113
incremental theory, 101–102
individual expression among Millennials, 39–41
individualism and culture, 293
individualization and teaching success, 140
inferiority and deficit models, 85–86

institutional effectiveness
  challenges to, 2
  a thriving community, 16–19
Integrated Developmental model, 193
intellectual development
  and academic self-efficacy, 103–104
  and attributional retraining, 115
  encouraging and enhancing, 99–100, 121–124
  factors contributing to, 100–101
  and implicit self-theory, 101–103
  shaping students' self-theories, 111–113
Intentional Growth Training, 228
intentionality and personal growth, 222–223
intercollegiate athletics
  and altruistic leadership, 302
  and building relationships, 304
  and personal growth and development, 230
  and spiritual growth and development, 273–274
  See also sports and exercise
International Coach Federation, 320
international students, interpersonal thriving among, 11–12
interventions and perceived academic control, 104–105
intrapersonal thriving, 10–11
intuition in decision making, 183–184
Involving Colleges (Kuh, Schuh, Whitt, & Associates), 32

James, William, reframing expectations, 168
Javidan, M., culture and leadership, 292
Jones, Janice E., 191–217
Jones-Smith, E., strengths-based supervision, 198
Joseph, S., life coaching, 321
Journal of Positive Psychology, founding of, 59
Juan, M. J. D., social networks, 242
justice, and strengthening teaching success, 145

Keen, C. H. and J. P., Common Fire, 32
Keeter, S.
  economic downturns and Millennials, 44
  educational level of Millennials, 37
  political views among Millennials, 38
Kennedy, Jessica, 343–357
Keyes, C. L. M.
  construct of positive relations, 11
  environmental mastery, 9
  social well-being, 66
Kidd, Vera
  leadership and Millennial generation, 280
  Millennials in higher education, 27–56

King, L. A., writing exercises in positive psychology, 272

Kinzie, J.
    admissions selectivity, 5–6
    enhancing student success, 322

Kottler, J. A., active listening skills, 243

Krauskopf, C. J., decision-making processes, 182

Krieshok, T. S., career counseling, 183

Krumboltz, J. D., career counseling, 174

Kuh, G. D.
    enhancing student success, 322
    Involving Colleges and *Student Success in College,* 32

Lambert, M. J., training *vs.* supervision, 191

Langer, E. J., concept of mindfulness, 9

Latino students
    and pathways to engaged learning, 10
    spirituality and intrapersonal thriving, 10–11

Lazarus, R. S., the broaden hypothesis, 61

leadership
    altruistic leadership and athletics, 302
    and civic engagement, *290*
    developing a language of strengths, 283–284
    and positive emotions, 289
    Relational Leadership model, 287
    Social Change model, 281, 282–283
    Transformational Leadership theory, 281–282

leadership development
    and academic efforts, 37
    applying principles of positive psychology, 290–292
    building emotional intelligence, 287–289
    case study in, 294–295
    and civic engagement, 289–290
    at colleges and universities, 279–280, 296
    developing a language of strengths, 283–286
    and fostering a sense of hope, 286–287
    models of, 280–281
    multicultural implications, 292–294
    opportunities for positive psychology, 15–16
    shifting to positive perspective, 281–283
    stages of, 285–286

Leadership Identity Development model, 285, 286

learning
    addressing problems in, 207–209
    continuing to learn, 210–212
    definitions of, 231
    and deliberate practice, 210–211
    encouraging curiosity, 110–111, 122
    engaged learning, 108–109

learning communities, 119

learning goals and growth mindset, 102

learning orientations in the workplace, 209–210

learning styles, 117–118
    reinforcing active role in, 114
    teachers as learners, 140

Letters to a Young Poet (Rilke), 177

Levine, A.
    classroom behavior among Millennials, 47
    economic downturns and Millennials, 44–45
    Generation on a Tightrope: A Portrait of Today's College Student, 33
    Millennials as "digital natives," 36
    self-expression among Millennials, 39–40
    sheltered upbringing of Millennials, 41, 42
    societal change and Millennials, 35
    traits of Millennials, 28–29

Levoy, G.
    and constructivist counseling, 180
    work as a calling, 170

Liesveld, R., identifying teaching talent, 135

life coaching
    on campus, 322–324
    case study, 335–336
    characteristics of coach and coachee, 320–321
    cultural considerations in, 333–335
    definition of, 320
    focusing on strengths, 331–333
    and goal-setting behavior, 325–328
    history of, 319
    methods and modalities for, 325
    positive psychology coaching interventions, 329–331
    in practice, 324–325
    role in mental health, 337
    vs. counseling, 323, 323
    vs. mentoring, 324

life experiences
    communicating to friends, 246–247
    transition from high school to college, 219–220

life purpose, and psychological well-being, 68

Lindholm, J. A., spirituality and higher education, 49

linguistic equivalence, 83

Linley, P. A.
    group work in classroom, 153
    knowing and using strengths, 332
    positive psychology and life coaching, 321

listening
    reflective listening, 203
    relationships and active listening, 242–243
    types of responses, 247–248

Locke, E. A., increasing self-efficacy, 196
locus of control, and academic success, 104
Lopez, S. J.
    capitalizing on strengths, 332
    creating opportunities for success, 173
    five-stage process of strengths development,
        344–345
    happiness in collectivist societies, 88
    hope and campus culture, 347
    meaningful sense of hope, 194
    positive psychology in higher education, 4
    strengths and goal-setting behavior, 199–200
    strengths-based supervision, 200
    strengths development model, 7, 133, 134
Louis, Michelle C.
    applying positive psychology in the
        classroom, 151
    developing student strengths, 147
    Enhancing Intellectual Development and
        Academic Success in College, 99–131
    five-stage process of strengths development,
        344–345
    strengths development model, 7, 133, 134
low-income students, interpersonal
    thriving, 11–12
Lucas, R. E., theory of subjective
    well-being, 5
Luthans, F.
    authentic leadership, 16, 296
    psychological capital, 18
Lyubomirsky, Sonja
    building positive emotions, 331
    discovering authentic meaning and
        purpose, 269
    intentional activity changes, 327
    intentional kindness, 330

Magyar-Moe, Jeana L.
    Positive Psychology 101, 57–79
    Positive Psychology in the Classroom,
        133–166
Mahoney, A., fostering spiritual
    development, 262
Maltby, J., positive psychology and life
    coaching, 321
Mamede, S., structure for reflection, 211
Mancuso, R. A., the undoing
    hypothesis, 63–64
Manor, H. L., facilitating feedback, 202
marijuana use, among Millennial generation, 40
market-driven education, 2–3
Marks, Lawrence I., Life Coaching for Students,
    319–341
Maslow, Abraham, hierarchy of needs, 319
Master, A., shaping students' self-theories, 112

mastery orientation, as response to failure,
    102–103
McCullough, Michael, promoting
    forgiveness, 269
McGovern, T. V., identifying and nurturing
    teaching talent, 142–143
McPherson, M., Millennials and social
    isolation, 39
measures for positive psychological strengths,
    69–70, 75
meditation, and positive emotions, 331
membership, and institutional sense of
    community, 19
Menninger, K., and treatment of mental
    illness, 58
mental health issues
    Complete State model of mental
        health, 68–69
    increasing frequency of among college
        students, 3, 15
    role of life coaching, 337
    routes to mental health, 66
mental illness, history of treatment, 57–58
mentoring
    importance of, 157
    vs. life coaching, 324
metric equivalence, 83
"Michelangelo effect," in friendships,
    250–251
microaggressions, and academic success,
    119–121
Mifune, N., appreciating diversity, 206
Millennial generation
    characteristics of, 33–34
    classroom behavior among, 46–48
    defining, 28–29
    dining options for students, 52–53
    and diverse student populations, 37–38
    and economic downturns, 44–45
    educational levels of, 37
    and environmental concerns, 31–32
    individual expression among, 39–41
    naming of, 33
    optimism of, 43, 45, 50, 55
    positive traits of, 27
    pressures and expectations faced by,
        49–50
    reaction to societal changes, 34–35, 43
    and self-assessment, 53
    self-knowledge among, 48
    service projects among, 45–46
    sheltered upbringing of, 41–43, 48
    similarities to past, 29–30
    spirituality among, 48–49
    student life programming for, 51–52, 53
    and technology, 35–37

Millennials Rising: The Next Great Generation (Howe & Strauss), 33, 39
Miller, Lisa M., Positive Psychology for Sport and Exercise, 299–317
Miller, S. L., identifying and nurturing teaching talent, 142–143
Milne, D., scaffolding training experiences, 192
Mindful Leadership model, 288
minorities, coping skills among, 91, 205
More Than Listening: A Casebook for Using Counseling Skills in Student Affairs Work (Harper), 243
motivation
    authentic motivation, 12–13
    and life coaching, 327
    and strengths development, 7
    and student success, 8
motivational interviewing, 202–203
multiculturalism
    and academic success, 119–121
    and campus sports and exercise, 308–310
    and career counseling, 184–185
    considerations in personal growth and development, 232–233
    cultivating safe environments for students, 95
    culturally relevant strengths, 91–92
    definition of, 82
    and leadership development, 292–294
    in life coaching with students, 333–335
    "multicultural personality," 92
    perspectives on training and supervision, 204–207
    staying abreast of research in, 93–94
Murray, H. A., constructivist counseling, 180–181
Murray, M. C., spiritual development, 265
mutuality
    definition of, 245
    significance of in relationships, 245–246

narrative counseling, 180–181
Nash, R. J., spiritual development, 265
National Institute of Mental Health, 58
National Survey of Student Engagement, 6, 17
Nelson, P., strengths theory, 59, 60
"New Tribalism," among Millennials, 40
Nicomachean Ethics (Aristotle), 49
Niemiec, R. M., strengths development, 200–201
Norcross, J. C., Stages of Change model, 327
Nordstrom, A. H., benefits of college friendships, 241

Ogles, B. M., training *vs.* supervision, 191
Oishi, S., theory of subjective well-being, 5
oppression and discrimination
    and academic success, 119–121
    dealing with external manifestations, 95
optimism
    among college students, 89–90
    among Millennial generation, 43, 45, 50, 55
    and increased motivation, 327
    and intrapersonal thriving, 10
    and leadership development, 281–283
    and sports and exercise, 304
organizational behavior, and institutional effectiveness, 17–18
Orlick, T., peer collaboration in sports, 305
Outliers: The Story of Success (Gladwell), 204
ownership, and institutional sense of community, 19

Pahl, R., types of friendships, 250
Palmer, P., identifying and nurturing teacher strengths, 135
Palmer, P. J., work as a calling, 33, 169–170
parents
    expectations of Millennial children, 50
    of Millennial generation students, 41–43
Pargament, K. I., fostering spiritual development, 262
Park, N.
    institutional effectiveness, 18
    positive psychology "theme semester," 303
Parks, S. D., *Common Fire*, 32
partnership, and institutional sense of community, 19
Pascarella, E. T., institutional effectiveness, 17
Pedersen, P., multicultural personality, 92
Pedrotti, Jennifer Teramoto, Cultural Competence in Positive Psychology, 81–98
peer support
    and fostering a sense of hope, 286–287
    learning communities, 119
    peer coaching, 323
    peer collaboration in athletics, 305, 307
    significance of autonomy support, 245–246
    in sports and exercise, 300
performance goals, and fixed mindset, 102
Perry, R. P., attributional retraining, 115
personal agency
    and academic success, 105–106
    and career planning, 176
    goals and agency thinking, 328
personal growth and development
    and academic advising, 229–230
    and career services, 229
    case study in, 233–235

college counseling centers, 227–229
  Intentional Growth Training, 228–229
  and intentionality, 222–223
  and intercollegiate athletics, 230
  multicultural considerations, 232–233
  and normative student development,
    223–225
  and psychological well-being, 68, 225–226
  transition from high school to college,
    219–220
personal growth initiative (PGI),
    significance of
  in academic advising, 229–230
  in career services, 229
  in the classroom, 230–232
  in college counseling centers, 227–229
  and intentionality, 222–223
  in intercollegiate athletics, 230
  and multicultural considerations, 232–233
  Personal Growth Initiative Scale, 222, 236
  and psychological well-being, 68, 225–226
pessimism
  among college students, 89–90
  cultural differences, 205
Peterson, C.
  discovering authentic meaning in life, 267
  positive psychology "theme semester," 303
  Values in Action Classification System,
    69–70, 136–137
Peterson, C. M., institutional effectiveness, 18
physical well-being, description of, 354
Pierce, G. R., increasing satisfaction with
    friendships, 252
Pitner, R. O., appreciating diversity, 206
planned happenstance theory, 174–176
playfulness, and personal growth, 222, 224
political views, among Millennials, 38
Ponterotto, J. G., multicultural personality, 92
Positive and Negative Affect Scale, 75
positive organizational behavior, and
    institutional effectiveness, 17–18
Positive Perspectives factor, in Thriving
    Quotient, 10
positive psychology
  and academic success (case example),
    121–124
  across cultures, 120–121
  and the advising relationship, 13–15
  applications in the classroom, 12–15
  applications in work and counseling, 75
  and campus counseling centers, 15
  cross-cultural and multicultural
    exemplars, 87–92
  cultural contexts and competence,
    81, 92–95

culturally relevant strengths, 91–92
  definition of, 4, 57
  and developing friendships, 39
  and developing self-knowledge, 48
  and ethnic stereotypes, 84, 85–86
  history of, 57–59, 280
  measures for psychological strengths,
    69–70, 70, 75
  optimism and subjective well-being,
    10, 65–66
  positive perspective on advising, 118–119
  and self-expression among Millennials, 41
  and student learning capacity, 30–31
  and student life programming, 15–16, 54
  use in higher education, 4–5
positive psychology, and campus culture
  case study, 346–347, 348–349, 351–352,
    355–356
  engagement in campus life, 349–351
  a sense of hope, 347–349
  sense of well-being, 352–355
  strengths-based approach, 344–347
positive psychology, and career counseling
  career flow, 171–172
  case example, 185–186
  counselor perspective, 186–187
  eliciting client wisdom, 176–181
  lifelong decision making, 182–184
  multicultural concerns, 184–185
  narrative and constructivist counseling,
    180–181
  planned happenstance perspective,
    174–176
  premises for, 167–168
  reframing expectations, 168–169
  and strengths-based approach, 172–174
  work as a calling, 169–171
positive psychology, and leadership
    development
  applying principles of positive psychology,
    290–292
  building emotional intelligence, 287–289
  case study, 294–295
  and civic engagement, 289–290, *290*
  at colleges and universities, 279–280
  developing a language of strengths,
    283–286
  and fostering a sense of hope, 286–287
  models of leadership development,
    280–281
  multicultural implications, 292–294
  shifting to positive perspective, 281–283
  stages of leadership development, 285–286
positive psychology, and life coaching
  case study, 335–336
  coaching interventions, 329–331

positive psychology, and life coaching (cont.)
cultural considerations, 333–335
focusing on strengths, 331–333
goal-setting behavior, 325–328
life coaching on campus, 322–324
overview of, 320–321
in practice, 324–325
positive psychology, and personal growth and
development
and academic advising, 229–230
and career services, 229
case study in, 233–235
college counseling centers, 227–229
Intentional Growth Training, 228–229
and intentionality, 222–223
and intercollegiate athletics, 230
multicultural considerations, 232–233
normative student development, 223–225
transition from high school to college,
219–220
well-being and distress, 225–226
positive psychology, and supervision and training
addressing problems and framing solutions,
207–209
continued learning and expert performance,
210–212
creating hope and fostering growth, 194
developmental perspective on, 192–193
evaluation and feedback, 201–204
fostering excellence, 209–212
multicultural perspectives on, 204–207
role of positive emotions in feedback, 204
setting the stage for effectiveness, 194–197
training vs. supervision, 191
uncovering potential, 197–201
positive psychology, in social development and
relationships
benefits of close relationships, 240–241
case study, 255–257
communication and capitalization, 246–248
conflict resolution, 248–249
empathy and communication skills, 242–245
friendship roles, 249–250
increasing satisfaction with friendships,
252–253
integrating friendship into university
programming, 253–255
mutuality and autonomy support, 245–246
selecting friends, 241–242
understanding relationship strengths, 250–252
positive psychology, in sports and exercise
benefits of sports and exercise, 300
benefits to students, 313–314
case study in, 310–313
and challenges faced by student athletes,
300–301

multicultural viewpoints, 308–310
practical applications of, 302–308
techniques and approaches to, 301–302
positive psychology, role in fostering spiritual
development
in academic advising and residence halls,
272–273
administration and academic
departments, 273
case example, 274–275
coursework in positive psychology,
270–272
defining spirituality and spiritual
development, 261–263
discovering authentic meaning and purpose,
267–268
a sense of calling, defining and describing,
263–264
spiritual development in college, 264–267,
269–274
positive psychology in the classroom
applying positive psychology theories,
151–159, 161–162
case study of, 159–161
identifying and nurturing student strengths,
143–148
identifying and nurturing teacher strengths,
135–143, 144–145
obstacles to strengths-based teaching,
148–151
positive psychology theories, 59–69
applying in the classroom, 151–159
authentic happiness and well-being
theory, 66, 68
broaden and build theory of positive
emotions, 60–66, 173
strengths theory, 59–60, 134
positive traits, cultural applicability of,
83–84, 85–86
potential, uncovering among trainees,
197–201
Prepare-Engage-Reflect model, for developing
friendships, 39
pressures and expectations, faced by Millennial
generation, 49–50
Prochaska, J. O., Stages of Change model, 327
Proctor, C., strengths-based practice, 148
psychological capital, and institutional
effectiveness, 18
psychological engagement, and student
success, 8
psychological vs. behavioral engagement, 6
psychological well-being
dimensions of, 67–68
five pillars of well-being, 301
and flourishing people, 65–66

and frequency of mental health issues,
6–7, 15
and life purpose, 68
psychology, courses in, 270–271
purpose well-being, 353
"Pygmalion effect," on students and trainees,
195–196

Quakers, tradition of "clearness committees,"
170–171

race and ethnicity
and access to higher education, 1–2
and career counseling services, 184–185
and coping skills, 91, 205
and cultivating safe learning environments,
95, 120
and Millennial generation, 38
and pathways to engaged learning, 10
stereotypes vs. multiculturalism, 84–86
and strengths development model, 7–8
Rath, T.
roles in friendship, 249
satisfying friendships, 253
sense of well-being, 353
Strengths Based Leadership, 284
Vital Friends Assessment, 251
rationality and reason
in decision making, 183–184
reflection, providing structure for, 211–212
reflective listening
in friendships, 242–243
in motivational interviewing, 203
reflective thinking, 211–212
Relational Leadership model, 287
relationships
benefits of close relationships, 240–241, 257
case study, 255–257
communication and capitalization in,
246–248
conflict resolution in, 248–249
cultivating through sports and exercise,
300, 304
developing among students, 253–255
empathy and communication in, 242–245
increasing satisfaction with friendships,
252–253
and institutional sense of community, 19
mutuality and autonomy support, 245–246
positive relationships with others, 67
selecting friends, 241–242
understanding relationship strengths,
250–252
various roles in, 249–250

remediation model
and studying student success, 31
vs. strengths-based model, 148, 149, 150
vs. strengths development, 6–7, 14
research
on academic self-efficacy, 104
cross-cultural research, 82, 83–84,
85–86, 89–90
on personal growth and development,
221–226
on shaping students' self-theories, 111–112
staying abreast of, 93–94
translational research, 306
residence halls, and fostering spiritual
development, 272–273
resilience, among college students
and personal growth initiative, 226
and sports and exercise, 304
resilience hypothesis, of Broaden and Build
theory, 64–65
resistance, and motivational interviewing
techniques, 203
Resonant Leadership model, 288
resourcefulness, and personal growth,
222, 224
resources, building durable, 63
Riemer, M., feedback in learning process, 201
Righetti, F., synergistic effect of friendship,
250–251
Rilke, Rainer Maria, 177
Roberts, D. R., Social Change model of
leadership, 283
Robinson, C., coaching for academic success,
322–323
Robitschek, Christine, Personal Growth and
Development, 219–238
Rogers, Carl
building supportive relationships, 242–243
empathy in the classroom, 154
Roksa, J., and market-driven education, 3
romantic relationships, skills for enhancing,
239–240
Ruch, W., strengths-based practice in the
workplace, 142
Rusbult, C., synergistic effect of friendship,
250–251
Ryan, R. M., authentic motivation, 12–13
Ryff, C. D.
construct of positive relations, 11
environmental mastery, 9
factors for well-being, 328
and psychological well-being, 65

Sakamoto, I., appreciating diversity, 206
Sanburn, J., Millennial generation, 27, 29

Sandage, S., forgiveness among Hmong Americans, 88
Saptya, J., feedback in learning process, 201
Sarason, B. R. & I. G., improving friendships, 252
Sarason, S. B., psychological sense of community, 18
Satisfaction with Life Scale, 75
Savickas, M. L.
　career counseling models, 168
　constructivist counseling, 181
Scannell, M., conflict resolution, 249
Schkade, D., intentional kindness, 330
Schmidt, H., structure for reflection, 211
Schneider, G. G., opportunities in higher education, 3
Schreiner, Laurie A.
　Clifton Strengths Finder and Self-Reflection Survey, 146
　coaching for academic success, 323
　concepts of student success, 100
　decision-making processes, 183
　developing a language of strengths, 283–284
　learning orientation among students, 197
　Positive Psychology and Higher Education, 1–25
　student thriving, 322
Schuh, J. H.
　enhancing student success, 322
　Involving Colleges and Student Success in College, 32
Schutt, D., appreciative inquiry, and career counseling, 179
Schwartz, B., strengths-based supervision, 200
self-acceptance, and psychological well-being, 67
self-actualization, 319
self-assessment, for Millennials, 53
self-assurance, and teaching success, 141
self-clarity, and career flow, 172
self-efficacy
　and academic success, 103–104
　and building positive emotions, 331
　increasing among trainees, 196
self-esteem, and sense of hope, 158–159
self-expression, among Millennials, 39–41
self-knowledge
　among Millennials, 48
　and leadership development, 286
　practical strategies for, 51–54
self-reflection, and career flow, 171–172
self-theories
　implicit self-theories, 101–103
　shaping students' self-theories, 111–113
self-verification theory, and empathy in relationships, 244

Seligman, Martin
　and academic thriving, 9
　discovering authentic meaning and purpose, 267, 268
　elements of well-being, 5, 328
　and history of positive psychology, 57, 59
　and intrapersonal thriving, 10
　optimism and leadership development, 281
　and origins of positive psychology, 280
　positive relationships and interpersonal thriving, 11
　strengths-based supervision, 198
　thriving communities, 17
　Values in Action Classification System, 69–70, 136–137
　well-being theory, 66
September 11, 2001 terrorists attacks, resilience in aftermath, 64–65
service learning
　and academic efforts, 37
　and leadership development, 290
　and multicultural understanding, 293
　opportunities for positive psychology, 15–16
　and student friendships, 253
service projects, among Millennials, 45–46
sexuality and gender roles, among Millennials, 38, 40
Shahbaz, P., Clifton Strengths Finder and Self-Reflection Survey, 146
Sharpe, K. E., strengths-based supervision, 200
Shaw, W. S.
　cross-cultural research, 90
　positive psychology and multiculturalism, 87
Sheldon, K. M.
　building positive emotions, 331
　intentional activity changes, 327
　intentional kindness, 330
Shushok, Frank, Jr.
　appreciating strengths in others, 185
　identifying student strengths, 173
　leadership and Millennial generation, 280
　Millennials in Higher Education, 27–56
　studying success, 319
Simon, T., early theories of student success, 133–134
Smith, Bruce W., 261–278
Smith-Lovin, L., Millennials and social isolation, 39
Snyder, C. R.
　academic success and sense of hope, 155, 156
　class goals, 157–158

cross-cultural research, 90
fostering a sense of hope, 286
hope and campus culture, 347
hope and self-esteem, 158–159
meaningful sense of hope, 194
pathways thinking and agency
thinking, 328
Sobell, L. C. & M. B., facilitating feedback, 202
Social Change model of leadership development,
281, 282–283, 285, 294
Social Connectedness factor, in Thriving
Quotient, 11
social development and relationships
benefits of close relationships, 240–241
case study, 255–257
communication and capitalization, 246–248
conflict resolution, 248–249
empathy and communication skills, 242–245
friendship roles, 249–250
increasing satisfaction with friendships,
252–253
integrating friendship into university
programming, 253–255
mutuality and autonomy support, 245–246
selecting friends, 241–242
understanding relationship strengths, 250–252
social inequality
and access to higher education, 1–2
and strengths development model, 7–8
social isolation, among Millennial
generation, 39, 41
social justice, student leadership on, 294
social media
effect on environmental concerns, 32
and Millennial generation, 35–36, 37, 40
social networks
among college students, 241–242
encouraging socializing opportunities on
campus, 253–255
social support, importance of, 239
social wellness
and campus culture, 353
dimensions of, 67–68
and flourishing people, 66
Spencer, L., types of friendships, 250
spiritual development
and administration and academic
departments, 273
college as context for, 264–267
coursework in positive psychology, 270–272
defining and describing a sense of calling,
263–264
defining spirituality and spiritual
development, 261–263
discovering authentic meaning and purpose,
267–268

fostering among college students, 269–274
fostering in academic advising and residence
halls, 272–273
spirituality
among Millennial generation, 48–49
fostering spiritual development,
261–263
and intrapersonal thriving, 10–11
a sense of calling, 263–264
Spirituality in Higher Education
project, 48–49
sports and exercise
applying positive psychology in, 302–308
benefits of, 300
and benefits of positive psychology to
students, 313–314
case study, 310–313
challenges faced by student athletes,
300–301
and multicultural viewpoints, 308–310
positive psychology approaches to,
301–302
See also athletics
Sriram, R., shaping students' self-theories, 112
Steele, C. M., effect of ethnic and racial
stereotypes, 120
Stein, J., Millennial generation, 27, 29
stereotypes
cultural and ethnic, 84–86
"stereotype threat," 120
Strauss, W.
expectations of Millennial generation, 50
generational change in society, 31
Millennials Rising: The Next Great
Generation, 33, 39
optimism of Millennial generation, 43
strengths-based approach
among collegiate athletes, 305
to campus culture, 344–347
and career counseling, 172–174, 186–187
leadership and a language of strengths,
283–286
in life coaching, 329–330, 331–333
and sports and exercise, 308–309
and supervision, 191–192, 197–201,
212–213
Strengths Based Leadership (Rath &
Conchie), 284
strengths-based practice
addressing problems and framing solutions
with, 207–209
case study, 159–161
and culturally competent practice, 92–95
educator perspective on, 134, 161–162
identifying and nurturing student strengths,
143–148

strengths-based practice (*cont.*)
  identifying and nurturing teacher strengths,
    135–143, *144–145*
  obstacles to strengths-based teaching, 148–151
  and perceived academic control, 114–117
strengths development
  Clifton Strengths Finder, 73–75
  culturally relevant strengths, 91–92
  measures for psychological strengths, 69–70
  and student life programming, 54
  and student success, 6–8
  Values in Action Inventory of Character
    Strengths, *71–72*
  vs. remediation model, 6–7, 14
StrengthsFinder survey instrument, 284
StrengthsQuest (Clifton, Anderson, & Schreiner),
    283–284, 344
StrengthsQuest self-assessment, 53, 70, 146, 147
strengths theory, in positive
    psychology, 59–60
stress, alleviating through exercise, 300
student advising and positive
    psychology, 13–15
student-centeredness, introduction of, 2–4
Student Engagement, National Survey
    of, 6, 17
student life programming
  and academic efforts, 37
  culturally competent practice, 92–95
  and Millennial students, 51–52, 53
  and personal growth initiative, 228–229
  and positive psychology, 15–16
  practical strategies, 54
students
  benefits of positive psychology in sports,
    313–314
  challenge of leadership roles, 287
  challenges faced by student athletes,
    300–301
  current characteristics of, 33–34
  emphasizing positive traits of, 30–31
  fostering spiritual development among,
    269–274
  friendships in college, significance of,
    241–242
  identifying and nurturing strengths,
    143–148, 332, 333, 334, 345
  normative student development, 223–225
  reinforcing active role in learning, 114
  and scheduled "quiet" time, 36–37
student success
  and coaching toward happiness and
    well-being, 328–329
  definitions of, 5–6
  facilitating student success, 32–33
  and strengths development, 6–8

Student Success in College (Kuh, Schuh, Whitt, &
    Associates), 32
Suh, E. M., happiness in collectivist
    societies, 87–88
supervision and training, positive model of
  addressing problems and framing solutions,
    207–209
  case study for, 212–213
  continued learning and expert performance,
    210–212
  creating hope and fostering growth, 194
  developmental perspective on, 192–193
  evaluation and feedback, 201–204
  fostering excellence, 209–212
  multicultural perspectives on, 204–207
  role of positive emotions in feedback, 204
  setting the stage for effectiveness, 194–197
  training *vs.* supervision, meanings of, 191
  uncovering potential, 197–201
supervision *vs.* training, 191
survival mentality *vs.* thriving perspective, 14
Syed, M., social networks among college
    students, 242

talents, development of
  combining with knowledge, 344
  and strengths development, 6–8, 60
  and successful teaching, *137–142*
  teaching talent, 135–136
targeted interventions, and perceived academic
    control, 104–105
Taylor, P.
  economic downturns and Millennials, 44
  educational level of Millennials, 37
  political views among Millennials, 38
Teacher Behaviors Checklist, The
  and identifying teaching talent, 142, 143
teaching
  appraising student learning styles, 117–118
  importance of mentoring, 157
  and student personal growth initiative, 231
  teachers as learners, 140
teaching, identifying and nurturing strengths,
    133–148
  obstacles to strengths-based teaching,
    148–151
  signature talents for successful teaching,
    137–142
  student strengths, 143–148, 332, 333,
    334, 345
  teacher strengths, 135–143, *144–145*
  values and character strengths applied to
    teaching, *144–145*
teaching, positive model of, 151–159
  active-constructive responding, 153–154

broaden and build theory of positive
emotions, 152–153
case study, 159–161
positive empathy, 154–155
sense of hope, 155–159
team work in classrooms, 153, 158
technology, and Millennial generation, 35–37
temperance, and strengthening teaching
success, 145
Terenzini, P. T., institutional effectiveness, 17
Terman, L. M.
early theories of student success, 7, 134
giftedness and marital satisfaction, 58
The Happiness Hypothesis (Haidt), 182
Thoen, Megan A., Personal Growth and
Development, 219–238
Thomas, F. N., solution-oriented
supervision, 209
thriving, as model of student success, 8–12
academic thriving, 9–10
definition of thriving, 8
encouraging and enhancing, 100
intrapersonal thriving, 10–11
and principles of positive psychology,
12–15
and strong sense of community, 19
Thriving Quotient, 9–12
Diverse Citizenship, 11, 16
Engaged Learning factor, 9
Positive Perspectives factor, 10
Social Connectedness, 11, 16
Tillich, Paul, spiritual development, 262, 263
training and supervision, positive model of
addressing problems and framing solutions,
207–209
case study, 212–213
continued learning and expert performance,
210–212
creating hope and fostering growth, 194
developmental perspective on, 192–193
evaluation and feedback, 201–204
fostering excellence, 209–212
multicultural perspectives on, 204–207
role of positive emotions in feedback, 204
setting the stage for effectiveness, 194–197
training *vs.* supervision, 191
uncovering potential, 197–201
transcendence, and strengthening teaching
success, 145
Transformational Leadership theory, 281–282
transitions, from high school to college,
219–220
translational research, on sports and
exercise, 306
Transtheoretical Model, of personal growth and
development, 221

Trevino, Y., blessings of diversity, 205
Triandis, H. C., definition of "culture," 82
trust, importance of in classroom, 157
Tugade, M. M., the undoing hypothesis,
63–64
Tyler, Leona, and development of positive
psychology, 58

Undoing Hypothesis, of Broaden and Build
theory, 63–64
Utsey, S. O., culturally relevant
strengths, 91–92

Vaillant, G., *Aging Well*, 32
Values in Action Classification System
case study, 159–160
identifying and nurturing student
strengths, 143
and identifying teaching talent,
136–137, 142
survey completion by students, 146
virtues as values in action, 268–269
Values in Action Institute on Character, 284
Values in Action Inventory of Character
Strengths
definitions of 24 strengths measured, 71–72
history and uses of, 69–70
Values Inventory of Strengths, The, 199
Vang, H. C., forgiveness among Hmong
Americans, 88
Veroff, J., savoring positive experiences, 331
Veterans Administration, and treatment of
mental illness, 58
VIA Classification Handbook (Peterson &
Seligman), 136
See also Values in Action Classification System
Vicuna, Belinda, 261–278
Vietnam War, and increases in college
enrollment, 2
virtues, categories of, 268–269
visioning, and career flow, 172
vocation, and sense of calling, 264
Vygotsky, Lev, developmental needs and
training, 192

Wade, John C.
Positive Career Counseling, 167–189
Positive Supervision and Training, 191–217
Wadsworth, D., and market-driven
education, 3
Watson, J., positive parenting skills, 58
Weigold, I. K., personal growth initiative and
student counseling, 227

well-being
    five pillars of, 301
    life coaching toward, 328–329
    and positive campus culture, 352–355
well-being, theory of
    authentic happiness and, 66, 68
    and flourishing people, 5, 65–66
    and intrapersonal thriving, 10
    and personal growth and development,
        225–226
wellness programs, 304
White, D. L., identifying teaching talent, 136
White, S. S., increasing self-efficacy, 196
Whitmore, J., life coaching and goal-setting, 326
Whitt, E. J.

enhancing student success, 322
    Involving Colleges and *Student Success in
        College,* 32
Wood, A. M., positive psychology and life
    coaching, 321
World War II, and increases in college
    enrollment, 2
Worthington, Everett, promoting
    forgiveness, 269
Wright, B. A., strengths-based
    supervision, 200

Yamagishi, T., appreciating diversity, 206
Youssef, C. M., psychological capital, 18